Reasoning With a Computer in PASCAL

Office hours

Pete Wentworth

TR 2:30 - 5:00

LH 315 A or B

LH 110

consulting

MV 7:00 - 9:00

LH 407 2:30 F

Auguste Rodin, The Thinker (about 1910). Courtesy of The Metropolitan Museum of Art, Gift of Thomas F. Ryan, 1910. (11.173.9)

Reasoning With a Computer in PASCAL

Daniel Solow
Case Western Reserve University

ADDISON-WESLEY PUBLISHING COMPANY
Reading, Massachusetts ■ Menlo Park, California ■ Don Mills, Ontario
Wokingham, England ■ Amsterdam ■ Sydney ■ Singapore ■ Tokyo
Mexico City ■ Bogotá ■ Santiago ■ San Juan

To My Brother, Jon

Mark S. Dalton • *Sponsoring Editor*
Susan Owen • *Development Editor*
Bette J. Aaronson • *Production Supervisor*
Debbie Stone • *Copy Editor*
Vanessa Piñeiro and Melinda Grosser • *Text Designers*
Kristin Belanger, Belanger Associates • *Illustrator*
Helen Wythe • *Production Coordinator*
Hugh Crawford • *Manufacturing Supervisor*
Marshall Henrichs • *Cover Designer*

Library of Congress Cataloging-in-Publication Data

Solow, Daniel.
Reasoning with a computer in Pascal.

Includes index.
1. Electronic digital computers—Programming.
2. PASCAL (Computer program language) I. Title.
QA76.6.S6447 1986 005.1 85-15753
ISBN 0-201-12060-7

ABCDEFGHIJ-DO-89876

PREFACE

In addition to teaching Pascal and good, structured programming style, I had two other goals in mind when writing this book, namely, to teach the underlying thinking process involved in programming, and to eliminate the fear and confusion associated with debugging. In the existing collection of introductory texts, one can see a fairly consistent approach to teaching programming, which is: "Let me show you the syntax for a particular programming statement. Watch me use that syntax . . . ; now you go use it." While this "do-as-I-do" approach might work well for gifted students, the results are less than satisfactory for the average student. In fact, many students, after struggling for some time, give up in frustration—leaving computing to "those who are talented."

Emphasis on Problem-Solving Techniques

In *Reasoning with a Computer in Pascal,* I make an effort to rectify this situation. My approach is based on the assumption that there is an underlying problem-solving process that is used, often subconsciously, by virtually all programmers. From the very first chapter, I attempt to make that thinking process conscious in several different ways. For example, in Chapter 1 I introduce and carefully describe a number of problem-solving techniques. Then, in subsequent chapters every program is developed with explicit reference to them; in other words, those techniques form the basis for the entire book.

For developing their own algorithms, I teach the students to think through their solution as a first step toward "translating" their own logic in terms that a computer can understand. While I do stress the need for careful algorithm development, at the same time, my approach acknowledges that students, like the rest of us, will inevitably introduce errors into the early versions of their programs; the important issue is how to deal with those errors. Hence, my second emphasis is on the process of tracing and debugging.

Tracing and Debugging

It is one thing to define a syntax, a run-time, and a logic error; it is quite another to teach a student what to do when these errors arise. In an effort to help students deal effectively with errors, the concept of debugging is introduced in the first chapter. Subsequently, debugging techniques are taught throughout the rest of the text. Specifically, when an algorithm is developed, I introduce subtle errors that any person is likely to make. I then use tracing to show how some of the errors can be detected *before* the program is run. I subsequently demonstrate the results of running the program and encountering run-time and logic errors. Finally, I show how systematic debugging techniques are used to track down, isolate, and identify the source of the errors, and how to correct the mistakes. The objective of this approach is to eliminate the fear associated with programming errors by showing the students that every error can be understood, has a logical explanation, and an appropriate correction. The final and correct program is then printed in color so that the students can easily distinguish it from the programs that contain errors. Color is used for other pedagogical purposes, as will be described presently.

Since this text is designed with the average student in mind, I maintain the emphasis on the problem-solving and debugging discussion throughout. Moreover, in order to focus greater attention on the problem-solving aspects of programming, the issue of coding in Pascal has been delayed until Chapter 3. From that point on, the coding and running of programs can be done without detracting from the problem-solving aspects. In the interest of putting the students on the computer as soon as possible, however, they are given a (complete) Pascal program to run at the end of Chapter 1. The objective of that exercise is not to introduce coding, but rather, to familiarize the students with the process of running a program, using the equipment, editor, printers, etc., by the time the coding material of Chapter 3 is taught.

Innovative Presentation of Procedures

In order to introduce top-down programming at an early stage, procedures without parameters are presented at the beginning of Chapter 5, immediately after the fundamental concepts of assignment statements, input/output operations, and IF/THEN statements. The use of procedures in conjunction with top-down programming is emphasized from that point on.

In addition, in Chapter 5 I use procedures as an introduction to the concept of repetition, which provides the basis for the following chapter on loops. I delay the more difficult concept of procedures with parameters until Chapter 7 so that students can adequately master the use of loops.

Focus on General Programming Concepts

As another special consideration for students, I have chosen to focus on general programming concepts rather than on specialized features available only in Pascal. To be sure, special Pascal features, such as user-defined values, CASE and REPEAT statements, and non-integer array subscripts, are presented in sufficient detail, but are not overly emphasized. Moreover, the Pascal data structures of records, sets, files, and pointers are presented in the final chapters, which can serve as an introduction to a more advanced course on Pascal.

Use of Pseudocode to Enhance Problem-Solving

The focus on problem solving is enhanced by the use of pseudocode. Specifically, each major programming concept is first introduced using a pseudocode statement that is closely related to the Pascal syntax, but leaves out some of the more distracting details. Then, a problem is solved, using pseudocode, to illustrate the new programming concept. The reason for using pseudocode first is to encourage the student to focus on the important issues of algorithm development, such as the problem-solving techniques, leaving the details of syntax to be handled subsequently.

It could be argued that the use of pseudocode in addition to a specific language could result in yet another level of learning for the student. For this reason, the pseudocode of this text is, in essence, Pascal with much of the punctuation and details of syntax removed. Furthermore, in order to avoid this extra level of learning, I recommend that students not be required to memorize or to use the pseudocode given here. Rather, they should be allowed to develop their own pseudocode, if they are so inclined.

Teaching Pascal Syntax

Naturally, this book teaches Pascal syntax. Numerous small examples as well as complete programs are presented. The objective is to insure that the student will be able to write structured programs that others can read easily. Good programming habits, such as the use of comments and descriptive identifiers, are instilled from the beginning.

In order to highlight the differences between pseudocode and Pascal, color has once again been used. Specifically, all correct Pascal statements (and programs) are printed in color, while all pseudocode statements appear in normal black print.

Applicability to Most Pascal Systems

In teaching Pascal syntax, this book has been written primarily for interactive systems. Particular attention has been given to many of the features that vary from one Pascal implementation to another. These include differences in input and output procedures, the ability (or inability) to display the value of user-defined and boolean variables, and what happens if the value of the expression in a `CASE` statement cannot be found in the list of given values. Primary focus is given to what happens in ISO standard Pascal and in UCSD Pascal. *If you are using Turbo Pascal, then in order for the inputting of data from a terminal to work as described in Chapter 3, you must be sure to have the students include the comment* `(*$B-*)` *immediately after the program heading, as has been done in the first program in the exercises of Section 1.6.* Generally speaking, this book should be usable for most Pascal systems—either batch or interactive.

Pedagogy

Exercises. Each section is followed by exercises that are graduated in difficulty. Beginning exercises test the basic principles taught in the section; subsequent exercises are designed to provide practice in problem-solving, tracing and debugging. Students are asked to run each complete program they develop using specific given data. Doing so simplifies the grading process since the output for each student's program should be the same.

Marginal Key Term Definitions. Each chapter contains a list of key terms (with page references) whose definitions appear not only in the body of the text, but also in the adjacent margins. A glossary is provided at the end of the book for quick reference.

Summaries and Recaps. Each chapter contains a short summary section that highlights the most important topics of the chapter. Many individual sections also contain a recap that reviews the key items in that section, and provides a transition to the subsequent section.

Logo. To encourage students to think carefully when developing an algorithm, a logo of Rodin's "The Thinker" has been used throughout the book. Specifically, whenever the text mentions the problem-solving technique of "thinking through your solution," the logo appears in the adjacent margin.

Color. As has already been mentioned, color is used to indicate all correct Pascal statements and programs. In contrast, all pseudocode statements as well as Pascal programs that contain errors, appear in normal black print.

ACKNOWLEDGMENTS

With regard to the preparation of the manuscript for this book, I am especially grateful to my student, Carolyn Cuff, who proofread the earlier versions, made substantive suggestions for improving the quality of the text, and prepared the solution and instructor's manual. With regard to typing the manuscript, I acknowledge Brenda Tate, Frances McKenney, and my wife, Audrey, for doing such a professional job. I am also grateful to Case Western Reserve University for the use of their word processing facilities, and for enabling me to test this book in class.

Numerous reviewers helped shape the final version of this text. I am particularly thankful to Gail Lefevre, Florida Junior College, and to Willard Shinn II for their enthusiastic support of this project and for their constructive suggestions. I also appreciated the useful comments of the following reviewers: Robert Del Zoppo, Jamestown Community College, Louis L. Gioia, Nassau Community College, Paul Bhatia, Middlesex County College, and Charles Engelke, University of Florida.

There are a number of professionals at Addison-Wesley I would like to acknowledge for making this book a reality. First, I thank my editor, Mark Dalton, for his recognition and support of my problem-solving approach and for his single-minded faith in the success of this project. Then there is Susan Owen, whose extensive editorial comments and hours of work led to a more concise and readable version of the text. I must also thank Bette Aaronson and her staff for producing the quality of book you see here.

Finally, I thank my wife, Audrey, for making it possible to complete this work so quickly. In fact, without her emotional support, this book would not exist at all.

Cleveland, Ohio *D.S.*

CONTENTS

3

CODING, READING, AND WRITING 71

4

IF SO THEN DO IT 131

5

REPETITION USING PROCEDURES AND LOOPS 189

6

ARRAYS 261

7 PROCEDURES (WITH PARAMETERS) AND FUNCTIONS 317

8 ADVANCED DATA STRUCTURES—PART I 373

9 ADVANCED DATA STRUCTURES—PART II 407

The creation myth, depicted by artist William Blake, reflects the belief that the universe was created according to logical principles. This concept—that we spring from rational beginnings—contributed to the birth of modern science. Once natural laws replaced the capricious whims of gods, men cast off their superstitions and sought to understand the universe through a systematic search for order. (THE BETTMANN ARCHIVE, INC.)

1

HOW COMPUTERS CAN BE MADE TO SOLVE PROBLEMS

1.1 WHAT IS COMPUTER PROGRAMMING?
1.2 THINKING IN TERMS OF A PROGRAMMING LANGUAGE
1.3 PROGRAM-DEVELOPMENT TECHNIQUES
1.4 DEBUGGING
1.5 OBTAINING AND MAINTAINING A CORRECT PROGRAM
1.6 RUNNING A PROGRAM
1.7 SUMMARY
EXERCISES FOLLOWING MOST SECTIONS

In this chapter, you will be introduced to the process of solving problems by computer. The first step of that process is to determine how you would solve the problem yourself. You will then be shown how to restructure your solution in terms that a computer will eventually be able to understand. Several helpful techniques for use in this critical process will also be presented. Most of these techniques will be used repeatedly throughout the book. Finally, you will learn about the three types of errors that typically arise when solving a problem by computer, and how to deal with them.

1.1 What Is Computer Programming?

A computer is an electronic device that, like a stereo, consists of a number of individual components. The names of these components and their functions will be presented, in part, at the end of this chapter, and in Chapter 3. More important, a computer is a powerful tool that you can use to help solve certain types of problems. The primary objective of this book is to teach you how computers can be used in that capacity.

In order for a computer to help solve a problem, the machine must be given a set of specific instructions to follow. The general process of giving those instructions to a computer is called **programming.** Unfortunately, computers cannot yet accept instructions in English (or any other spoken language). Instead, computers "speak" *computer* (or *programming*) *languages*. Learning to give instructions to the computer in a language that the computer can understand will be the primary objective of this book. While there are many different computer languages, each with its advantages and disadvantages, this book will focus on one specific computer language called **Pascal.** A comparison of some of these different languages is given in Appendix F.

Programming The process of giving instructions to the computer.

Pascal A specific computer language.

Relative to a spoken language, computer langauges are very limited in the size of their "vocabulary." Thus, you will not have a lot of memorizing to do. On the other hand, all programming languages are extremely precise. When you speak a foreign language and you leave out a word in a sentence, most of the time you will be understood. With computer languages, however, the slightest mistake can make it impossible for the computer to understand your instructions. Ultimately, in order to program a computer successfully, you will have to pay attention to details of "grammar."

Aside from the need to be careful, what is it that makes computer programming so challenging? Precisely the same things that makes it challenging to express an idea from one spoken language to another. For example, suppose you wanted to translate a thought from English into Japanese. After clearly understanding the thought in English, you would have to restructure this thought completely, so that the same idea could be expressed in Japanese. When translating your thoughts into a computer language, the limited vocabulary of the language can require some effort on your part to express your thoughts correctly. For the most part, it is this process of learning to think in a new language that makes problem solving with computers seem difficult at first.

Throughout this book, much time will be devoted to teaching you how to think in terms of the programming language Pascal so that you can program a computer to perform the desired tasks. In fact, the next section is designed to show you more precisely what is involved in this process.

1.2 Thinking in Terms of a Programming Language

To understand what it means to think in terms of a programming language, suppose you are living in a town called Smallville (Fig. 1.1). From the planet Runga, a family of Orks has come to visit you. (The family of Orks should be thought of as the computer.) Among themselves, the Orks speak a language of their own. Although the Orks can neither speak nor understand English, they have learned to read and to write just a bit of the language. Now suppose you are faced with the following.

Problem: Looking at the map in Fig. 1.1, you want to tell the Orks how to walk from where they are on Maple Street to your house on Redwood Street.

The first step in solving this problem (and all computer problems) is to determine how you would solve the problem yourself. If you cannot do so, then you will be unable to provide the appropriate instructions to the computer. After looking at the map in Fig. 1.1, you might think, "This is easy. I will simply write the following instructions for the Orks":

Solution: Take Maple Street heading east until you reach Oak Avenue. Make a left and go to Pine Street. From there, turn right and

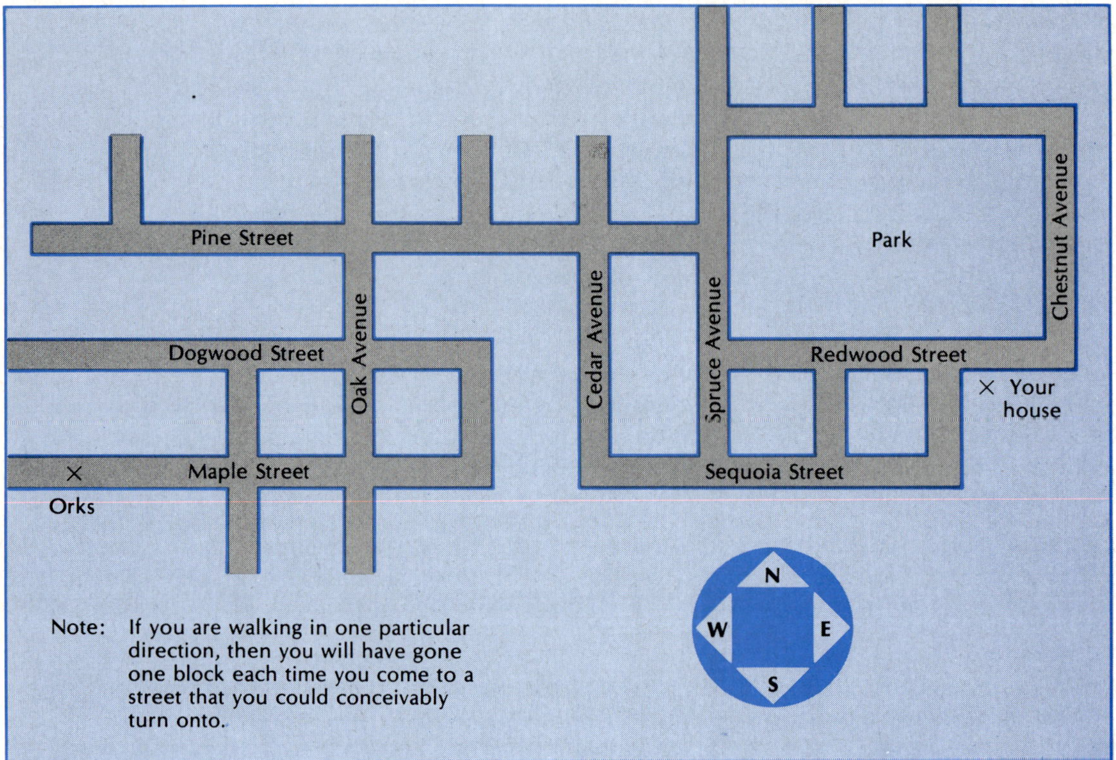

Figure 1.1 A map of part of Smallville.

follow Pine Street until you reach the park. Then make a right and go one block to Redwood Street. At Redwood you can only turn left. Do so and follow Redwood for two blocks. On that corner you will find my house. (With regard to the concept of a "block": if you are walking in one particular direction, each time you come to a street that you could conceivably turn on, that constitutes one block.)

Unfortunately, if you were to give the above instructions to the Orks, they would not be able to understand them, for their vocabulary is far too limited. Clearly, in order to help the Orks, you must know precisely what their vocabulary and rules of grammar are. Their vocabulary is limited to the following:

Ork Vocabulary: "go," "block(s)," "East," "West," "North," "South." The Orks are also familiar with all of the numbers when written as numerals and not when they are spelled out.

Ork Grammar Rules: (1) When writing instructions for the Orks, each sentence must end with a period. (2) The first letter of each sentence must be *upper case* (i.e., capitalized). (3) All other letters must be *lower case* except for the first letter of a compass direction, which must be capitalized.

Now your job is clear. You must rephrase the original instructions in terms that the Orks can understand. In other words, you must think in terms of the Ork language so that you can explain to the Orks, in their vocabulary, how to reach your house.

For the problem above, the process of translating the first instruction is straightforward. That is, the instruction, "Take Maple Street heading east until you reach Oak Avenue," can be translated into the Ork vocabulary as, "Go East 2 blocks." Similarly, "Make a left and go to Pine Street," will translate to, "Go North 2 blocks."

Although in this example the translation process is easy, in most computer problems this task can require a great deal of time and effort. One reason for this difficulty is that the way in which *you* solve a problem can be quite different from the way in which a computer solves the problem. In other words, human and machine problem-solving processes are often different. Thus, you might not know how to express the way you solve a problem in terms that the computer can understand.

To illustrate this situation in the Ork problem, consider the instruction that you want the Orks to follow once they reach the corner of Pine Street and Oak Avenue, namely:

> From there, turn right and follow Pine Street until you reach the park.

You clearly understand what it means to say "until you reach the park," but the Orks do not. As you can see, your problem-solving process is different from that of the Orks. Thus, if you want to communicate with the Orks, you will not only have to think in terms of their language, but actually begin to reason as the Orks would.

Without looking at the map, can you rephrase the above instruction so that the Orks will be able to understand? Evidently, thinking in terms of the Ork langauge and reasoning as they would is not always a simple matter. This and the next section will present several techniques that you might find useful in learning to do so.

To illustrate one such technique, consider, once again, the instruction:

> From there, turn right and follow Pine Street until you reach the park.

In order to explain this instruction to the Orks, you need to understand more precisely how you are actually solving the problem. For example, you might ask yourself:

> Exactly how do I follow Pine Street until I reach the park?

In answering the question, you must keep in mind the Ork vocabulary, which, as you recall, consists of: "go," "block(s)," "East," "West," "North," "South," and all of the numbers when written as numerals. Thus you might come up with the following answer:

> What I am really doing is heading east on Pine Street for a certain number of blocks.

From this understanding, it is somewhat easier to express the desired instruction in the Ork vocabulary, specifically:

> Go East 3 blocks.

Thinking through your solution The process of going over your initial solution very slowly and carefully in order to understand more precisely what individual steps you are performing to solve the problem.

The technique of trying to determine more precisely what steps are involved in solving a problem yourself will be referred to as **thinking through your solution.** When humans solve a problem, they are often unaware of their thought process. Many steps are taken for granted, or understood subconsciously at best. Thinking through your solution is a technique to make you more conscious of what you are doing when you solve a problem. After you have solved the problem in your own mind, you must learn to go over that solution very slowly, with the objective of identifying, more precisely, what individual steps you are performing to solve the problem.

In so doing, you should always keep in mind how a computer "thinks," that is, its vocabulary. By thinking through your solution, you will have a much better chance of translating your own solution procedure into a sequence of instructions that can be understood by a computer. As each problem in this text is solved, the process of thinking through your solution will be discussed and illustrated for you. This technique will be indicated by the logo . Whenever you see this symbol in the margin of this text, you will know that you should think through your solution. Doing so will be a crucial step toward developing good programming skills.

1.3 Program-Development Techniques

You have learned that the first and most important step in the computer programming process is to determine how you would solve the problem yourself. Once you have expressed the solution to a problem in terms that you understand, your ultimate objective is to translate that solution in terms of a specific programming language that a computer can understand. Developing a step-by-step solution procedure for a given word problem will be referred to as the *algorithm development* phase of computer problem solving. An **algorithm** is, in fact, a step-by-step method that can be used to solve a problem. One example of an algorithm is the set of instructions that was developed for the Orks in the previous section. To aid you in developing algorithms, the technique of thinking through your solution can, and should, be used. Several other techniques will be introduced now to help you in the translation process.

Algorithm A step-by-step method that can be used to solve a problem.

Stepwise Refinement

In the Ork problem of the previous section, it was a relatively easy matter to go, sentence by sentence, from your original solution to expressing the answer using the Ork vocabulary. In most problems for which you will use computers, this transition cannot be done so readily.

To handle these more difficult problems, a technique known as **stepwise refinement** can be very useful. Simply stated, stepwise refinement is the process of gradually expressing your original solution to a problem more and more in terms that a computer can understand, until finally the entire solution can be written as a sequence of instructions in the vocabulary of a specific computer language.

Stepwise refinement The process of gradually expressing the original English solution to a problem in terms that can be understood by the computer.

To illustrate the process of stepwise refinement, recall the original (English) solution to the Ork problem: "Take Maple Street heading east until you reach Oak Avenue. Make a left and go to Pine Street. From there, turn right and follow Pine Street until you reach the park. Then make a right and go one block to Redwood Street. At Redwood you can only turn left. Do so and follow Redwood for two blocks. On that corner you will find my house." Instead of attempting to translate these instructions directly into the Ork vocabulary, you might find it easier to use the technique of stepwise refinement, whereby you first reword your original solution so that it more closely resembles the Ork vocabulary. For example,

Refinement. Go East 2 blocks on Maple Street. Turn left and go North 2 blocks. Turn right and go East 3 blocks. Turn right on Spruce Avenue. Go straight 1 block. Turn left on Redwood and go straight 2 blocks.

This refined solution is closer to the Ork vocabulary than was the original. Further refinement will be necessary, however, before the Orks will understand how to reach your house. In fact, the refinement process must be continued until you can state the entire solution as a sequence of instructions in a specific programming language. The final act of obtaining the list of instructions in the computer language is called **coding.** At that stage, you will at last have a **computer program.**

Coding The final act of expressing the solution to a problem as a list of computer instructions in a specific langauge.

Computer program A sequence of computer instructions written in a specific computer langauge.

A coded program can sometimes be difficult to read and to understand. A *flowchart* is a pictorial method for representing the steps of a program. Although this book will not use flowcharts, many textbooks and other computer literature do use them. Therefore, for reference purposes, Appendix E of this book contains an explanation of how to read and to draw flowcharts.

When solving computer problems, always begin with your original English solution. As you apply the refinement process, you should continually use a vocabulary (chosen by you) that consists of fewer English words and more "computer words." Using this increasingly more restricted vocabulary will facilitate your ability to state the solution in the appropriate computer language. Collectively, these limited English vocabularies are called **pseudocode.** Conveniently, when using pseudocode, you need not be overly concerned about punctuation, spelling, or rules of grammar. Those can be dealt with in the final coding phase.

Pseudocode A limited English vocabulary used when applying stepwise refinement.

In the refined solution above, a pseudocode was used that consisted of the words in the Ork vocabulary together with the words: "turn," "left," "right," "and," "on," "straight," and the names of the streets. Although there are no specific rules, in order to be useful, the vocabulary of the pseudocode you choose should contain enough words so that you can adequately describe the solution of the problem, and be kept relatively close to that of the computer language into which the algorithm will finally be coded.

The use of pseudocode and refinement in the programming process is depicted in Fig. 1.2. During the refinement process in this text, a pseudocode will always be used to rephrase the solution; however, you need not memorize the particular pseudocode used here. Feel free to design your own.

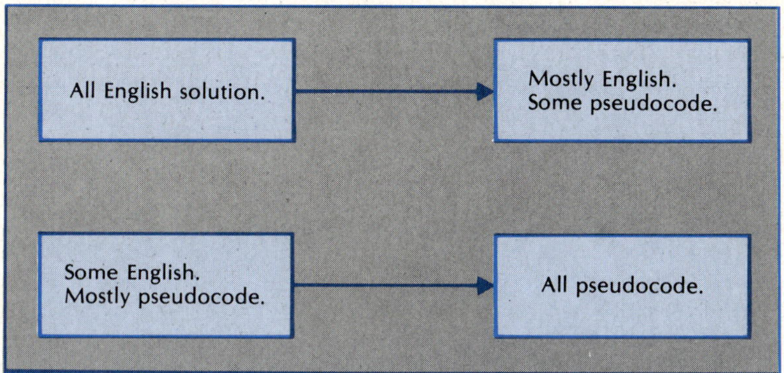

Figure 1.2 Refinement and pseudocode in problem solving.

Top-Down Programming

When a problem is complex, you might well have some difficulty in developing an algorithm (i.e., a solution), and even in describing how you would solve the problem yourself. Suppose, for example, that you were faced with the following problem.

Problem: The Orks want an algorithm that will enable them to get from any street corner in Smallville to your house.

If you find that a problem is so complicated that you have difficulty beginning, then you might use a technique called **top-down programming,** which is designed to help you structure your thoughts so that you can get started. Simply stated, the technique of top-down programming suggests that you decompose the original problem into smaller, more manageable subproblems. In so doing, you should focus your attention on the larger and more important aspects of the overall problem first, leaving minor details to be handled later. To draw an analogy, top-down programming is like designing an outline for a term paper. You begin by identifying the individual topics. Then you focus on each topic, developing the sections and subsections. Only when the outline is complete do you begin the actual writing. To summarize, with top-down programming, you first determine *what* tasks have to be done. Then you can determine (in greater detail) *how* to accomplish those tasks.

Top-down programming A technique designed to help you develop an algorithm for a complicated problem by decomposing the overall problem into smaller, more manageable subproblems.

Applying the technique of top-down programming to the Ork problem above, you might first choose certain landmarks in Smallville and concentrate on how to get from those landmarks to your house. Once those major tasks have been accomplished, you can then focus on the details of how to get from a particular (starting) intersection to the nearest landmark.

As another example, consider the problem of preparing for a camping trip. In the spirit of top-down programming, you might begin by identifying what tasks have to be done, for example: buy food, prepare the camping equipment, check the car. The details of how you accomplish these tasks are addressed subsequently. If the individual details for performing a specific task are still unclear, you can use top-down programming again to decompose that task into further subtasks that might be easier to handle. In Chapter 5 you will see this technique used in the computer problem-solving process.

Inputting, Processing, and Outputting

During the algorithm-development phase, you will first develop a solution to your problem expressed in terms that you understand. Then, by thinking through your solution, and through the process of stepwise refinement, you should begin to think in terms of the programming language so that you can restate the solution in terms that a computer can understand. One way to do so is to use the technique of **inputting, processing, and outputting.** In order to understand this technique, consider the following problem.

Inputting, processing, and outputting A problem-solving technique whereby you identify each of the three parts of a computer program.

Inputting The process of supplying to the computer information (i.e., data) that will be needed when the program is used to solve a problem.

Data Information provided by you to the computer in order to be able to solve a problem.

Processing The method of using, manipulating, and/or performing computations with the data in order to obtain the solution to a problem.

Problem: Chocolate chip cookies are packaged 12 to a box and 24 boxes to a carton. Given the number of cookies baked on a certain day, determine the number of cartons that can be obtained.

In designing the algorithm, you could begin with the **inputting** phase, which consists of identifying the information that must be made available to the computer at the time the program is to be used. That information is often referred to as the **data** of the problem. The specific manner in which the data are entered into the computer will be discussed in Chapter 3. For the cookie problem above, the data consist of the specific number of cookies that were baked together with the number of cookies per box and boxes per carton. In order to identify the inputting phase of a program, ask yourself what information you will need to be given in order to solve the problem.

The **processing** phase consists of manipulating, using, and/or calculating with the data obtained from the inputting phase so as to produce the solution to a problem. In order to identify the steps involved in the processing phase, you will have to think through your solution. A technique that can often help you to do so is the process of **working through a specific example.** This technique will now be demonstrated.

Working through a specific example The process of choosing specific values for the data and solving the problem by hand. As you do so, attempt to describe the general computations that would have to be performed when the values of the data are not specified explicitly.

For the cookie example, the processing phase consists of using the [given] number of cookies baked to calculate the number of cartons that can be obtained. In order to understand how to do so, work through a specific example. Suppose, for example, that 2080 cookies were baked. To compute the number of cartons, you must first divide 2080 by 12 to obtain the number of boxes (in this case, 173 boxes with 4 leftover cookies). Then you must divide 173 boxes by 24 to obtain the number of cartons (in this case, 7 cartons with 5 leftover boxes).

The objective of working through a specific example is not to obtain the answer for this one specific situation. Rather, the objective is to make you conscious of what computations would have to be performed in general, when the values of the data are not specified explicitly. Thus, as you work through a specific example, attempt to identify what computations would have to be performed in general. For the cookie example, the result of working through a specific example should lead you to identify the following processing phase:

1. Given the number of cookies baked, divide that number by 12 (eating any leftover ones) to obtain the number of boxes.
2. Divide the number of resulting boxes by 24 (eating any leftover ones) to obtain the number of cartons.

Finally, the **outputting** phase consists of having the computer make available to you the answer to the problem, in this case, the number of cartons that can be produced. (The specific manner in which the computer reports the solution of a problem will be addressed in Chapter 3.)

Outputting The process of having the computer report to you the solution that the machine obtained during the processing phase.

Recap

To recap the programming process so far, you should follow these general steps:

1. *Algorithm development:* After thoroughly understanding the word problem, you should describe in your own words how you would go about solving the problem. If you have difficulty in getting started, attempt to identify the inputting, processing, and outputting phases of the problem. In general, to help you during the processing phase, you will find it useful to work through a spe-

cific example. If the problem is complex, then you might wish to use the technique of top-down programming to decompose the original problem into smaller, more manageable subproblems.

2. *Stepwise refinement:* This technique (in conjunction with the use of pseudocode) will help you express your solution to a problem more and more in terms that can ultimately be written in a computer language.
3. *Coding:* When you have refined your algorithm "sufficiently," you must then provide a list of instructions in a specific programming language. (Remember, the more refinement you do, the easier will be the coding phase.) As you do so, pay particular attention to details of spelling, punctuation, and rules of grammar.

In this section you have learned various techniques for converting a word problem into a sequence of instructions that the computer can ultimately perform. No matter how careful you are, you might still make mistakes. The next section will discuss the types of errors you might encounter, and what to do when they arise.

Exercises for Section 1.3

Use the technique of stepwise refinement to rewrite each of the following groups of instructions. Specifically, think through your solution and use pseudocode to rewrite the given word instructions. Then, from that solution, use refinement again to code the instructions in terms of the Ork vocabulary and rules of grammar (see page 5).

1. Head north from the corner of Pine Street and Spruce Avenue. Take every possible right turn until your house is reached.
2. Head south from the corner of Pine Street and Cedar Avenue. Each time you reach a point where you can no longer go straight, turn left. Stop when you reach Redwood Street.
3. Beginning at the far west end of Pine Street, always walk east or south, and always walk as far as you can on a given street. When you can no longer follow these directions, go north one block.

In each of the following word problems, identify the inputting, processing, and outputting phases.

4. Bob the grocer has kept a list of the total amount of money received during each of the past 30 days. Determine the combined total sales figure for those 30 days. Also, find the maximum amount that was sold on any single day.

5. From a paragraph of text, count the number of times each letter occurs.
6. Look up a person's phone number in the telephone book.
7. Sort 13 given playing cards into four suits.

For each of the following problems, use the technique of top-down programming to decompose the problem into a group of subproblems that might be easier to solve. Then, for each subproblem, use top-down programming to propose further subproblems to be solved. As you do so, focus on identifying a group of tasks that have to be accomplished rather than on specifying the details of how to perform those tasks.

8. Drive from your house to the airport to meet a friend at the arrival gate.
9. Change a flat tire.
10. Plan a party.

For each of the following word instructions, work through a specific example using the given data. As you do so, try to describe how you would solve the problem if you had different unspecified data instead of the given specific data.

11. Count the number of times the letter "e" occurs in a given sentence.

    Given data: Use the specific sentence above.
12. Given the number of eggs ordered, compute the total cost as 54 cents for each of the first 20 dozen, 50 cents for each of the next 30 dozen, 45 cents for each of the next 50 dozen, and 40 cents for each dozen thereafter.

    Given data: 720 eggs ordered.
13. Look at a given list of numbers. Whenever you find two consecutive numbers that are not in an increasing order, interchange the positions of those two numbers. Repeat the entire process until the whole list is in increasing order

    Given data: 10 14 11 12

1.4 Debugging

No matter how careful you are in the algorithm-development, refinement, and coding phases, you might still make mistakes. A mistake in a computer program is called a *bug*. **Debugging** is the process of locating and correcting all such mistakes. The debugging phase is often the most challenging aspect of computer programming for a novice (and sometimes for an expert). Therefore it will be well worth your while to learn proper debugging procedures from the beginning. Many techniques and examples will be presented throughout this book to help

Debugging The process of locating and correcting errors in a program.

you master the "art" of debugging. The sooner you learn correct debugging procedures, the more quickly you will get your programs to run correctly, and the less frustrated you will be. Moreover, if you are confident of your debugging abilities, then you will know that you can *always* find and correct any mistake, for a computer is nothing but a fast, dumb machine, doing exactly what you tell it to do.

There are three different types of errors you can make during the programming process, all of which will be illustrated in the following example. Suppose that after sufficient refinement, you code the following algorithm for the original Ork problem of Section 1.2 and give it to the Orks:

```
Go East 2 Blocks.
Go North 2 blocks, then go West 4 bocks
Go North 1 block.
Go east 2 blocks.
```

Syntax Errors

When you hand these written instructions to the Orks, they will not immediately try to follow them. Rather, they will first read what you have written to see that it makes sense, i.e., that they can at least understand what you are trying to say. To that end, recall the Ork vocabulary and rules of grammar, which will be repeated here for your convenience.

Ork Vocabulary: "go," "block(s)," "East," "West," "North," "South." The Orks are also familiar with all of the numbers when written as numerals and not when they are spelled out.

Ork Grammar Rules: When writing instructions for the Orks, each sentence must end with a period. The first letter of each sentence must be upper case (i.e., capitalized). All other letters must be lower case except for the first letter of a compass direction, which must be capitalized.

Syntax error An error caused by not following the grammatical rules of a computer language. These errors usually arise from misspellings, bad punctuation, omitting special words, etc.

Errors that are caused by not following the rules of a computer language are referred to as **syntax errors.** These errors usually arise from misspellings, bad punctuation, omitting special words, and similar careless mistakes. Looking now at the first sentence of your instructions, you can see that you have capitalized the "B" in "Blocks," which should have been lower case. The Orks cannot deal with this "unknown" situation. It would be nice if the Orks would write you a note saying:

> The first letter in the word "Blocks" of the first sentence should be lower case.

In fact, it would be even better if the Orks would correct the mistake themselves and proceed. Unfortunately, computers, like Orks, are currently incapable of performing such tasks. Sometimes computers can be intimidating by printing caustic and often mysterious messages. For the mistake above, you might see something like this:

```
Go East 2 Blocks.
    ***Warning—unauthorized use of upper-case
    letter.
```

The computer might or might not tell you exactly where the error is, although the approximate location will be indicated. Sometimes you will have to do some thinking and searching to find out what the computer is complaining about. Also, it can happen that an error in one part of the program causes the computer to think that there are other errors later in the code when, in reality, there are none. You will see this situation in a moment. In any event, for the program above, the computer might provide the following list of *error messages:*

```
Go East 2 Blocks.
    ***Warning—unauthorized use of upper-case
    letter.
Go North 2 blocks, then go West 4 bocks
    ***Error—unrecognizable punctuation.
    ***Fatal Error-undefined word.
    ***Fatal Error-undefined word.
Go North 1 block.
    ***Warning—unauthorized use of upper-case
    letter.
Go east 2 blocks.
    ***Warning—unauthorized use of lower-case
    letter.
```

The first error message has already been discussed. Can you determine what is causing the other error messages? To do so, you might wish to review thoroughly the Ork vocabulary and rules of grammar.

In general, in order to find and to correct syntax errors, you must have a complete and thorough knowledge of the grammatical rules of the computer language you are using.

Each of the remaining error messages will now be discussed briefly.

```
***Error—unrecognizable punctuation.
```

This error is caused by the comma appearing in the second sentence. No punctuation other than a period is permitted.

```
***Fatal Error—undefined word.
```

This error is caused by the word "then" in the second sentence. The word "then" is not part of the Ork vocabulary.

```
***Fatal Error—undefined word.
```

The second appearance of this error message is caused by the misspelled word "bocks" in the second sentence. The Orks do not realize that you meant "blocks" instead of "bocks."

```
***Warning—unauthorized use of upper-case
letter.
```

At first glance, there seems to be nothing wrong with the third sentence and, indeed, that is true. This error message is caused by the omission of a period at the end of the *previous* sentence. Thus the Orks did not understand why the first letter of the word "Go" in the third sentence was being capitalized. Notice how an error in one part of the program can cause the computer to think, incorrectly, that there are other errors later in the program.

```
***Warning—unauthorized use of lower-case
letter.
```

In the last sentence, the first letter of the word "east" should have been capitalized.

In general, you might not be able to correct all of the syntax errors on the first attempt. This is natural. Generally, after you have repeated the process of correcting errors and having the computer read your revised program two or three times, you will have found all of the syntax errors.

Run-Time Errors

After correcting all of the syntax errors, the Ork program becomes:

```
Go East 2 blocks.
Go North 2 blocks.
Go West 4 blocks.
Go North 1 block.
Go East 2 blocks.
```

The Orks, having been able to read and to understand your program, will now proceed to *execute* your instructions. That is, the Orks will now read each instruction of your program and attempt to perform them one at a time from top to bottom. The process of performing the instructions is called *running* or *executing* the program.

When the Orks run the above program, you will receive an error message that might read as follows:

```
***Execution Error—unable to perform sentence
3 due to "end of street."
```

With a cursory look at the third sentence and at the map in Fig. 1.1, perhaps you realize that from the corner of Pine and Oak the Orks should be heading *east*, not west as you requested in the third sentence of the program. No wonder the Orks ran into the [west] end of Pine Street. Correcting this error, the program becomes:

```
Go East 2 blocks.
Go North 2 blocks.
Go East 4 blocks.
Go North 1 block.
Go East 2 blocks.
```

Once again the Orks will check for syntax errors in your program. Finding none, they proceed to execute the instructions from the beginning, one at a time. This time you will get the error message:

```
***Execution Error—unable to perform sentence
3 due to "end of street."
```

Note that this error message is precisely the same one that you had a moment ago. You might very well ask yourself how this error is possible. Maybe the Orks (i.e., the computer) have made a mistake. No, they did not. The mistake is in the program. Can you determine what went wrong this time?

To answer this question, put yourself at the corner of Pine Street and Oak Avenue in Fig. 1.1. Now read the third sentence of the program and attempt to follow the instructions. In doing so, you should realize that the program tells the Orks to go 4 blocks east instead of 3 blocks. Looking at Fig. 1.1, it is no wonder that the Orks, once again, ran into the end of the street.

Run-time error An error caused by asking the computer to perform an instruction that the machine cannot perform.

In summary, a **run-time error** is an error that is caused by asking the computer to perform an instruction that the machine cannot possibly perform. A run-time error might, for example, be caused by asking the computer:

1. To divide a number by 0.
2. To take the square root of a negative number.
3. To store some information in a "forbidden" area of the machine.

If a program contains more than one run-time error, you will have to run (and to correct) the program many times in order to find all of the errors. The reason is that, as soon as the computer encounters one run-time error, the machine will stop (with an error message) and will not continue to find other run-time errors.

Logic Errors

After correcting the last run-time error, the new program becomes:

```
Go East 2 blocks.
Go North 2 blocks.
Go East 3 blocks.
Go North 1 block.
Go East 2 blocks.
```

Once again, the Orks will check for syntax errors before running the program. Finding none, the Orks proceed to perform the instructions one at a time. This time, there will be no run-time errors. In fact, there will be no error messages at all. Unfortunately, the Orks will not arrive at your house. Instead, they will end up at the house directly north of yours across the park (see Fig. 1.1). Can you determine why this is so?

Once again, to discover what has caused the error, put yourself in the role of the Orks (i.e., the computer) and execute the instructions in the program. After the third sentence, you will find yourself at the end of Pine Street next to the park. The problem is that the fourth sentence of the program instructs you to go *north* one block instead of south. It is no wonder that the Orks never made it to your house. The final (and correct) program for solving this problem is.

```
Go East 2 blocks.
Go North 2 blocks.
Go East 3 blocks.
Go South 1 block.
Go East 2 blocks.
```

A **logic error** is an error that is caused by giving the computer an incorrect sequence of instructions to follow (although each instruction by itself can be performed by the computer). An example of a logic error is when you accidentally instruct the computer to add two numbers that should have been subtracted. Sometimes, a logic error in one part of a program will subsequently lead to a run-time error later in the program. The reason is that, at the time the logic error is encountered, the computer can still perform the (incorrect) instruction. However, as a result of doing so, the computer might not be able to perform a subsequent instruction, thus producing a run-time error.

Logic error An error caused by giving the computer an incorrect sequence of instructions (although each instruction by itself can be performed by the computer).

Logic errors are probably the most difficult to deal with because the computer will provide no error message. Nonetheless, with good debugging techniques, you will always be able to locate and to correct these errors.

Recap

There are three types of errors you might encounter in a computer program. They are

1. A syntax error, which is an error caused by not following the grammatical rules of the specific programming language.
2. A run-time error, which is caused by asking the computer to execute an instruction that the machine cannot possibly perform.
3. A logic error, which is the result of giving the computer an incorrect sequence of instructions (although each instruction by itself can be performed by the computer).

In this section, you have learned the three types of errors you might encounter during the programming process. However, you have also seen that, with proper debugging techniques, those errors can always be located and corrected. The next section provides several other techniques to ensure that you obtain a correct and working program.

Exercises for Section 1.4

Reread Exercises 1, 2, and 3 in Section 1.3. Each of the following three programs has been coded to direct the Orks from their given starting positions to their ending positions, as specified in Exercises 1, 2, and 3, respectively. First, rewrite each program, correcting all the syntax errors. Then, using the map in Fig. 1.1, perform the instructions as though you were the Orks. Indicate each time you encounter a run-time error, and write a corrected program. After all of the run-time errors are eliminated, run the program again and indicate any logic errors you encounter. Finally, rewrite the program correctly, being sure that the new program performs precisely the same instructions as given in the corresponding exercise of the previous section.

1. Go 1 block North.
Go east 2 blocks.
Go South 1 block.
Go East 1 block.
Stop.

2. Go South 1 block.
Go East 2 blocks.
Go North 1 block.

3. Go East 4 blocks.
Go South two blocks.
Go 2 Blocks East.

1.5 Obtaining and Maintaining a Correct Program

In this section, you will learn what is involved in obtaining a correct, working program. In addition, you will learn that continuous monitoring and revisions of a program may be necessary.

Tracing

In the previous section, you learned about syntax, run-time, and logic errors. Syntax errors are probably the easiest errors to deal with because they are clearly indicated by the computer and they are caused by a grammatical mistake. Run-time and logic errors are more difficult to resolve.

In the Ork example, when a run-time or logic error was encountered, you had to determine precisely how and why that error arose. In general, one of the best ways to do this is to pretend that you are the computer following the instructions. You must then execute the instructions one at a time to see what goes wrong. The process of playing the role of the computer and performing the instructions of the program yourself is referred to as *tracing the flow of the program*, or, more simply, **tracing.**

Tracing The process of playing the role of the computer and performing the instructions of the program yourself.

In the Ork example, each time a run-time or logic error occurred, you had to trace the program. You could have saved the Orks (and yourself) a great deal of time and trouble had you traced the program *before* the errors occurred. In fact, had you traced the algorithm when you first coded the program, you probably would have detected (and corrected) all of the run-time and logic errors.

Although tracing a program can be time consuming, the time spent will, most likely, be amply rewarded. As a general rule, you should trace your program either immediately before or immediately after you code the algorithm, but certainly before the computer starts to perform the instructions.

If a program is long and complicated, you should probably trace only those parts of the program that are most likely to cause problems. In any event, when a run-time or logic error arises, you will have to trace at least part of the code in order to determine what is wrong. In Chapter 2 you will be shown how to trace a program.

Testing and Validating

In the original Ork problem, you only wanted to give the Orks instructions for reaching your house from one specific starting point. Suppose, however, that you had to provide an algorithm for reaching your house from every possible intersection in Smallville. Once you have developed the algorithm, coded it, and removed all of the syntax and run-time errors, how will you know if your program really does what it is supposed to do?

One possibility is to *test* your algorithm starting with every intersection in Smallville. While this strategy is ideal, there are probably too many intersections to make this feasible. Such detailed testing is usually prohibitive in terms of the time and effort (computer and human) that is required. Therefore, another strategy is needed.

Unfortunately, there are no specific rules to follow in this situation. You will probably end up testing your algorithm on a limited number of selected cases. You might try following these general guidelines:

1. Test the algorithm on several easy cases for which you can trace the program and for which you know the answers.
2. Test the algorithm on several of the most difficult or tricky cases.
3. Try to think of situations that might cause the algorithm to perform incorrectly; then test the algorithm on those cases.

Much research is currently being done to determine when an algorithm performs correctly on all possible data values. That topic, however, is beyond the scope of this book.

Documentation

When a program has only a few instructions, you should have little difficulty reading and understanding the purpose of each instruction. However, when a program is long and complicated, reading and understanding the program can be a monumental task, especially if someone else wrote the program.

Often, programs are so big and so complex that teams of programmers are required to accomplish the job. Sometimes one person will work on a program for a while, and then another person will take over. In order for a program to be understandable to many possible users, it is helpful if the program contains frequent and explicit *comments*, written in English, that explain the purpose of various instructions. For example, a set of comments describing the inputting, processing, and outputting phases of the program can be very useful. Most programming languages have the facility for allowing you to place such comments virtually anywhere in the program. In this text, appropriate comments will be enclosed by the symbols { }.

When the computer encounters a comment within the program, the machine will ignore that comment completely. In other words, comments in a program are for the reader's convenience only. For instance, the original Ork program might have been written as follows:

```
{The next two instructions direct the Orks to Oak and Pine.}

Go East 2 blocks.
Go North 2 blocks.

{The next instruction directs the Orks to the park.}

Go East 3 blocks.
```

{The next two instructions direct the Orks around the park to my house.}

```
Go South 1 block.
Go East 2 blocks.
```

Other techniques for improving the *readability* of a program, and for writing "good" code will be discussed throughout the book.

In addition to comments within the program, it might be advisable (and necessary) to supply the user of the program with some additional written information (in English) outside the program. This information might detail how the program was designed, how to use the program, or what to do if something goes wrong. Such supporting information is referred to as *program documentation* (or sometimes, *user's manual*).

Program Maintenance

In some cases, a computer program is never completely finished. The reason is that, over time, certain factors might change, thus necessitating modifications to the original program in order to maintain its correctness and usefulness. Needed changes might arise in the Ork problem, for example, if new streets were added to the city, and old ones blocked off or made into one-way streets. Other changes might be needed if, as a program gets used more and more, certain bugs (undetected during the testing and validating phase) make themselves evident. In such cases, the program must be corrected. The process of continually monitoring a program and making such changes is called *program maintenance*.

1.6 Running a Program

After you have coded a program into a specific language, you will, at last, be ready to "face" the computer. After developing your program, preparing a set of instructions in your pseudocode, tracing, and coding, you will finally have a (handwritten) computer program that you believe will solve the original problem. You are now at a point where you would like to have the computer run the program. In so doing, you will enter the debugging phase so as to locate and to correct the syntax, run-time, and logic errors.

Unfortunately, computers cannot yet read handwriting. Thus, your first task is to prepare your materials in a *machine-readable form*, i.e., a form that the computer can read. Specifically, a complete *computer job* will usually consist of three machine-readable parts, namely,

1. The computer program itself.
2. The input values (i.e., the data), if any.
3. Some *system commands*, which are designed to provide the computer with certain necessary information. (Since the specific system commands vary from one computer to another, your instructor and/or someone at your computing facility will have to provide that information.) Some examples of the type of information included in the system commands are

   a) Identification—your name, department, course, etc.

   b) Account information—account number where the bill can be sent (computer services are not free), limits on the amount of computer resources you wish to use (e.g., computer time, amount of storage space, number of pages to be printed, etc.).

   c) Password—which you alone know so that no one else can use your account.

   d) Language information—indicating which computer language you are using.

   e) Delimiter information—to indicate where the program and/or data begins and/or ends.

All three of the above components must be prepared in a machine-readable form. The specific way you do so depends on which of two methods you are using to communicate with the computer. The two methods are described below.

Batch Processing

Batch processing The original method developed for communicating with the computer.

The original method developed for communicating with the computer is called **batch processing.** To use this method, you will prepare your job in a machine-readable form by using *off-line* equipment, that is, equipment not connected to the computer. Most likely, you would do so by typing your job on 80-column punch cards (Fig. 1.3). A *keypunch* machine (Fig. 1.4) will convert each character you type on the keyboard into a combination of punched holes that appear in one column of the card. The computer will subsequently be able to read the cards on a machine called a *card reader*, where those punched holes will be converted back into the original character you typed. Your

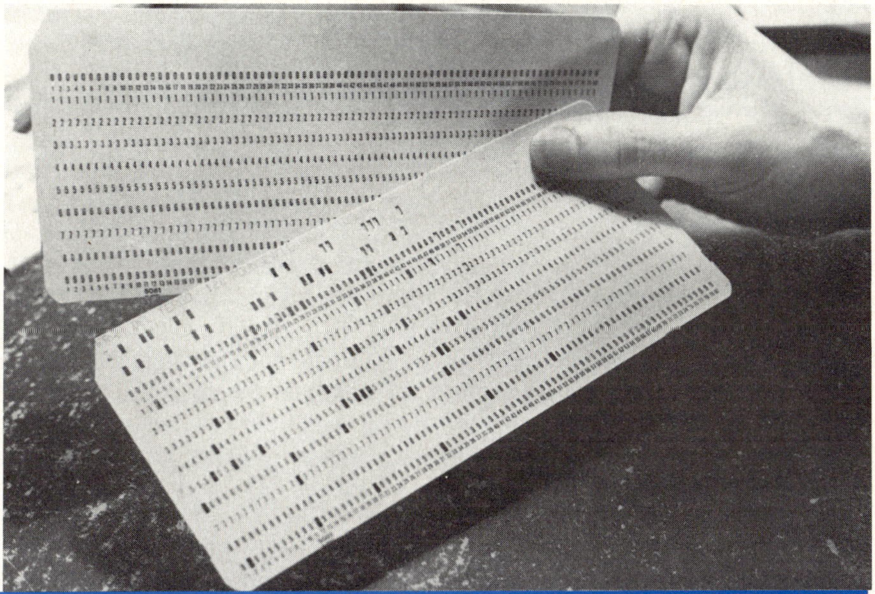

Figure 1.3 Punch cards. Photo by Darlene Bordwell.

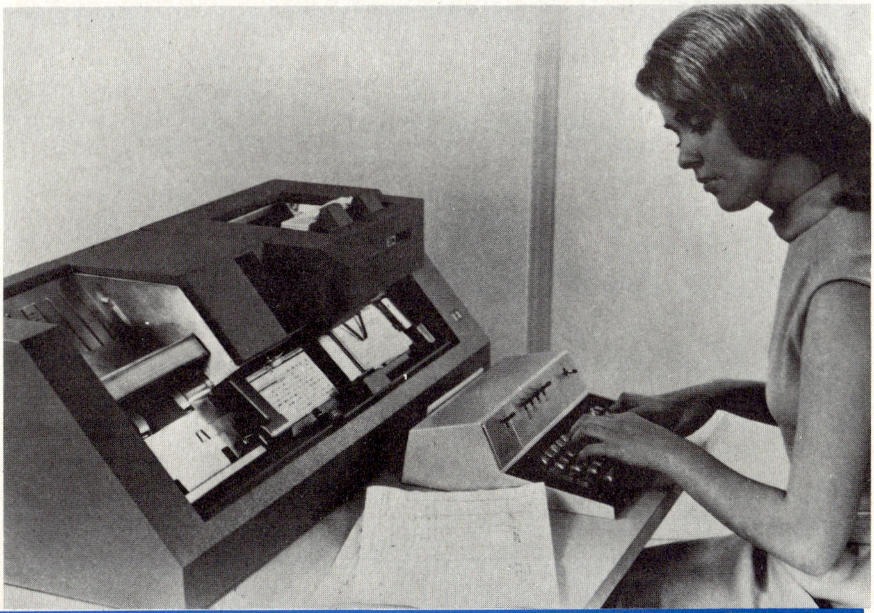

Figure 1.4 A keypunch machine. Courtesy of Data 100 Corporation.

instructor and/or someone at your computing facility will be able to show you how to use a keypunch, how to correct typing mistakes, etc.

When the typing is completed, you submit the resulting *deck* (of cards) to an *input/output station*. There, the deck will be put on a card reader that is connected to the computer. At some installations, you will operate the card reader yourself; at others, your deck is collected in a group, and a "batch" of jobs is entered (via a card reader) at one time.

Sometime later, if the computer does not break down, if your deck is not lost, and if the card reader does not accidentally destroy some of the cards, the results will be returned to you in the form of a *listing* of the program and the results, on computer paper, printed on a *printer* (Fig. 1.5). The amount of time it takes to get your job back can vary from seconds to days, depending on many factors, most of which you cannot control. It can be frustrating to wait for the listing to come back, only to discover that you made a careless typing mistake. Therefore it is advisable to check each card carefully before submitting the job, especially the system commands. A sample batch job is illustrated in Fig. 1.6.

Figure 1.5 A printer.

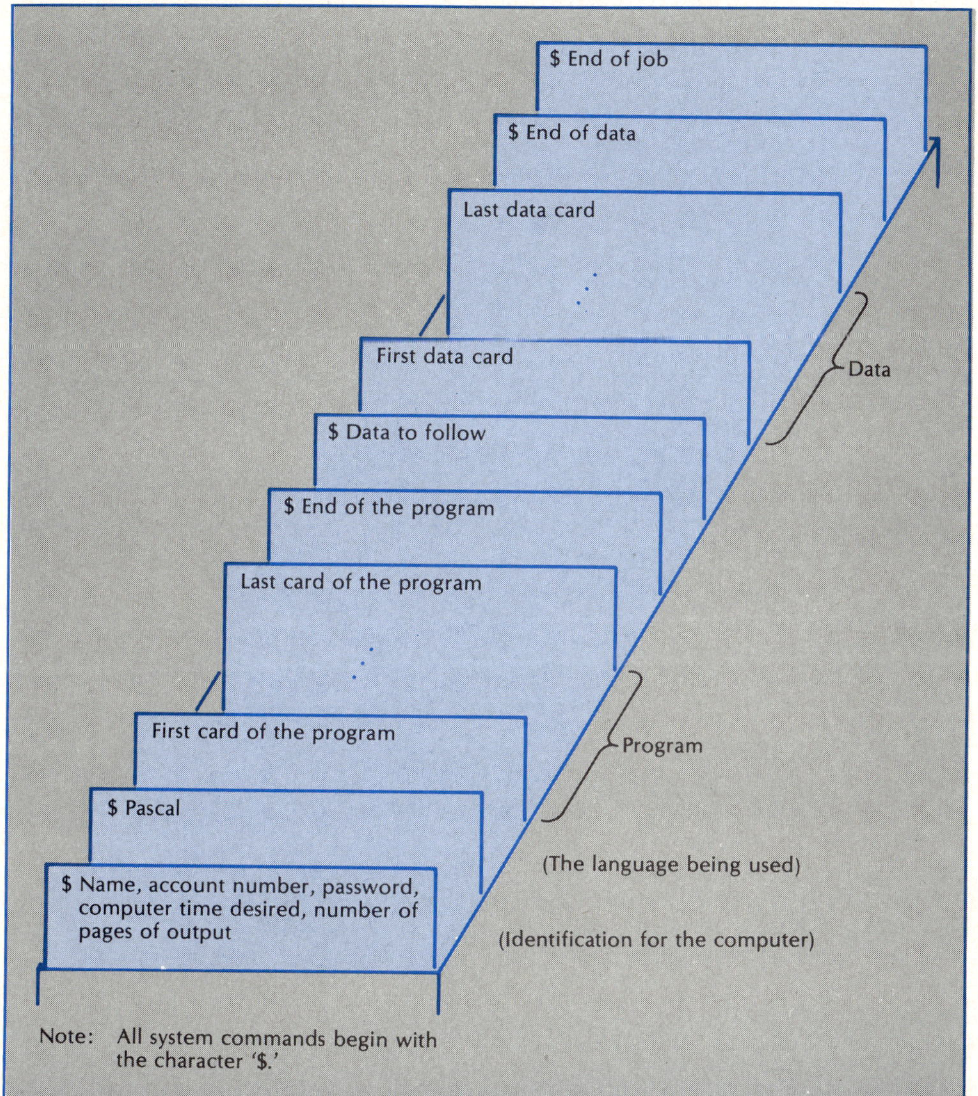

Figure 1.6 A sample batch job.

There are two major disadvantages to using batch processing. First of all, once the computer begins to execute your program, it is impossible for you to interact with the machine. Thus, for example, all data for the program must be available to the computer when you submit the job. Either that data must be included with the deck, or else the data must have been prepared beforehand. Second, you are not, in any way, using the computer to help you with the arduous task of preparing the job in a machine-readable form. This is because the keypunch is not connected to the computer. Both of these problems have been overcome with the development of the second method for communicating with the computer.

Interactive Processing

Interactive processing A method of communicating with the computer both as you code and as you run a program.

Interactive processing is a method that was designed to allow you to interact directly with the computer, both as you prepare the program and as the computer runs the program. A *microcomputer* is one form of an interactive system in which the computer will work exclusively for you. In contrast, with *time-sharing systems,* the computer will be interacting with many users at once, i.e., you will be sharing the computer's time with other users. In essence, the computer "moves" from one user to the next, spending a small amount of time working exclusively with each one, eventually returning to the first user. The greater the number of users, the longer it will take the computer to return to your job.

As was already pointed out, the primary advantage of an interactive system is that you can interact with the computer. Thus, for example, you could instruct the computer to terminate your program halfway through the execution. Alternatively, the computer can stop while executing your program to request certain information (e.g., data values) from you.

To communicate with the computer in an interactive mode, you will, most likely, use a *terminal* that is *on-line* (linked to the computer) (Fig. 1.7). The terminal usually consists of a *keyboard* (where the data will be typed when needed by the program), a television screen (called a *CRT,* which stands for cathode-ray tube), and possibly a printer. The system commands, program, and data will all be entered at the terminal. Each character you type on the keyboard will appear on the CRT and will ultimately be transmitted to the computer. (Since there are many different types of terminals, your instructor and/or someone at your computer facility will show you how to use a terminal, how to correct typing mistakes, etc.)

In an interactive mode, when the computer is running your program, the machine might display a *prompt* on your CRT, i.e., a request for you to type data. Often, the prompt is in the form of a character (such as a "?"). The computer will continue running your program

Figure 1.7 A keyboard and computer terminal. Courtesy of Apollo Computer Inc.

only after you have typed the necessary information in response to the prompt. A sample interactive session is illustrated in Fig. 1.8.

Although batch processing was the first method developed (and is still used extensively), interactive systems are quickly becoming dominant in the marketplace. In addition to being interactive, these systems usually provide the user with many sophisticated methods for entering, storing, *editing* (i.e., correcting typographical errors), and debugging programs. Using these tools can significantly reduce the time, effort, and frustration involved in getting a program to work correctly. The examples throughout the rest of this book are written for an interactive system; however, you can also run those examples on a batch system.

How a Computer Runs a Program

Once you have prepared the program, system commands, and data in a machine-readable form, and once you have submitted the job, the computer will finally be put to work. You might recall, from the discussion of the Orks, that a computer works with a language all its

Note: Underlined words have been produced by the computer; other words were typed by the user.

```
Account number: CS231   (identifying yourself)
Password: ■ ■ ■ ■   (not displayed for security reasons)
Command: Edit   (ask the computer to create a program)
Program name: Test   (provide a name for the program)
  No such existing program. Creating a new program.
Ready
  Program              (begin typing the program here)
  .
  .
  .
  End of program       (end typing the program here)
Command: Save   (ask the computer to store this program)
  Program Test saved
Command: Run   (ask the computer to run this program)
Language: Pascal   (the computer language to be used)
  Compiling. . .          (Here, the computer is compiling the program.)
  No errors detected      (Since no syntax errors were found, the computer
                          will now run the program.)
Running. . .
Enter your name   (a message displayed by the program)
Danny             (entering the requested data)
Hello Danny.      (a message displayed by the program)
  End execution   (the program is finished)
Command: Bye      (signing off)
  User CS231 logged off
```

Figure 1.8 A sample time-sharing session.

own. That language is called *machine language*. You might very well ask: "Why not write a program directly in machine language? Why use some other programming language?" The reason is that machine language consists exclusively of numbers; no letters or other symbols are allowed. To program in machine language would be very difficult.

You can, of course, write programs in many other computer languages besides Pascal. Languages that are "close" to machine language are called *low-level* languages. Languages that allow you to use names, symbols, and other concepts that are more closely related to English are called *high-level* languages. Generally speaking, the lower the level of the language, the harder it is to write a program, but the faster the program will run.

Since the computer only understands instructions written in machine language, your program will have to be translated into machine language. This process is called **compiling a program.** Fortunately, the computer has the capability to do so. In fact, some of the system commands that are included with your job will instruct the computer to do just that.

Compiling a program The act of translating a program into machine language.

A *compiler* is a [very large] program stored inside the computer. The compiler will take your program as input data (at this point, your program is referred to as **source code**), and will then attempt to translate your program into machine language. However, if you have syntax errors in your program, the compiler will be unable to complete its task. Indeed, it is the compiler that will produce all of the syntax error messages.

Source code The original program coded into a specific programming language.

Only when your program contains no syntax errors can the compiler successfully translate your program into machine langauge. The resulting machine-language translation that comes out of the compiler is called **object code** (Fig. 1.9). At that point, the computer will finally begin executing the instructions (and encountering run-time errors, if any).

Object code The resulting machine-language translation that comes out of the compiler.

Once you have debugged and tested a program, and deemed it to be correct, there is no need for the computer to recompile the program each time it is used. (To do so would require valuable computer time.) Instead, the final program is compiled once, and the resulting object code is saved for later use. However, if you need to change the source code, the computer must, of course, recompile the new program.

In this chapter, you have learned the steps involved in the computer problem-solving process. In Chapter 2, you will begin to learn how a computer "thinks." Specifically, you will learn several types of instructions that the computer will be able to understand.

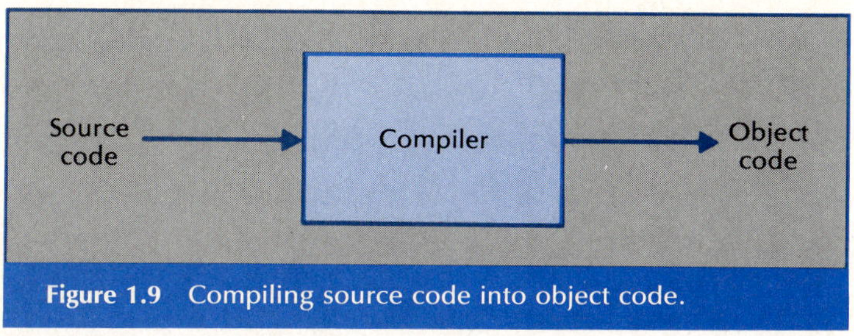

Figure 1.9 Compiling source code into object code.

Exercises for Section 1.6

Run one of the following two programs on your computer, depending on whether you are working with a batch system (Exercise 1) or an interactive system (Exercise 2). If you are working with a microcomputer, do Exercise 2. In any event, become familiar with all aspects of your computing facility including (as appropriate): location and operation of terminals and keypunches, preparation of system commands, storing and editing the program, and location of computer manuals and consultants to help you when you encounter a problem you cannot resolve. Be sure to type the program *exactly* as you see it here; otherwise, you will encounter syntax errors (from the compiler) that you might not understand at this time. In this event, look for (and correct) any careless typographical errors in the program.

1. (This program is for users of a batch system only.)

```
PROGRAM Test(INPUT, OUTPUT);  (*$B-*)
VAR
   Name :ARRAY[1..50] OF CHAR;
   I, J :INTEGER;
   Ch   :CHAR;
BEGIN
   I := 0;
   READ(Ch);
   WHILE (Ch <> '*') AND (I < 50) DO
          BEGIN
             I := I + 1;
             Name[I] := Ch;
             READ(Ch)
          END;
   WRITE('Congratulations ');
   FOR J := 1 TO I DO
        WRITE(Name[J]);
   WRITELN('.');
   WRITELN('You have just run your first Pascal program!')
END.
```

You should note that the data for this program consists of one card on which you type your name followed by the symbol ∗. When you are successful, the computer should return to you the following result:

```
Congratulations [your name].
You have just run your first Pascal program!
```

2. (This program is for users of an interactive system only.)

```
PROGRAM Test(INPUT, OUTPUT); (*$B-*)
VAR
   Name :ARRAY[1..50] OF CHAR;
   I, J :INTEGER;
   Ch   :CHAR;
BEGIN
   WRITELN('Type your name followed by the symbol *');
   WRITELN('and then a carriage return');
   I := 0;
   READ(Ch);
   WHILE (Ch <> '*') AND (I < 50) DO
         BEGIN
            I := I + 1;
            Name[I] := Ch;
            READ(Ch)
         END;
   WRITELN;
   WRITE('Congratulations ');
   FOR J := 1 TO I DO
       WRITE(Name[J]);
   WRITELN('.');
   WRITELN('You have just run your first Pascal program!')
END.
```

You should note that the data for this program consists of your name followed by the symbol * and then a carriage return. The computer will "ask" you to type this information on your keyboard by displaying a message on your screen. When you are successful, the computer shoud display on your CRT the following result:

```
Congratulations [your name].
You have just run your first Pascal program!
```

1.7 Summary

In this chapter, the process of using a computer to solve a problem has been broken down into the following seven phases: Algorithm

Development, Coding, Running, Debugging, Testing and Validating, Documenting, and Program Maintenance. The phase that requires the most creativity (and is often the most challenging) is the algorithm-development phase, for which you can use the techniques of stepwise refinement; thinking through your solution; pseudocode; inputting, processing, and outputting; working through a specific example; and top-down programming.

After you have developed a coded program for solving a problem, you must then prepare that program in a machine-readable form. How you do so depends on whether you are using a batch-processing or an interactive system. In the former case you might prepare your job on a keypunch; in the latter, you will be working on a terminal.

Once the program is prepared in a machine-readable form, you submit the job to the computer. Using the compiler, the computer will attempt to translate your program into machine language. In so doing, you begin the debugging process.

The three types of computer errors that can arise in the debugging process are (1) syntax errors, which are caused by not following the grammatical rules of the specific programming language; (2) run-time errors, which are caused by asking the computer to perform an instruction that the machine cannot possibly perform; and (3) logic errors, which are caused by giving the computer an incorrect sequence of instructions to follow (although each instruction by itself can be executed).

Syntax errors are the easiest to correct because the computer generally indicates the error clearly. To resolve run-time and logic errors, however, you will have to determine what instructions are causing the error and why. To find the problem, you will have to trace at least part of the program, i.e., play the role of the computer and execute the instructions yourself. As a general rule, tracing should be done sometime before the computer runs the program for the first time. The more time and effort you put into the algorithm-development, coding, and tracing phases, the less time you will need in the debugging phase.

Key Terms

Programming 2

Pascal 2

Thinking through your solution 6

Algorithm 7

Stepwise refinement 7

Coding 8

Computer program 8

Pseudocode 8

Top-down programming 9

Inputting, processing, and outputting 10

Inputting 10

Data 10

Processing 10

Working through a specific example 11

Outputting 11

Debugging 13

Syntax error 14

Run-time error 18

Logic error 19

Tracing 21

Batch processing 24

Interactive processing 28

Compiling a program 31

Source code 31

Object code 31

Galileo was the first to use the telescope for astronomy. Having heard that a telescope had been invented in Holland, the indomitable scientist set out to duplicate the device. In August 1609, he presented to the Venetian senate a 9-power telescope, an instrument three times as powerful as its predecessors, thus opening up exploration of our universe. (THE BETTMAN ARCHIVE, INC.)

2

USING THE MEMORY OF THE COMPUTER

From Chapter 1, you should realize that it will not be possible to program a computer until you understand how the machine "thinks." As a first step in that direction, in this chapter you will learn how the computer can be made to store information in its memory. Also, you will learn how to perform certain operations with that information. Then, using a simple example, many of the problem-solving techniques of Chapter 1 will be illustrated. Pseudocode will be used throughout the chapter to allow you to focus on important problem-solving issues instead of on the details of Pascal syntax. Pascal will be taught in Chapter 3.

2.1 How Computers Can Be Made to Store Information

A computer, like a human, has a memory. The purpose of the computer's memory is to store information for later use. Programming languages like Pascal allow you to access and to use part of the computer's memory. In this section, you will learn how that storage can be performed from within a program. To that end, you should think of the computer's available memory as a [very large but limited] book. On each page of the book you can instruct the computer to write (i.e., *store*) information, or to read (i.e., *retrieve*) information. The first of these operations will be discussed in this section, and the second operation will be addressed in Section 2.2.

Using Variables to Store Information

On each "page" of the computer's available memory, you can instruct the computer to write certain information, such as the number 3, or 4.18. However, the computer can write *only one number per page*. Thus, for example, you can give the computer an instruction of the form:

Write the number 3.14 on page 2037.

One of the problems with doing this, however, is that if you ever want to retrieve (and to use) the number 3.14 from the computer's memory, you will have to remember on what page the computer wrote that number. Clearly, if you have stored many numbers in the computer's memory, you will quickly forget which number was written on which page.

One way to resolve this problem is to use **identifiers** (i.e., names, words, letters, etc.) instead of page numbers, for names are more easily remembered than numbers. The names you give to the pages of memory are called variable identifiers, or, more simply, **variables.** When working in pseudocode, the variable identifiers you choose can consist of any sequence of letters and/or characters because there are no rules of grammar that must be followed. The number that you store into a variable is called the **value of a variable.** Thus, instead of instructing the computer to "write the number 3.14 on page 2037," you could give the computer the equivalent instruction:

> Write the number 3.14 on the page whose name is `Price` (i.e., store the value 3.14 into the variable whose name is `Price`).

Now, when you wish to retrieve the number 3.14, you need only refer to the variable `Price`. You do not need to remember on which page the number 3.14 was written; the computer will do that for you. The actual page number is called the **address of the variable** (Fig. 2.1).

During the development of an algorithm, the programmer will typically "create" variables to store values. Since the values have a physical, real-world meaning, the corresponding variables also have a real-world meaning, which you can associate with the value. For instance, in the example above, the value 3.14 stored in the variable `Price` might represent a price of three dollars and fourteen cents for some item in a particular problem.

Identifiers Names that are used for various purposes in a program.

Variables Names that are used by you in a program to refer to specific memory locations of the computer.

Value of a variable The number that is stored into the variable.

Address of a variable The actual "page" number that corresponds to a variable.

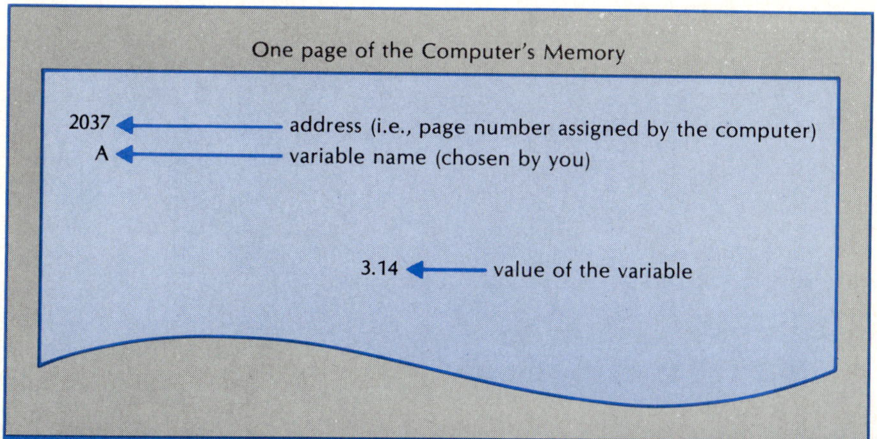

Figure 2.1 Storing a value into a variable.

In order to enhance the readability of your program, the name you choose for a variable should be indicative of the purpose of that variable, to whatever extent possible. For example, suppose that you needed to develop an algorithm to determine the amount of money a newspaper girl earns. In order to do so, you might need to know the number of papers she sold. If so, then you should create a variable whose name, say, is *Papers*. At the same time, you should consciously say to yourself that the meaning of the value of the variable *Papers* is the actual number of papers sold.

Declaring a Variable

Declaring a variable Telling the computer the name of a variable and the type of information that will be stored into that variable.

Before you can store a value into the memory of the computer, you must **declare** (i.e., create) **the associated variable**. In so doing, you instruct the computer to associate a specific variable name (e.g., *Price*) with a page in the memory. When you declare a variable, you must provide the computer with the name of the variable and the type of information that will be stored into the variable because, as you will soon learn, numbers are not the only information that can be stored in the computer's memory.

For each variable you declare, the computer will automatically assign a page number to that variable. Fortunately, you need not be concerned with which variable corresponds to which page. The computer will always keep an accurate list so that when you refer to the variable by its name, the computer will know the associated page number.

In Pascal, the variables are declared once and only once at the beginning of a program. The specific way in which you do so will be described in Section 3.1. However, when working in pseudocode, you need not declare your variables; you can simply use variables in designing your algorithm. The reason is that pseudocode is not a computer language, and so the details of declaring variables can be temporarily ignored.

Assigning a Value to a Variable in Pseudocode

Assignment statement The instruction that tells the computer to store a value into a variable.

During the algorithm-development phase of solving a problem, you will often have to store a particular value into a variable. This process is called *assigning* a value to the variable, or *defining* the variable. The associated computer instruction is called an **assignment statement.** In order to assign a value to a variable, you could write the English instruction

Store the following Value into the following Variable (assuming that the Variable has been declared).

In this text, however, pseudocode will be used to write the above instruction more simply as

```
Variable := Value
```

The symbol := should be read as "gets the value of," or "is assigned the value of." (Throughout this text, a name that is underlined, as was Variable above, can be replaced by any (allowable) name of your choosing. In a similar sense, Value above can be replaced with any allowable value.) Do not confuse the symbol := with the symbol =, which stands for "equals." Some books use the symbol ←, or some other symbol instead of :=, but the meaning is the same.

Note that in an assignment statement the variable must appear to the left of the :=, while the value of the variable must be to the right. Thus, for instance, the assignment statement

```
Price := 3.14
```

will instruct the computer to store the value 3.14 into the variable whose name is *Price*. The subsequent assignment statement

```
Price := 2.5
```

instructs the computer to turn to the page corresponding to *Price*, to erase the previous value of 3.14 *(because only one number can be written on each page)*, and to write the new number 2.5 on that page.

Constants

One of the major reasons for using a variable in a computer program is because you can change the value of the variable at different places in the program. However, you can also assign a number, or other known and fixed value, to an identifier that will not be changed anywhere in the program. Such an identifier is called a constant identifier, or, more simply, a **constant**. At this point, you might very well ask why you would want to assign a fixed number to an identifier. In other words, why not work with that fixed number directly? There are several possible answers.

Constant An identifier whose value will not change anywhere in the program.

Suppose, for instance, that you were going to use the number 3.1415927 in many different places in a program. If you store that number into an identifier, say *Pi*, then you would not have to retype the entire number every time you needed it. Instead, you could refer, more simply, to the identifier `Pi`. Using an identifier in this way is particularly beneficial if, at some future time, you need to change that number throughout the entire program. To do so, you need only alter the one statement where the value was originally assigned to the identifier, instead of having to locate and to correct that number everywhere it occurred.

Moreover, by using an identifier instead of a specific number, your program will be easier for someone else to read. For instance, *you* might know that the number 0.18 is being used in your program as a tax rate, but someone else will not. If, on the other hand, you use an identifier whose name is `TaxRate` instead of 0.18, another person will be able to understand your program more easily.

Reading a Value into a Variable

`READ` **statement** The instruction that tells the computer to obtain the value for a variable from somewhere outside the program.

You have learned that the assignment statement can be used to store a value into a variable. Another instruction for storing a value into a variable is called a `READ` **statement.** (Throughout this text, words such as `READ` whose letters are all in UPPER CASE are words that have a special meaning to the computer, and you will use those words when coding an algorithm into Pascal. Therefore you should not use those words as identifiers in your program.)

A `READ` statement should be used when the value of a variable will not be known until the program is actually run. For example, suppose you want to write a program for instructing the Orks on how to get from an intersection in Smallville to your house. You will not know the specific intersection from which the Orks will start until the program is used.

Therefore imagine that you are writing a program for someone else, and that you wish to allow that user to determine the value of a variable when the program is run. For this situation, it would indeed be convenient to have the following type of programming instruction:

> Go ask the user for the value of a variable, say, `Intersection`.

More generally, in a program, you would like to be able to write the following type of instruction:

> Obtain the value of the following Variable from somewhere "outside" this program.

The equivalent pseudocode statement

```
READ Variable
```

instructs the computer to do precisely that. However, in order for the computer to be able to perform this instruction, you will have to specify precisely where the value for the variable can be obtained. For example, the value might be obtained from the keyboard at which you are working, or from a magnetic tape or cassette (where the value has been previously typed and stored), or from punch cards that accompany your program. The details of how and where the computer obtains the value for the variable using a READ statement will be addressed in Chapter 3.

In any event, the pseudocode statement

```
READ Variable
```

will be used in this text to tell the computer (1) to obtain the value for the Variable from somewhere outside the program, (2) to turn to the page of the memory corresponding to the Variable, (3) to erase whatever is on that page (because only one number can be written on each page), and (4) to write the new value of the Variable on that page.

For example, the pseudocode statement

```
READ Lowest, Highest
```

tells the computer to obtain the values for the variables *Lowest* and *Highest* from somewhere outside the program. (Observe that more than one variable can appear in a READ statement.)

Comparison of Assignment and READ Statements

Both the assignment and the READ statements can be used to store information into the computer's memory; either statement will assign a value to a variable. There are, however, three important differences. First, you should use a READ statement when the value of a variable is not known beforehand. Second, the READ statement will instruct the computer to obtain the value of the variable from outside the program, whereas in an assignment statement, the value of the variable must appear on the right side of the := . Third, the READ statement will allow you (or someone else who does not know programming) to change the value of a variable from outside the program.

To illustrate the first difference between a READ and an assignment statement, suppose you had to write a program to compute the amount of money obtained by selling a certain number of cookies. The data for this problem consist of the number of cookies sold and the price per cookie. Thus you might create two variables, say *Cookies* and *Price*, whose values represent the number of cookies baked and the price per cookie, respectively. However, the specific values of these variables (i.e., the data) will not be known until the program is run. Therefore, when writing the instructions to obtain the values for those variables, you should use the READ statement

```
READ Cookies, Price
```

In contrast, suppose that you know, beforehand, that the number of cookies is 2080, and that the price per cookie is 12 cents. Then, instead of the READ statement, you should use the assignment statements

```
Cookies := 2080
Price := 0.12
```

to store the values of the variables.

In this book, whenever you encounter a word problem in which it says "Given a value for. . . ," this means you *will* be given the appropriate value at the time the program runs. In these cases, you should use a READ statement (instead of an assignment statement) to store the value (that will be given to the computer when the program runs) into an appropriate variable.

What should you do if the value of a variable could be determined conveniently either by using an assignment statement or a READ statement, as in the following?

Problem: For each of the past 30 days, Bob the grocer has kept a list of the total amount of money he received on each day. He wants you to write a program to determine the combined total he earned during those 30 days.

In developing your program, suppose that you decide to create a variable, say *Days*, whose value represents the 30 days (i.e., the value of *Days* will be 30). To store the value of 30 into the variable *Days*, you could use either the assignment statement

```
Days := 30
```

or the READ statement

```
READ Days
```

Both statements are, of course, acceptable.

The advantage of using the assignment statement is that the computer will not have to search outside the program to obtain the value for *Days*. There is, however, a greater advantage to using the READ statement if, at some future time, this value will change. Imagine, for example, that several months in the future, Bob says to you that he now wishes to obtain the total money he earned every 15 days (instead of 30 days). Had you used the assignment statement originally, you would now have to go into the program and change the assignment statement to

```
Days := 15
```

On the other hand, had you originally used a READ statement to assign a value for *Days*, you would not have to modify the program at all. Rather, from outside the program, you (or, more importantly, Bob the grocer, who knows nothing about programming) could go to the place where the computer will obtain the value for *Days*, and simply change that value from 30 to 15. Thus, by having used a READ statement in the first place, the proposed change could have been implemented by someone who knows nothing about programming.

In conclusion, use a READ statement when the value of a variable will not be known until the program is run. Use an assignment statement when you know, beforehand, what the value of a variable is. When both options are available, it is sometimes better to use a READ statement than an assignment statement because of the ability to change the value of the variable from outside the program.

In this section, you have learned how to create a variable and how to use the assignment and READ statements to store information into those variables. In Section 2.2, you will learn how to retrieve and how to use that information.

Exercises for Section 2.1

Convert each of the following word instructions into an appropriate assignment statement.

1. Store the current interest rate of 0.09 into the variable *Interest*.
2. Create a constant E whose value is 2.718.
3. Set the value of the variables *Minute*, *Hour*, *Day*, *Week*, and *Year* to the number of seconds in a minute, minutes in an hour, hours in a day, days in a week, and weeks in a year, respectively.

In each of the following groups of statements, after performing the last instruction, identify all of the variables and their final values.

4.
```
READ First, Second, Third
First := 3.5
Second := 3.6
First := 3.2
Third := 4
First := 3.0
First := 3.0
Second := 1.5
First := 2.9
```

5.
```
READ Temp
High := 1000
Low := 0
Temp := 500
Low := 500
High := 750
READ Low, High
```

2.2 Using Information from the Computer's Memory

In Section 2.1 you learned two ways for storing information into the computer's memory: the assignment and READ statements. In this section, you will learn how to retrieve and use that information in the problem-solving process. As a general rule, there are two reasons for wanting to retrieve information from the computer's memory. First, there will be times when you will want to calculate, manipulate, and/or process that information, particularly during the processing phase of solving a problem. Second, you will want the computer to report that information to you during the outputting phase. Both of these topics will be addresssed in this section.

Performing Arithmetic Operations

Like calculators, computers can add (+), subtract (−), multiply (*), and divide (/) numbers. Unlike calculators, however, computers do not automatically "display" the results of their calculations. Rather, those results are usually stored back into the computer's memory for later display or use. Consequently, the assignment statement can, and should, be used to store the result of an arithmetic calculation.

For example, if you want to perform the multiplication of 3 times 5, then the instruction

```
3 * 5
```

is not valid because the result (namely, 15) has not been stored anywhere. On the other hand, the statement

```
Amount := 3 * 5
```

is valid because the result (15) will be stored into the variable *Amount*, assuming, of course, that the variable *Amount* has been declared properly.

In pseudocode, it is acceptable to omit the symbol * (e.g., you can write 3(5) instead). However, in Pascal, you must always use the symbol *. Therefore, when writing pseudocode, it is advisable to use the symbol * to indicate multiplication.

In addition, computers can use the values of variables when performing arithmetic operations. Once again, the end result of the calculations (i.e., the answer) should be stored into a variable by using an assignment statement. As always, the variable into which you wish to store the result must be by itself on the left of the := . The variables and/or numbers you are using in the calculations must appear to the right of the := .

From here on, such a sequence of calculations to the right of a := will be referred to as an **expression.** Thus to calculate and to store the result of an expression in pseudocode, you would write

Expression A sequence of calculations to be performed.

```
Variable := Expression
```

For example, the statement:

```
Second := First + 1
```

will cause the computer to retrieve the value for the variable *First* from the machine's memory, to add 1 to that value, and to store the result into the variable *Second*.

When the computer retrieves the value of a variable that appears in an expression on the right of the := , in this case, *First*, the value of that variable will *not* be changed. Rather, the computer simply "reads" the value of that variable from the appropriate page in the memory, leaving the value of the variable unchanged.

The computer then performs the calculations in the expression on the right side of the := . For all practical purposes, you can think of these calculations as being performed "on a piece of scratch paper." The computer then stores the final result of the computations into the variable that is on the left of the := , e.g., *Second* in the example above. In so doing, any previous value of that variable is erased.

As another example, suppose that you have used the assignment statements

```
Amount := 3
Price := 5
```

to store the values of 3 and 5 into the variables *Amount* and *Price*, respectively. The calculation

```
Amount := Amount * Price
```

would have the following effect. First, looking at the right side of the := above, the computer would retrieve the values of *Amount* and *Price* from the memory. (In so doing, the values of *Amount* and *Price* remain unchanged.) Next, using these values for *Amount* and *Price*, the computer would perform the multiplication of 3 times 5. Finally, looking at the left side of the := above, the computer would store the result of the computation (i.e., 15) into the variable *Amount*. In so doing, the old value of 3 for *Amount* is erased, and the new value of 15 is written on the page corresponding to *Amount*.

Precedence of Arithmetic Operators

As simple as arithmetic operations are, you must still be very careful. For instance, after performing the instruction

```
Amount := 7 - 2 * 3
```

what will be the value of *Amount*? Is it

```
(7 - 2) * 3 (i.e., 15)?
```

Or is it

```
7 - (2 * 3) (i.e., 1)?
```

Once again, you must learn how a computer thinks. Computers, unless told otherwise, will follow these rules: (1) All multiplications and divisions are performed first. In so doing, the computer works from the left of the expression to the right. (2) All additions and subtractions are performed next. In so doing, the computer again works from the left of the expression to the right. However, a minus sign that is used in front of a single variable (e.g., −*B*) will be evaluated before multiplications and divisions. This minus sign is called a *unary* operator. Thus

```
-B + A * C - D
```

will be computed as

```
(-B) + (A * C) - D
```

Example

In the following assignment statement, parentheses are used to indicate the next operation that would be performed by the computer.

```
Amount := 5 + 8 / 2 * 3 - 6 / 3 * 2
Amount := 5 + (8 / 2) * 3 - 6 / 3 * 2
Amount := 5 + (4 * 3) - 6 / 3 * 2
Amount := 5 + 12 - (6 / 3) * 2
Amount := 5 + 12 - (2 * 2)
Amount := (5 + 12) - 4
Amount := (17 - 4)
Amount := 13
```

The order in which operators are performed is called the **precedence of the operators.** You must keep the issue of precedence in mind whenever you come across a new arithmetic operator, such as the operator MOD that will be described in Chapter 3. In such instances, you should always inquire as to the precedence of that operator in relation to the other arithmetic operators.

Precedence of operators The order in which the operators are performed.

It is, of course, possible to change the normal precedence of operators. To do so, you need only enclose in parentheses the expression that you want computed first.

Example

Under the normal precedence of operators, the expression

```
A + B * C
```

will cause the value of *B* to be multiplied by that of *C* first, and the result to be added to the value of *A*. However, the expression

```
(A + B) * C
```

will cause the value of *A* to be added to that of *B* first, and the result to be multiplied by the value of *C*.

Example

Suppose that the values of *A*, *B*, and *C* are 8, 2, and 3, respectively. Also, suppose that you want to compute and to store the value of

$$\frac{A - B}{2C}$$

into the variable D. The resulting value of D should, of course, be 1. However, if you carelessly wrote the statement

```
D := A - B / 2 * C
```

the value of D will turn out to be 5, because of the normal precedence. The result is a logic error because you gave the computer an incorrect (but executable) instruction (see Section 1.4). Similarly, if you wrote the statement

```
D := (A - B) / 2 * C
```

the value of D would turn out to be 9; still a logic error. The correct assignment statement is

```
D := (A - B) / (2 * C)
```

When working in pseudocode, you need not be overly concerned about parentheses and precedence—after all, the reason for using pseudocode is to avoid worrying about details. However, during the coding phase, you must be *extremely* careful of parentheses and precedence. For this reason, you are well advised to get into the habit of using parentheses even in pseudocode. When in doubt, use parentheses.

Displaying the Value of a Variable

WRITE statement The instruction that tells the computer to display the value of a variable (or an expression).

In accordance with the outputting phase of problem solving, you will eventually want the computer to report to you the values of certain variables, for those values will constitute the solution to the original problem. Indeed, programming languages, including Pascal, have this capability. In this text, the associated pseudocode instruction, referred to as a WRITE **statement,** will be

```
WRITE Variable
```

Specifically, such a statement will be used to tell the computer (1) to retrieve the value of the Variable from the computer's memory (in so doing, the value of the Variable will remain unchanged); and (2) to display the value of the Variable in some form—perhaps on paper, perhaps on a television screen, or perhaps in some other part of the computer. The issue of how, where, and in what form the computer displays the value of a variable will be addressed in Chapter 3. For now, consider the following examples.

Example

The pseudocode statement

```
WRITE Lowest, Highest
```

tells the computer to retrieve the values for the variables *Lowest* and *Highest* from the computer's memory, and to display those values.

Example

The value of a computation can also be displayed with a WRITE statement, for example:

```
WRITE 5 * Highest - 3
```

More generally, the following instruction is acceptable:

```
WRITE Expression
```

In this section, you have learned how to retrieve information from the computer's memory. In addition, you have learned how to use an assignment statement to perform simple arithmetic operations with that information. Finally, you have learned about the concept of displaying the values of variables. From this and Section 2.1, you now have enough pseudocode instructions to handle the inputting, processing, and outputting phases of simple problems. In fact, in Section 2.3, you will be shown how to do precisely that.

Exercises for Section 2.2

What, if anything, is wrong with the following pseudocode instructions?

1. 3.14159 * *Radius* * *Radius* := *Area*
2. *Counter* := *Counter* + 1
3. Compute 2 * 3.14159 * *Radius*
4. *First* + 1 := 5 * 3

5. `READ Amount + 1`
6. `Amount = 3(Amount * Price)`

Suppose that all of the following variables have been declared, and that these assignment statements have been performed:

```
Amount := 3.5
First := 2
Second := 1
```

In each of the following assignment satements, determine the resulting value of the variable on the left of the := . (Use the usual rules of precedence.)

7. `Total := 1.0 + First * Amount`
8. `Second := Second + First / 2 - 1`
9. `First := (First + 3) - 4 * Amount / 7`
10. `Amount := Amount + 2.0 * Amount`

Recalling the rules of precedence, write each of the following instructions with an assignment statement using parentheses together with the operators +, −, *, and /.

11. D gets the value of $1 + \frac{A - B}{C}$.
12. Store the value of $\frac{A}{B} + \frac{C}{2}$ into D.
13. Compute $\frac{A(2B)}{C}$ and put the result into D.
14. The value of D should be computed as $\frac{\frac{1 + A}{2B} - 1}{C}$.

2.3 Solving a Problem

In this section, you will put into practice the problem-solving techniques of Chapter 1, together with the concepts of Sections 2.1 and 2.2. The objective is to convert a given word problem into a sequence of pseudocode instructions that, if performed by the computer, will result in the solution to the problem.

Problem: Given the values of two variables, switch the values of those two variables and display the results thus obtained.

This problem is so simple that you might wonder why a computer is even needed; indeed the problem could easily be solved by hand. The point of this example, and of many examples in this book, is to teach you a particular programming concept that demonstrates techniques that are used in solving more complex problems. When you begin to solve these more complex problems, you will see that the value of a computer lies in the speed with which the machine can carry out instructions (sometimes millions of instructions per second). As a general rule, you should use a computer when the amount of time needed to solve a problem by hand exceeds the amount of time needed to prepare the program and the data.

Algorithm Development

The first step is to describe in your own words how you would solve the above problem yourself. To that end, you might come up with the following

Solution: To solve the problem, I simply interchange the values of the two variables.

While this statement is perhaps true, you cannot give those instructions to a computer, for the machine does not understand English. The computer does, however, understand the concept of assignment, `READ`, and `WRITE` statements. Therefore, your objective is to describe the above solution in terms that the computer can understand.

Thinking Through Your Solution. The next step is to think through your solution in an attempt to understand more precisely how you are solving the problem. Can you do so for the above problem?

If you are having difficulty, one way to begin is to identify the inputting, processing, and outputting phases of the problem.

Inputting. To identify the inputting phase of the problem, learn to ask yourself "What information will I have to be given in order to solve the problem?" In this problem, you will need to be given the original values of the two variables.

In order to store these values into the memory of the computer, you will need to declare (i.e., create) two variables, say *`First`* and *`Second`*. Since their original values will not be known until the program is run, those values (i.e., the data) should be stored into the computer using a READ statement, instead of an assignment statement (see Section 2.1). However, as you will soon see, another part of this problem will require the use of an assignment statement. Thus, the first (pseudocode) statement in the algorithm should be

```
READ First, Second
```

This instruction tells the computer to go somewhere outside the program to obtain the values for *First* and *Second*, and to store those values into the computer's memory.

Processing. To identify the processing phase of the problem, learn to ask yourself "What do I want to do with the data once that information is stored in the computer?" For this problem, you will need to switch the values of the two variables.

Now you should think through your solution (i.e., switching the values of the two variables) so as to understand, more precisely, how you accomplish that task. Try to isolate and to identify the individual steps you are performing. As you do so, you must keep in mind how the computer thinks. Specifically, recall the concept of an assignment statement. Thus, for example, by thinking through your solution, you might provide the following more detailed solution.

Solution: To switch the values of the two variables, I must take the value of the second variable and put that value into the first variable. Then, I take the value of the first variable and put that value into the second variable.

Observe that the answer obtained by thinking through your solution is being expressed more in terms that the computer can understand because the concept of "putting" a value into a variable is precisely that of an assignment statement.

Refinement. Recall from Chapter 1 that refinement is the process of gradually rephrasing your English solution in terms of a specific programming language. To that end, pseudocode should be used first. Can you express the last solution above in terms of pseudocode?

If you understand assignment statements correctly, then you might write the following two statements:

```
First := Second     {Assigning the value of the second variable to the first variable.}
Second := First     {Assigning the value of the first variable to the second variable.}
```

What you will soon discover is that these two statements will not quite accomplish the desired task. The reason is that you have not yet thought through your solution carefully enough. For now, you have developed the inputting and processing phases to obtain the following pseudocode algorithm:

```
READ First, Second
First := Second
Second := First
```

Outputting. To identify the outputting phase of the problem, learn to ask yourself, "What information do I want the computer to display so that I will then know the solution to the problem?" Obviously, here you want the computer to display the new values of the variables *First* and *Second*.

The next step is to convert that answer into a pseudocode statement. Recalling the WRITE statement from Section 2.2, the appropriate statement is

```
WRITE First, Second
```

Combining the inputting, processing, and outputting phases, the pseudocode algorithm that has been developed for solving this problem is

```
READ First, Second
First := Second
Second := First
WRITE First, Second
```

Since the above algorithm has been developed in pseudocode, the issue of declaring the variables has been temporarily omitted.

Debugging

In theory, the next step in developing a computer program might be to code the above algorithm. That is to say, the above pseudocode statements must be rewritten in terms of a specific programming language, such as Pascal. In so doing, you must pay particular attention to spelling, punctuation, and the rules of grammar of the particular language. At this time, however, you have not learned a specific programming language. Therefore the coding process will be delayed until Chapter 3. For now, assume that the computer can understand the algorithm above.

Once an algorithm has been coded into a specific computer language, the next step is to locate and to correct the syntax, run-time, and logic errors. You must correct the syntax errors first because the computer will not attempt to execute the instructions until all of these errors are eliminated. However, since the above program has not been coded, the process of eliminating syntax errors will not be demonstrated at this time. The remainder of this section will illustrate the process of finding and correcting logic errors.

Therefore assume that the computer can now run the program. Also, suppose that the original values of the variables *First* and *Second* that will be read by the computer are 3 and 7, respectively. The user of the program would have to supply these values to the computer, either at the terminal when the program is run, or in some other manner. The details of doing so will be discussed in Chapter 3.

On running the above program using the values of 3 and 7, the computer will return to you the following information as specified in the final WRITE statement:

(i.e., *First* equals 7 and *Second* equals 7)

The answer is definitely not what you wanted. You expected the results to be

(i.e., *First* equals 7 and *Second* equals 3)

Clearly, an error has been made. However, since the computer did not display an error message, it is apparent that the machine was able to perform all of the instructions in the program. Consequently, the above error is a logic error and not a run-time error (see Section 1.4).

Ideally, you should have traced the program *before* the computer ran the program. However, now that you know the program has an error, you must attempt to discover the cause. Although you might be tempted to do so, you should *not* have the computer run the program again without making some [intelligent] changes. Otherwise, you will obtain the same results. Nor should you make random changes in the program to "see what happens." Instead, you should begin a systematic search for the error. To that end, the computer can be a useful tool as you will now see.

Finding the Error. For the above program, observe that the only time the computer was instructed to display information was in the last statement. Perhaps it would be helpful if additional information were displayed as the computer performs the various instructions. To do so, you can use additional WRITE statements. For instance, compare the following program to the original one:

```
READ First, Second
WRITE First, Second      {This is a new statement.}
First := Second
WRITE First, Second      {This is a new statement.}
Second := First
WRITE First, Second
```

The two new WRITE statements will be used to help track down precisely where the error occurs.

Since this program consists of very few instructions, you could place a WRITE statement after each and every statement. However, you will not be able to do so when a program contains many instructions. The reason is that with large programs too many WRITE statements can produce so much displayed information that you will probably be unable to follow or to analyze the flow of the program. Therefore you must choose the location and number of WRITE statements with care and forethought.

Having introduced WRITE statements into this short program, it is time to have the computer run the program again. Assuming that no new syntax errors have been introduced, the computer will display the following values for *First* and *Second* corresponding to each of the three WRITE statements:

First	*Second*
3	7
7	7
7	7

The first WRITE statement has confirmed that, indeed, the READ statement has properly assigned the original values of 3 to *First* and 7 to *Second*. It is the second WRITE statement that indicates that the values for *First* and *Second* are incorrect. So, what has happened between these two WRITE statements? The only instruction that has been performed is the assignment statement

```
First := Second
```

Can you determine what has happened?

To answer the question, play the role of the computer, and recall how an assignment statement works (see Section 2.1). Specifically, the computer will (1) retrieve the value of the variable to the right of the := (namely, *Second*) from the computer's memory, (2) turn to the page of the book corresponding to the variable to the left of the := (namely, *First*), and (3) *erase* whatever appears on that page (namely, the previous value of 3 for `First`), and then write the new value obtained from (1) above (namely, 7).

When performing the third step above, you should be able to see that the logic error arises when the previous value of 3 for `First` is erased permanently from the computer's memory. It is no wonder that the second `WRITE` statement has produced the value of 7 for both `First` and `Second`.

Correcting the Error. Finding errors is half the battle; the other half is correcting them. You discovered that the second statement below (marked with an arrow) caused the computer to erase the original value for `First` from the machine's memory, thus resulting in a logic error:

```
READ First, Second
First := Second        ←
Second := First
WRITE First, Second
```

Can you determine how to overcome this problem?

The answer is to "save" the original value of `First` *before* the computer loses that value. In order to accomplish this objective, you can create and declare a new variable, say `Hold`, which you can use to preserve the original value of `First`. Then, before the instruction

```
First := Second
```

(which will destroy the original value of `First`), you should put the statement

```
Hold := First
```

The result will be that, after executing the two statements

```
Hold := First
First := Second
```

the original value of `First` (namely, 3) will be stored safely in `Hold` for later use. Indeed, that original value for `First` can subsequently be put into `Second` with the statement

```
Second := Hold    (instead of Second := First)
```

In addition, after all the errors are located and corrected, the `WRITE` statements that were added to the program for debugging purposes should be removed. In Chapter 4, you will learn about a debugging technique that does not require the physical removal of these additional WRITE statements. In any event, there is one group of WRITE statements that should not be removed. Whenever you enter data into the computer by using a READ statement, there can always be doubt as to whether the correct values were assigned to the appropriate variables. For example, when preparing the data outside the program, a typing or other careless mistake could have been made. To remove any such doubt, all original data should be displayed (with a WRITE statement) after being stored into the computer. The process of doing so is referred to as **echo printing.** The one exception to echo printing is if the amount of data for a program is very large (e.g., an entire telephone directory). Thus, the corrected program is

Echo printing The process of displaying the values of all variables that are obtained as a result of using a READ statement.

```
READ First, Second       {Obtain the original values for First
                          and Second.}
WRITE First, Second      {Echo print the data.}
Hold := First      {Save the original value of First in Hold.}
First := Second      {Put the original value of Second into
                      First.}
Second := Hold      {Put the original value of First (which is now
                     in Hold) into Second.}
WRITE First, Second      {Display the new values of First and
                          Second.}
```

At this point, it is worth examining a bit more closely how the logic error arose in the first place. Recall, from the algorithm-development phase, the first English solution describing how you would solve the problem:

Solution I: I simply switch the values of the two variables.

By thinking through your solution, and through the process of refinement, you restated the solution to obtain

Solution II: I put the value of *Second* into *First*, and then I put the value of *First* into *Second*.

At that time, what you failed to realize was that when you "put the value of *Second* into *First*," your mind automatically remembers the original value of *First* somewhere else. For the computer, that "somewhere else" had to be made explicit by using the variable *Hold*.

When solving a problem, you can often be unaware of what your mind is doing. For this reason, you must learn to think through your solution as carefully and methodically as possible. In order to do so effectively, you must always keep in mind how a computer thinks.

Tracing

No matter how careful you are, errors can occur in the early versions of a computer program. The only way you will obtain a correct and working program is to apply systematic and carefully planned debugging techniques. Nevertheless, a great deal of time and frustration can be saved by tracing the program (or part of the program) before having the computer run it. The process of tracing will now be illustrated for the corrected program obtained above.

Recall from Section 1.5 that in order to trace a program you must play the role of the computer and perform the instructions yourself. One of the best ways to do so is to make a list of every variable in the program. Then, after you perform each statement, change the values of the variables just as the computer would do. Remember that when tracing you should provide the values of *all* variables after each and every statement. That process has been done for the corrected program above, and the results are

	First	*Second*	*Hold*
READ *First, Second*	3	7	—
WRITE *First, Second*	3	7	—
Hold := *First*	3	7	3
First := *Second*	7	7	3
Second := *Hold*	7	3	3
WRITE *First, Second*	7	3	3

Looking at the first and last row of numbers in the list above, you can see that, indeed, the values of *First* and *Second* were correctly interchanged.

When tracing a READ statement, you might not know what specific values to choose for the variables appearing in that statement. In Chapter 4 you will see that, as a result of choosing certain values for those variables, you might end up tracing only part of the program. For now, when you trace a READ statement, choose any values for the variables.

In this text, tracing will be done just before coding an algorithm. When doing your own programming you might find it better to do so immediately after coding the algorithm but before the computer runs the program.

In this section, you have seen the computer problem-solving process in action. Specifically, by thinking through your solution, and by stepwise refinement, you learned how to express an original solution to a problem in terms of the pseudocode `READ`, `WRITE`, and assignment statements. Then, the process of locating and correcting errors was illustrated. In Section 2.4, you will learn about the different types of information that can be stored in the computer's memory.

Exercises for Section 2.3

Given that the initial values of *First*, *Second*, and *Result* are going to be 0, −1, and 2.5, respectively, trace the following pseudocode algorithms. Specifically, make a list of all variables used in each exercise. Then, after each statement, provide the current values for *all* of the variables.

1.
```
READ First, Second
First := First + 1
Second := Second + 3 * First
READ Result
Total := (Second * Result + 5.0) / 2.0
Result := 2 * Total
WRITE First, Second, Result, Total
```

2.
```
READ Result
First := Result - 2
READ Second
Sum := First - Second / 4
Sum := Second * Sum + 1
READ First
First := First + Second + Sum * 8
WRITE First, Second, Result, Sum
```

Using the techniques learned in Chapter 1, convert each of the following word problems into a sequence of pseudocode instructions consisting of assignment, `READ`, and `WRITE` statements. In the assignment statements of your algorithm, use only parentheses and the operators +, −, *, and /. Also, when performing calculations on the right side of the := , use variables only; do not use explicit numerical values. All numerical values needed should be stored into appropriate constants at the beginning of your algorithm. Finally, trace each algorithm using data of your own choosing. As you solve the problem, be conscious of identifying the inputting, processing, and outputting phases. Also, be aware of the process of thinking through your solution and of refinement. (In this and all subsequent exercises, any values that are "given" should be stored in appropriate variables by using a `READ` statement.)

3. Given the number of hours that an employee has worked (rounded to the nearest whole hour), together with an hourly wage rate, determine the amount of tax to be withheld and the remaining amount of money to be paid to the employee. To do so, use a tax rate of 18% (i.e., 0.18).

4. For a circle of known radius, compute and display the area and the circumference by the respective formulas: 3.14159 times the square of the radius; two times 3.14159 times the radius.

5. Convert some given measurements in feet, pounds, and degrees Fahrenheit (°F) into the corresponding measurements expressed in meters, kilograms, and degrees Centigrade (°C), respectively. The associated formulas are

$$1 \text{ ft} = 0.30479 \text{ m}$$
$$1 \text{ lb} = 0.453592 \text{ kg}$$
$$^\circ\text{C} = (5/9)\,(^\circ\text{F} - 32)$$

6. Given the values of the four variables `First`, `Second`, `Third`, and `Fourth` (representing four Zip codes) in increasing order, interchange the values so that they are in decreasing order. Also, display the new values of the variables.

2.4 Types of Values and Variables

So far, you have learned that numbers can be stored (and retrieved) from the computer's memory by using variables. In this section you will learn that other types of information, such as letters, can also be stored in the computer's memory. You will see that, because these different types of information are stored differently by the computer, certain programming concerns are necessary.

Integers

Integer values Any of the positive and negative numbers that contain no decimal point.

An **integer** is any number like the following:

. . . −3, −2, −1, 0, 1, 2, 3, . . .

Each computer is constrained by a largest positive integer (and a smallest negative integer) that can be used. In Pascal, the value of that largest positive integer is automatically stored in a predefined identifier called MAXINT. However, the smallest negative integer that can be used will be approximately −MAXINT. You will, however, need to find out what those values are on your computer by using a WRITE statement to display the value of MAXINT. Thus, for instance, if the value of MAXINT on your computer is 32767, then the largest positive integer you can use is 32767.

If you attempt to work with a larger integer than the computer can handle, the computer might display a run-time error. However, with some Pascal implementations, the computer will not display an error message. In these cases you are likely to discover the mistake only when you see that some of the numerical answers you obtain are incorrect.

Although you can use a comma when writing an integer in pseudocode (e.g., 5,320), Pascal does not allow the use of a comma. Therefore, it is advisable to get into the habit of writing an integer without a comma. You should also note that when you use a positive integer, the plus sign (+) is optional. However, for a negative integer, you must precede the number with the minus sign (−).

Reals

Computers can also store **real numbers,** which are numbers that contain a single decimal point. For example:

Real values Any numbers that contain a decimal point.

3.14159, −2.0, +1378.124, −0.00000081, 5000000.0

Scientific notation. When working with very large real numbers such as 5,000,000.0 or very small real numbers, such as 0.00000081, you can represent them without writing all of the zeroes. That representation is referred to as *floating-point,* or *scientific notation.*

One way to express a real number in scientific notation is to rewrite the number so that only one digit appears to the left of the decimal point. The resulting real number is called the *characteristic.* As you rewrite the original real number, count the number of positions you have to move the decimal point. That integer is called the *exponent.* The exponent should be positive if you moved the decimal point to the left, and negative if you moved the decimal point to the right. Finally, to write the original number in scientific notation, write the characteristic, followed by the letter "E," followed by the exponent. The following is a list of real numbers written in scientific notation:

Real Number	**Scientific Notation**
5000000.0	5.0E6
+0.00000081	+8.1E−7
−932000.0	−9.32E+5
−0.00005140	−5.14E−5

To convert a number expressed in the scientific notation

Characteristic E Exponent

back into a real number, you reverse the process. Specifically, move the decimal point in the Characteristic to the right as many positions as is indicated by the integer Exponent. If, however, the Exponent is negative, then move the decimal point to the left the appropriate number of spaces. Each time you move the decimal point, fill in another zero. For example:

Scientific Notation	**Real Number**
5.1E+3	5100.0
−1.4E−4	−0.00014
−2.31E+2	−231.0
+1.75E−3	0.00175

Accuracy of Real Numbers. For the moment, think of a real number as being expressed in the scientific notation:

Characteristic E Exponent

As with storing integers, the computer is constrained, i.e., there are limits on the number of digits that can be used in the Characteristic. This restriction is called the precision of real numbers of the computer. A typical precision for the Characteristic might be six decimal digits. There are also restrictions on the allowable values of the integer Exponent. This restriction is called the *range* of real numbers of the computer. A typical value for the range of the Exponent might be between −38 and +38. As with the integers, if you attempt to work with a real number that is beyond the precision and/or range of your computer, you can encounter errors.

The fact that computers cannot work with all real numbers (because of limited precision and range) can result in some unusual problems. For example, computers do not work with fractions such as $\frac{1}{2}$. Rather, the computer must convert these fractions into their decimal representations (e.g., $\frac{1}{2}$ = 0.5). In so doing, the number of digits in the decimal representation can be very large: for example, $\frac{1}{3}$ =

0.3333. . . . Since a computer cannot store all of these digits, the number $\frac{1}{3}$ cannot be represented exactly in a computer. That number must be stored in the computer using a finite number of digits according to the precision of the particular computer. The remaining digits will be dropped. The dropping of these excess digits is referred to as *truncation error.*

The result of truncation errors is that, when you perform calculations with real numbers, the results you obtain might be off slightly in the last decimal positions. These truncation errors can cause peculiar results in a computer. For instance, you know that

$$\tfrac{1}{3} + \tfrac{1}{3} + \tfrac{1}{3} = 1.$$

However, to a computer with a precision of six digits,

$$\tfrac{1}{3} + \tfrac{1}{3} + \tfrac{1}{3} = 0.333333 + 0.333333 + 0.333333 = 0.999999.$$

The study and analysis of truncation errors are beyond the scope of this text.

Characters

In addition to storing numbers, computers have the capability of storing characters. A **character** is any letter, digit or other symbol that is available on a particular computer. The number of different characters that are available can vary from one machine to another. Typically, a computer might work with 64, 128, or 256 different characters. With regard to programming, characters are used, for example, when you want to read and to process textual information.

Character values Any letters, digits, or other symbols that are available on your computer.

When you write the symbol A, it is not clear whether you are referring to the character A or to the variable whose name is `A`. Something must be done to avoid this confusion. In Pascal, and in this text, a character value will be enclosed in apostrophes (i.e., single quotation marks). For example:

```
'A'    {Refers to the character A, not to the variable A.}
'a'    {Lower-case letters, if available on your computer, are different from
        upper-case letters.}
'2'    {This is the character 2, not the integer 2.}
'.'    {Other symbols are also characters.}
' '    {A blank space is considered to be a character.}
```

You can store a character value into an appropriately declared variable by using an assignment statement in much the same way as you would store numbers. For instance, if the variables *LastLetter*, *One*, and *Blank* have been declared properly, then the following assignment statements are valid:

```
LastLetter := 'z'
One := '1'
Blank := ' '
```

In this book, it will be assumed that only one character can be stored in each variable. However, a group of characters, such as 'House' or '***' will be referred to as a *string*.

Boolean Values

When writing computer programs, it is often necessary to compare two numbers (in terms of their size). For example:

1 is less than 7 (which is TRUE),

3 equals 4 (which is FALSE).

Boolean values The values TRUE and FALSE.

As you can see, the result of comparing two numbers is always TRUE or FALSE. These two values are called **boolean values.** In Pascal, you can store either of these two boolean values into a properly declared variable using an assignment statement. Thus, when using pseudocode, for example, it would be valid to write:

```
OverSpent := TRUE
FoundPiece := FALSE
```

At this point, you might very well ask why you would want to store a boolean value, and how those values are useful in problem solving. You will see the answer to these questions in Chapter 4.

In this chapter, you have learned how computers store and retrieve various types of information. You have also seen four different types of variables and values that can be used in programs. In Chapter 3, you will learn a new programming concept, and you will be introduced to the process of coding.

Exercises for Section 2.4

Express each of the following real numbers in scientific notation.

1. 528000.0

2. −0.00804

3. 105000.00
4. +0.000000182
5. 1000.0002

Express each of the following as a real number.

6. −1.52E4
7. 4.003E6
8. −4.275E2
9. +1.333E−1

For each of the following algorithms that you wrote for the exercises in Section 2.3 (see page 62), indicate the type of each variable in the algorithm, i.e., the type of value that will be stored in that variable (e.g., integer, real, character, or boolean).

10. The algorithm for Exercise 3.
11. The algorithm for Exercise 4.
12. The algorithm for Exercise 5.
13. The algorithm for Exercise 6.

2.5 Summary

In this chapter, you have learned about four types of information that can be stored in the memory of the computer, namely: integer values, real values, characters, and booleans. You have also learned how the computer stores and displays information. If you think of the computer's memory as a large (but limited) book, then you can imagine that on each page of the book, the computer can write one (and only one) piece of information. So as to avoid having to remember the page number on which a particular value was written, names (of your choosing) can be given to the pages. Those page names are called variables.

There are three distinct aspects associated with working with variables. These are: (1) declaring a variable, which involves telling the computer at the beginning of the program the name of each variable and the type of value that will be stored into that variable; (2) defining the variable, which is the process of storing an appropriate type of value into the variable by using an assignment or `READ` statement; and (3) referencing a variable, which is the process of using the value that is currently stored in the variable in a `WRITE` statement or to perform a calculation. To retrieve the desired value from the memory of the computer, you simply refer to the name of the variable into which the value was stored.

You learned that in order to store information into a variable, you can use assignment and `READ` statements. These will instruct the computer to turn to the page of memory corresponding to the variable, to erase whatever is on that page, and to write the value on that page.

There are two important differences between a `READ` and an assignment statement. First, the `READ` statement will instruct the computer to obtain the value for the variable from somewhere outside the program. Second, you should use the two statements for different situations. Use a `READ` statement to assign a value to a variable when that value will not be known until the program is run; use an assignment statement when the value of a variable is known beforehand.

When performing a sequence of arithmetic calculations using the arithmetic operators addition (+), subtraction (−), multiplication (*), and division (/), you can use numbers and/or variables. You should always store the result of a sequence of arithmetic calculations (i.e., an expression) into a variable of the appropriate type. To do so, you can use the assignment statement

```
Variable := Expression
```

to instruct the computer to retrieve from its memory the values of the variables appearing in the Expression; to perform the calculations in the Expression; and to store the final result into the Variable. Do not forget the rules of precedence when working with arithmetic operators.

After the data has been processed, you can use the `WRITE` statement to have the computer display the value of a variable. The form of the `WRITE` statement is

```
WRITE Variable (or WRITE Expression)
```

`WRITE` statements can be placed virtually anywhere in the program, not just at the end to display the solution. Consequently, `WRITE` statements can be useful in echo printing and in debugging a program to locate the exact point at which an error occurs.

Key Terms

Identifiers 39
Variables 39
Value of a variable 39
Address of a variable 39
Declare a variable 40
Assignment statement 40

Prior to the mid-fifteenth century, most books and pamphlets were expensive, laboriously handwritten manuscripts. Then Johann Gutenberg, a skilled metallurgist, invented movable type and the printing press. Borrowing an idea from winemaking, Gutenberg built a crude press that spread ink on type cast from soft metal and then forced the ink onto the surface of paper. The introduction of mass printing brought books within reach of the common people and revolutionized education and learning during the Renaissance. (HISTORICAL PICTURES SERVICE, CHICAGO)

3

CODING, READING, AND WRITING

In this chapter you will begin to learn the rules of grammar for the Pascal programming language. That is, you will learn how to code an algorithm developed in pseudocode into its equivalent Pascal syntax. In order to avoid confusion between pseudocode and syntax, note that all initial presentation of Pascal syntax will be in blue type. Moreover, the first completely correct Pascal program in this and in all subsequent chapters will also be in blue.

Also in this chapter you will learn more precisely how the inputting and outputting of information is accomplished. Specifically, the `READ` and `WRITE` statements will be examined in greater detail. Finally, the entire problem-solving process will be demonstrated with an example. Special attention will be given to the process of locating and correcting syntax errors.

3.1 Introduction to Coding

From the work that has been done so far, you probably realize that there are a large number of details that must be considered carefully when developing a program. However, the real attention to detail comes during the coding phase, for it is here that you must follow precisely the specified rules of grammar, or the computer will not be able to perform the desired instructions. In this section, you will begin to learn the rules of grammar for the Pascal programming language.

Introductory Comments on Pascal

Pascal was developed by Professor Niklaus Wirth in Zurich, Switzerland, in 1968; the first documentation was presented by him in 1971 ("The Programming Language Pascal." *Acta Informatica* 1971; 1(1): 34–65). Pascal was designed with the objective of making you conscious, at all times, of how the computer thinks. Thus, for example, if `Card` is declared to be an integer variable, then the assignment statement

```
Card := 8 / 2
```

will cause an error. The reason is that in Pascal the value of 8 / 2 is 4.0, which is a real number, and a real number cannot be stored into an integer variable. In addition, correctly placed punctuation is critical in Pascal. A misplaced colon (:), comma (,), or period (.) will probably result in a syntax error.

A complete Pascal program consists of three parts, which appear in the following order: (1) the *program heading*, which provides a name for the entire program; (2) the *declaration section*, which informs the computer of certain identifiers and other items used in the program; and (3) the *executable section*, which consists of the actual statements to be performed by the computer. Each of these parts will now be described in greater detail. For your convenience, a summary of the syntax for all Pascal statements can be found in Appendix A.

The Program Heading

One purpose of the program heading is to provide the computer with a name (of your choosing) for the entire program. The heading will also tell the computer where to obtain the values for variables that appear in the READ statements, and where to display the values of variables that appear in the WRITE statements.

The program heading consists of one Pascal statement, which is the first statement that appears in a Pascal program. The syntax for the program heading is

```
PROGRAM Name(FileName, FileName, ..., FileName)
```

Throughout the coding sections of this textbook, items in upper-case type—e.g., PROGRAM above—together with all associated punctuation, must appear in your program exactly as you see them here (except that it does not matter whether you type those words in upper-case or lower-case letters). However, the three dots (. . .) are not allowed; you must always replace them with specific names. Underlined items, such as Name and FileName above, are also to be provided by you, and these can vary from one program to another.

The Name that appears in the program heading above is the name you choose to give to the entire program. Currently, the only names you should use for the FileName are INPUT and OUTPUT. To the computer, the name INPUT means that the values for variables that appear in subsequent READ statements will be entered either at your terminal (if you are working with an interactive system), or on punch cards that accompany your program (if you are working with a batch-processing system). Similarly, the name OUTPUT means that the computer will display values of variables appearing in subsequent WRITE statements either at your terminal, or on a printer, whichever is applicable.

Example

```
PROGRAM Taxes(INPUT, OUTPUT);
```

Example

```
PROGRAM Doit(OUTPUT);        {This program will not read data.}
```

In Section 3.2, you will see that other names can (and should) sometimes be used inside the parentheses of the program heading.

The Declaration Section

The objective of the declaration section of a Pascal program is to inform the computer of the existence of certain identifiers and other items that will be used in the subsequent instructions. For example, you have already learned the concept of declaring variables. In addition to variables, in Pascal there are up to five other items that must also be declared. The general form for the six declarations of a Pascal program is

```
LABEL      Declarations;
CONST      Declarations;
TYPE       Declarations;
VAR        Declarations;
FUNCTION   Declarations;
PROCEDURE  Declarations;
```

These declarations, if used at all, must appear immediately after the program heading, in the specific order given above (with the exception that the order of the FUNCTION and PROCEDURE declarations can be interchanged).

The LABEL declarations are described in Appendix C; the TYPE declarations are given in Chapter 6; the FUNCTION declarations are presented in Chapter 7; the PROCEDURE declarations appear in both Chapter 5 and Chapter 7. In this section, you will learn about the CONST and VAR declarations.

Constant Declarations. Recall, from Section 2.1, that a constant is an identifier whose value, once assigned, will not be changed anywhere in the program. The possible reasons for using a constant were discussed in Section 2.1.

In Pascal, it is necessary to declare separately those identifiers that will be used as constants. Once an identifier has been declared as a constant (and given a value), the value of that constant cannot be changed anywhere in the program. The Pascal syntax for a constant declaration is

```
CONST
    Identifier = Value;
    Identifier = Value;
    .
    .
    .
    Identifier = Value;
```

Example

```
CONST
    Pi = 3.1415927;
    TaxRate = 0.18;
    Period = '.';
```

Observe the use of the symbol = instead of := . The reason for using an equal sign is to make you aware that defining a constant is not quite the same as assigning a value to a variable.

Variable Declarations. In Pascal, each variable can be used to store one and only one type of value throughout the entire program. In the variable declaration, you will tell the computer the name of each variable and the type of value that will be stored in that variable. The syntax for the variable declaration is

```
VAR
    Variable, Variable, ..., Variable :TypeName;
```

The TypeName can be INTEGER, REAL, CHAR, or BOOLEAN. (Note the use of the word CHAR instead of CHARACTER.)

Example

```
VAR
    First, Second  :REAL;
    Day, Month     :INTEGER;
    Temp           :REAL;
```

You should note that spaces before and after the colon (:) are optional. Also, the order in which you declare the variables and their corresponding types is irrelevant, and you can use as many lines as necessary.

Example

```
VAR
    Char1              :CHAR;
    Sec, Hour, Min     :INTEGER;
    Strike, Spare      :BOOLEAN;
    Letter, Digit      :CHAR;
```

Choosing Names in Pascal

Thus far, you have seen the need to create names (identifiers) in a program (e.g., constant names, variable names, program names, etc.). In pseudocode, you have complete freedom over how you choose names; however, in Pascal, the names you choose must follow these rules:

1. A name must always begin with one of the letters A through Z (or a through z if your computer allows the use of lower-case letters).
2. The name can contain any number of letters and/or digits (0 through 9), but no other characters are allowed (e.g., +, *, etc.). On some Pascal systems, the computer uses only the first eight characters of a name; additional characters are simply ignored. In this case, the variables `NumberOfCards` and `NumberOfLines` are the same variable because the first eight characters are the same. Verify this feature on your system.
3. The name cannot be any of the **reserved words** that have a special meaning in Pascal. For instance, the following names cannot be used:

   ```
   CONST    VAR    TYPE    BEGIN    END    AND    OR
   ```

   Appendix B contains a complete list of reserved words in Pascal.
4. There are certain words called *predefined* or **standard identifiers** that also have a special meaning in Pascal. For example:

   ```
   TRUE    FALSE    INTEGER    INPUT    OUTPUT
   ```

Reserved words Words that have a special meaning in Pascal and cannot be used as identifiers in your program.

Standard identifiers Words that have a special meaning in Pascal. Although you could use them as identifiers in your program, you are advised not to do so.

While it is possible for the programmer to redefine these words (e.g., use them as variable names), you should remember that, once a standard identifier has been redefined, its original meaning is lost for the remainder of the program. In this book a standard identifier will never be redefined, and you are strongly urged to follow the same policy so as to avoid accidentally changing the meaning of a standard identifier. Appendix B also contains a list of all Pascal standard identifiers. Here, then, are some examples of valid and invalid Pascal identifiers.

Example

The following are valid Pascal names:

```
A
X10            {In this text, all names will begin with an upper-case letter.}
T1a
CounterValue
CounterVariable   {This is acceptable but, on some implementations
                  of Pascal, this variable will be considered the
                  same as the previous one because the first eight
                  characters of both names are identical.}
Real   {This is acceptable, but the standard identifier REAL has now lost its
       original meaning for the rest of the program.}
```

Example

The following are invalid Pascal names:

```
1A     {Does not start with a letter.}
Client-name    {Contains the symbol - .}
End    {This is a reserved word.}
```

In any event, to improve readability, you are advised to choose names that are descriptive of the purpose for which the name is being used. For example, `InterestRate` is a more descriptive variable name than `I`.

The Executable Section

After writing the program heading and declaration section, it is finally possible to give Pascal instructions to the computer to be executed. The syntax for the executable section is

```
BEGIN
   Statement;
   Statement;
   .
   .
   .
   Statement
END.
```

The [first] occurrence of the reserved word BEGIN signifies the beginning of the executable section of a Pascal program. The [last] occurrence of the word END signifies the end of the executable section, and of the entire program. Each Statement can be any valid Pascal instruction, such as an assignment, READ, or WRITE statement. You will subsequently learn various other types of statements. Finally, a Pascal program ends with a period (.) as the very last character.

Example

```
BEGIN
   A := 5.8;
   B := 2.3;
   C := A * B
END.
```

Perhaps the single largest cause of syntax errors in the executable section of a Pascal program is the misplacement of semicolons. To help clarify this issue, a description of the proper use of a semicolon will be given now.

In the program heading and declarations, you saw that a semicolon was used to end a statement. In the executable section, however, a semicolon is used to *separate* one statement from another (not to end a statement). Thus, a semicolon is placed at the end of a statement only if there is a following statement. In the next example, note that there is no semicolon at the end of the last statement.

Example

```
Statement; Statement; Statement
```

Clearly, in order to place a semicolon in the proper location, you must know precisely where one Pascal statement ends and the next one begins, and that might take some care. For instance, as you will soon learn, the words BEGIN and END have a special meaning in Pascal. When taken as a whole, the words BEGIN and END (and all the statements in between these two words) constitute one big Pascal statement. With this understanding, the following example illustrates the proper use of semicolons as statement separators.

Example

<u>Statement</u>;	{This semicolon separates this statement from the following BEGIN-END statement.}
BEGIN	{There is no semicolon here because the word BEGIN by itself is not a statement.}
<u>Statement</u>;	{This semicolon separates this statement from the next one.}
<u>Statement</u>	{There is no semicolon here because the subsequent word END by itself is not a statement.}
END;	{This semicolon separates the entire BEGIN-END statement from the next statement.}
<u>Statement</u>	{There is no semicolon here because there is no statement following this one.}

From the discussion above, you might think that Pascal is a very rigid language, and with regard to programming concepts it is. In other aspects, however, Pascal is very flexible. For example, Pascal statements can appear anywhere in a line, and any number of statements per line is allowed. Thus the example above could have been written equally well as

```
Statement; BEGIN Statement; Statement END;
Statement
```

although this form is, perhaps, not as easy to read. In addition, whenever one blank character is allowed, you may use any number of blank characters—i.e., extra blank characters will automatically be ignored. The only concern regarding the end of a line in a Pascal program is that a name or number cannot be split between two lines. If necessary, leave blank spaces at the end of one line and put the name or number on the next line.

Comments, written in English and enclosed by { } (braces), can also be used to improve the readability of a program. Comments can be placed anywhere that a blank character could be placed legally. If brace symbols are not available on your system, Pascal will allow you to enclose a comment with (* at the beginning and *) at the end. Now, you will learn more details regarding the various Pascal statements that can appear in the executable section of a program.

Assignment Statements. In Chapter 2, you learned that any of the four types of values (integer, real, character, and boolean) can be stored into the computer's memory by using the pseudocode assignment statement (which is also the correct Pascal syntax)

```
Variable := Value
```

As you have already learned, in Pascal each variable can be assigned one and only one type of value throughout the program. For this reason, to code an assignment statement in Pascal, you should keep in mind that the Value must be of the same type as that of the Variable (as specified in the VAR declaration).

In the event that a variable is declared to be of one type and then, subsequently, a different type of value is assigned to that variable, the following rules hold in Pascal: (1) When the assignment statement is "hopeless" (e.g., trying to assign a real number to a boolean variable), a syntax error will occur. (2) When an integer value (e.g., 2) is assigned to a real variable, no error occurs; the computer automatically adds the necessary decimal point (in this case, 2.0) and performs the assignment. (3) When a real value (e.g., 12.64) is assigned to an integer variable, a syntax error will occur.

Example

Suppose that *I*, *R*, *C*, and *B* have been declared as integer, real, character, and boolean variables, respectively. Then the following would happen:

Assignment	Result
R := 3	Acceptable because the computer will add the necessary decimal point.
C := 3	Not acceptable to store an integer value into a character variable.
C := '3'	Acceptable.
B := *I*	Not acceptable to store an integer value into a boolean variable.
I := 2.333	Not acceptable to store a real value into an integer variable.

Finally, with regard to using real numbers, you should know that in Pascal any number that contains a decimal point must also contain at least one digit to the left and one digit to the right of the decimal point. For example, .18 is not a valid real number, but 0.18 is valid. You can, of course, express a real value either as a real number or in scientific notation (see Section 2.4).

Performing Calculations in Pascal. In Chapter 2, you also learned about the arithmetic operators +, −, *, and /, and the pseudocode statement (which is also the correct Pascal syntax)

```
Variable := Expression
```

To code such a statement in Pascal, you need only keep three items in mind. First, in the Expression, each operator must be written explicitly [e.g., (A) (B) is not a valid expression, but A * B is valid]. Second, recall that the precedence rules of Appendix B will be followed when evaluating the Expression. Third, the resulting value of the Expression must be of the same type as that of the Variable; otherwise, an error will occur. The only exception is that an Expression resulting in an integer value can be stored into a real Variable without causing an error.

In view of this last issue, you must be careful when using the arithmetic operators in assignment statements. In Pascal, the following rules hold: (1) when using the operators +, −, and * together with two integer values (or variables), the result of the calculation is an integer; (2) when using these same operators together with at least one real number (or variable), the result of the calculation is a real number; and (3) the result of using the operator / in Pascal will always be a real number (e.g., the value of 8 / 2 is 4.0, and so this result cannot be stored into an integer variable). If you want the result of dividing two integers to be an integer, use the reserved word DIV in place of /.

Example

Calculation	Type of Result
3 * 2	6 (integer)
3 * 2.0	6.0 (real)
8 / 2	4.0 (real, not integer)
8 DIV 2	4 (integer, not real)
3 / 2	1.5 (real)
3 DIV 2	1 (integer, the remainder is discarded)

What Happens If . . .?

Whenever you encounter a new programming concept (e.g., the assignment statement), you should learn to ask questions along this line: "What happens if . . .?" Anticipating questions will help you to avoid errors when writing programs because you will understand precisely how each programming instruction is performed. Thus, for instance, for an assignment statement you might ask what happens if a variable appearing on the left or the right side of the := has not previously been declared. In Pascal the computer will be unable to perform the appropriate calculations, resulting in an error.

This section has introduced you to the grammar of the Pascal programming language. The program heading, declaration, and executable sections were explained in some detail. Section 3.2 will address issues pertaining to the READ statement in Pascal and to the associated syntax; Section 3.3 does the same for the WRITE statement.

Exercises for Section 3.1

Rewrite each of the following program segments eliminating all of the syntax errors you can find.

1.
```
PROCRAM Bcgin(INPUT, OUTPUT)
CONSTANT
    Pi := 3.1415927;
    E := 2.718;
VARIABLES
    A, C    :REAL;
    B       :BOOLEAN;
    I       :INTEGER
```

2.
```
PROGRAM First(INPUT, OUTPUT);
CONST
    Blank = ` ';
    Star = *;
    Period(.) = `.'
VAR
    I, J:          INTEGER
    Ch, Blank     :CHARACTER.
```

3.
```
PROGRAM Last(INPUT, OUTPUT);
VAR
    Integer C1, C2   :CHAR;
    TotalScore, R   :REAL;
    End,         :INTEGER;
CONST  Workdays = 5
```

For each of the following pseudocode algorithms, prepare the appropriate program heading and declaration section.

4.
```
READ Principal, Final     {Both of these variables are real.}
WRITE Principal, Final
Balance := (1 + (InterestRate/100))(Principal)
                {InterestRate is the integer constant nine.}
Initial := Final / (1 + (InterestRate / 100))
WRITE Balance, Initial
```

5.
```
Ch1 := Period
Ch2 := Comma
Ch3 := Colon
Ch4 := Semicolon     {Period, Comma, Colon, and Semicolon are
                      constants whose values are the corresponding
                      punctuation symbol.}
Punc := TRUE
```

Assume that the following declarations have been made:

```
VAR
    Irate, Jrate                 :INTEGER;
    Arate, Brate, Crate          :REAL;
    Truth, Consequences          :BOOLEAN;
    Ch1                          :CHAR;
```

Also assume that all variables have been assigned values. Explain what, if anything, is wrong with each of the following Pascal statements. When possible, correct the mistake.

6. `Irate := Irate + Brate`
7. `Truth := Irate`
8. `Truth := FALSE`
9. `Arate := (Arate) (Brate + Crate)`
10. `Truth := Consequences`
11. `Crate := Irate DIV Jrate`
12. `Ch1 := 1`

Suppose that *I* and *R* have been declared as integer and real variables, respectively. Also, suppose that the following assignment statements have been performed:

```
I := 2;
R := 2.0
```

Using the standard rule of precedence, determine the value of each of the following expressions, and indicate what type of variable the result should be stored into.

13. `R * 2.5 + 6 / 3 + I`

14. `I / 2`

15. `I * I + 2 * I + 3`

16. `I * 1.2E1 - 4`

Suppose that *I*, *R*, *C*, and *B* have been declared as integer, real, character, and boolean variables, respectively. Also, suppose that these variables have been assigned some initial values. Identify the mistakes and/or possible mistakes, if any, that might arise when the computer performs the following assignment statements:

17. `C := 7`

18. `B := I + 1`

19. `R := I * I * I + 4 * I * I - 5`

20. `I := 2 * R - 1`

21. `B := TRUE`

22. `R := R + 1.33E1.4`

23. `I := I / 2 + 32000000000000000`

24. `R := R * 1.333333333E-2 + 4.8E400`

Code the following word instructions into Pascal using only parentheses and the operators +, −, *, /, and `DIV`. Include the program heading and the `VAR` declarations, but do not be concerned with the `READ` and `WRITE` statements.

25. Given the value of the integer *Irate*, compute the value of the variable

Factor as $\dfrac{1}{1 + \dfrac{Irate}{100}}$.

26. Compute the value of *M* as the maximum number of playing cards that can be dealt to each of *K* players from a deck of *N* cards, provided that each person is to receive the same number of cards.

27. Given the integer variable *Card* whose value is between 1 and 52, use an assignment statement to compute a value for the integer variable *Suit* according to the following:

1 if $1 \le Card \le 13$
2 if $14 \le Card \le 26$
3 if $27 \le Card \le 39$
4 if $40 \le Card \le 52$

Check your assignment statement when the value of *Card* is 26. (*Hint:* The value of *Suit* is closely related to the number of times you can divide 13 into the value of *Card*.)

3.2 Reading

Recall, from Section 2.1, that the pseudocode statement

```
READ Variables
```

is used to instruct the computer to obtain the values from the Variables from somewhere outside the program, perhaps from a terminal. In this section you will learn more about this process, and you will learn the answers to the following questions: (1) From what different locations can the computer obtain the values for the Variables? (2) How, precisely, does the computer locate and assign the values to the Variables? (3) What issues must a programmer be concerned with when using a READ statement, and where can errors potentially arise? (4) What is the specific Pascal syntax for this statement?

Files

A READ statement can instruct the computer to obtain the necessary data from any of various computer components called **input devices:**

Input devices Electronic components from which the computer can obtain values for the data when instructed to do so in a program.

1. A *card reader*—where the data will be typed (and subsequently read) on punch cards (see Fig. 1.3).
2. A *terminal*—where the data will be typed on a keyboard (which is part of the terminal) when needed by the computer (see Fig. 1.7).
3. A *magnetic tape* or *cassette*—onto which the data has been previously typed and stored. (In many ways, a computer tape is very similar to an audio tape.)
4. A *magnetic hard disk* or *floppy disk*—onto which the data has been previously typed and stored (Fig. 3.1). (In many ways, a magnetic disk is very similar to a phonograph record.)

A computer can have one or more of these input devices. To complicate matters further, the data for a program can be split up so that some data is on one input device and some on another. You might therefore ask, "How will the computer know which data is to be read from which device?" In fact, you, the programmer, must provide the computer with that information. You must do so when coding an algorithm into Pascal. The general programming concept that allows you to do so is a **file**. A file is a collection of information that is located or stored, as a unit, in some part of the computer. Just a few of the many different types of files are

File A collection of information stored as a unit in some part of the computer.

Figure 3.1 A magnetic hard disk. Courtesy of Memorex Corporation.

1. An *input file*—a collection of data located on an input device.
2. An *output file*—a collection of information to be displayed by the computer. Output files will be discussed in more detail in Section 3.3.
3. A *program file*—a program, coded in a specific language, that is located or stored in some part of the computer.
4. A *text file*—a collection of characters that, as a unit, is stored or located in some part of the computer.

Just as you learned to choose variable names in the previous chapter, you will need to select and to provide the computer with a *file name* for each file you use in your program. In Pascal, you do so in the program heading. For example, in the program heading

```
PROGRAM Exchange(INPUT, Books);
```

the file name INPUT refers to your terminal (if you are using an interactive system), or to punch cards that accompany your program (if you are using a batch-processing system). The file name *Books* is also being used. At this point in the program, however, there is no way to know if this file is being used as an input or as an output file. You will only be able to tell when you see if the file name *Books* appears in a subsequent READ or a WRITE statement, as will be described momentarily.

You will also need to tell the computer the locations of the files (i.e., on what disk, tape, or other part of the computer the file can be found). The specific way in which you do so varies from one computer to another, and so those details will not be provided in this text.

Reading from a File

For programming purposes, you can think of an input file as a collection of individual lines of information (Fig. 3.2). The lines are separated by a special symbol called the **end-of-line marker** which, in this textbook, will be denoted by the symbol ■. Each line, in turn, consists of a (possibly different) number of columns. Each column can contain one digit, letter, or other character. Finally, at the end of a file, there is a special **end-of-file marker,** which, in this textbook, will be denoted by the symbol □. Although the end-of-line and end-of-file markers will not be visible to you, they are there nevertheless. For example, if you are typing data at a terminal, then the carriage return button is the end-of-line marker. The corresponding end-of-file marker varies from one computer to another.

End-of-line marker A special character used to indicate the end of each line in a file.

End-of-file marker A special character used to indicate the end of a file.

In general terms, the pseudocode statement

```
READ FileName, Variables
```

will instruct the computer to go to the file whose name is FileName to search for the needed values of the variables. As those values are found, they are assigned to the variables in the order listed in the READ statement. For example, if you are working with a file whose name is *DiskFile*, and with the three variables *First*, *Second*, and *Third*, then the pseudocode statement

```
READ DiskFile, First, Second, Third
```

```
Line
Number                     Column

                   1111111111222222
          1234567890123456789012345

    1     This file contains■
    2     4 lines of characters■
    3     and numbers.■
    4      3   -2  1.4  3.33E-5■
    5     □
```

Figure 3.2 An example of a file.

will instruct the computer to go to the file whose name is `DiskFile`, and attempt to assign the first value encountered to the variable `First`, the second value encountered to the variable `Second`, and the third value encountered to the variable `Third`.

In an input file, there is no need to make explicit reference to which value corresponds to which variable. This is because the computer always matches the position of the value in the input file to the corresponding variable in the `READ` statement. Thus an input file must contain only values; the variable names should be confined to the `READ` statement.

More details about how to work with files will be given in Chapter 8. For now, the file name will no longer be included in the `READ` statement. In Pascal, when a `READ` statement does not contain a file name, the computer will obtain the values for the variables either from your screen (if you are working with an interactive system), or from the punch cards that accompany your program (if you are using a batch-processing system).

The next issue that must be addressed is exactly how the computer "encounters" a value in an input file. The answer depends on the type of variable for which a value is being sought (in particular, searching for numbers and searching for characters are treated differently).

Looking for the First Numerical Value. When the computer is instructed (by a `READ` statement) to obtain the value for an integer or a real variable, the computer will go to the appropriate file and begin searching from the first column of the first line, looking for the first value you requested. The computer will then scan from left to right (one column at a time) until it encounters the first digit or sign of the desired number. In so doing, the computer will ignore any blank spaces that appear in front of the number. When "scanning" you might think of the computer as using a **pointer** that moves from column to column, left to right. Once the first digit has been found, the computer will continue to read the desired number until encountering any character that is not part of the number, such as a blank space or a letter. Finally, the computer will assign the desired number to the variable in your `READ` statement.

Pointer A method for keeping track of the next character to be read in a file.

Looking for Other Numerical Values. When more than one variable occurs in the `READ` statement, the computer must have some way of knowing when the first numerical value in the input file ends and the next numerical value begins. Generally, some symbol, called a **delimiter,** is used to separate one value from the next in an input file. In Pascal, the specific delimiters that are used to separate numerical values are blank spaces or end-of-line markers.

Delimiter Any character used to separate values in a file.

When typing numbers in a file, you should not type part of a number on one line and the rest of the number on the next line. This is because as soon as the computer encounters the end-of-line marker, it will assume that the number being read ends at the end of the current line.

As long as there are variables in the `READ` statement that have not been assigned values, the computer will continue to scan the file (from where the machine left off) looking for the next value to assign to the next variable. Whenever an end-of-line marker is encountered, the pointer is automatically set to the first column of the next line. Thus, the computer can (and will) scan as many lines of the file as necessary.

Example

Suppose that the computer is executing the pseudocode statement

```
READ I, R, J
```

Any of the following three sample input files would serve to assign the values of 20, −1.23, and 33 to *I*, *R*, and *J*, respectively. (Throughout this text, the first [nonblank] character in the first line of an input [or output] file is always located in the first column of that file, unless otherwise specified.)

First Input File

```
20 −1.23          33 ■
□
```

Second Input File

```
20 −1.23          ■
33 ■
□
```

Third Input File

```
20 ■
−1.23 ■
33 ■
□
```

What Happens When a READ Statement Is Completed?

When all variables in a READ statement have been assigned values, the READ statement is completed, and the computer will proceed to the next instruction in the program. At that time, however, the pointer could be located in either of two places, depending on which of two possible Pascal READ statements you have used. The first READ statement will cause the pointer to remain just to the right of where the last value was encountered; the second one will automatically position the pointer at the beginning of the next line of the input file. The syntax for the first statement, which leaves the pointer to the right of the last value encountered, requires the use of parentheses, and commas to separate the variables. That syntax is

```
READ(Variable, Variable, ..., Variable)
```

The syntax for the second statement (called a "read line" statement), which automatically sets the pointer at the first column of the next line of the input file is

```
READLN(Variable, Variable, ..., Variable)
```

The difference between these two statements is illustrated in the following examples.

Example

Recall the second input file in the example above. If you are using the Pascal READ statement (in which the pointer is not reset at the beginning of the next line when completed), then the statements

```
READ(I);
READ(R)
```

will assign the value of 20 to *I* and −1.23 to *R*. However, if, instead, you are using READLN statements (in which the pointer is reset at the beginning of the next line when completed), then the statements

```
READLN(I);
READLN(R)
```

will assign the value of 20 to *I* and 33 to *R*. This is because after the first READLN statement is completed, the pointer (which is located just to the right of the value 20) will automatically be repositioned at the first column of the second line of the file, thus skipping over the value −1.23.

Example

Suppose that the input file for a program is

```
-10      20      30■
 40     -50      60■
□
```

The Pascal statement

```
READLN(I, J)
```

will assign the values of −10 to *I* and 20 to *J*. Subsequently, since the READLN statement is completed, the pointer will automatically be set at the first column of the next line. In this case, the pointer skips over the value 30 and the first end-of-line marker, and is set just to the left of the value 40. Thus, the subsequent Pascal statement

```
READ(K, L)
```

will assign the values of 40 to *K* and −50 to *L*. This time, however, the pointer remains just to the right of −50 because a READ statement has been used instead of a READLN statement. Thus the subsequent Pascal statement

```
READLN(M)
```

will assign a value of 60 to *M*. Then, since the READLN statement is completed, the pointer is reset at the beginning of the next line (just at the end-of-file marker).

Reading a Character Value

Reading a character value from an input file can require more care than reading numerical values, especially when one of the characters you wish to read from the file is the delimiter itself (e.g., a blank space or an end-of-line marker). For example, recall that the blank character is one delimiter that is used for separating numbers in an input file. Logically, then, the following blank character:

```
S T■
□
```

should separate the two character values 'S' and 'T' in the above input file. (Note that, in the input file, the quotation marks are not included with the character values.) Hence, the Pascal statement

```
READ(First, Second)
```

should assign the value of 'S' to the variable *First* and 'T' to the variable *Second*.

Evidently, if a blank character is used as a delimiter when reading character values, it would be impossible to assign the value of a blank character to a variable by using a READ statement. Such a situation is not desirable. To overcome this problem, when reading characters in Pascal, the blank space and the end-of-line markers are, themselves, treated as actual characters. Thus for the above [character] input file, the Pascal statement

```
READ(First, Second, Third, Fourth)
```

would assign the value of 'S' to *First*, ' ' (i.e., a blank character) to *Second*, 'T' to *Third*, and the end-of-line marker to *Fourth* (remember, the end-of-line marker is itself a character). In such a situation, the pointer moves one column at a time, assigning the character in the current column to the corresponding variable in the READ statement.

You should note that, in Pascal, after the end-of-line marker is read (and recognized), that character is automatically converted and stored as a blank space, and not as an end-of-line marker. The reason for this is that when you read an end-of-line marker in the course of reading other characters, the end-of-line marker is not really part of the rest of the text. Therefore to "protect" you from using the end-of-line marker inadvertently as part of the textual data, that character is converted to a blank space.

When reading character values, you might want to instruct the computer to skip over the end-of-line marker (if you do not want to read that character into a variable). In order to accomplish that goal, there are two issues that must be addressed. The first is how you, the programmer, will know when the pointer has reached the end-of-line marker so that you can instruct the computer to proceed to the next line without reading the end-of-line marker. The second issue is how to instruct the computer to skip over the end-of-line marker.

Unfortunately, the answers to these questions depend on which particular version of Pascal you are using. In other words, "not all Pascals are created equally." Because there are different versions, you will have to investigate the specific Pascal on your system to determine how certain input and output procedures are performed. Below are some of the difficulties you might encounter.

Standard Versions of Pascal. In order to be able to skip over an end-of-line marker when reading characters from a file, the computer must have the capability of "looking ahead" to detect an upcoming end-of-line marker. Indeed, "standard" versions of Pascal have this capability, and they provide a special boolean variable (technically referred to as a "function") whose value is `TRUE` if the next character to be read is the end-of-line marker. Otherwise, the value of this variable is `FALSE`. The boolean variable is

`EOLN` (or `EOLN(`*FileName*`)` if you are working with a file other than `INPUT`)

Example

Suppose that the input file and the current position of the pointer is

```
                          pointer
                          ↓
This is a line of text.■
This is the next line of text.■
□
```

In this case, the value of `EOLN` is `FALSE` because the next character to be read is the period (`.`), not the end-of-line marker (recall that the pointer points to the next character to be read). Thus if a program is now to perform the statement

`READ(`*Ch*`)`

the period will be assigned to the [character] variable *Ch*. Subsequently, however, the value of `EOLN` will be `TRUE` because the next character to be read is the end-of-line marker. If the next instruction in the program is to perform the statement

```
READ(Ch)
```

the value of `Ch` will be that of the end-of-line marker, which is itself a character. However, as was explained previously, in all versions of Pascal, if you read an end-of-line marker into a character variable, the computer will automatically convert the end-of-line marker into a blank space.

The second issue you need to address is how (when the value of `EOLN` is `TRUE`) to skip the end-of-line marker (which you do not want to read) and proceed to the next line of the file. The answer is that the instruction

```
READLN
```

(with no variables) will do precisely that. Then, the pointer will be located at the first column of the next line.

The use of the Pascal variable `EOLN` will be further illustrated in Chapter 4. For now, however, you should be aware of another problem regarding the use of `EOLN`. In order for the computer to assign an initial value to `EOLN` (at the beginning of the program), the computer must find the first character in the file (to determine if it is or is not the end-of-line marker). Indeed, with standard versions of Pascal, the first instruction the computer performs (without your telling the machine to do so) is to find the first character in the input file. In the event that the data is being read from a file that has been prepared before the computer runs the program, the computer will have no difficulty in finding the first character; the computer will simply go to the file and look at the first character. If that character is an end-of-line marker, then the value of `EOLN` will be `TRUE`, otherwise the value of `EOLN` will be `FALSE`.

On the other hand, imagine the problem that will arise if you enter the data at a terminal (which you will do at the time the program runs) when the computer "asks" you to. Unfortunately, with standard versions of Pascal, the computer will not, in any formal way, ask you to type the first character so that the value of `EOLN` can be determined. Rather, the computer will stop at the beginning of your program and will not continue processing until that first character is typed. For a user who is not familiar with this problem, one solution is to tell the user to type a carriage return (which is an end-of-line marker) immediately after the program begins to run. In that way, the computer can assign a value to EOLN and can continue running the program.

Nonstandard Versions of Pascal. Other versions of Pascal have been designed to handle the problem of finding the initial value of EOLN in a more practical way, especially when you are entering data from a terminal. This process will be described for two nonstandard versions of Pascal called Turbo Pascal and UCSD Pascal (because it was developed at the University of California at San Diego).

With these versions of Pascal, the computer will not attempt to find the first character in the input file. Thus you will not have to type that first character at your terminal. As a result, however, the computer no longer has the capability of "looking ahead" to detect an upcoming end-of-line marker. Therefore, with these versions of Pascal, the value of EOLN cannot be set to TRUE until *after* the end-of-line marker has been read (and stored as a blank space). Consequently, with these versions of Pascal, when reading character values from an input file it will not be possible to avoid reading the end-of-line marker into a variable by using the boolean variable EOLN. Rather, you will have to read the end-of-line marker and, after doing so, you will have to "ignore" the value of that variable if you want to "skip" over the end-of-line marker.

Some differences between these standard and nonstandard versions of Pascal will be pointed out at the appropriate places in this book. For the time being, assume that a standard version of Pascal is being used and, as a result, that the pointer in an input file will always refer to the next character to be read.

Avoiding the End-of-File Marker

Recall that when reading numbers and/or characters, you must never instruct the computer to read past the end-of-file marker. If you do, a run-time error will result. As with the end-of-line marker, you might ask how you, the programmer, will know when the pointer has reached the end-of-file marker. In fact, standard Pascal provides the special boolean variable (technically referred to as a "function")

> EOF (or EOF(FileName) if you are working with a file other than INPUT)

that works very much like the variable EOLN for handling end-of-line markers. The value of EOF is TRUE if the next character to be read is the end-of-file marker. Otherwise the value of this variable will be FALSE.

Example

Suppose that the input file and the current position of the pointer is

```
pointer
↓
10 ■
□
```

Assuming that *N* is an integer or a real variable, the Pascal statement

```
READ(N)
```

will assign the value of 10 to *N* and move the pointer just to the right of the number 10—i.e., to the end-of-line marker. At that point, the value of the variable EOLN will be TRUE; however, the value of the variable EOF will be FALSE because the computer is not yet aware of the upcoming end-of-file marker. On the other hand, had the original statement been

```
READLN(N)
```

then, after assigning the value of 10 to *N*, the pointer would move to the first column of the next line. At that time, the value of the variable EOF will be TRUE.

From this example, you can see that after completing a READ statement (instead of READLN) the value of the variable EOF can never be TRUE. The reason for this is that the end-of-file marker can never be the character immediately to the right of a value because first there will be an end-of-line marker.

Reading Boolean Values in Pascal

Currently, it is not possible to read boolean values in Pascal. Therefore if you need to assign a value to a boolean variable, the only way to do so is to use an assignment statement.

What Happens If . . .?

It is now time to see how and where potential errors can arise when using a READ or READLN statement. As you have learned, one of the best ways to do so is to ask the question "What happens if . . .?" Regarding READ or READLN statements, one could, for example, ask what happens if there are more variables in the statement than there are corresponding values in an input file?

Recall, from the discussion above, that the computer will continue to search the input file for values so long as there are variables in the READ statement that have not been assigned values. However, it is not possible for the computer to search past the end-of-file marker. Consequently, by having more variables in a READ statement than there are values in the input file, you are, in essence, asking the computer to search past the end-of-file marker, which the machine cannot do. Therefore the result will be a run-time error with an associated error message of the form

```
***Insufficient data
```

or

```
***End of file encountered
```

You might also ask what will happen if there are fewer variables in a READ or READLN statement than there are values on a line in an input file. In this case, the computer will locate and assign only as many values as there are variables in the READ statement. If you are using a Pascal READLN statement, then the remaining values on the line will be ignored because the pointer is set at the beginning of the next line. If, however, you are using a Pascal READ statement, then those remaining values will be used when the next READ statement is performed because the pointer remains to the right of the last value encountered.

Another situation that could be anticipated is if during a READ or READLN statement, the type of value encountered does not agree with the type of variable in the READ statement (e.g., trying to read a character value into an integer variable). In this case, remember that a READ statement is performed exactly like an assignment statement, with the exception of where the value for the variable is obtained. Consequently, the computer will encounter the same difficulties with an inappropriate type of value here as with the corresponding assignment statement (see Section 3.1 for details).

Finally, you might ask what happens if a given READ statement contains both character and numerical variables? Simply stated, if the next variable to obtain a value is a numerical variable, then the blank space and the end-of-line marker are treated as delimiters, and hence they are ignored when the computer searches for a value. On the other hand, if the next variable to obtain a value is a character variable, then its value will be the next character in the input file, as indicated by the current position of the pointer (regardless of whether that character is a blank space or an end-of-line marker).

Example

(As you follow this example, be conscious of where the pointer is located after each variable obtains its value.) Suppose that *Ch1* and *Ch2* are character variables, and that *Number1* and *Number2* are numerical variables. If the input file is

```
10 68■
□
```

then the Pascal statement

```
READ(Number1, Ch1, Ch2, Number2)
```

would have the following effect:

Variable	Value
Number1	10
Ch1	' ' (the blank space)
Ch2	'6' (the character six)
Number2	8

Once again, you should be aware of the fact that not all versions of Pascal are the same. For instance, in some nonstandard versions of Pascal (notably, Turbo Pascal), a numerical value in an input file *must* be followed by a blank space or an end-of-line marker. In this case, if you were to instruct the computer to read the value for a numerical variable followed by a character variable, the character variable would be assigned the blank space that immediately follows the numerical value in the input file. In conclusion, be sure to understand precisely how READ and READLN statements are performed on the version of Pascal you are using.

In this section you have learned more precisely how the READ statement works and how to code that statement into Pascal. In Section 3.3 you will learn similar details regarding the WRITE statement.

Exercises for Section 3.2

Suppose that the input file is

```
-10      22.3■
1.0E-2■
   2     1.23      57■
-9999■
□
```

For each of the following exercises, determine the values that would be assigned to the numerical variables by the given Pascal statements. Always be conscious of where the pointer is located after each variable obtains its value and after each statement is completed.

1. ```
   READ(I);
   READ(R)
   ```
2. ```
   READLN(I);
   READLN(R)
   ```
3. ```
   READ(I, R, S, J);
   READ(T);
   READ(K)
   ```
4. ```
   READLN(I, R, S, J);
   READLN(T);
   READLN(K)
   ```

Suppose that READ and READLN statements were going to be used to assign the seven following values to the corresponding variables, respectively:

Variables	**Desired Values**
I, R, J, S, K, T, L	1, 1.23, 2, 0.15, 3, −2.05, 4

Under the assumptions given in each of the following exercises, design an input file using the fewest possible lines that would accomplish the desired assignments of values to variables for the given Pascal statements.

5. Assume that no more than four values are to be put on one line, and that the following Pascal READ statements are being used.

   ```
   READ(I, R, J, S);
   READ(K, T);
   READ(L)
   ```

6. Use the same assumptions as in Exercise 5, except that the following Pascal READLN statements are being used.

   ```
   READLN(I, R, J, S);
   READLN(K, T);
   READLN(L)
   ```

7. Use the same assumptions as in Exercise 5, except that no more than three values are to be put on a line.
8. Use the same assumptions as in Exercise 6, except that no more than three values are to be put on a line.
9. Use the same assumptions as in Exercise 5, except that no more than two values are to be put on a line.

10. Use the same assumptions as in Excercise 6, except that no more than two values are to be put on a line.

The seven values in the input file

```
-8      1.23       3■
4.01       0     -2.8■
7■
□
```

if used at all, are to be assigned to the seven numerical variables *I*, *R*, *J*, *S*, *K*, *T*, and *L*, respectively. Replace each of the following pseudocode statements with a Pascal READ or READLN statement so as to accomplish the desired assignment of values to variables.

11.
```
READ I, R
READ J, S
READ L
```

12.
```
READ I, R
READ S, K
READ L
```

13.
```
READ I, R, J, S
READ K, T
READ L
```

Recall that in Pascal, after a numerical value has been assigned to a variable in a READ statement, the pointer remains at the column immediately to the right of the value encountered. Also recall that when reading a character value, the pointer moves one column at a time from left to right, assigning each character encountered to the corresponding variable in the READ statement. If the input file is

```
2H     5 S■
8Clubs  3D■
□
```

what values would be assigned to the integer variables *V1*, *V2*, *V3*, and *V4*, and to the character variables *C1*, *C2*, *C3*, *C4*, and *C5* by the following Pascal statements? Assume that standard Pascal is being used. Also, be conscious of precisely where the pointer is located after each variable is assigned a value. For each exercise, start at the beginning of the input file.

14.
```
READLN(V1, C1, V2, C2)
```

15.
```
READLN(V1, C1, C2, V2);
READLN(V3)
```

16. `READLN(C1, C2, V1, C3, C4, V2, C5, V3)`

Suppose that the following Pascal declarations have been made:

```
VAR
    I, J, K       :INTEGER;
    A, B, C       :REAL;
```

In each of the following input files, identify all errors that would occur while performing the Pascal statements

```
READLN(I, J, A);
READLN(B, K);
READLN(C)
```

17.
```
I = 1  J = 2  A = 1.3■
2.8 3■
2.0■
□
```

18.
```
1  2  3■
4.0  5.0  6.0■
□
```

Suppose that a particular input file is

```
-10    15  1.0E-07■
1.85    2  -12T■
New■
□
```

Determine the value that would be assigned to the variables in each of the following Pascal statements, and indicate what type each variable should be declared as. Also, after each statement is completed, indicate the value of the variables `EOLN` and `EOF` using standard Pascal.

19. `READ(I, J); READLN(S, T); READ(K, Ch1)`

20. `READLN(I); READ(S, J, K, Ch1, Ch2, Ch3)`

21. `READLN(I); READ(S, J, K, Ch1, Ch2); READLN;`
`READLN(Ch2, Ch3)`

For the input file above, prepare Pascal `READ` statements that would accomplish the following assignments.

22.

Variable	**Value**
I	−10
S	1.85
J	2
K	−12
Ch1	' '
Ch2	'N'
Ch3	'e'
Ch4	'w'

23.

Variable	**Value**
S	1.85
I	2
J	−12
Ch1	'T'
Ch2	'N'

3.3 Writing

Recall, from Section 2.2, that the pseudocode statement

```
WRITE Variables
```

is used to instruct the computer to display the current values for the Variables in some part of the computer. This section will address the following questions: (1) In what different places can the computer display the values of the Variables? (2) Exactly how does the computer display the values of the Variables? (3) When using a WRITE statement, what issues must a programmer be concerned with, and where can errors potentially arise? (4) What is the specific Pascal syntax for this statement?

Files

Output devices
Electronic components on which a computer can display values when instructed to do so in a program.

By using a WRITE statement, you can instruct the computer to display the desired values on any of various computer components called **output devices,** of which a computer can have more than one. These are

1. A *printer*—where the values will be printed on paper (see Fig. 1.5).
2. A *terminal*—where the values will be displayed on a television screen (i.e., a CRT) (see Fig. 1.7).
3. A *magnetic tape* or *cassette*—where the values will be written and stored, but not displayed for you to see.

4. A *magnetic hard disk* or *floppy disk*—where the values will be written and stored, but not displayed for you to see (Fig. 3.1).
5. A *card punch*—where the values will be typed and punched onto cards (that might later be read on a card reader).

As with the READ statement, you, the programmer, can control which values are displayed on which output devices, by using a file. As with input files, you must provide the computer with a file name for each output file to be used in the program. Once again, in Pascal you do so in the program heading. For example, in the program heading

```
PROGRAM Exchange(OUTPUT, Books);
```

the file name OUTPUT refers to your terminal (if you are using an interactive system), or to the printer (if you are using a batch-processing system). The file name *Books* is also being used. At this point in the program, however, there is no way to know if this file is being used as an input or an output file. You will only be able to tell when you see if the file name *Books* appears in a subsequent READ or a WRITE statement, respectively. In view of this uncertainty, if you were writing this program, perhaps you should put a useful comment after the program heading, written in English and enclosed in braces, to provide the reader with additional information pertaining to the file *Books*.

When working with output files, you will also have to tell the computer where the file is to be located (i.e., on what disk, tape, or other output device). The specific way in which you do so varies from one computer to another, and so those details will not be provided in this book.

You should note that there is one major difference between an output file and an input file. An output file is created by the computer program, whereas an input file is not; an input file is created by you (or someone else) before (or at the time) the program is run. The computer program does not create its own input file.

Writing onto a File

Except for the difference mentioned above, you can think of an output file in much the same way as an input file (Fig. 3.2). Specifically, an output file consists of a collection of individual lines of information that will be separated by end-of-line markers. Each line, in turn, consists of a [possibly different] number of columns. Each column can contain one digit, letter, or other character. On each output device there is a maximum number of columns per line that can be used. That number varies from device to device, and from one computer to another, but typical values might be 72, 80, 120, or 132 columns per line.

Finally, at the end of the file, there will have to be an end-of-file marker. Under some circumstances, you will have to instruct the computer explicitly to put the end-of-file marker at the end of the output file. In other circumstances, the computer will do so by itself. In this book, unless told otherwise, assume that the computer will automatically insert the end-of-file marker.

In general terms, the pseudocode statement

```
WRITE FileName, Variables
```

will instruct the computer to go to the file whose name is FileName, and to write the values of the Variables. Those values are written in the same order as they appear in the WRITE statement. In so doing, the variable names are not written on the output file; only their values are written.

Example

If you are working with a file whose name is *TapeFile*, and with the three variables *Deposits*, *Withdrawals*, and *Balance*, then the statement

```
WRITE TapeFile, Deposits, Withdrawals, Balance
```

will write, on the file named *TapeFile*, the value of *Deposits* first, the value of *Withdrawals* second, and the value of *Balance* third.

More details about how to work with output files will be given in Chapter 9. For now, the file name will no longer be included in the WRITE statement. In Pascal, when the file name is omitted in a WRITE statement, the values will be displayed either at your screen (if you are working with an interactive system), or at a printer (if you are working with a batch-processing system).

Field Widths

The next issue that must be addressed is that of precisely where, within a line, the computer will write the values. In that regard, you should be concerned with (1) how many columns you should use to display one value (the number of columns that are used is called the **field width** of the value), and (2) choosing which columns (within a line) you should use to display the values. Later in this section, you will see that you can, in fact, control both the field width and the exact location of a value within the line.

Field width The number of columns used to display one value.

For the moment, however, assume that you are not exercising this control. The computer will still follow certain general guidelines that vary, to some extent, from one computer to another. For example, unless told otherwise, the computer will allow a fixed (but possibly different) field width for each type of value (e.g., integer, real, string, etc.). The specific field widths depend on the computer being used, and are often called the *default field widths*. For a real value, the default field width will always include adequate space for displaying the sign, decimal point, and/or exponent of the value, if necessary. For demonstration purposes, this book will use the default field widths given in Fig. 3.3.

In Pascal, the computer will also *right justify* (as opposed to *left justify*) the value within the field width:

	Right Justification
Integer	−20
Real	1.234E2
String	word
	⟵ field width ⟶

As you can see, when right justifying a value within a specified field width, blanks are inserted to the left of the value as necessary to

Type of Variable	Field Width
REAL	22 (10 significant digits; exponent in the form E ± nn)
INTEGER	11
BOOLEAN	6
CHARACTER	1

Figure 3.3 Default field widths used in this text.

use the exact number of columns in the field width. Thus in a field width of 10, the integer −12 would be augmented (or *filled*) with seven blanks, while the integer −123 would be filled with six blanks. In addition, note that the computer will display the sign of a negative number; however, the sign of a positive number will be displayed as a blank space.

The computer will display subsequent values in a `WRITE` statement beginning in the column immediately to the right of where the previous field width ended. When the values of all the variables in a `WRITE` statement have been displayed on one line in the file, you might wonder if the computer will insert an end-of-line marker or not. In that regard, Pascal has two different `WRITE` statements, one that does not insert an end-of-line marker upon completion, and one that does. The syntax for the first statement, which does not insert an end-of-line marker in the file when completed, is

```
WRITE(Variable, Variable, ..., Variable)
```

The syntax for the second statement called a "write line" statement, which does insert an end-of-line marker in the file when completed, is

```
WRITELN(Variable, Variable, ..., Variable)
```

Observe the use of commas to separate the variables, and also the required use of parentheses. Also, the statement

```
WRITELN
```

(with no variables) will simply insert an end-of-line marker into the file just after the last value that was displayed. Finally, do not forget that in Pascal you can display the value of an expression as well as a variable, for example:

```
WRITE(Amount + Balance)
```

To illustrate these statements, consider the following examples.

Example

If the values of the variables *First* and *Second* are 123 and −45, respectively, then, using right justification and a field width of 10, the Pascal statement

```
WRITE(First, Second)
```

would display the values as follows:

```
                    1 1 1 1 1 1 1 1 1 1 2
1 2 3 4 5 6 7 8 9 0 1 2 3 4 5 6 7 8 9 0    (Column)

                  1 2 3             - 4 5    (Values)
```

Example

Suppose that the value of the variable *R* is 0.1234, that of *I* is −10, and that of *C* is '*'. Using the default field widths in Fig. 3.3, the statements

```
WRITELN(R);
WRITE(I);
WRITE(C)
```

will display those values as

```
1.234000000E-1■
-10*
```

In the last example above, observe that there is no end-of-line marker at the end of the second line because the last instruction was a `WRITE` statement, not a `WRITELN` statement. Therefore a subsequent `WRITE` or `WRITELN` statement will display values beginning immediately to the right of the '*'.

Recall that each output device has a maximum line length (i.e., number of columns per line). Thus you must be sure to put an end-of-line marker in the file (with the `WRITELN` statement) before exceeding the amount of displayed information that can fit on a line, as illustrated in the following example.

Example

If an output device has a maximum of 72 columns per line, all of the following are real variables, and the default field width of 22 is used for a real variable, then the statement

```
WRITE(A, B, C, D)
```

would cause a run-time error because you have instructed the computer to display information in 88 columns of one line, which the machine cannot do. One way to correct the problem is to use the statements

```
WRITELN(A, B, C); WRITE(D)
```

Displaying Readable Output

When you obtain the results of a program, you might have difficulty interpreting the displayed values. For example, suppose that, as a result of a group of WRITE statements, your computer program displayed the following results:

```
          181           2.13E0
2300                4.96290E3
```

How will you know which of these values corresponds to which variables in the program? You could, of course, search through the entire program until you found the appropriate WRITE statements. Then you would have to match the displayed values to the corresponding variables in the WRITE statement.

In order to simplify the process, there is a standard way to display variable names (and other textual information) in the Pascal WRITE statement. To do so, you simply put single quotation marks around the string you want to display. If you want to display a single quotation mark itself, replace that symbol with two single quotation marks. Thus, for example, the Pascal statement

```
WRITELN('Bob''s house')
```

will display

```
Bob's house
```

Textual information can also be displayed along with the values of variables. Thus, for example, instead of the Pascal statements

```
WRITELN(I, P);
WRITELN(N, T)
```

which will display only the values of these variables, you could use, for example,

```
WRITELN('I =', I, '  P =', P);
WRITELN('N =', N, '  T =', T)
```

which will display, before the value of each variable, the variable name together with an equal sign, as follows:

```
I =     181     P =        2.13E0
N =    2230     T =    4.96290E3
```

In this way, you would know immediately which variable has which value. Observe that, when performing a `WRITE` statement, items in quotation marks are displayed exactly as they appear; however, the surrounding quotation marks are automatically removed.

Imagine, for a moment, that you are preparing a program for someone else to use. While it is true that you, the programmer, know the meaning of the variables *I*, *P*, *N*, and *T* above, the user might not. To such a person, the following output would probably be more understandable:

```
Product Number  =   181  Unit Price   =       2.13
Units Sold      =  2230  Total Sales  =    4962.90
```

Naturally, your first task as a programmer is to make sure that your program does indeed solve the desired problem. Thus when you are developing the program, no one cares how the output is displayed except you. However, once the program is working correctly, you should take the time to format the output in a coherent and readable fashion so that others can understand and use what you have done.

Preceding READ Statements With WRITE Statements

There is another common use for displaying textual information with a `WRITE` statement. Suppose that you are entering data at a terminal. Recall that when the computer encounters a `READ` statement the machine will go to the terminal to find the data values, which you will type at that time. However, how will you know precisely when to type the data, and in what form (e.g., should you type an integer, a real number, or a character)?

One solution to this problem is to precede each such `READ` statement in the program with an appropriate `WRITE` statement that, when performed by the computer, will display information on the screen to tell the user what and how to enter the data.

Example

If you are writing a program in which you use a `READ` statement to allow the user to enter a value corresponding to the variable *Cookies*, for example, then you should precede that `READ` statement with `WRITELN` statements such as the following:

```
WRITELN('Enter an integer value for Cookies');
WRITELN('then press return');
READ(Cookies)
```

The message in quotation marks will then appear on the screen and the user will know when and how to enter the appropriate value.

Throughout the coding sections of this text, such WRITE statements will always precede each READ statement. If, however, you are working with a batch-processing system, you should omit these WRITE statements because all of the data for the program must be prepared beforehand.

Controlling the Field Width

In Pascal it is a simple matter to control the field width yourself. In either a WRITE or WRITELN statement, you need only follow the item being displayed with a colon and then an integer that specifies the desired field width. The value will then be right justified in the specified field width, as illustrated in the following example.

Example

Using the value of −10 for *I*, the Pascal statement

```
WRITE('I =':10, I:5)
```

will produce

```
                  1 1 1 1 1 1
1 2 3 4 5 6 7 8 9 0 1 2 3 4 5   (Columns)

                I =     - 1 0   (Values)
```

If your field width is too small for the value being displayed, Pascal will automatically increase the width to a sufficient size. Moreover, the value for the field width can itself be an integer variable. Thus, for example, if *FieldWidth* is an integer variable that has been declared and assigned a value of 5, then the following statement would produce the same result as above:

```
WRITE('I =': 2 * FieldWidth, I: FieldWidth)
```

Displaying Real Numbers

Recall, from Section 2.4, that you can write a real value either as a real number, or by using scientific notation (e.g., you can write either 124000.0 or 1.24E5). In Pascal, when you instruct the computer to display the value of a real variable, the machine will normally do so in scientific notation. However, you can specifically instruct the computer to display the value as a real number. To do so, immediately following the variable name in the `WRITE` statement, you first specify a field width. Then, you follow that field width with a second colon and another integer that represents the number of digits to be displayed to the right of the decimal point, as illustrated in the following example.

Example

If the value of *R* is 1.238E−1, then the statement

```
WRITE(R:10:3, R:10, R)
```

will display

```
         11111111112222222222333333333344
12345678901234567890123456789012345678901 2   (Columns)

     0.124   1.238E-1          1.238000000E-1   (Values)
```

Observe that, in the first number, the last digit in the value of *R* (i.e., 8) has been dropped and the number has been rounded up because the `WRITE` statement allowed only three digits to be displayed to the right of the decimal point.

Recap

Thus far, you have learned many issues relating to the pseudocode statement

```
WRITE Variables
```

For instance, in Pascal unless otherwise specified, the computer will allocate certain default field widths (i.e., number of columns) for displaying each data type (i.e., integer, real, etc.). When displaying values in Pascal, no matter what the field widths are, the following rules hold: (1) all numbers are right justified within the field width (so blanks are filled in on the left of the number, as necessary); (2) all real values are displayed in scientific notation; however, you have also learned how to display such values as real numbers; and (3) character variables are always displayed in a field width of one.

Pascal also has two statements for displaying values of variables and expressions: the WRITE statement, which does not put an end-of-line marker in the file after the statement is completed, and the WRITELN statement, which does. With either statement, you can display string values by enclosing the string in single quotation marks. To display a single quotation mark itself, replace that symbol with two single quotation marks.

Some Complete Pascal Programs

In this and the previous two sections, you have learned enough Pascal syntax to enable you to write complete Pascal programs. The general form of a Pascal program is

```
PROGRAM Name(FileName, ..., FileName);
LABEL      Declarations;
CONST      Declarations;
TYPE       Declarations;
VAR        Declarations;
FUNCTION   Declarations;
PROCEDURE  Declarations;
BEGIN
   Statement;
   Statement;
   .
   .
   .
   Statement
END.
```

Here are several simple but complete Pascal programs.

Example 1

```
PROGRAM Square(INPUT, OUTPUT);     {This program reads a value
                         for an integer, squares that value, and displays the results.}
```

```
VAR
   I, Isquared :INTEGER;     {Declare the variables.}
BEGIN
   WRITELN('Enter an integer value for I');     {This
                          statement displays a message to the terminal.}
   READ(I);
   WRITELN('I =', I:3);     {Echo print the data.}
   Isquared := I * I;
   WRITELN('I squared =', Isquared:5)     {Note that no
                                  semicolon is required here.}
END.
```

What will the output look like if the value of *I* is 11?

Example 2

```
PROGRAM Switch(INPUT, OUTPUT);     {This program reads the
                  values for two real variables, displays those values,
                  interchanges the values of the two variables, and displays the
                  final results.}
VAR
   First, Second, Hold :REAL;     {Declare the variables.}
BEGIN
   {The next statement displays a message to the terminal.}
   WRITELN('Enter two real numbers please.');
   READ(First, Second);
   WRITELN('First =', First:12:6, ' Second =',
           Second:12:6);     {Echo print the data.}
   Hold := First;
   First := Second;
   Second := Hold;
   WRITELN;     {Leave one blank line.}
   WRITELN('First =', First:12:6, ' Second =',
           Second:12:6)
END.
```

In this and the previous two sections, you have learned how to code programs in Pascal, and how to use READ and WRITE statements. In Section 3.4, the whole problem-solving process will be demonstrated.

Exercises for Section 3.3

Suppose that the following assignment statements have been made:

Integer	Real	Character
`I := 1250`	`A := -5 / 3`	`C1 := 'E'`
`Total := 325`	`B := -1.0E-3`	`C2 := 'r'`
		`C3 := 'h'`
		`C4 := 'a'`
		`C5 := 't'`

Using the default field widths in Fig. 3.3, what, precisely, will the following Pascal statements produce? Show which values occur in each column of each output line.

1. `WRITELN(A, B, I, C1)`
2. `WRITE('The total for', I, ' people is:', Total)`
3. `WRITE('The', C1, C4, C2, C5, C3, ' is round.')`

Using the default field widths of Fig. 3.3, determine whether the following Pascal `WRITE` statements would fit on one line of an output device having a maximum of (a) 72, (b) 80, and (c) 132 columns per line. (Note: Any variable beginning with the letter "I" is an integer variable; any variable beginning with the letter "R" is a real variable.)

4.
```
WRITE(' Column', I1, ' Column', I2, ' Column', I3,
      ' Column', I4, ' Column', I5, ' Total =', R)
```
5.
```
WRITE(' Test score 1 =', R1,
      ' Test score 2 =', R2)
```

What will the following Pascal statements produce? You need not be concerned with field widths and/or justification; however, indicate which values will be displayed on which lines.

6.
```
WRITE('I =', I, ' J =', J);
WRITE(' K =', K, ' A =');
WRITELN(A, ' M =', M)
```
7.
```
WRITELN('Total Gross Salary =', Total);
WRITE('Total Taxes Paid =');
WRITELN(Taxes);
WRITELN('------------------');
WRITELN('Net Pay Remaining =');
WRITE(Net)
```

Assume that the following assignments have been made:

```
A := 0.045; B := TRUE; Ch1 := 'F';
```

```
Ch2 := 'f'; Iss1 := 236; Iss2 := 49;
Iss3 := 187; Cont := 2823.25
```

Show precisely what the following Pascal statements would produce using the default field widths of Fig. 3.3. Be sure to indicate which values appear in which columns.

8.
```
WRITE('A =', A);
WRITE(' A =', A:8);
WRITE(' A =', A:8:3);
WRITELN;
WRITE('Iss1 =', Iss1, ' Iss2 =', Iss2);
WRITELN(' Iss3 =', Iss3);
WRITE('Cont =', Cont)
```

9.
```
WRITE('It is ', B, ' that ', Ch1,
      ' is less than ', Ch2);
WRITELN; WRITELN;
WRITELN('This looks like one big number',
        Iss1, Iss2:2, Iss3:3);
WRITELN('Cont =', Cont:10)
```

Using the values of the variables above, prepare Pascal `WRITELN` statements that would produce precisely the following output.

10. Social Security Number: 236-49-187
Contribution Factor: 0.045
Total Contributions: $ 2823.25

11. It is true that

```
 187
+ 49
----
 236
```

Suppose that the following assignment statements have been made:

```
Iss1 := 292                 Part1 := 18
Iss2 := 44                  Part2 := 1443469
Iss3 := 3110                UnitPrice := 5.41
Day := 19                   Inventory := 320
Month := 11                 Ivalue := 1731.20
Year := 83                  Sold := 40
AreaCode := 415             Income := 216.40
Phone1 := 369               Finventory := 280
Phone2 := 7214              Fvalue := 1514.80
Deposits := 986.62
```

For each of the following problems, prepare Pascal `WRITELN` statements that would produce precisely the given outputs. The numbers appearing in each problem correspond to the values of the variables above. Your `WRITELN` statements, however, should contain the associated variable names, not the numbers. After each variable in your

WRITELN statements, indicate the exact field width that should be used so that when the value of the variable is displayed no blanks would be inserted when right justifying the value.

12. Social Security Number: 292-44-3110 Date: 11/19/83
Phone Number: (415) 369-7214
Total Deposits: $ 986.62

13.

Part Number:	18-1443469	Unit Price:	$ 5.41
Initial Inventory:	320	Value:	$ 1731.20
Units Sold:	40	Value:	$ 216.40
Final Inventory:	280	Value:	$ 1514.80

Rewrite the following Pascal program eliminating all of the syntax errors you can find.

14.
```
PROGRAM Loan(INPUT, OUTPUT);
CONST
    InterestRate := 9;
VAR
    Principal, Final, Balance, Irate :REAL;
READLN Principal, Final
Irate := InterestRate / 100 + 1;
Initial := Final / I
Balance := (Principal) (Interest)
WRITE('If', Principal:10.2
      ' dollars are invested at', InterestRate,
      ' percent for one year,')
WRITELN(' then the balance will be',
        Balance:10:2, 'dollars.');
WRITELN('If you want', Final:10:2,
        ' dollars at the ', ' end of the year');
WRITELN(' you should invest; Initial:10.2,
        ' at the beginning of the year.');
```

3.4 Putting It All Together

Through an illustrative example, the problem-solving techniques of Chapter 1, the programming concepts of Chapter 2, and the coding material of this chapter will now be brought together.

Problem: Each day, the Chocolate Chip Cookie Company bakes a different number of cookies. The cookies are packaged 12 to a box, and 24 boxes to a carton. Any leftover boxes are sold to a children's hospital for 57 cents, which is exactly half the normal price per box. Naturally, any remaining cookies are eaten by the employees. Given the number of cookies produced, the company wants you to write a program to determine the number of cartons and leftover boxes that can be sold, their associated values, and a total of how much money the company will earn.

Algorithm Development

Your first step is to determine how you would solve the problem yourself. Without a great deal of thought, you might provide the following:

Solution: From the number of cookies purchased, I somehow determine how many cartons and how many leftover boxes there will be. I then compute the associated values and add them to obtain the total amount of money earned.

Refinement. Your objective now is to use the process of refinement to express this answer more in terms of pseudocode, until finally you can code the solution into Pascal. The objective of using pseudocode first is to free your mind of the details of Pascal syntax so that you can concentrate on the problem-solving aspects.

To begin, you should think through your solution so you will understand more precisely how you solve the problem. Start by identifying the inputting, processing, and outputting phases of the problem.

Inputting. As usual, you should ask yourself what information you need to be given in order to solve this problem. First of all, you need to know the number of cookies that were baked. Therefore the variable *Cookies* will be used to store that information.

Since the value of the variable *Cookies* will not be known until the program is run, a READ statement should be used to store that value instead of an assignment statement. Thus one is led to the pseudocode statement

```
READ Cookies
```

Of course you should echo print the data with the pseudocode statement

```
WRITE Cookies
```

Other information you will need to solve this problem includes: the number of cookies per box, the number of boxes per carton, and the associated selling prices. Since these numbers are known before the program is to be run, you can either work with these numbers directly, or else store these values into constants.

Processing. To identify this phase of the program, you should ask yourself what you want to do with the data once the values have been entered into the computer. In fact, the following computations must be made using the value of the variable *Cookies*:

1. Compute the number of cartons that can be sold and the associated value.
2. Compute the number of leftover boxes and the associated value.
3. Compute the sum of the values obtained in (1) and (2) to obtain the total amount of money the company will earn.

Now, you should think through your solution so as to determine precisely how you perform the above computations. To that end, you might find it beneficial to use the technique of working through a specific example.

Working Through a Specific Example. Recall, from Chapter 1, that, in order to work through a specific example, you should choose values for the data and then perform the necessary calculations by hand, using those values. Thus, for example, how would you proceed if 3318 cookies were baked?

Each of the three computations above will now be analyzed using the specific example.

Computing the Number of Cartons. As you work through the specific example, you will realize that the first step is to calculate the number of boxes of 12 cookies that can be obtained. To do so, you would divide the number of cookies by 12 (disregarding the remainder, since those cookies will be eaten by the employees). Using the variable *Boxes* to represent the number of boxes that can be obtained, you are led to the assignment statement

```
Boxes := Cookies / 12     {With the remainder being
                           disregarded.}
```

Thus for the specific example of 3318 cookies there will be 276 boxes.

Using this value for the variable *Boxes*, it is now possible to compute the number of cartons that can be sold. Once again you should use the specific example to help you think through your solution. If you have done so, then you should realize that you can obtain the number of cartons by dividing the number of boxes by 24 (disregarding remainder, if any) because there are 24 boxes per carton. Using the variable *Cartons* to represent the number of cartons that can be obtained, you are led to the assignment statement

```
Cartons := Boxes / 24     {With the remainder being
                           disregarded.}
```

For this example in which there are 276 boxes, there will be 11 cartons.

Computing the Value of the Cartons. One way to obtain the total dollar value of the cartons is to multiply the selling price of each carton by the number of cartons to be sold. Proceeding along this line of reasoning, each box in a carton sells for $1.14. Since there are 24 boxes per carton, the selling price of one carton is 24 * 1.14. Using the variable `CartonSales` to represent the total value of all the cartons that will be sold, you are led to the assignment statement

```
CartonSales := 24 * 1.14 * Cartons
```

Computing the Number of Leftover Boxes. Work through the specific example to determine the number of leftover boxes. In so doing, you might notice that the number of leftover boxes is precisely the remainder obtained when dividing the total number of boxes by 24—in this case, 12. Using the variable `LeftOvers` to represent the number of leftover boxes, you could, in fact, write the assignment statement

```
LeftOvers := the remainder on dividing Boxes
             by 24
```

At this point, however, further refinement is necessary to restate the above instruction in terms that the computer can understand by using the operators *, −, etc. (At the end of this section, you will learn a simple method for performing the above computation.) For now, using the specific example, can you determine how to use the values of `Boxes` and `Cartons` to compute the desired value of `LeftOvers`?

After some effort, you might realize, once again, that the process of converting word instructions into a sequence of computer statements is not always simple. The correct assignment statement for computing the value of `LeftOvers` is

```
LeftOvers := Boxes - 24 * Cartons
```

Computing the Value of the Leftover Boxes. As is stated in the original problem, each leftover box sells for 57 cents. Using the variable `LeftSales` to represent the value of the leftover boxes, you are led to the assignment statement

```
LeftSales := .57 * LeftOvers
```

Computing the Total Sales. The total sales is simply the sum of *CartonSales* and *LeftSales*. Using the variable *Total* to represent the total money earned, you have the assignment statement

```
Total := CartonSales + LeftSales
```

The processing phase is now complete.

Outputting. According to the original problem statement, you are led to the pseudocode instruction

```
WRITE Cartons, CartonSales, LeftOvers,
      LeftSales, Total
```

Putting together the inputting, processing, and outputting phases, the pseudocode algorithm for solving the problem is

```
READ Cookies
WRITE Cookies
Boxes := Cookies / 12        {With the remainder being disregarded.}
Cartons := Boxes / 24        {With the remainder being disregarded.}
CartonSales := 24 * 1.14 * Cartons
LeftOvers := Boxes - 24 * Cartons
LeftSales := .57 * LeftOvers
Total := CartonSales + LeftSales
WRITE Cartons, CartonSales, LeftOvers,
      LeftSales, Total
```

Coding

In the exercises following this section, you will have the opportunity to trace the above algorithm using various values of the variable *Cookies*. Now, however, it is time to convert the above pseudocode instructions into a sequence of Pascal statements. The following is such a coded program, which you could type into your computer. It includes a program heading, a declaration section, an executable section, and the use of punctuation and semicolons.

```
PROGRAM Sales(INPUT, OUTPUT);
CONST
   CookiesPerBox = 12;
   BoxesPerCarton = 24;
   BoxPrice = 1.14;
   LeftPrice = .57;
VAR
   Cookies, Boxes, Cartons, LeftOvers   :INTEGER;
   CartonSales, LeftSales               :REAL
```

```
BEGIN
   WRITELN('Enter the number of cookies baked and',
          ' press return.');
   READ(Cookies);
   WRITELN('Today, ', Cookies:4, ' cookies were baked.');
   Boxes := Cookies / CookiesPerBox;
   Cartons := Boxes / BoxesPerCarton;
   CartonSales := BoxesPerCarton * BoxPrice * Cartons;
   LeftOvers := Boxes - BoxesPerCarton * Cartons;
   LeftSales := LeftPrice * LeftOvers;
   Total := CartonSales + LeftSales;
   WRITELN;
   WRITE('The', Carton:5, ' cartons can be sold for',
        ' a value of');
   WRITELN(CartonSales:8:2);
   WRITELN;
   WRITE('The, LeftOvers:5, ' leftover boxes can be',
        ' sold for a value of');
   WRITELN(LeftSales:8.2);
   WRITELN;
   WRITELN('The company has earned a total of');
   WRITELN(Total:8:2)
END
```

Debugging

As you run a program, you will begin to locate and to correct the syntax, run-time, and logic errors. That process will now be illustrated for you using the program above.

Debugging the Syntax Errors. After each pair of Pascal statements below, you will see a syntax error message produced by the compiler, followed by a discussion of what caused that error and how to correct the mistake. You need not look back at the original program. After reading the error message, try to determine what is causing the problem *before* reading the subsequent discussion.

Pascal Statement I:

```
      BoxPrice = 1.14;
      LeftPrice = .57; ←
*** Error in constant
```

Discussion: Recall that, in Pascal, a real number must have at least one digit to the left and to the right of the decimal point. The value for `LeftPrice` should have been written as 0.57.

Pascal Statement II:

```
     CartonSales, LeftSales  :REAL
  BEGIN ←
*** Semicolon expected
```

Discussion: A semicolon is missing after the word `REAL`.

Pascal Statement III:

```
  WRITELN('Today, ', Cookies:4,
          'cookies were baked.');
  Boxes := Cookies / CookiesPerBox; ←
*** Type conflict of operands
```

Discussion: All three variables in the marked statement were declared as integers; however, the operator / will produce a real number, which in Pascal cannot be stored in an integer variable. The / should be replaced with `DIV`.

Pascal Statement IV:

```
     Boxes := Cookies / CookiesPerBox;
     Cartons := Boxes / BoxesPerCarton; ←
*** Type conflict of operands
```

Discussion: This error is caused for precisely the same reason as the previous one. Replace / with `DIV` in the marked statement.

Pascal Statement V:

```
     LeftSales := LeftPrice * LeftOvers;
     Total := CartonSales + LeftSales; ←
*** Undeclared identifier
```

Discussion: Indeed, the variable `Total` was not declared as a real variable, as it should have been.

Pascal Statement VI:

```
     WRITELN;
     WRITE('The', Carton: 5, ' cartons can be',
          ' sold for a value of'); ←
*** Undeclared identifier
```

Discussion: The variable `Carton` is misspelled; that variable should have been `Cartons`.

For the next two statements, numerous error messages will be displayed prior to the discussion. Can you discover what is causing all these errors?

Pascal Statement VII:

```
     WRITELN;
     WRITE('The, LeftOvers:5, ' leftover boxes can be',
          ' sold for a value of'); <---
*** Illegal symbol (terminator expected)
*** Error in variable
*** ')' expected
*** Undeclared identifier
*** ':=' expected
*** String constant must not exceed source line
```

Discussion: Have you discovered what is causing all of these errors? The answer is that a single quotation mark has been omitted accidentally after the word 'The' in the marked `WRITE` statement. As a result of this mistake, the compiler "thinks" (often incorrectly) that there is something wrong with all of the subsequent statements. Those statements and their [rather meaningless] error messages will not be included here. Rather, all of the mistakes encountered so far will be corrected first, and the new program will then be recompiled.

Debugging the Syntax Errors (Again). After making all of the corrections needed so far, the resulting program is

```
PROGRAM Sales(INPUT, OUTPUT);
CONST
   CookiesPerBox = 12;
   BoxesPerCarton = 24;
   BoxPrice = 1.14;
   LeftPrice = 0.57;
VAR
   Cookies, Boxes, Cartons, LeftOvers  :INTEGER;
   CartonSales, LeftSales, Total       :REAL;
BEGIN
   WRITELN('Enter the number of cookies baked and',
          ' press return.');
   READ(Cookies);
   WRITELN('Today, ', Cookies:4, ' cookies were baked.');
   Boxes := Cookies DIV CookiesPerBox;
   Cartons := Boxes DIV BoxesPerCarton;
   CartonSales := BoxesPerCarton * BoxPrice * Cartons;
   LeftOvers := Boxes - BoxesPerCarton * Cartons;
   LeftSales := LeftPrice * LeftOvers;
   Total := CartonSales + LeftSales;
```

```
    WRITELN;
    WRITE('The', Cartons:5, ' cartons can be sold for',
          ' a value of');
    WRITELN(CartonSales:8:2)
    WRITELN;
    WRITE('The', LeftOvers:5, ' leftover boxes can be',
          ' sold for a value of');
    WRITE(LeftSales:8.2);
    WRITELN;
    WRITELN('The company has earned a total of');
    WRITE(Total:8:2)
END
```

Here are the syntax error messages for the new program followed by a discussion of what caused those errors and how to correct the mistakes.

Pascal Statement VIII:

```
WRITE ('The', LeftOvers:5,
       ' leftover boxes can be ',
       ' sold for a value of');
WRITE(LeftSales:8.2); <——
*** '.' expected
```

Discussion: This error message is deceiving. The problem is that the period in the marked statement should have been a colon. A more appropriate error message would have been

```
':' expected
```

Pascal Statement IX:

```
END <——
*** Unexpected end of input
```

Discussion: A period is missing after the last END in the program. Because of that omission, the compiler "thought" that there would be some statements following this final END. When looking for those instructions, the machine "unexpectedly" discovered that there were none.

After making these last two corrections, all of the syntax errors will have been removed and the compiler will be successful in translating the Pascal program into machine language. Now the computer can run the program and you can begin to debug the run-time and logic errors, as illustrated below.

Debugging the Run-Time and Logic Errors. On running the corrected program using the data in which 3318 cookies are baked, the following output is obtained:

```
Enter the number of cookies baked and press return.
3318 ⟵ This number was typed by the user at the terminal
Today, 3318 cookies were baked.

The 11 cartons can be sold for a value of 300.96

The 12 leftover boxes can be sold for a value of 6.84
The company has earned a total of
   307.80
```

Checking these computations by hand, you can easily verify that the numbers are correct, and since the computer performed all of the instructions, there are no run-time errors. Only the manner in which the answer is being displayed should be improved. For example, there should probably be a blank line just before the sentence "The company has. . . ." Also, the value 307.80 should be displayed on the previous line (after the word "of"). Can you change the above program to accomplish these alterations?

One solution is to change the statement

```
WRITE(LeftSales:8:2);
```

to

```
WRITELN(LeftSales:8:2);
```

Also, the statement

```
WRITELN('The company has earned a total of');
```

should be changed to

```
WRITE('The company has earned a total of ');
```

The final corrected program is

```
PROGRAM Sales(INPUT, OUTPUT);
CONST
   CookiesPerBox = 12;
   BoxesPerCarton = 24;
   BoxPrice = 1.14;
   LeftPrice = 0.57;
VAR
   Cookies, Boxes, Cartons, LeftOvers  :INTEGER;
   CartonSales, LeftSales, Total       :REAL;
```

```
BEGIN
   WRITELN('Enter the number of cookies baked and',
         ' press return.');
   READ(Cookies);
   WRITELN('Today, ', Cookies:4, ' cookies were baked.');
   Boxes := Cookies DIV CookiesPerBox;
   Cartons := Boxes DIV BoxesPerCarton;
   CartonSales := BoxesPerCarton * BoxPrice * Cartons;
   LeftOvers := Boxes - BoxesPerCarton * Cartons;
   LeftSales := LeftPrice * LeftOvers;
   Total := CartonSales + LeftSales;
   WRITELN;
   WRITE('The', Cartons:5, ' cartons can be sold for',
         ' a value of');
   WRITELN(CartonSales:8:2);
   WRITELN;
   WRITE('The', LeftOvers:5, ' leftover boxes can be',
         ' sold for a value of');
   WRITELN(LeftSales:8:2);
   WRITELN;
   WRITE('The company has earned a total of');
   WRITE(Total:8:2)
END.
```

On running this final program, you will, at last, obtain the following more readable output:

```
Enter the number of cookies baked and press return.
3318 ←— This number was typed by the user at a terminal
Today, 3318 cookies were baked.

The 11 cartons can be sold for a value of 300.96

The 12 leftover boxes can be sold for a value of 6.84

The company has earned a total of 307.80
```

The Operator MOD

In the cookie example above, you saw the need to compute the remainder obtained on dividing one integer by another. Specifically, the number of leftover boxes was precisely the remainder obtained on dividing the number of boxes by the number of boxes per carton. Using the operators −, *, and DIV, and after some thought, time, and effort, the value for the leftover boxes was calculated by using the two Pascal assignment statements

```
Cartons := Boxes DIV BoxesPerCarton;
LeftOvers := Boxes - BoxesPerCarton * Cartons
```

The need to compute the remainder from dividing one integer, say `Numerator`, by a second integer, say `Denominator`, is so common that in Pascal there is a built-in operator called `MOD` that can be used directly to perform that computation. Specifically, the value of

```
Numerator MOD Denominator
```

is precisely the remainder you obtain when you divide the integer `Numerator` by the integer `Denominator`.

Example

The number of leftover boxes from the cookie example above could have been computed by

```
LeftOvers := Boxes MOD BoxesPerCarton
```

Since `MOD` is a new operator, you should ask, "What is the precedence of `MOD` in relation to other operators?" The answer is that, in Pascal, `MOD` has the same precedence as *, /, and `DIV` (see Appendix B).

Now you are ready to run programs. The remainder of this book will be devoted to teaching you new programming concepts and how to implement those concepts in Pascal. In addition, the problem-solving steps of Chapter 1 will continually be demonstrated with each example.

Exercises for Section 3.4

Trace the pseudocode algorithm of this section (see page 120) for the following values of the variable `Cookies`.

1. 288,000

2. 128,377

Code, run, and debug each of the following algorithms that you wrote in Section 2.3 (see page 62) into Pascal, using the given sets of data values.

3. The algorithm for Exercise 3.
   a) 40 hours at $4.00 per hour.
   b) 48 hours at $5.25 per hour.
   c) 34 hours at $6.35 per hour.

4. The algorithm for Exercise 4.
   a) radius is 4.0.
   b) radius is 1.5.
   c) radius is 5.2.

5. The algorithm for Exericse 5.
   a) 20.5 feet, 18 pounds, 0 degrees Fahrenheit.
   b) 32.0 feet, 145 pounds, 212 degrees Fahrenheit.
   c) 45.3 feet, 98 pounds, −20 degrees Fahrenheit.

6. The algorithm for Exercise 6.
   a) 24106, 24108, 24118, 24121.
   b) 30206, 30419, 31309, 36406.
   c) 11202, 13139, 21804, 30166.

3.5 Summary

In this chapter, you have learned the details of how a computer reads and displays information. In addition, you have begun to learn how to code an algorithm into Pascal, and how to debug syntax errors. A review of some of the more important issues will be given here.

A file is a collection of information stored, as a unit, on an input or output device. Each file consists of a collection of individual lines that are separated by an end-of-line marker. Each line, in turn, has a certain number of columns, each of which contains one character. In an input file, individual numerical values must also be separated by some type of delimiter. In Pascal, the standard delimiters for separating numerical values are a blank space and the end-of-line marker. At the end of the file is the end-of-file marker.

When the computer performs the pseudocode instruction

```
READ FileName, Variables
```

the machine will attempt to find the values for the variables from the specified file. In so doing, the computer uses a pointer to scan each line of the file (from left to right) looking for the necessary values of the Variables. When encountered, those values are assigned to the Variables in the order as listed in the `READ` statement.

When a `READ` statement is completed (i.e., all variables have been assigned values), you will need to know where the pointer is finally positioned. In Pascal, the pointer will either be located at the column just to the right of the last value encountered, or else the pointer will be set at the first column of the next line in the file, depending on whether you use the Pascal `READ` or `READLN` statement, respectively.

The pseudocode statement

```
WRITE FileName, Variables
```

will instruct the computer to display the values of the variables (in the order listed) in the appropriate output file. Each value will be displayed within a certain number of columns (called the field width), which you can control. In Pascal, the value will be right justified within the field width.

When working with WRITE statements, you must always be aware of how and when an end-of-line marker is inserted into the file. In Pascal, a WRITE statement does not put an end-of-line marker in the file when completed, whereas a WRITELN statement does. Potential errors can arise when more information is displayed on a single line than is allowed. (Recall that each output device has a maximum number of characters per line that can be displayed.)

You have learned that a Pascal program consists of a program heading, a declaration, and an executable section. Specifically, the general form of a Pascal program is

```
PROGRAM   Name(FileName, ..., FileName);
LABEL     Declarations;
CONST     Declarations;
TYPE      Declarations;
VAR       Declarations;
FUNCTION  Declarations;
PROCEDURE Declarations;
BEGIN
   Statement;
   Statement;
   .
   .
   .
   Statement
END.
```

Key Terms

Reserved words 76
Standard identifiers 76
Input devices 85
File 85
End-of-line marker 87
End-of-file marker 87
Pointer 89
Delimiter 89
Output devices 102
Field width 105

Most of the everyday inventions we take for granted actually date from the last half of the 19th century. To name just a few: the typewriter, the phonograph, the electric light bulb, the automobile, the telephone, X-rays, and the washing machine. Of course, many devices—such as this swimming life buoy created by Monsieu Barathon—never saw the light of day. According to Barathon's plan, a shipwrecked person would float on an inflated rubber buoy attached to a frame. The passenger could operate the buoy's propeller by pedalling her feet, much like riding a bicycle.

4

IF SO THEN DO IT

In this chapter you will learn a new programming concept that will enable you to instruct the computer to perform an action only under certain conditions, which you can specify. Solving a word problem involving this concept will be illustrated for you with an example. As in the previous chapters, you will use the problem-solving techniques of Chapter 1, and particular emphasis will be placed on the debugging phase.

4.1 IF/THEN Statements

IF/THEN statement A programming statement that instructs the computer to perform an action only if a certain condition is true.

In this section you will learn the basic idea of the IF/THEN **statement,** which instructs the computer to perform an action only if a certain condition is true. You will also see where that concept arises in the problem-solving process. In addition, you will learn how to write the IF/THEN statement in pseudocode.

To illustrate the need for an IF/THEN statement, suppose that the Orks (of Chapter 1) have decided to spend the afternoon shopping on Main Street (Fig. 4.1). At the end of the day, they want to go to the theater on Division Boulevard. Can you supply them with the instructions for doing so?

Perhaps you realize that the correct instructions depend on precisely where (on Main Street) the Orks will be when they start toward the theater. For example, if the Orks are starting from West Third Street, then you might provide the instructions:

Go East 3 blocks.

Go North 1 block.

Alternatively, if the Orks are starting at East Second Street, then the instructions:

Go West 2 blocks.

Go North 1 block.

would be appropriate.

Surely you do not want to write a separate set of instructions for every possible starting point. In order to come up with an appropriate set of instructions, irrespective of where the Orks begin, you need to think through the solution given above. Notice that West *Third* Street is *three* blocks from Division Boulevard, and that East *Second* Street is *two* blocks from Division Boulevard. If you were to assign the num-

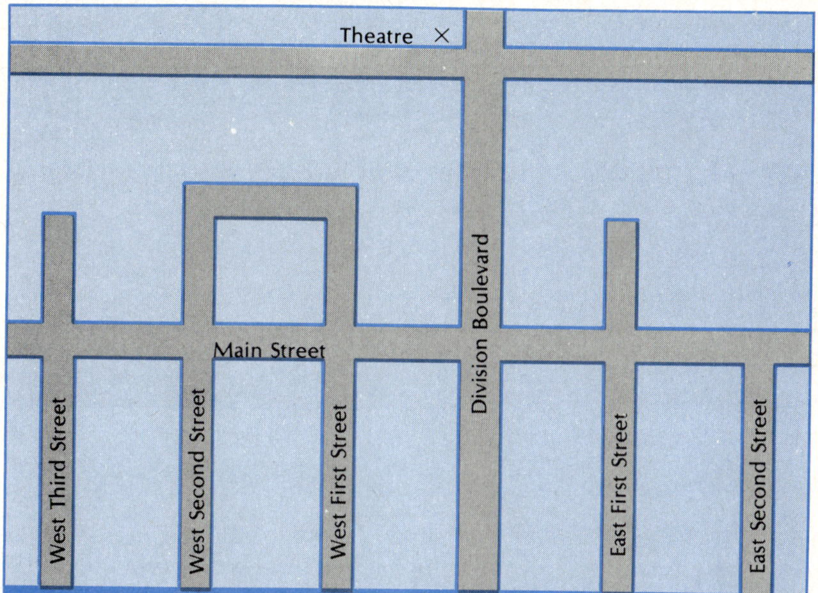

Figure 4.1 A section of Smallville.

ber of the street from which the Orks are starting to the variable K, then you might provide the following instructions:

> IF you are starting from West K Street, THEN
> go east K blocks (K is the street number, e.g., third street, and hence 3 blocks).

Alternatively,

> IF you are starting from East K Street, THEN
> go west K blocks.

Fortunately, computers can understand these IF/THEN statements (when properly coded into Pascal). The general form of the IF/THEN statement in pseudocode is

```
IF some Condition is true, THEN perform some
   Action
```

The Condition is an expression whose value is either TRUE or FALSE (recall these two boolean values from Section 2.4). The Action is any instruction (or group of instructions) that the computer is able to perform. These instructions might consist of assignment, `READ`, or `WRITE` statements, or even another `IF/THEN` statement; but remember, the computer will perform the Action only if the Condition is true. After the `IF/THEN` statement is completed, the computer proceeds to the instruction immediately following the Action. In this book the above `IF/THEN` statement will be shortened to

```
IF Condition THEN
   Action
```

Example

The pseudocode statement

```
IF Balance > 1000 THEN
   InterestRate := 0.12
```

will cause the computer to determine whether the value of the variable *Balance* is greater than 1000. Only if this comparison is true will the value of 0.12 be assigned to the variable *InterestRate*. Otherwise, this assignment statement will not be performed.

Relational Operators

Relational operator Any of the six operators (<, >, =, ≤, ≥, ≠) used to compare two numbers, characters, or variables.

From the example above, you can see that the condition in the `IF/THEN` statement was obtained by comparing two numbers to determine if the value of the variable *Balance* was (or was not) greater than 1000. The result of the comparison is either true or false, depending on the specific value of *Balance*. In problem solving, the need to compare the values of two numbers (or variables)—and to take appropriate action based on the result of the comparison—often arises, and it is in such situations that the `IF/THEN` statement should be used. In general, you can use any of the six **relational operators** to compare numbers when forming the condition in an `IF/THEN` statement, namely:

Relational Operator	Pseudocode Symbol
is less than	$<$
is greater than	$>$
is equal to	$=$
is less than or equal to	$\leq$
is greater than or equal to	$\geq$
is not equal to	$\neq$

The result of using these relational operators to compare two numbers will always be a boolean value, for example:

Comparison	Value
$1.5 < 2.83$	TRUE
$3 = 4$	FALSE
$2 \geq 2$	TRUE
$1.8E1 > 1.8E1$	FALSE

It is also possible to compare the values of variables. For example, if the value of the variable *X* is 1.5 and the value of the variable *I* is −2, then the following comparisons result in valid boolean values:

Comparison	Value
$X < 0.0$	FALSE
$X \geq I$	TRUE
$I = -1$	FALSE
$I \neq -1$	TRUE

In Pascal, you can store the result of a comparison into a boolean variable for later use. Thus, for example, you could use the following assignment statement:

```
B := X < I
```

In this case, the result of the comparison, which is FALSE, is stored into the boolean variable *B*.

In Pascal, it is also possible to compare other types of values and/or variables. For instance, if *Ch* is a character variable, then the result of the comparison

```
Ch = 'A'
```

will be true if the value of *Ch* is the character 'A' and false otherwise.

Other types of allowable comparisons will be discussed in Section 4.4. There is, however, one type of comparison you should avoid, namely, comparing two real numbers for equality. This should be avoided because of truncation errors. For example, on a computer with a precision of six digits, the value of the apparently true comparison:

```
1/3 + 1/3 + 1/3 = 1.0
```

will be false because the expression to the left of the equal sign will be evaluated as 0.999999, which indeed is not equal to 1.0.

Boolean Expressions

Boolean expression A sequence of comparisons and calculations whose final result is either of the values TRUE or FALSE.

Boolean operator Any of the three operators (AND, OR, NOT) that can be used to form boolean expressions.

In Chapter 2, you learned to create arithmetic expressions by using variables together with the operators +, −, *, /, DIV, and MOD. In a similar manner, it is possible to create **boolean expressions** (calculations whose result is either TRUE or FALSE) by using variables together with the relational operators, or the following three **boolean operators:**

```
AND    OR    NOT
```

Example

The pseudocode statement

```
IF (A > 0) AND (B > 0) THEN
   C := 1 / (A * B)
```

will cause the computer to determine whether the values of the variables *A* and *B* are both greater than 0. Only if this condition is true will the computer perform the assignment statement

```
C := 1 / (A * B)
```

The operators AND and OR require two boolean values in order to be evaluated—one to the left of the operator and one to the right of the operator. The operator NOT, however, requires only one boolean value. In order to use these operators effectively, you must understand how the computer performs "calculations" with these operators. Therefore for illustration purposes, suppose that *P* and *Q* are expressions whose values are either TRUE or FALSE (you can think of *P* and *Q* as the results of performing two separate comparisons, as in the example above). Then, when using *P* and *Q* together with the boolean operators AND, OR, and NOT, the computer will obtain the following results:

Expression	Result
P AND Q	TRUE if both *P* is TRUE and *Q* is TRUE. Otherwise, the value of (*P* AND *Q*) is FALSE.
P OR Q	TRUE if either *P* is TRUE or *Q* is TRUE (or both are TRUE). Otherwise, the value of (*P* OR *Q*) is FALSE.
NOT P	TRUE if *P* is FALSE. Otherwise, the value of (NOT *P*) is FALSE.

Example

According to the table above, if the value of *P* is TRUE and that of *Q* is FALSE, then the value of

1. (*P* AND *Q*) is FALSE.
2. (*P* OR *Q*) is TRUE.
3. (NOT *P*) is FALSE.

When working with boolean conditions, keep in mind the fact that the computer must be able to evaluate the entire condition. Thus, for example, if the value of the variable *Number* is 0, then the computer would be unable to evaluate the boolean condition in the statement

```
IF (Number < 0) OR ((10 / Number) < 3) THEN
    Number := Number + 1
```

The reason is that the computer cannot perform the division of 10 by 0 in the expression following the word OR.

Nested IF/THEN Statements

As mentioned previously, the action associated with an IF/THEN statement can be an assignment, READ, WRITE, or another IF/THEN statement. When the action is another IF/THEN statement, the result is called a *nested* IF/THEN statement (an IF/THEN statement within an IF/THEN statement). This situation is illustrated below.

Example

The pseudocode statement

```
IF A > 0 THEN
    IF B > 0 THEN
        C := 1 / (A * B)
```

will cause the computer to determine whether *A* is greater than 0. Only if this condition is true will the computer perform the statement

```
IF B > 0 THEN
    C := 1 / (A * B)
```

Solving a Problem

The following example illustrates how the IF/THEN statement is used in developing a computer program to solve a problem.

Problem: Given the normal and overtime hourly wages of an employee together with the number of hours worked, compute the wages earned by the employee. Use the normal rate for those hours worked under 40 hours; use the overtime rate for those hours worked over 40 hours.

Algorithm Development. As always, the first step is to determine how you would solve the problem yourself. Without giving the issue much thought, you might provide the following solution.

Solution: I compute the wages by using the normal and overtime hourly rates and the number of hours worked.

Now it is necessary to think through your solution so that you can express this answer more in terms that a computer can understand. To get started, identify the inputting, processing, and outputting phases of the problem.

Inputting. As usual, begin by asking yourself, "What specific data will I need to be given in order to solve the problem?" Obviously, you will need the normal and overtime hourly rates, and the number of hours worked. Thus you are led to using the pseudocode statements

```
READ NormalRate, OvertimeRate, Hours
WRITE NormalRate, OvertimeRate, Hours
```

to assign the data (that will be given to you when the program is run) to the associated variables, and to echo print (i.e., immediately display) those values, respectively.

Processing. This is where the IF/THEN statement will be used. To see how, ask yourself, "What do I want to do with the data once that information has been entered into the computer?" Use the original solution given above, which was:

Solution: Compute the wages by using the normal and overtime hourly rates and the number of hours worked.

Now you must continue thinking through your solution to determine more precisely how you will accomplish this task. You might find it helpful to use the technique of working through a specific example in which, for instance, the values of the variables are

```
NormalRate := 4.00
OvertimeRate := 6.00
Hours := 20
```

Here, because the number of hours worked is less than 40, you do not need to worry about overtime hours. Indeed, it is not difficult to calculate the total wage earned—$80. This value was obtained by using the formula

```
Wages := NormalRate * Hours
```

On the other hand, if

```
Hours := 50
```

then the overtime rate is involved. If you have worked through this example, then you should realize that, in this case, the total wage—$220—is computed as follows:

```
Wages := NormalRate * 40 +
         OvertimeRate * (the number of
                         overtime hours)
```

For this situation, it is necessary to compute the number of overtime hours. By working through the specific example, you can see that the calculation for the number of overtime hours is *Hours* − 40.

Combining these observations, evidently, the correct formula for computing the wages depends on whether the value of *Hours* is greater than 40 or not. If not, then you can use the formula

```
Wages := NormalRate * Hours
```

However, if the value of *Hours* is greater than 40, then the correct formula is

```
Wages := NormalRate * 40 + OvertimeRate *
         (Hours - 40)
```

Thus using IF/THEN statements, you could write

```
IF Hours ≤ 40 THEN
   Wages := NormalRate * Hours
IF Hours > 40 THEN
   Wages := NormalRate * 40 +
            OvertimeRate * (Hours - 40)
```

In the example above, you should note that, no matter what the value of *Hours*, the boolean expression in only one of these two IF/THEN statements will be true; the other will be false.

For most problems, there is more than one way to perform the desired computations. In this "wage" problem, for example, one could also obtain the same value for *Wages* by using the instructions

```
Wages := NormalRate * Hours
IF Hours > 40 THEN
   Wages := NormalRate * 40 +
            OvertimeRate * (Hours - 40)
```

To see that these instructions are also correct, trace these statements for yourself using the specific examples above. You will see that, when the value of *Hours* is less than or equal to 40, the first statement will compute the value of *Wages* correctly. Then, in the second statement, the boolean condition

```
Hours > 40
```

will be false, and this fact will prevent the computer from performing the assignment statement that would change the value of *Wages*. Alternatively, when the value of *Hours* is greater than 40, the first statement will compute the value of *Wages* incorrectly; however, the second statement will subsequently recompute the value of *Wages* correctly.

Outputting. Since the only requested information in the problem is the total wage, the outputting phase consists of the single statement

```
WRITE Wages
```

Combining the inputting, processing, and outputting phases, the pseudocode algorithm becomes

```
READ NormalRate, OvertimeRate, Hours
WRITE NormalRate, OvertimeRate, Hours
IF Hours ≤ 40 THEN
   Wages := NormalRate * Hours
IF Hours > 40 THEN
   Wages := NormalRate * 40 + OvertimeRate *
            (Hours - 40)
WRITE Wages
```

Since this algorithm is correct, the tracing, coding, and debugging issues will not be addressed here.

Compound Statements

In the preceeding "wage" example, the action associated with each IF/THEN statement consisted of only one instruction. However, in other problems, the action might consist of several statements. Such a group of statements is often referred to as a **compound statement,** which can be thought of as one big statement. In this book, the individual statements comprising the compound statement will always be indented as a group. For example:

Compound statement A group of statements that, when considered as a whole, can be thought of as one big statement.

```
IF Condition THEN
    Statement 1 ┐
    Statement 2 ├ Compound Statement
    Statement 3 ┘
```

In this example, if the Condition is true, then the compound statement consisting of Statement 1, Statement 2, and Statement 3 will be performed; otherwise, none of these statements will be performed.

In contrast, compare the IF/THEN statement above with

```
IF Condition THEN
    Statement 1 ┐
    Statement 2 ┘ Compound Statement
Statement 3
```

Here, because Statement 3 is not indented, only Statement 1 and Statement 2 constitute the compound statement; Statement 3 is not part of this IF/THEN statement at all. Thus, in this instance, if the Condition is true, then Statement 1 and Statement 2 will be performed (as a group). Subsequently, since the IF/THEN statement is completed, Statement 3 is performed. However, if the Condition is false, then Statement 1 and Statement 2 are not performed. Subsequently, however, since the IF/THEN statement is completed, Statement 3 is performed. Note that when Statement 3 is part of the compound statement, it is performed only if the Condition is true. However, when Statement 3 is not part of the compound statement, it will always be performed (no matter whether the Condition is true or false).

Example

```
NetWages := Wages
Taxes := 0.0
IF Wages ≤ 300.00 THEN
   Taxes := 0.13 * Wages             } Compound
   NetWages := Wages - Taxes         } Statement
WRITE Wages, Taxes, NetWages
```

For these instructions, the compound statement will be performed only if the value of the boolean condition *Wages* ≤ 300.00 is TRUE. On the other hand, the WRITE statement, which is not part of the compound statement, will be performed irrespective of the value of the boolean condition.

For coding purposes, it is extremely important to note that, while a human can usually interpret the meaning and purpose of indentation, a computer cannot. Thus when coding a compound statement into Pascal, there will be a special way to indicate that a group of statements is to be considered as a compound statement, as will be described in Section 4.4.

Special Uses for IF/THEN Statements

You have just seen the use of IF/THEN statements in problem solving. In addition, there are several other common uses for these statements in computer programs, as will now be described.

Using IF/THEN Statements for Data Verification. Another typical use for IF/THEN statements in programming is testing whether the value of a variable is within an allowable range. This process is often referred to as **data verification,** or testing the data for validity.

Data verification
Testing whether the values of the data are within some allowable range.

To illustrate this process, imagine that, in a particular program, the variable *Month* is to contain an integer value that represents the month of a year. After performing the statement

```
READ Month
```

the value for this variable should, of course, be an integer between 1 and 12. However, suppose that when you prepare the data for this program, you accidentally type the value of 15 instead of 5. In the program, you can use an IF/THEN statement to display an appropriate message in the event that the value of *Month* is not valid, for example,

```
IF (Month < 1) OR (Month > 12) THEN
   WRITE 'The value of Month is invalid'
```

Also, in the event that the value of *Month* is not valid, it is probably better not to perform the rest of the instructions in the program because the output you obtain might be meaningless. A subsequent IF/THEN statement can be used to do precisely that. For example, you could write

```
IF (Month ≥ 1) AND (Month ≤ 12) THEN
   ⟨Here is the rest of the program⟩
```

In this case, the rest of the program will be performed only if the value of *Month* is between 1 and 12.

Unfortunately, it can happen that the data is *valid* (i.e., within the allowable range) but still incorrect. For instance, in the example above, the value for *Month* could have been entered accidentally as 6 (which is in the valid range of 1 to 12) when you meant to type a value of 5. It is for this reason that a good programmer not only checks for validity, but also echo prints the data. That way, a visual check can detect the incorrect value. The exception to this rule is when the amount of data is exceedingly large. You would not, for example, want to echo print the entire telephone directory.

Continuing with the issue of data verification, suppose that, in addition to the value of *Month*, you want to verify that the value of the variable *Year* is between 1948 and 1972. If you want the computer to perform the rest of the program only if the values of both *Month* and *Year* are acceptable, then you could write, for instance,

```
READ Month, Year
WRITE Month, Year
IF (Month < 1) OR (Month > 12) THEN
   WRITE 'Month is invalid'
IF (Year < 1948) OR (Year > 1972) THEN
   WRITE 'Year is invalid'
IF (1 ≤ Month ≤ 12) AND (1948 ≤ Year ≤ 1972)
   THEN
   ⟨Here is the rest of the program⟩
```

However, if there are many variables to verify, then the boolean condition that is used in the final IF/THEN statement (to determine whether to perform the rest of the program) can be exceedingly long. Can you see a way to accomplish the same result more easily?

One solution is to use a boolean variable, say *Error*, whose value is to be TRUE if there is any error in the data, and FALSE otherwise. The following instructions will have the same results as the three IF/THEN statements on page 143:

```
READ Month, Year
WRITE Month, Year
Error := FALSE     {At this point, there is no error.}
IF (Month < 1) OR (Month > 12) THEN
   WRITE 'Month is invalid'
   Error := TRUE     {Now there is an error in Month.}
IF (Year < 1948) OR (Year > 1972) THEN
   WRITE 'Year is invalid'
   Error := TRUE     {Now there is an error in Year.}
IF NOT Error THEN
   ⟨Here is the rest of the program⟩
```

Observe that the boolean expression in the final IF/THEN statement is much shorter than in the previous example. Yet, as before, the computer will perform the rest of the program only if all of the data are valid, i.e., if the value of *Error* is FALSE.

In the example above, consider what would happen if you omitted the first assignment statement. In the event that the value of *Month* is 10, for instance, and that of *Year* is 1950, the computer would be unable to evaluate the condition in the final IF/THEN statement. The reason is that the variable *Error* will not have been assigned a value. Trace these statements for yourself.

Using IF/THEN Statements in Debugging. In Chapter 2, you saw that WRITE statements could be very useful during the debugging process. One approach is to wait until a run-time or logic error arises, and then to insert appropriate WRITE statements to help trace the program and to locate the error. Finally, after correcting all of the mistakes, you would have to remove all the additional WRITE statements that are no longer needed (until the next error arises).

With the use of IF/THEN statements, a better approach is available to you. The idea is to anticipate, from the beginning, that your initial program might contain errors. Thus you should consider including with your program some additional `WRITE` statements for debugging purposes. However, by using `IF/THEN` statements, when the program is finally working correctly, there will be no need to remove those `WRITE` statements.

To see how this time-saving strategy can be accomplished, construct a boolean variable, say *Debug*, whose value, at the beginning of the program, should be set to `TRUE` provided that you want the `WRITE` statements to be executed, and to `FALSE` otherwise. Then, at various places in your program, you would write

```
IF Debug THEN WRITE Variables
```

These `WRITE` statements will be performed only if the value of *Debug* is `TRUE`. Then, when the entire debugging process is complete, you can simply go to the beginning of the program and set the value of *Debug* to `FALSE`. This will prevent the `WRITE` statements from displaying information when the program is run next time.

In this section, you have learned how to use the `IF/THEN` programming concept to instruct the computer to perform an action only if some condition is true. In addition, you have learned how to use a compound statement when the desired action consists of several individual statements. Finally, you have seen several typical uses for `IF/THEN` statements. In Section 4.2 you will learn a convenient extension of the `IF/THEN` statement.

Exercises for Section 4.1

Suppose that the following assignment statements have been made:

```
Leg1 := 3                      Price := 3.5
Leg2 := 4                      Buy := FALSE
Hypotenuse := 5
```

Indicate whether each of the following expressions would be a valid condition in an `IF/THEN` statement. For those that are valid, determine whether the condition is true or false. For those that are not valid, explain what is wrong.

1. `5 * Price - 1.50`
2. `Leg1 * Leg1 + Leg2 * Leg2 = Hypotenuse * Hypotenuse`

3. `(NOT B) AND (Price + 2.25)`
4. `(Price > 3 + 0.1 * Price) OR Buy`

For what values of the integer variable *Irate* will the assignment statements be performed in the following IF/THEN statements?

5.
```
IF NOT (Irate / 4 ≤ 12) THEN
   Total := Amount * 4
```
6.
```
IF ((Irate > 1) AND (Irate < 5)) OR (Irate = 8)
   THEN
   Value := 0.15
```
7.
```
IF Irate > 1 THEN
   IF (Irate < 5) OR (Irate = 8) THEN
      Value := 0.15
```

Write pseudocode statements to perform the following word instructions. You need not be concerned with reading values for the variables.

8. Display the larger of the two variables *Check* and *Balance*. (In case of a tie, it does not matter which variable is displayed.)
9. Compute the value of *Y* as that of *X* provided that *X* is greater than or equal to 0; otherwise the value of *Y* should be that of -*X*. Display the value of *X* in the former case and the value of *Y* in the latter case.
10. Given the number of gallons of oil ordered (denoted by the variable *Order*), compute the total ordering cost (denoted by the variable *Cost*) as: $50 plus $1.18 for each of the first 150 gallons ordered; plus $1.12 for each of the next 100 gallons ordered; plus $1.07 for each subsequent gallon ordered.

For each of the following problems, after the data are read, use IF/THEN statements to write appropriate error messages when the associated values are invalid. Also, use a boolean variable so as to perform the rest of the program only if there is no error in any of the data.

11. The time of day (on the 24-hour system) will be read and stored into the variables *Hours*, *Minutes*, and *Seconds*.
12. *Ball1* and *Ball2* are two variables whose values, respectively, are the number of pins knocked down by each of two balls in a bowling frame. (Remember, no more than a total of ten pins can be knocked down in one frame.)
13. The value and suit of a card from a deck of playing cards is to be read and stored into the integer and character variables *Value* and *Suit*, respectively. The value of each card should be between 1 and 13 while the suit should be one of 'C', 'D', 'H', or 'S'.

For the following word problem, explain why the given pseudocode instructions produced the given (incorrect) output. Correct the pseudocode instructions.

14. Word Problem

Given the values of the integer variables *Ball1* and *Ball2*, compute and display the values of the boolean variables *Spare* and *Strike* according to the following rules. The value of *Spare* should be TRUE only if the sum of the values of *Ball1* and *Ball2* is 10 and the value of *Ball1* is less than 10. The value of *Strike* should be *TRUE* only if the value of *Ball1* is 10.

Pseudocode Instructions

```
Ball1 := 6
Ball2 := 4
IF (Ball1 + Ball2 = 10) AND (Ball1 < 10) THEN
   Spare := TRUE
   Strike := FALSE
IF Ball1 = 10 THEN
   Strike := TRUE
Spare := FALSE
WRITE Strike, Spare
```

Output

```
FALSE (= Strike)
FALSE (= Spare)     {This value is incorrect.}
```

4.2 IF/THEN/ELSE Statements

In the previous section you learned how to use the IF/THEN programming concept to instruct the computer to perform an action only if some condition is true. From many of the examples presented there, you might have noticed that often you need to perform one action when a condition is true and a second action when that same condition is not true. For example, if the data are invalid, then display an error message; otherwise (if the data are valid), perform the rest of the program. In general, such a situation could be handled with the two statements

```
IF Condition THEN
   Action 1
IF NOT Condition THEN
   Action 2
```

In this section, you will see how to write these two instructions with a single statement. Specifically, these two statements can be

IF/THEN/ELSE statement A programming statement that instructs the computer to perform one action if a certain condition is true and an alternative action if that same condition is false.

combined into the following equivalent pseudocode IF/THEN/ELSE **statement:**

```
IF Condition THEN
   Action 1
ELSE
   Action 2
```

Such a statement will first instruct the computer to determine whether the value of the Condition is TRUE or FALSE; to perform Action 1 (and not Action 2) if the Condition is true; and to perform Action 2 (and not Action 1) if the Condition is false. Once the IF/THEN/ELSE statement is completed, the computer will proceed to the instruction following Action 2.

Example

```
IF Hours ≤ 40 THEN
   Wages := NormalRate * Hours
ELSE
   Wages := NormalRate * 40 +
            OvertimeRate * (Hours - 40)
```

You must be particularly careful if the actions in an IF/THEN/ELSE statement are themselves nested IF/THEN/ELSE statements. For example, in the statement

```
IF Condition 1 THEN IF Condition 2 THEN
   Action 1 ELSE Action 2
```

it is not clear whether the word ELSE is attached to the second or to the first IF/THEN statement. Looking very carefully at the indentation below, the above statement could mean either

```
IF Condition 1 THEN
   IF Condition 2 THEN
      Action 1
   ELSE
      Action 2
```

or

```
IF Condition 1 THEN
   IF Condition 2 THEN
      Action 1
ELSE
   Action 2
```

In the first situation, Action 2 will be performed only if Condition 1 is true and Condition 2 is false. In the second situation, however, Action 2 is performed only if Condition 1 is false.

The problem encountered in this example is similar in nature to that of the order in which arithmetic operations are performed by the computer. With IF/THEN/ELSE statements, as with arithmetic operators, there is a normal precedence for performing operations. In the case of IF/THEN/ELSE statements, unless told otherwise, the computer will associate the word ELSE with the closest IF/THEN statement. Thus of the two possible interpretations above, the computer will follow the first one. Just as the precedence for arithmetic operators can be overriden by using parentheses, there is a way to override the normal process of associating the word ELSE with the closest IF/THEN statement. The details for doing so in Pascal will be described in Section 4.4.

Again, it is important to note that, even though a computer cannot interpret the meaning and purpose of indentation, it is always advisable to use some form of *consistent* indentation policies so that the program is more readable. Although there are no universally accepted guidelines for rules of indentation, Fig. 4.2 illustrates two possible indentation schemes. The first one will be used in this book. Keep in mind that the objective of indentation is to facilitate the reading and understanding of the program.

Solving a Problem

Now that you have learned the concept of an IF/THEN/ELSE statement, it is time to work through a complete example. In so doing, you will see for the first time how logic errors can arise.

Problem: Gary Gambler has been using his computer to keep track of his gambling accounts. Recently, it occurred to him that he might be able to use the machine to help him play poker. As a first step in that direction, he has asked you to write a program

```
IF    Condition THEN          IF Condition
      Statement               THEN  Statement
      .                             .
      .                             .
      .                             .
      Statement                     Statement
ELSE                          ELSE  Statement
      Statement                     .
      .                             .
      .                             .
      .                             Statement
      Statement
```

Figure 4.2 Two possible indentation policies.

that will read the values of five playing cards and determine whether those cards constitute a "straight" or a "flush" (or both).

A straight is when the face values of the five cards can be arranged in a consecutive, increasing order (irrespective of the suit). In that regard, a jack has a face value of 11, a queen has a face value of 12, and a king has a face value of 13. However, you can count the face value of an ace as either 1 or 14. Thus, except for the last two, each of the following are straights:

```
5 7 4 6 8                {This is the straight 4 5 6 7 8.}
ace 2 3 4 5              {In this straight, the ace is a 1.}
10 jack queen king ace   {In this straight, the ace is a 14.}
queen king ace 1 2       {Not a straight—the face values are not in
                          increasing order.}
7 4 3 5 8                {Not a straight.}
```

A flush, on the other hand, is when all five cards are from the same suit (irrespective of their face values).

Algorithm Development. As usual, the first step in computer problem solving is to determine how you would solve the problem yourself. Without giving the issue too much thought, you might provide the following solution.

Solution: I look at the five cards and see if they constitute a straight or a flush (or both).

The next step is to think through your solution so as to understand more precisely how you solve the problem. First, pseudocode will be used to describe the solution steps. Eventually, however, a sequence of instructions must be coded into Pascal. To help you think through your solution, begin by identifying the inputting, processing, and outputting phases of the problem.

Inputting. Again, to begin the inputting phase, you must ask yourself what information you will need to be given in order to solve the problem. Obviously, you will need to know the specific five cards with which you are working. Therefore you might be tempted to use the instruction

```
READ Card1, Card2, Card3, Card4, Card5
```

to read the values of the five cards. However, a little further thought should lead you to some of the following questions: (1) Are the values of the variables integers or characters? (2) In what specific ways will the values of the variables relate to the actual playing cards? (3) From the values of the variables, how will you know the suit of a card?

The way in which you create and store the data can greatly affect the way in which you solve a problem (and even the speed with which the resulting algorithm works). Therefore, when solving problems, it is worthwhile to give careful thought as to how the data should be represented. Particular emphasis will be given to this topic in Chapters 6 and 8.

To answer the questions posed above, observe that for each card you will need to know its face value and its suit. Therefore it seems reasonable to represent each card by two variables. The first variable, whose value will be an integer between 1 and 13, will represent the face value of the card; specifically, the ace will be represented by the integer 1, and the jack, queen, and king, by the integers 11, 12, and 13, respectively. The second variable, whose value will be a character, will represent the suit of the card; specifically, a value of 'C' will stand for clubs, 'D' for diamonds, 'H' for hearts, and 'S' for spades. Furthermore, in order to simplify the process of determining if the five cards constitute a straight, their face values will be entered in increasing order.

With these items in mind, you are led to the statement

```
READ Value1, Suit1, Value2, Suit2, Value3,
     Suit3, Value4, Suit4, Value5, Suit5
```

As usual, you should echo print the data with the statement

```
WRITE Value1, Suit1, Value2, Suit2, Value3,
      Suit3, Value 4, Suit4, Value5, Suit5
```

However, recall, from the Section 4.1 that you can use IF/THEN statements to check the data for validity. You should do so for this problem. Specifically, for the first card, you could write

```
IF (Value1 < 1) OR (Value1 > 13) THEN
   WRITE 'the face value of the first card is invalid'
IF NOT ((Suit1 = 'C') OR (Suit1 = 'D')
   OR (Suit1 = 'H') OR (Suit1 = 'S')) THEN
   WRITE 'the suit of the first card is invalid'
```

A similar set of IF/THEN verification statements should be written for each of the other cards.

Also, in order to check that the face values of the cards are entered in increasing order, you could use the following statement

```
IF NOT ((Value1 ≤ Value2) AND (Value2 ≤ Value3) AND
        (Value3 ≤ Value4) AND (Value4 ≤ Value5)) THEN
   WRITE 'the face values are not in increasing order'
```

Of course, these data-verification statements should be put together in such a way that the rest of the program is performed only if all of the data are valid. However, the details for doing so will not be given.

Processing. To determine the processing portion of the program, you should ask yourself what you want to do with the data once those values have been entered into the computer. Obviously, from the original [English] solution given above, you should check to see if the five cards constitute a straight or a flush (or both).

Once again, you must think through your solution to determine how to do so. Only then will you be able to supply the computer with the appropriate instructions. For instance, recalling that the face values of the five cards are entered in increasing order, you might provide the following more refined solution.

Solution: If the face values of the five cards are consecutive, then WRITE 'straight'; otherwise, if the suit values are all the same, then WRITE 'flush'.

Already you can see the concept of an IF/THEN/ELSE statement arising. By using appropriate indentation, the IF/THEN/ELSE statement is even more evident. For example,

```
If ⟨the face values are all consecutive⟩ THEN
   WRITE 'straight'
ELSE
   IF ⟨the suit values are all the same⟩ THEN
      WRITE 'flush'
```

However, further refinement is necessary in order to rephrase the English items in angle brackets (which you see above) in terms of equivalent boolean expressions that a computer can understand. Specifically, looking at the first IF/THEN statement in the answer above, you must translate the English concept of "consecutive" into computer terminology. Can you use the values of the variables *Value1*, . . . , *Value5* to create a boolean expression that will be true when the five cards are consecutive?

If you are having difficulty, then you might find it helpful to use the technique of working through some specific examples in which you consider several specific values for these variables. Which are consecutive and which are not? After some experimentation, you might realize that, in order for the cards to be consecutive, the face value of each successive card should be one more than that of the previous card. Thus you might provide the following more refined solution:

```
IF Value2 = Value1 + 1 AND
   Value3 = Value2 + 1 AND
   Value4 = Value3 + 1 AND
   Value5 = Value4 + 1 THEN
   WRITE 'straight'
ELSE
   IF ⟨the suit values are all the same⟩ THEN
      WRITE 'flush'
```

Looking at the second IF/THEN statement in the solution above, it remains to convert the concept of "all cards are of the same suit" into a boolean expression that the computer will be able to understand. For instance, the [English] concept of "same" can be changed into the [computer] concept of "equality." Thus, to verify that the suits of the five cards are the same, you can use the values of the appropriate variables to check if

```
Suit1 = Suit2 = Suit3 = Suit4 = Suit5
```

Thus using this expression, the processing portion of this program would appear to be

```
IF Value2 = Value1 + 1 AND
   Value3 = Value2 + 1 AND
   Value4 = Value3 + 1 AND
   Value5 = Value4 + 1 THEN
   WRITE 'straight'
ELSE
   IF Suit1 = Suit2 = Suit3 = Suit4 =
      Suit5 THEN
      WRITE 'flush'
```

Outputting. As you can see in the IF/THEN/ELSE statement above, the outputting for this problem has already been included in the processing phase and need not be discussed further. Thus by putting together all components the pseudocode algorithm is

```
READ   Value1, Suit1, Value2, Suit2, Value3,
       Suit3, Value4, Suit4, Value5, Suit5
WRITE Value1, Suit1, Value2, Suit2, Value3,
       Suit3, Value4, Suit4, Value5, Suit5
{To save space, the IF/THEN statements that were used to check the data for
validity will be omitted here.}

IF Value2 = Value1 + 1 AND
   Value3 = Value2 + 1 AND
   Value4 = Value3 + 1 AND
   Value5 = Value4 + 1 THEN
   WRITE 'straight'
ELSE
   IF Suit1 = Suit2 = Suit3 = Suit4 =
      Suit5 THEN
      WRITE 'flush'
```

Tracing

In order to trace this algorithm, you will have to choose values for the variables that are being read. Up until now, the choice for those values has not been critical. However, when a program contains a statement of the form

```
IF Condition THEN
   Action
```

the choice of values for the variables can be extremely important. The reason is that some choices will result in the Condition being true (and hence the Action being performed), while other choices will result in the Condition being false (and hence the Action being skipped).

Ideally, it would be best to trace the program using values that test both cases; for this example that can be done. However, when a program contains a large number of IF/THEN statements, it is generally not feasible to choose data that test every possible combination of conditions. Therefore careful thought should be given to the issue of selecting "useful" test values for the data. While there are no specific rules, you should at least select values that are likely to arise when someone else uses the program. Also, you should choose values that test some of the more important aspects of the program. For the poker example, for instance, you might create data to test the following cases:

1. Neither a straight nor a flush.
2. A straight (and not a flush).
3. A flush (and not a straight).
4. A straight and a flush.

For this discussion, only the first of these four situations will be traced. To that end, suppose, for example, that you had the following cards, and associated variables and values:

Card	Variable	Value	Variable	Value
4 of hearts	*Value1*	4	*Suit1*	'H'
5 of spades	*Value2*	5	*Suit2*	'S'
6 of spades	*Value3*	6	*Suit3*	'S'
6 of clubs	*Value4*	6	*Suit4*	'C'
9 of clubs	*Value5*	9	*Suit5*	'C'

In order to refer to the four parts of the IF/THEN/ELSE and IF/THEN statements in the algorithm above, the labels "S1," "S2," "S3," and "S4" will be added. Then, using the above values for the variables together with the labels, the following statement will be traced:

```
S1:  IF Value2 = Value1 + 1 AND
        Value3 = Value2 + 1 AND
        Value4 = Value3 + 1 AND
        Value5 = Value4 + 1 THEN
S2:     WRITE 'straight'
     ELSE
S3:     IF Suit1 = Suit2 = Suit3 = Suit4 =
           Suit5 THEN
S4:        WRITE 'flush'
```

To begin the tracing, recall how an IF/THEN/ELSE statement works. First you must examine the condition in S1 to see if that boolean expression is true or false. After carefully doing so, you should conclude that the condition is false because the value of *Value4* is not equal to that of *Value3* + 1. Accordingly, the action in S2 is skipped, and the action following the word ELSE is performed (i.e., S3 and S4).

Since S3 and S4 constitute an IF/THEN statement, the condition in S3 must now be checked. For the current values of the variables, that condition is false because the value of *Suit1* is not equal to that of *Suit2*. Thus the action in S4 is not performed. At this point, the entire IF/THEN/ELSE statement (beginning with S1) is completed. Consequently, the computer proceeds to the instruction immediately following this IF/THEN/ELSE statement (i.e., following S4). In this case, however, there are no subsequent statements, and so the entire program is over. Observe that, other than echo printing the data, no other information has been displayed at all!

While *you* know that, for the current values of the variables, the cards constitute neither a straight nor a flush, you should probably have the program display that fact. Can you modify the above program to do so? One solution is to change S3 and S4 into the statement

```
IF Suit1 = Suit2 = Suit3 = Suit 4 =
   Suit5 THEN
   WRITE 'flush'
ELSE
   WRITE 'neither a straight nor a flush'
```

The tracing phase is now complete.

In this section, you have learned how the pseudocode `IF/THEN/ELSE` statement is used to perform one action if a specified condition is true, and an alternative action if that same condition is false. In addition, you have seen how these statements arise in the problem-solving process. For the problem of this section, the next step would be to code the algorithm into Pascal, which you will learn how to do in Section 4.4. After preparing the coded program in a machine-readable form, you could then begin to locate and to correct the syntax, run-time, and logic errors. Part of the debugging process will be illustrated in detail in Section 4.3.

Exercises for Section 4.2

1. How does the instruction

```
IF Condition THEN
    Action 1
    Action 2
```

differ from the instruction

```
IF Condition THEN
    Action 1
ELSE
    Action 2
```

Specifically, for each set of instructions, indicate under what value of the Condition, Action 1 and Action 2 will be performed.

Rewrite each of the following instructions using `IF/THEN/ELSE` statements only.

2.
```
IF X ≥ 0 THEN Y := X
IF X < 0 THEN Y := X
```

3.
```
IF Balance > Amount THEN
    WRITE 'Balance is greater than Amount'
IF Balance < Amount THEN
    WRITE 'Balance is less than Amount'
IF Balance = Amount THEN
    WRITE 'Balance equals Amount'
```

4.
```
IF Order ≤ 150 THEN
    Cost := 50 + 1.18 * Order
IF (Order > 150) AND (Order ≤ 250) THEN
    Cost := 50 + 1.18 * 150 + 1.12 *
            (Order - 150)
```

```
IF Order > 250 THEN
   Cost := 50 + 1.18 * 150 + 1.12 * 100 +
           1.03 * (Order - 250)
```

Write pseudocode algorithms to solve each of the following problems. Be sure to include data-verification statements when appropriate.

5. Given five playing cards in the same form as was used in the poker problem of this section (i.e., in increasing order of face value), determine if four of the five cards have the same face value or not. (You need not read the suit values.)
6. Mr. Smith is in a 30% tax bracket, which means that 30 cents of each dollar he earns goes to the government. He has a certain amount of money that can be invested in either (a) a money market fund that pays 11% annual interest on the first $1,000, and 12% on the amount over $1,000 (if any), or (b) a government bond that pays 8% annual interest (which is exempt from income tax). Given the initial amount of money that Mr. Smith can invest, determine which of these two investment strategies is better, and indicate how much interest he will earn, after taxes, at the end of one year using the best strategy.
7. A playing card will be represented by an integer between 1 and 52. The values of 1 through 13 are clubs, 14 through 26 are diamonds, 27 through 39 are hearts, and 40 through 52 are spades. Within a given suit, the first number corresponds to the ace of that suit, the second number to the two of that suit, and so on. Thus, for example, the number 17 corresponds to the 4 of diamonds. Given an integer between 1 and 52, display the associated card, e.g., the integer 8 should be displayed as: 8 of clubs; the integer 37 should be displayed as: jack of hearts. (*Hint:* After reading the data into a variable, say `Card`, use the value of `Card` to create a variable, say `Suit`, whose value is to be 1, 2, 3, or 4, depending on the suit of the given card. Then create a variable, say `FaceValue`, whose value is to be an integer between 1 and 13 corresponding to the face value of the given card. Try to use assignment statements instead of `IF/THEN` statements to calculate the values of `Suit` and `FaceValue`.)

4.3 Debugging

The objective of this section is to take you step by step through part of the debugging process. To that end, recall that after tracing (and correcting) the poker program of the previous section the new algorithm is

```
READ Value1, Suit1, Value2, Suit2, Value3,
     Suit3, Value4, Suit4, Value 5, Suit5
WRITE Value1, Suit1, Value2, Suit2, Value3,
      Suit3, Value4, Suit4, Value5, Suit5
```

{To save space, the data-verification statements will be omitted here.}

```
IF Value2 = Value1 + 1 AND
   Value3 = Value2 + 1 AND
   Value4 = Value3 + 1 AND
   Value5 = Value4 + 1 THEN
   WRITE 'straight'
ELSE
   IF Suit1 = Suit2 = Suit3 = Suit4 =
      Suit5 THEN
      WRITE 'flush'
      ELSE
      WRITE 'neither a straight nor a flush'
```

Since the process of coding will be described in Section 4.4, assume that the above algorithm has already been coded into Pascal. After preparing the program, data, and control cards in a machine-readable form, and after correcting all of the syntax errors, you are ready to deal with the run-time and logic errors.

Suppose, for example, that you are going to test the program with a straight consisting of the 10 of hearts, jack of spades, queen of spades, king of hearts, and ace of diamonds. Recalling that the data must be entered so that the face values are in increasing order, the data for this problem is

```
1D   10H   11S   12S   13H
```

You, of course, know that this is a straight (i.e., 10, jack, queen, king, ace). Unfortunately, when you run the program with this data, the computer displays:

```
1D   10H   11S   12S   13H
neither a straight nor a flush
```

Now what do you do? In general, besides panicking, you should follow these steps:

1. Locate the part of the program that is causing the error. (Do not attempt to guess the cause of the error.)
2. Trace that portion to identify the specific cause of the error.
3. Correct the mistake.
4. Retrace the new program with the current data to make sure that the error has indeed been corrected.

Locating the Error

The first step is to locate the part of the program that is causing the error. Fortunately, the first `WRITE` statement in the program caused the data to be echo printed and, as you can see, the correct values have been assigned to the variables. Thus the error is not due to incorrect data values. Since this program is very short, the source of the error can only be in the statement (with labels added):

```
S1    IF Value2 = Value1 + 1 AND
         Value3 = Value2 + 1 AND
         Value4 = Value3 + 1 AND
         Value5 = Value4 + 1 THEN

S2:      WRITE 'straight'
      ELSE

S3:      IF Suit1 = Suit2 = Suit3 = Suit4 =
            Suit5 THEN

S4:         WRITE 'flush'
         ELSE

S5:         WRITE 'neither a straight nor a flush'
```

Tracing

Now it is time to trace the above statement so as to understand precisely why there is an error. To do so, begin by using the values of the variables to determine whether the condition in S1 is true or false. In fact, the condition in S1 is false because the boolean expression

```
Value2 = Value1 + 1
```

is not true (since the value of *Value2* is 10 and that of *Value1* is 1). Thus the entire condition

```
Value2 = Value1 + 1 AND
Value3 = Value2 + 1 AND
Value4 = Value3 + 1 AND
Value5 = Value4 + 1
```

is false. If you thought that the condition was true, then you did not trace the statement correctly. In general, when tracing it is very easy to perform what you were thinking about when you wrote the program instead of what is actually written in front of you at the moment. This problem can be avoided only if you are extremely careful during the tracing process. When tracing, remember to act like a computer, not like a programmer.

Correcting the Error

Now that you have located the error, can you modify the condition in S1 so that the program will perform correctly on the current data? Since the condition in S1 does not cover the straight in which *Value1* = 1, *Value2* = 10, *Value3* = 11, *Value4* = 12, and *Value5* = 13, you must change that condition somehow. For example, one possibility is

```
IF (Value2 = Value1 + 1 OR
    Value2 = Value1 + 9) AND
    Value3 = Value2 + 1 AND
    Value4 = Value3 + 1 AND
    Value5 = Value4 + 1 THEN ...
```

The boolean expression following the word OR has been added to allow for the possibility of having a straight in which *Value1* = 1 and *Value2* = 10, i.e., a straight in which the cards are a 10, jack, queen, king, and ace.

Retracing

Once you have made the correction, you should retrace the program with the current data to ensure that the error has been fixed. For the current problem, since it is so easy to do this, the details will not be illustrated.

More on Debugging

After locating and correcting the above logic error, the new program (with labels added for reference purposes) is

```
READ Value1, Suit1, Value2, Suit2, Value3,
     Suit3, Value4, Suit4, Value5, Suit5
WRITE Value1, Suit1, Value2, Suit2, Value3,
      Suit3, Value4, Suit4, Value5, Suit5
{To save space, the data-verification statements will be omitted here.}
  S1:  IF (Value2 = Value1 + 1 OR
           Value2 = Value1 + 9) AND
           Value3 = Value2 + 1 AND
           Value4 = Value3 + 1 AND
           Value5 = Value4 + 1 THEN
  S2:      WRITE 'straight'
       ELSE
```

```
S3:        IF Suit1 = Suit2 = Suit3 = Suit4 =
              Suit5 THEN
S4:           WRITE 'flush'
           ELSE
S5:           WRITE 'neither a straight nor a flush'
```

Once again you must recompile the program and remove the syntax errors, if any. Suppose that you have done so, and that you now run the program with the following data:

```
5H   6H   7H   8H   9H
```

In this case, you would expect the answer to be

```
straight
flush
```

Unfortunately, when you run the program, the computer displays:

```
5H   6H   7H   8H   9H
straight
```

Go through the debugging steps above in an attempt to find and to correct the mistake.

Locating the Error Again

As before, after scanning the values that have been echo printed, you can see that the correct values have been assigned to the variables. Therefore in this program you can be sure that the error is once again in the statement consisting of S1 to S5 above.

Tracing Again

Now you must trace the statement to understand why there is an error. To that end, you should begin by checking whether the condition in S1 is true or false. Since that condition is true, the computer should have (and has) performed the WRITE statement in S2. Now what?

If you think that the computer will now check the condition in S3, then you have forgotten how an IF/THEN/ELSE statement is performed. Recall from Section 4.2 that for the statement

```
IF Condition THEN
   Action 1
ELSE
   Action 2
```

if Action 1 is performed (as is the case here), then Action 2 is not performed. Thus for the current problem the computer will not check the condition in S3. In fact, since S3, S4, and S5 together constitute Action 2, the computer will now proceed to the instruction following S5. Since there is none, the program is over! Now that you know what is causing the problem, can you correct the mistake?

Correcting the Error Again

As you have seen, the "culprit" is the word ELSE (just before S3), for it is this word that prevents the computer from performing the desired instructions (beginning in S3), which determine whether the cards constitute a flush. One way to correct the problem is simply to remove the word ELSE. Thus the corrected group of statements becomes

```
S1:  IF (Value2 = Value1 + 1 OR
        Value2 = Value1 + 9) AND
        Value3 = Value2 + 1 AND
        Value4 = Value3 + 1 AND
        Value5 = Value4 + 1 THEN
S2:       WRITE 'straight'
S3:  IF Suit1 = Suit2 = Suit3 = Suit4 =
        Suit5 THEN
S4:       WRITE 'flush'
     ELSE
S5:       WRITE 'neither a straight nor a flush'
```

By eliminating the word ELSE, the new program above will allow the computer to check the given cards for both a straight and a flush.

Retracing Again

It is not difficult to trace this new program with the current data. When you do so, you will indeed get the desired result:

```
straight
flush
```

However, whenever you change a program to correct one mistake, you might unknowingly introduce a new error that will arise only when a different set of data is used. For this reason, when making a change, you should look carefully at the proposed change and perhaps trace several other values of the data to see what happens. Also, you should test the new program using all of the existing data values (even those that you have already tested). Unfortunately, the above program is still incorrect, for when you run the latest version of the program with the original straight in which *Value1* = 1, *Value2* = 10, *Value3* = 11, *Value4* = 12, and *Value5* = 13, you will obtain the following results:

```
1D   10H   11S   12S   13H
straight
neither a straight nor a flush
```

If you use the techniques you have learned to locate the error, then you will discover that the word `ELSE` (between S4 and S5) is causing the problem. For the given data, the condition in S4 is false because the suits are not all the same. Consequently, the action in S5 is performed, resulting in the `WRITE` statement producing the unwanted output, "neither a straight nor a flush." Can you correct the error?

You could resolve the problem simply by removing the word `ELSE`, as you did previously. In so doing, you would have to change S5 to

```
IF ⟨neither a straight nor a flush⟩ THEN
   WRITE 'neither a straight nor a flush'
```

You would then have to replace the English expression in angle brackets with an equivalent boolean expression using the variables in the program. Doing so is possible but quite cumbersome. A better approach is available.

Evidently, you only want to display the last message if neither of the previous `WRITE` statements in S2 and S4 were performed. To determine whether that happened, you can create a new boolean variable, say *Neither*, whose value should be `TRUE` if the cards constitute neither a straight nor a flush, and `FALSE` otherwise. Just prior to S1, the hand (at that point) constitutes neither a straight nor a flush, so you should set the value of *Neither* to `TRUE`. Now, if either S2 or S4 is performed—that is, the computer writes "straight" or "flush"—then you should set the value of *Neither* to `FALSE` after S2 (in the event that a straight is encountered), and again after S4 (in the event that a flush is encountered). Finally, after removing the word `ELSE`, S5 should be changed to

```
IF Neither THEN
   WRITE 'neither a straight nor a flush'
```

The final (and correct) processing portion of this algorithm is then

```
Neither := TRUE
IF (Value2 = Value1 + 1 OR
    Value2 = Value1 + 9) AND
    Value3 = Value2 + 1 AND
    Value4 = Value3 + 1 AND
    Value5 = Value4 + 1 THEN
    WRITE 'straight'
    Neither := FALSE
IF Suit1 = Suit2 = Suit3 = Suit4 = Suit5 THEN
    WRITE 'flush'
    Neither := FALSE
IF Neither THEN
    WRITE 'neither a straight nor a flush'
```

This section has shown you what to do when you encounter a logic error. However, there are two things that you should definitely *not* do. First, do not rerun the program without making some intelligent change, just in the hope that, "perhaps this time the program will work." Invariably, you will obtain the same results. Second, do not attempt to "guess" what is causing the error and then say to yourself, "Well, let's see what that does," or, "I'll try this—it probably won't hurt anything." The only reasonable way to proceed is to isolate and to understand the error using systematic debugging techniques. Only then will you be able to correct the program.

Exercises for Section 4.3

In each of the following exercises, you will be given a word problem together with a pseudocode algorithm and the results of running that algorithm with a specific set of data. Use the debugging techniques you have learned in this section to locate the cause of the indicated error. Explain, in English, why the error arose. Finally, write a corrected algorithm that works for the given data.

1. The following algorithm is designed to determine if the poker hand, as described in this section, contains "two pairs." Two pairs is a hand in which there are two distinct pairs of cards having the same face value, and the face value of the fifth card should be different from that of the two pairs; e.g., a hand consisting of two fives, two tens, and a queen is "two pairs."

Algorithm

```
READ Value1, Value2, Value3, Value4, Value5
WRITE Value1, Value2, Value3, Value4, Value5
IF ((Value1 = Value2) AND
   (Value3 = Value4)) OR
   ((Value2 = Value3) AND
   (Value4 = Value5)) THEN
   WRITE 'two pairs'
ELSE
   WRITE 'no two pairs'
```

a) The output obtained for one set of data is

```
2 2 6 7 7
no two pairs      {This is not correct.}
```

b) The output obtained for another set of data is

```
8 8 8 8 9
two pairs      {This is not correct.}
```

c) The output obtained for another set of data is

```
5 5 6 6 6
two pairs      {This is not correct.}
```

2. The following algorithm is supposed to determine the cost of ordering a given number of light bulbs. Provided that there are enough light bulbs in inventory to meet the order, the cost for this order is to be computed as either $15 + 0.50 * (number of light bulbs ordered), or 0.75 * (number of light bulbs ordered), whichever is smaller. On the other hand, if there is not enough inventory to meet this order, then the cost is to be 0.75 * (number of available light bulbs) and, in this event, a suitable message should be displayed.

Algorithm

```
READ BulbsOrdered, Inventory
WRITE 'BulbsOrdered =', BulbsOrdered,
      'Inventory =', Inventory
IF BulbsOrdered ≤ Inventory THEN
   IF 15 + 0.50 * BulbsOrdered ≤
      0.75 * BulbsOrdered THEN
      Cost := 15 + 0.50 * BulbsOrdered
ELSE     {Assume that this ELSE is associated with the first IF/THEN
         statement, not the second one.}
   WRITE 'not enough inventory available'
   Cost := 0.75 * BulbsOrdered
WRITE 'Cost = ', Cost
```

a) The output obtained for one set of data is

```
BulbsOrdered = 100    Inventory = 50
not enough inventory available     {This is correct.}
Cost = 75.00    {This is incorrect.}
```

b) The output obtained for another set of data is

```
BulbsOrdered = 50    Inventory = 100
***A variable has not been assigned a value
```

4.4 Coding IF/THEN and Related Statements

Now that you have seen how to work with IF/THEN and IF/THEN/ELSE statements in pseudocode, it is time to learn how to code these instructions into Pascal. As usual, when coding, you must pay particular attention to the rules of grammar. In this section, you will see precisely how to write boolean expressions in Pascal. In addition, you will learn to be careful of the precedence of the relational and boolean operators, just as you did with the arithmetic operators. Finally, you will learn about a special Pascal statement that can save you time and effort when working with nested IF/THEN/ELSE statements.

Creating Boolean Expressions in Pascal

As you learned earlier in this chapter, when using IF/THEN and IF/THEN/ELSE statements, you often need to create boolean expressions in order to compare two values. One way to do so is to use the six relational operators: >, <, =, ≥, ≤, ≠ to compare numbers. As you saw in Section 4.1, the result of such a comparison is a boolean value (i.e., TRUE or FALSE). The first three of these symbols will always be available on your typing equipment; however, the latter three symbols probably will not. Therefore Pascal replaces ≥, ≤, and ≠ with >=, <=, and <>, respectively. The following table summarizes these facts:

English Meaning	Pseudocode Symbol	Pascal Symbol
greater than	>	>
less than	<	<
equal to	=	=
greater than or equal to	≥	>=
less than or equal to	≤	<=
not equal to	≠	<>

In addition to comparing numbers, Pascal has the capability of comparing any two values of the same type, for example, two boolean values or two character values. The two boolean values are ordered so that `FALSE` is less than `TRUE` (i.e., the value of `FALSE < TRUE` is `TRUE`). Comparing two character values, however, requires some care and understanding on your part.

Comparing Character Values in Pascal. In Section 4.1, you learned to compare two character values for equality. For example, suppose that *Ch* is a character variable that has been assigned a value. When performing the comparison

```
Ch = 'M'
```

it is quite clear that the result of the comparison will be true if the value of *Ch* is `'M'`, and false otherwise. However, what would be the meaning (if any) of the comparison

```
Ch < 'M'
```

In order for this comparison to be meaningful, the various characters must be "ordered" in such a way that some characters come "before" the character `'M'` while others come "after" `'M'`. Then, using this ordering, the computer can determine that the above comparison is true if the value of *Ch* is a character that comes before `'M'`, and false otherwise.

Unlike numbers, which have a "natural" ordering, there are many possible ways to order characters. One ordering could have the digits '0' to '9' come before the letters, while another ordering could have those same digits come after the letters. Thus there are many different possible orderings and, in fact, different computers can (and do) use different orderings.

Collating sequence A list that associates an integer with each available character in the computer.

Collectively, these orderings are called **collating sequences.** In other words, the collating sequence is a list that associates an integer with each available character; the integer represents the "position" of that character in the ordering. Thus when comparing two character values (or variables), the computer will use its collating sequence to compare the integers that correspond to the character values in order to determine which character is "smaller."

Example

With one particular collating sequence, the integer 59 is associated with the character `';'`, while the integer 65 is associated with the character `'A'`. For a computer that uses that collating sequence, the comparison

```
';' < 'A'
```

will be true because the integer associated with the character `';'` (namely, 59) is indeed less than the integer associated with the character `'A'` (namely, 65).

As was mentioned above, there are many different collating sequences currently in use. Two of the common ones are the *American Standard Code for Information Interchange,* or ASCII (pronounced, "as—key"), and the *Extended Binary Coded Decimal Interchange Code,* or EBCDIC. (These collating sequences are given in Appendix D.) Moreover, since different machines might use different collating sequences, the processing of characters in a program can depend very much on the particular computer being used. What is more, the number of different characters available can vary from one machine to another. Thus a particular character might be available on your computer but not on another computer. This can sometimes make it difficult to transfer programs that compare characters from one machine to another.

Example

The value of the comparison

```
'a' > 'A'
```

is `TRUE` when working with the ASCII collating sequence, but `FALSE` when working with the EBCDIC collating sequence (see Appendix D).

If you need to work with characters, you should keep these differences in mind, and you should obtain a list of the available characters together with the collating sequence from your local computer facility. Also, be very careful when trying to use such a program on different computers.

Using Boolean Operators in Expressions. In Section 4.1, you learned that the (pseudocode) operators `NOT`, `AND`, and `OR` can be used to form more complicated boolean expressions. Those same reserved words are available in Pascal. Thus, for example, provided that the variable *`Radius`* has been declared and assigned a value, the following is a valid Pascal boolean expression:

```
NOT ((Radius <= 1.5) AND (Radius >= 0.5))
```

Whenever you work with any operator, be it arithmetic, relational, or boolean, there are two items you should be concerned with when coding those expressions into Pascal, as will now be described.

Using Correct Operator Values

You have learned to use the arithmetic, relational, and boolean operators to form expressions. In that regard, you can think of an operator (such as +, <, or AND) as a "black box." That is, you can supply *input* value(s) and/or variables to the black box and, after performing the operation, you will obtain a resulting *output* value from the black box (Fig. 4.3).

Using the operator +, for example, you might supply the input values consisting of the integers 1 and 2. After performing the operation 1 + 2, you obtain the result, namely 3. In this case, two integers were supplied to the operator, and an integer output value was obtained from the operator.

As another example, using the relational operator <, you might supply the input values `'a'` and `'A'`. After performing the operation, `'a' < 'A'`, you obtain the boolean value TRUE or FALSE, depending on the collating sequence of the computer. In this case, two character values were supplied to the operator, and a boolean output value was obtained from the operator.

From these examples, and by looking at Fig. 4.3, you can see that there are two items you should be concerned with when using operators. First, the input values should be of the correct type for that operator. For instance, with the operator AND, the only allowable types

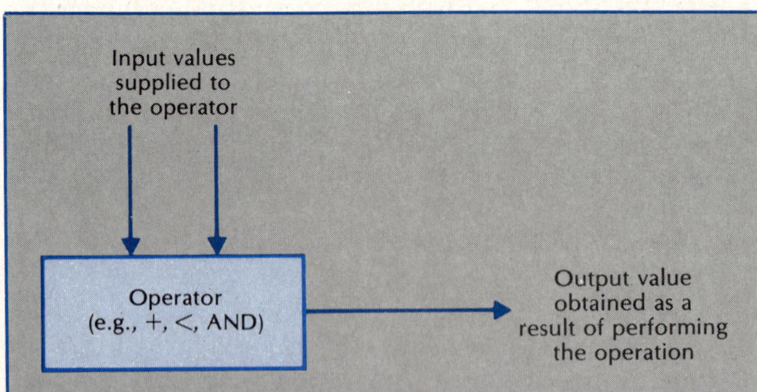

Figure 4.3 Operators.

of input values are boolean values (TRUE or FALSE). The computer cannot, for example, evaluate the expression 10 AND 11. In contrast, for the operator +, the allowable types of input values are numerical (integer or real). The computer cannot, for example, evaluate the expression 'a' + 'b'.

Second, the type of output value obtained as a result of performing the operation must be of the appropriate type. For instance, with the operator =, the result of performing the operation is a boolean value, either TRUE or FALSE, which could only be stored in a boolean variable. So, in the assignment statement

```
B := 3 = 5
```

the variable *B* must have been declared as a boolean variable using the declaration

```
VAR
    B :BOOLEAN;
```

In conclusion, for each and every operator, you must know precisely what types of input values are allowed, and what type of output value is obtained. Attempting to supply a wrong type of value to an operator, or storing the result of an operator in the wrong type of variable will result in an error, or provide incorrect results.

When coding expressions involving operators, there is a second major concern you should be aware of, as will now be described.

Precedence of Operators

When coding arithmetic expressions, you learned to be aware of precedence (i.e., which operation is performed first). A similar concern arises when coding boolean expressions. For instance, if P, Q, and R are all expressions whose values are TRUE or FALSE, then what is the meaning of

```
NOT P OR Q AND R
```

Is it

```
NOT [(P OR Q) AND R]
```

or

```
NOT [P OR (Q AND R)]
```

or

```
[(NOT P) OR Q] AND R
```

In fact, in Pascal, it is none of these. In general, unless told otherwise, the computer will perform all NOTs (from left to right) first, all ANDs (from left to right) second, and all ORs (from left to right) third. Thus the above expression really means

```
(NOT P) OR (Q AND R)
```

Just as with the arithmetic operators, you can use parentheses to override the normal precedence of boolean operators, since expressions in parentheses are always evaluated first. Thus to change the normal precedence in the example above, you could write, for instance,

```
NOT ((P OR Q) AND R)
```

Finally, the issue of precedence arises when an expression contains, simultaneously, arithmetic, relational, and/or boolean operators. For example, how will the computer evaluate the expression

```
3 * 5 < 10 AND 11 = 8 + 3
```

Again, unless parentheses are used, in Pascal the computer will perform the operations in a prespecified order, as given in Appendix B. Thus the above expression would lead to an error because the computer would be unable to evaluate the expression, indicated by parentheses, that results from the normal precedence:

```
3 * 5 < (10 AND 11) = 8 + 3
```

However, you can use parentheses to "force" the computer to evaluate the expression correctly in the following way:

```
((3 * 5) < 10) AND (11 = (8 + 3))
```

In fact, you can always ensure that the computer will follow the desired order of operations by using parentheses, and you are therefore strongly advised to develop the habit of doing so (even when working in pseudocode). You will find the precedence for all Pascal operators in Appendix B.

Coding IF/THEN Statements

To code the pseudocode statement

```
IF Condition THEN
   Action
```

in Pascal, you need only replace the <u>Condition</u> by a valid boolean expression that uses parentheses where necessary, and in which the correct types of input values are supplied to each operator (as has been described above). The <u>Action</u> must be replaced by any valid Pascal statement, such as an assignment, `READ`, or `WRITE` statement, properly coded in Pascal. In the following example, assume that *Amount*, *Level*, *Quantity*, and *Max* are integer variables.

Example

```
IF (Level = Quanitity) AND (Quantity = Max) THEN
   READLN(Amount)
```

In the example above, the use of parentheses is absolutely necessary to override the normal precedence of the operators. Also, note that it would be incorrect to write

```
IF (Level = Quantity = Max) THEN
   READLN(Amount)
```

The reason is that the expression

```
Level = Quantity = Max
```

is not a valid boolean expression in Pascal because the implied word "and" in the expression above must be written explicitly as

```
(Level = Quantity) AND (Quantity = Max)
```

Coding Compound Statements

In Section 4.1, you learned that when the action associated with a pseudocode `IF/THEN` instruction is to consist of several statements (called a compound statement), those statements should be indented as a group. However, recall that, to a computer, indentation has no meaning whatsoever. Therefore when coding a compound statement into Pascal you must precede the first statement of the group with the reserved word `BEGIN`, and follow the last statement with the reserved word `END`, as illustrated in the following example.

Example

```
IF Amount >= 0.0 THEN
   BEGIN
      Balance := Balance + Amount;
      WRITELN('Balance =', Balance:10:2)
   END
```

In this example, the words BEGIN and END can be thought of as left and right parentheses, respectively. Thus the compound statement, together with the words BEGIN and END, can be thought of as one big Pascal statement.

Using Semicolons. Recall that in the executable section of a Pascal program, semicolons are used to separate statements. Keeping in mind that the entire IF/THEN statement begins with the word IF and ends at the end of the action that follows the word THEN, the following illustrates the proper use of semicolons as statement separators:

```
Statement;          {This semicolon separates this statement from the next
                     IF/THEN statement.}
IF Condition THEN       {There is no semicolon here because no
                         statements are being separated.}
   BEGIN     {There is no semicolon here because the word BEGIN by
              itself is not a statement.}
      Statement;        {This semicolon separates this statement from
                         the next one.}
      Statement       {There is no semicolon here because the word
                       END on the next line is not a statement.}
   END;     {This semicolon separates the entire IF/THEN statement
             from the next statement.}
Statement     {There is no semicolon here because we assume that there is
               no statement on the next line.}
```

Empty statement A Pascal statement that does nothing. This statement is sometimes inserted by the computer automatically so as to avoid a syntax error caused by incorrectly placing a semicolon before an END.

In the example above, observe that the very last statement is not part of the compound statement and therefore is not part of the IF/THEN statement at all. Also, if you were to place a semicolon after the last statement inside the compound statement (just before the word END), you would technically make a syntax error because the word END, by itself, is not a statement. However, in this situation, Pascal will automatically insert what is called the **empty statement,** i.e., a statement that does nothing, after this semicolon and before the word END so that no syntax error will occur. Thus, for example,

```
BEGIN
   Statement;
   Statement;
                    ←—     {The empty statement will be inserted here.}
END
```

Coding IF/THEN/ELSE Statements

In Section 4.2 you learned about the pseudocode statement

```
IF Condition THEN
   Action 1
ELSE
   Action 2
```

The coding of this statement in Pascal is similar to that of the IF/THEN statement. Just keep the following items in mind:

1. The Condition should be replaced by any valid boolean expression in Pascal, and Action 1 and Action 2, by any valid Pascal statement.
2. When either action is to consist of several statements, those statements must be surrounded with the words BEGIN and END.
3. With regard to the placement of semicolons, the entire IF/THEN/ELSE statement begins with the word IF and ends at the end of Action 2.

In the following example suppose that *Ball1* and *Ball2* are integer variables, and *Spare* and *Strike* are boolean variables.

Example

(Pay careful attention to the use of semicolons.)

```
READ(Ball1, Ball2);        {This semicolon separates this statement
                           from the next big IF/THEN/ELSE
                           statement.}
IF Ball1 = 10 THEN
   BEGIN
      Strike := TRUE;      {This semicolon separates this statement
                           from the next one.}
      Spare := FALSE;      {This semicolon is incorrect, but the
                           empty statement will be inserted.}
   END
```

```
ELSE
   BEGIN
      Strike := FALSE;     {This semicolon separates this
                            statement from the next IF/THEN
                            statement.}
      IF Ball1 + Ball2 = 10 THEN
         Spare := TRUE
   END;    {This semicolon separates the big IF/THEN/ELSE statement
            from the next statement.}
WRITELN('Strike = ', Strike, ' Spare = ', Spare)
```

As was stated in Section 4.2, in the statement

```
IF Condition 1 THEN
   IF Condition 2 THEN
      Action 1
   ELSE
      Action 2
```

the word ELSE is normally associated with the second IF. However, the words BEGIN and END can be used to associate the word ELSE with the first IF, as follows:

```
IF Condition 1 THEN
   BEGIN
      IF Condition 2 THEN
         Action 1
   END
ELSE
   Action 2
```

In this situation, if Condition 1 is false, then only Action 2 is performed. However, if you were to omit the words BEGIN and END, Action 2 would be performed if Condition 1 were true and Condition 2 were false, because the ELSE would be associated with the second IF/THEN statement.

Using the Pascal Variables EOLN and EOF

Recall from Section 3.4 that in standard Pascal EOLN is a boolean variable whose value is TRUE if the next character to be read is the end-of-line marker. Careful use of this variable together with an IF/THEN statement is often needed when processing textual data in Pascal so as to avoid reading the end-of-line markers.

For instance, suppose that *Ch1* and *Ch2* are two character variables whose values are to be read, and suppose that you do not know whether the input file will consist of

```
AB■
□
```

or

```
A■
B■
□
```

If the first data file is being used, then the statement

```
READ(Ch1, Ch2)
```

would assign the value of 'A' to *Ch1* and 'B' to *Ch2*. However, if the second data file is being used, then the same READ statement would assign 'A' to *Ch1* and the first end-of-line marker (instead of 'B') to *Ch2*. Remember, however, that after the end-of-line marker is read and recognized, it will automatically be converted to a blank space.

If you want to avoid reading the end-of-line marker irrespective of which input file is being used, then you can do so in standard Pascal by using the variable EOLN as follows:

```
READ(Ch1);        {This will assign 'A' to Ch1.}

IF EOLN THEN
   READLN;        {This will skip to the next line of the input file if an end-of-
                  line marker occurs after the 'A'.}

READ(Ch2)         {This will assign 'B' to Ch2 no matter which of the
                  two input files is used.}
```

Recall that, in some nonstandard versions of Pascal (notably, UCSD and Turbo Pascal), the computer does not "look ahead" to compute the value of EOLN (and EOF). For those versions of Pascal, the above instructions will not work. In fact, you cannot avoid reading the end-of-line marker by using the variable EOLN. However, you can use the instructions

```
READ(Ch1, Ch2);
IF EOLN THEN
   READ(Ch2)
```

If the second input file is being used, then after the first read statement is completed, the value of *Ch1* will be 'A' and that of *Ch2* will be a blank space (corresponding to the first end-of-line marker). At that point, the value of EOLN will be TRUE because the end-of-line marker has just been read. Consequently, the subsequent IF/THEN statement will instruct the computer to read another value for *Ch2*, which, in this case, will be the value 'B' on the second line of the input file.

Similar precautions are needed to avoid reading past the end-of-file marker, for otherwise you will get a run-time error. To that end, the boolean variable EOF can be used in standard versions of Pascal. For instance, if you want to read a value for the variable *Amount* only if the pointer is not yet at the end-of-file marker, then you could write

```
IF NOT EOF THEN
   READ(Amount)
```

Be sure to inquire as to the specific version of Pascal being used on your system; and how the variables EOLN and EOF are handled.

The CASE Statement

For certain programming situations, Pascal has a special statement that can simplify your work. Suppose, for example, that you wish to compute the value of the variable *TaxRate* based on the value of the variable *Dependents* as follows:

Dependents	*TaxRate*
0	0.22
1	0.20
2	0.18
3	0.15
4	0.14
5 or 6	0.12
7, 8, or 9	0.10

You could, of course, use a very long Pascal IF/THEN/ELSE statement to compute the desired value of *TaxRate*. For example,

```
IF Dependents = 0 THEN
   TaxRate := 0.22
ELSE
   IF Dependents = 1 THEN
      TaxRate := 0.20
```

```
ELSE
 .
 .
 .
```

The following Pascal CASE **statement** accomplishes the same task:

CASE statement A Pascal statement that instructs the computer to perform one of an alternative number of actions based on the value of an expression that you specify.

```
CASE Dependents OF
     0       :          TaxRate := 0.22;
     1       :          TaxRate := 0.20;
     2       :          TaxRate := 0.18;
     3       :          TaxRate := 0.15;
     4       :          TaxRate := 0.14;
     5, 6    :          TaxRate := 0.12;
     7, 8, 9 :          TaxRate := 0.10
  END
```

More generally, the syntax for a CASE statement is

```
CASE Expression OF
     Value, ..., Value : Action;
     .
     .
     .
     Value, ..., Value : Action
  END
```

Such a statement will instruct the computer (1) to compute the value of the Expression (for instance, *Dependents* in the example above); (2) to locate the value in the list of Values following the reserved word OF (for example, 2); (3) to perform the Action (that appears to the right of the colon) associated with that Value (for example, *TaxRate* := 0.18); and (4) to proceed to the instruction immediately following the END when finished.

When using a CASE statement, the Expression must be an integer, boolean, or a character expression, but never a real expression. Also, each Value must be of the same type as the Expression. You might also observe that there is an END but no corresponding word BEGIN, because the reserved word CASE serves the same function as the word BEGIN. Finally, the Values cannot be a range of values. In other words, you cannot assume that the computer will understand what you mean by "7 through 9" or "7 . . . 9"; you must list each and every value, separated by commas.

If the value of the expression cannot be found in the list of given Values, then the computer will not know what to do. In standard Pascal, a run-time error would occur. In UCSD Pascal, the computer would simply proceed to the statement following the word END. In some nonstandard versions of Pascal (notably, Turbo Pascal), you can add, after the last Action, a final instruction of the form:

```
ELSE Action
```

In view of these differences, you should inquire as to how your version of Pascal handles the situation when the value of the Expression cannot be found in the list of given Values.

Here, then, is a final example of the CASE statement.

Example

Suppose that *Ch* is a character variable whose value is going to be a certain type of punctuation mark.

```
CASE Ch OF
       '.' :        WRITELN('Period');
       ',' :        WRITELN('Comma');
       '!' :        WRITELN('Exclamation point');
       '?' :        WRITELN('Question mark');
       ';' :        WRITELN('Semicolon');
       ':' :        WRITELN('Colon')
    END
```

A Sample Problem

In Sections 4.2 and 4.3, a pseudocode algorithm was developed for the poker problem of determining whether a group of five cards constituted a straight, a flush, or both. In coding that program into Pascal, you must prepare a program heading and a declaration section. In addition, all statements in the executable section must conform to Pascal syntax (by correctly using parentheses, semicolons, and other punctuation and reserved words). Here, then, is a coded Pascal program corresponding to the last (and correct) pseudocode version of the poker program of Section 4.3.

```
PROGRAM Poker(INPUT, OUTPUT);      {This program will read
                                    the values of five playing
                                    cards and will determine
                                    if they constitute a
                                    straight or a flush or
                                    both.}

VAR
   Value1, Value2, Value3, Value4, Value5  :INTEGER;
   Suit1, Suit2, Suit3, Suit4, Suit5       :CHAR;
   Invalid, Neither                        :BOOLEAN;
BEGIN
   {This next set of WRITE statements displays a message to the terminal.}
   WRITELN('Enter each of the five cards in increasing');
   WRITELN('order of face value, as follows:');
   WRITELN('An integer between 1 and 13 for the face');
   WRITELN('value, immediately followed by one of the');
   WRITELN('upper-case letters: C, D, H, or S, for the suit.');
   READ(Value1, Suit1, Value2, Suit2, Value3, Suit3,
        Value4, Suit4, Value5, Suit5);
   WRITELN;
   WRITELN('First card is:', Value1:4, ' of ', Suit1);
   WRITELN('Second card is:', Value2:4, ' of ', Suit2);
   WRITELN('Third card is:', Value3:4, ' of ', Suit3);
   WRITELN('Fourth card is:', Value4:4, ' of ', Suit4);
   WRITELN('Fifth card is:', Value5:4, ' of ', Suit5);
   {Only one set of data-verification statements will be included here. A similar set is
   needed for each card. Also, note the use of parentheses in all boolean conditions.}
   Invalid := FALSE;
   IF (Value1 < 1) OR (Value1 > 13) OR
      NOT ((Suit1 = 'C') OR (Suit1 = 'D') OR
         (Suit1 = 'H') OR (Suit1 = 'S')) THEN
      BEGIN
         WRITELN('The first card is invalid.');
         Invalid := TRUE
      END;
   IF NOT ((Value1 <= Value2) AND (Value2 <= Value3) AND
         (Value3 <= Value4) AND (Value4 <= Value5)) THEN
      BEGIN
         WRITELN('Face values are not in increasing order.');
         Invalid := TRUE
      END;
   IF NOT Invalid THEN
      BEGIN
         Neither := TRUE;
         WRITE('This poker hand is: ');
```

```
          IF ((Value2 = Value1 + 1) OR
             (Value2 = Value1 + 9))
             AND (Value3 = Value2 + 1)
             AND (Value4 = Value3 + 1)
             AND (Value5 = Value4 + 1) THEN
             BEGIN
                WRITE('straight ');
                Neither := FALSE
             END;
          IF (Suit1 = Suit2) AND (Suit2 = Suit3)
             AND (Suit3 = Suit4) AND
             (Suit4 = Suit5) THEN
             BEGIN
                WRITE('flush');
                Neither := FALSE
             END;
          IF Neither THEN
             WRITE('neither a straight nor a flush')
       END
    END.
```

You should note that the READ statement in the program above will work correctly in standard Pascal, but not necessarily in some nonstandard versions, such as Turbo Pascal. The reason is that in Turbo Pascal, for example, a nonblank character value cannot immediately follow a numerical value in an input file, as can be done in standard Pascal. For these nonstandard versions, each face value of a card in the input file would have to be followed by a blank space, and then a character value representing the suit of the card. The associated READ statement would be:

```
READ (Value1, Suit1, Suit1, Value2, Suit2,
      Suit2, Value3, Suit3, Suit3, Value4,
      Suit4, Suit4, Value5, Suit5, Suit5)
```

The first occurrence of each *Suit*-variable in the READ statement above will assign the blank space following the face value in the input file to the *Suit*-variable; the second occurrence of that same *Suit*-variable will then reassign it the subsequent character value from the input file that corresponds to the actual suit of the card.

In this chapter, you have learned how to use IF/THEN and related statements in problem solving. In Chapter 5 you will learn the true power of a computer. Specifically, you will see how to instruct the machine to perform a group of instructions any number of times while having to write those instructions only once.

Exercises for Section 4.4

Suppose that *C* and *B* have been declared as character and boolean variables, respectively. Also, suppose that the following assignment statements have been made:

```
C := '7';
B := TRUE
```

Using the standard rules of precedence, determine the value of each of the following expressions.

1. `(C = '7') OR NOT B`
2. `NOT (C <= 'A') AND B` {First use the ASCII collating sequence of Appendix D, then repeat this problem using the EBCDIC collating sequence.}

For each of the following operators, indicate all of the allowable types of input values, and the corresponding type of the output value in Pascal.

3. −
4. /
5. DIV
6. <=
7. NOT

Find and correct all syntax errors in the following Pascal statements. Use semicolons only when absolutely necessary. Assume that the variables *I* and *J* are integers, *B* is boolean, *C* is character, and *R* is real.

8.
```
IF R ≤ 0.15 AND NOT (I = 1) THEN
     BEGIN
        J := J + 1;
        IF J > 5 THEN
           J := 5;
     END;
  ELSE
     WRITELN('I =', I:3)
```

9.
```
IF B THEN
   IF I = J THEN
      BEGIN
         R := R * R
         WRITELN('R =', R:12)
      END
   ELSE
      I := J;
ELSE
   B := NOT B
```

10.
```
CASE C OF:
   'a', 'b', 'c', : I := 3
   0, 1, 2, 3, 4, 5, 6, 7, 8, 9 :
           WRITELN('C is a digit')
   ';', ':', :

     BEGIN
        I := 1
        J := 1
        WRITELN('C is a punctuation mark')
     END
```

11. Suppose that, for the instructions

Set the value of the integer variable *Draw* to 0. Display the value of the integer variable *Suits*. If that value is 5, then display the word 'flush'. If the value of *Suits* is not 5, set the value of the variable *Draw* to 5 − *Suits* and, at the same time, display the message 'too bad, you do not have a flush'. No matter what the value of *Suits* is, display the value of the variable *Draw*

the following Pascal statements have been coded:

```
Draw := 0;
WRITELN('Suits =', Suits:1);
IF Suits = 5 THEN
   WRITELN('flush')
ELSE
   Draw := 5 - Suits;
   WRITELN('too bad, you do not have a flush');
WRITELN('Draw =', Draw:1)
```

Explain how the following output was obtained, and correct the mistake:

```
Suits = 5
flush
too bad, you do not have a flush     {This line should not
                                      have been displayed.}
Draw = 0
```

Use only CASE statements to code each of the following instructions in Pascal. You need not declare the variables.

12. Compute the value of the integer variable `Days` depending on the integer variable `Month` (whose value will be the number of a month) according to: 30 days has September, April, June, and November; all the rest have 31 except for February which has 28 (assume a non–leap year).

13. Given the value of the character variable `Day` (which represents the first letter of a day of week), and given the value of the boolean variable `Day-time`, compute the value of the variable `PayFactor` as follows:

1.0 if working on a weekday during daytime hours,
1.3 if working on a weekday and not during daytime hours,
1.2 if working on a weekend during daytime hours,
1.5 if working on a weekend and not during daytime hours.

14. Compute the value of the variable `WaterTax`, which depends on the value of the variable `GallonsUsed` as follows:

`GallonsUsed`	`WaterTax`
0–500	2
501–1000	3
1001–1500	4
1501–2000	5
2001–3000	6
over 3000	7

Hint: Since you cannot have a range of values in a `CASE` statement, create an integer variable `Units` whose value corresponds to the number of units of 500 gallons that were used. After computing the value of `Units`, use this variable in the `CASE` statement. Be careful when the value of units is greater than 6. Test your `CASE` statement when 2800 gallons are used and when 4300 gallons are used.

Code, run, and debug a Pascal program for each of the following problems from Section 4.2 (see page 158). Use the given data to test your program.

15. The algorithm in Exercise 5.

a) 6 6 6 6 9

b) 4 7 7 7 8

c) 2 5 5 5 5

16. The algorithm in Exercise 6.

a) 800

b) 1000

c) 1500

17. The algorithm in Exercise 7.

a) 13

b) 25

c) 54

4.5 Summary

In this chapter, you learned how to use the IF/THEN statement to perform an action only if a certain boolean condition is true. Specifically, the pseudocode statement

```
IF Condition THEN
   Action
```

will instruct the computer to determine if the value of the Condition is TRUE or FALSE, and to perform the Action only if the Condition is true. The Action can consist of a single statement or a group of statements. A group of statements, when considered as a unit, is called a compound statement and, in Pascal, must be surrounded by the words BEGIN and END.

In addition to performing arithmetic calculations, computers can compare the values of numbers, characters, and/or variables using the six relational (Pascal) operators: <, >, =, <=, >=, <>. The result of such a comparison is one of the values TRUE or FALSE. When comparing character values, the corresponding integers in the collating sequence are compared.

Just as the operators +, −, *, and / can be used to combine numbers, so the operators NOT, OR, and AND can be used to combine boolean values so as to create other boolean values. When evaluating a boolean expression in Pascal, the computer will observe the precedence rules given in Appendix B. However, you can control the order by using parentheses.

Whenever you use arithmetic, relational, or boolean operators, you should always be sure that the input values supplied to the operator are of the correct type for that operator. Similarly, be aware of the type of output value obtained as a result of performing the operation, for that output value can be stored only in an appropriate type of variable.

The pseudocode statement

```
IF Condition THEN
   Action 1
ELSE
   Action 2
```

will instruct the computer (1) to determine if the value of the Condition is TRUE or FALSE, (2) to perform Action 1 (and not Action 2) if the value of the Condition is TRUE, and (3) to perform Action 2 (and not Action 1) if the value of the Condition is FALSE. When the IF/THEN/ELSE statement is completed, the computer proceeds to the instruction immediately following Action 2.

Key Terms

IF/THEN **statement 132**

Relational operator 134

Boolean expression 136

Boolean operator 136

Compound statement 141

Data verification 142

IF/THEN/ELSE **statement 148**

Collating sequence 168

Empty statement 174

CASE **statement 179**

Philo T. Farnsworth, lone wolf and somewhat eccentric inventor, diagrammed his idea for a television system on a high school blackboard when he was only 16. Here the television pioneer works on the device that permitted the first simultaneous visual and oral reception of film in the home, which he patented in 1930. This device was the first to "tear down" an image at the point of transmission, then rebuild it at the receiving end. By the close of the 1950s, almost 90 percent of American homes had at least one TV. (THE BETTMANN ARCHIVE, INC.)

5

REPETITION USING PROCEDURES AND LOOPS

Repetition The process of repeating a group of instructions so as to solve a problem.

In this chapter you will learn a new and powerful programming concept called **repetition.** The concept of repetition, as used in programming, refers to a sequence of instructions that are to be performed over and over again. To use repetition in problem solving, you will learn how (1) to view the solution of certain problems as that of performing a sequence of steps repeatedly, (2) to identify the individual operations to be repeated, and (3) to write the appropriate instructions in Pascal, so that the computer will be able to perform the repetition.

5.1 Procedures (without Parameters)

Procedure A group of instructions that, as a unit, is given a name. By subsequently referring to that name in the program, you can instruct the computer to perform the instructions any number of times.

A **procedure** is a programming concept that will enable you to perform a group of instructions many times while only having to write those instructions once. There are two types of procedures: those without parameters, and those with parameters. Procedures *with* parameters will be discussed in Chapter 7, so for now you need not be concerned with the concept of a parameter.

A procedure can be thought of as a program within a program. To distinguish a procedure from the actual program, the program is often referred to as the *main program* and the procedures are sometimes called *subprograms, subroutines,* or *modules.* Procedures can be very useful because, while human beings quickly get bored performing the same operations repeatedly, a computer is exceptionally adept at accomplishing such monotonous tasks. That fact, in part, accounts for the power of a computer. Can you imagine performing the same operation ten thousand times? Computers do so routinely (without ever complaining).

The following problem illustrates the idea of repetition, although the repetition will be performed only twice.

Problem: The cost of material needed to make a rectangular tablecloth depends on the size of the tablecloth, as follows. The cost is $1.50 per square foot for each of the first 12 square feet of material, and $1.25 for each subsequent square foot. Given the length and width of a tablecloth, first compute the associated cost for the material. Then add two feet to the length and one foot to the width, and compute the cost for the new tablecloth. Display the two costs and the associated lengths and widths.

In this problem, you can immediately identify the need to perform a group of instructions twice. Specifically, the cost of the material must be computed once for the original length and width, and once for the increased length and width. In order to accomplish this repetition, you will first need to provide the computer with the instructions for computing the cost of the material for a tablecloth of a given size. Next, you will have to instruct the computer to perform these instructions the appropriate number of times within the program, in this case twice. The process of accomplishing the first step is called **declaring the procedure;** that of implementing the second is called *invoking,* or **calling the procedure.** Both of these issues will be discussed in more detail below.

Declaring a procedure Providing the computer with the specific instructions and the name that constitutes a procedure.

Calling a procedure The act of instructing the computer to perform the instructions in a procedure by referring to the name of the procedure in the program.

Declaring a Procedure (without Parameters) in Pseudocode

The act of declaring a procedure is the process of providing the computer with the list of instructions that eventually will be performed by the program. Observe that when you declare a procedure you are not telling the computer to perform the given instructions; rather, you are telling the computer what the instructions are, and where to locate them when necessary.

To declare a procedure, you must supply the computer with a **procedure name** (much like any other name), and with the **body of the procedure,** which is the specific group of instructions that constitutes the procedure. The procedure name refers to the entire list of instructions in the body of the procedure, which you subsequently develop similarly to the way in which you develop the processing portion of a program.

Procedure name The name you choose to give to a procedure.

Body of a procedure The specific instructions that constitute a procedure.

Example

The following procedure declaration (in pseudocode) provides the instructions needed to compute the cost of the material for a tablecloth whose length and width are stored in the variables *Length* and *Width*, respectively:

```
PROCEDURE ComputeCost     {ComputeCost is the procedure
                           name.}
    Area := Length * Width              }
    IF Area ≤ 12 THEN                   }
       Cost := 1.50 * Area              } Body of the
    ELSE                                } procedure
       Cost := 1.50 * 12 +              }
               1.25 * (Area - 12)       }
```

You should note that, in order for the computer to perform these instructions, the values of the variables *Length* and *Width* would have to have been assigned previously. Also, when declaring a procedure in Pascal, it is necessary to indicate the beginning and the end of the body of the procedure, as will be described in Section 5.4. However, when using pseudocode to declare a procedure, the first and last statements will be clear from the indentation.

After you have prepared the procedure declaration, you must place all of those statements somewhere the computer can find them. In Pascal, the procedure declarations are put in the declaration section at the beginning of the program (the details will be given in Section 5.4). Under some circumstances, it is even possible to store the procedure declaration outside of the program altogether (i.e., in some other part of the computer). Such procedures are called *external procedures*, but they will not be discussed further in this book. In any event, after a procedure has been declared, you are finally in a position to use the procedure in a program.

Using a Procedure (without Parameters)

To "use" a properly declared procedure in a program means to instruct the computer to perform the statements that constitute the body of the procedure. To do so in pseudocode, you simply write in the main program the name of the procedure you wish the computer to perform. That is, you can instruct the computer to perform the instructions in the body of the procedure by referring to the procedure name in the actual program itself. Specifically, the pseudocode statement:

```
ProcedureName
```

will instruct the computer to (1) locate the procedure whose name is ProcedureName (i.e., locate the appropriate procedure declaration), (2) perform all of the instructions in the body of that procedure, (3) return to the main program when finished, and (4) perform the statement immediately following the place at which the procedure was called.

Example

Recall the procedure *ComputeCost* that was declared in the previous example. The following instructions in the main program invoke (i.e., call) the procedure *ComputeCost* two times.

```
READ Length, Width
WRITE Length, Width
ComputeCost     {This statement requests the computer to perform the
                 instructions in the body of the procedure
                 ComputeCost. When completed, the following
                 WRITE statement will be performed.}
WRITE Cost     {Displays the result of computing the cost of the material.
                The value of Cost was computed during the preceding
                procedure call.}
Length := Length + 2     {Changes the value of the length.}
Width := Width + 1      {Changes the value of the width.}
WRITE Length, Width
ComputeCost     {This statement requests the computer to perform the
                 instructions in the body of the procedure
                 ComputeCost again. This time, however, the new
                 values of Length and Width will be used. When
                 completed, the following WRITE statement will be
                 performed.}
WRITE Cost     {Displays the cost of the material for the new tablecloth.}
```

After the first call to the procedure *ComputeCost* above, the statements

```
Length := Length + 2
Width := Width + 1
```

were used to add two feet to the length, and one foot to the width, respectively. Observe that these new values are then stored back into the same variables, *Length* and *Width*, rather than into two new variables. The reason for doing so is that, when the procedure *ComputeCost* is called for the second time, those instructions will then use the new values of the variables *Length* and *Width*. The occurrence of a variable on both the left and right side of a := is quite common in programming, and will be discussed at greater length in Section 5.3.

Using Procedures in Conjunction with Top-Down Programming

Because the use of procedures can greatly improve the readability of a program, there are times when it is beneficial to use them even though they will be invoked only once. The next example demonstrates this use of procedures by having a main program that calls four procedures whose names are indicative of their respective functions.

Example

Assuming that each of the following four procedures has been declared properly, this is a valid main program in pseudocode:

```
ReadStockPrices
ReadSharesOwned
ComputeShareValues
DisplayResults
```

From the example above, you can see that the creation of procedures is very closely linked to the technique of top-down programming. Specifically, top-down programming suggests that you decompose a complex problem into a collection of more easily solved subproblems. In so doing, you focus on the major tasks to be accomplished first, leaving details to be filled in later. Each subproblem that you identify can be thought of as a separate procedure that merits its own name. With regard to "filling in the details later," that process is accomplished when you specify the instructions that constitute the body of the procedure. The following problem illustrates the use of procedures in conjunction with top-down programming.

Problem: Given the test results of a class of students, first sort the scores in decreasing order. Then, next to each score, display a letter grade based on a given grading scale.

By using top-down programming, you might decompose this problem into the following subproblems:

Read (and verify) the test scores.
Echo print the data.
Sort the scores in decreasing order.
Assign appropriate letter grades.
Display the results.

If you were to provide an appropriate procedure name for each of these tasks, the main program for solving this problem might consist of the following five procedure calls:

```
ReadScores
DisplayScores
SortScores
AssignGrades
DisplayResults
```

The next step in solving this problem would be to fill in the details of each of these subproblems. Specifically, you would have to supply the instructions constituting the body of each of these procedures. To do so, it would be advisable to think through your solution for each of these tasks. If a particular task is complicated, then you might wish to use top-down programming again to create further subproblems and procedures.

Other Uses for Procedures

There is another potential benefit to using top-down programming and procedures. As you may have noticed, the problems in this book are quite simple and short. However, in "real-world" problems, the programs can be enormously complex, perhaps consisting of thousands of individual instructions. To prepare such large programs, often a team of programmers will be assigned to work together. By using top-down programming, the manager of the team can decompose the big problem into smaller subproblems and give a procedure name to each one. Then, the manager can assign to each programmer the task of writing the code for a particular procedure. In so doing, the manager must take care to see that the procedures fit together and function properly. Thus the individual programmers will have to do a good job of documenting and commenting their work.

Yet another benefit of using procedures arises in the area of debugging. It is quite a bit easier to locate and to correct an error in a "short" procedure than to do so for a "large" program. There are no fixed rules as to how many instructions a program, procedure, or module should contain; however, if a module contains more than 100 instructions, you might consider breaking the module into smaller modules. As a general rule, it is better to have a lot of modules, each of which is short in length and easy to work with.

Local versus Global Variables

When the computer performs the instructions in a procedure, the machine will need the values of certain variables. In addition, after executing the procedure, the computer must transmit the results that were obtained back to the main program for possible further processing. In this section, you will learn one way to pass values for the variables from the main program to the procedure, and how to send the resulting values from the procedure back to the main program.

Global variables
Variables that are declared in the main program, and whose values can also be used (and changed) in the body of a procedure.

Local variables
Variables that are declared within (and can only be used within) a procedure.

One way of passing information to and from the procedure is by using **global variables**—variables that have been declared in the main program. The advantage of global variables is that you can use them in any and all procedures as well as in the main program. **Local variables,** in contrast, are variables that are declared within (and can only be used within) a specific procedure. The values of those variables are not available to the main program or to any other procedure.

Recall the procedure for obtaining the cost of the material for a tablecloth:

```
PROCEDURE ComputeCost
   Area := Length * Width
   IF Area ≤ 12 THEN
      Cost := 1.50 * Area
   ELSE
      Cost := 1.50 * 12 + 1.25 * (Area - 12)
```

By examining the function and role of each variable in the above procedure, you will see some of the types of variables that are used in a procedure, and whether those variables should be declared as local or global variables. Here, then, is a list of all of the variables used above, together with an explanation of their functions.

Variable	Purpose
Length	A global variable because its value must be provided outside of the procedure, i.e., from the main program.
Width	Same as *Length*.
Area	A local variable because its value is used only within the procedure. Once the procedure is completed, the value of this variable is no longer needed.
Cost	A global variable because its value will contain the desired result after performing all of the instructions in the procedure. This value must be returned to the main program for further processing.

From this example, it is possible to identify three categories of variables: (1) *input* variables, which are global variables because their values must be supplied by the main program to the procedure (e.g., *Length* and *Width* above); (2) *output* variables, which are global variables because their values will be computed by the procedure and returned to the main program for further processing (e.g., *Cost* above); and (3) local variables whose values are computed and used within the procedure, but not needed once the procedure is completed (e.g., *Area* above). These observations are summarized in Fig. 5.1. Notice the similarity to inputting, processing, and outputting.

The following example illustrates more precisely how local and global variables are used in programs.

Example

```
{The following pseudocode declarations pertain to the main program.}
Length, Width :REAL     {Length and Width are global
                         variables.}
PROCEDURE ComputeCost    {Declare a procedure.}
   Area :REAL     {Area is a local variable.}
   Area := Length * Width
   IF Area ≤ 12 THEN
      Cost := 1.50 * Area
   ELSE
      Cost := 1.50 * 12 + 1.25 * (Area - 12)
{The main program begins here. All variables are global ones.}
   READ Length, Width
   WRITE Length, Width
   ComputeCost
   WRITE Cost     {The value of Cost is computed and stored when
                   the procedure ComputeCost is called (and
                   executed) in the previous statement.}
   Length := Length + 2
   Width := Width + 1
   WRITE Length, Width
   ComputeCost
   WRITE Cost
```

It is possible to have and to declare both a local variable and a global variable that have the same name. For example, in the main program above, you could also declare a global variable whose name is *Area*. Yet, for all practical purposes, the local and global variables are treated as two separate variables—when performing instructions in the main program, the computer works with the global variable; when performing instructions in the procedure, the computer works with the local variable.

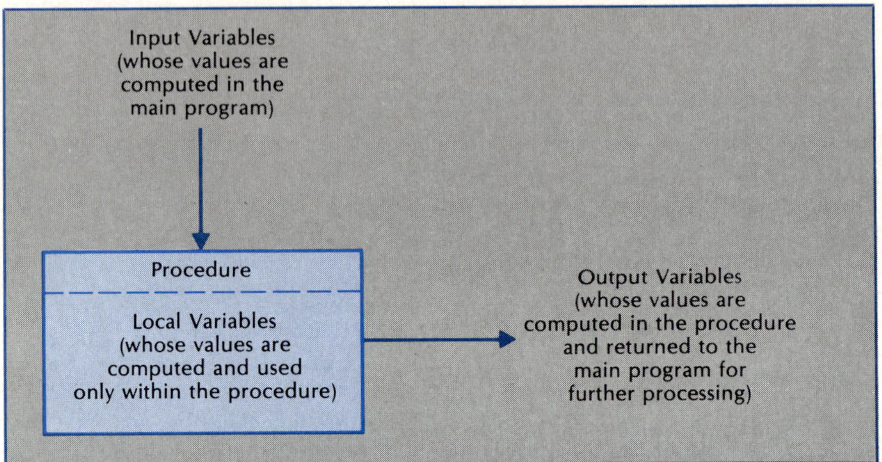

Figure 5.1 Types of variables used in procedures.

Now that you know about local and global variables, you might very well ask when and why you should declare and use local variables. Why not use only global variables for all computations within a procedure? The reason is that there is always the danger of permanently changing the value of a global variable by mistake. Locating and correcting such an error can be difficult. You might therefore keep in mind the following rules: (1) Use a global variable when the value of that variable must be supplied by (or to) the main program. (2) Use a local variable when the value of that variable is used only in the procedure, not in the main program. (3) Use different names for each so as to avoid confusion.

Recap

In this section you have learned about the concept of a procedure, which allows you to assign a name to a particular group of instructions. By referring to that name you can then instruct the computer to perform that sequence of instructions as often as needed in the program. In addition, you have learned about the use of local and global variables for working with information in a procedure. In the next section, you will learn another method for performing a group of instructions repeatedly.

Exercises for Section 5.1

For each of the following word problems, first use top-down programming to identify subproblems that might be easier to solve. In so doing, provide the name of a procedure for accomplishing each subproblem. As you use top-down programming, look for and identify a group of instructions that needs to be repeated. For each procedure, describe, in English, the purpose and objective (i.e., the input and output) of the procedure; however, you need not specify the details that constitute the body of the procedure. Finally, write a main program that consists exclusively of calls to the procedures.

1. Read and display the given positions of a tic-tac-toe game. Then, given one move by each player, display the resulting positions of the game after each move.

2. You will be given three paragraphs of text that represent the chorus of a song and two verses. Display the given text as follows:

> Chorus
> First Verse
> Chorus
> Second Verse
> Chorus

In each of the following word problems, identify a group of instructions that needs to be repeated. In so doing, create an appropriate procedure declaration that includes the body of the procedure for accomplishing the task. Identify each variable in the procedure as pertaining to input, output, or local information, and indicate whether the variable should be local or global. Finally, write the main program to call the procedure the appropriate number of times.

3. An author earns a royalty rate of 12% on each of the first 5000 copies of her book that are sold, and 15% on each copy thereafter. Given the number of copies sold and the selling price per copy, compute and display the amont of money to be paid to the author. Also, display the amount of money that would be paid to the author if twice as many copies were sold.

4. The letters 'a', 'b', and 'c' are to be represented by the integers 5, 14, and 8, respectively. Given, as data, a three-letter "word" in which each letter is either 'a', 'b', or 'c', display the associated integer code for that word. For example, the word "cab" should be displayed as the code 8, 5, 14. (*Hint:* Read and process each letter before going on to the next letter, i.e., do not read all three letters at one time.)

5.2 The Concept of a Loop

In the previous section, you learned to use a procedure to perform a set of instructions several times; you need write the instructions only once and from then on refer to the set of instructions by name. However, what if you had to perform a group of instructions 100 (or 1,000,000) times? Surely you would not want to write the procedure name each time to call the procedure. In this section, you will learn how to overcome this problem by using a new programming concept that will enable you to repeat a group of instructions any number of times.

Loop A group of instructions to be repeated together with an associated rule to indicate when the repetition should end.

The concept is that of a **loop,** which in computing refers to a sequence of instructions that is to be performed over and over again. The use of the word "loop" is derived from Fig. 5.2. In some respects, a loop is similar to a procedure; but there are also differences. A comparison of these two programming concepts is provided at the end of this section.

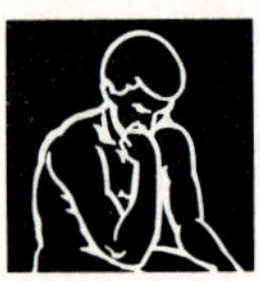

To illustrate the concept of a loop in problem solving, consider the problem of hammering a nail into a piece of wood on the floor. Suppose, for simplicity, that the nail has already penetrated the wood. Without much thought you might say that, to solve the problem, "I just hammer the nail into the wood." While this statement is perhaps true, as always it is advisable to think through your solution more carefully so as to recognize the need for repetition. In the previous section, the need to perform repetition was quite obvious. In this sec-

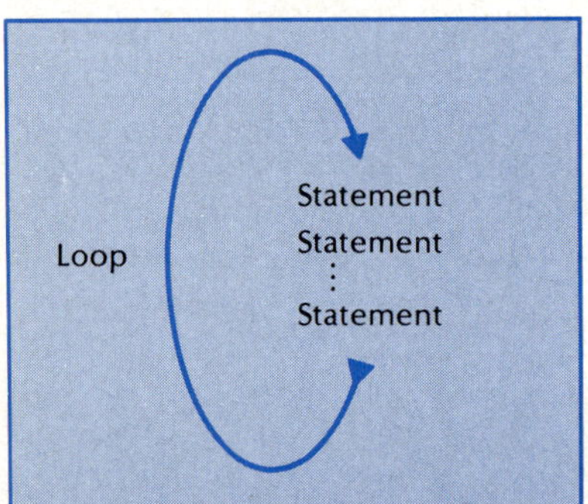

Figure 5.2 The concept of a loop.

tion, however, you will see that, when solving a problem, you must often make a conscious effort to identify the use of repetition in the solution. Returning to the hammer-and-nail example, and looking for repetition in the solution given above, one stroke on the nail might be described as follows:

Step 1: Place the head of the hammer on the head of the nail.

Step 2: Pull the hammer back.

Step 3: Bring the hammer forward (with force) making the head of the hammer strike the head of the nail.

To solve the original problem, the three steps above must be performed over and over again, and that fact is precisely the concept of a loop. When considered as a whole, the steps that must be performed repeatedly are called the **body of the loop** (which is analogous to the body of a procedure).

Body of a loop The specific instructions of a loop that are to be repeated.

Stopping Rules

There is one issue that has been overlooked in the "loop" formulation of the problem above: namely, how many times should you repeat the three steps? In other words, when should you stop? In fact, in order to stop, each loop must be accompanied by a **stopping rule** that is used to indicate when the body of the loop should no longer be performed. For the example above, such a rule might be one of the following:

Stopping rule A part of a loop that tells the computer when the body of the loop should no longer be performed.

Stopping Rule 1: Perform the three steps exactly 10 times.
Stopping Rule 2: Perform the three steps until the head of the nail is flush against the wood.

Notice that with Rule 1 you know beforehand how many times the body of the loop is to be executed, while with Rule 2 you do not know. The former situation gives rise to what is called a `FOR` **loop,**and the latter is referred to as a `WHILE` **loop.** This and the next two sections describe the `FOR` loop in detail. Subsequently, the `WHILE` loop (and its variations) will be addressed.

`FOR` **loop** A loop in which the stopping rule specifies precisely how many times the body of the loop is to be performed.

As you have seen, the key to using a loop in problem solving is to identify a sequence of operations that must be performed repeatedly, together with an associated stopping rule. To illustrate this process once more, recall the Orks (of Chapter 1). Looking at Fig. 5.3, can you provide the Orks with instructions for going from where they are on Maine Street to the corner of California and Nevada?

`WHILE` **loop** A loop in which the body is performed an unspecified number of times, so long as a boolean condition is true.

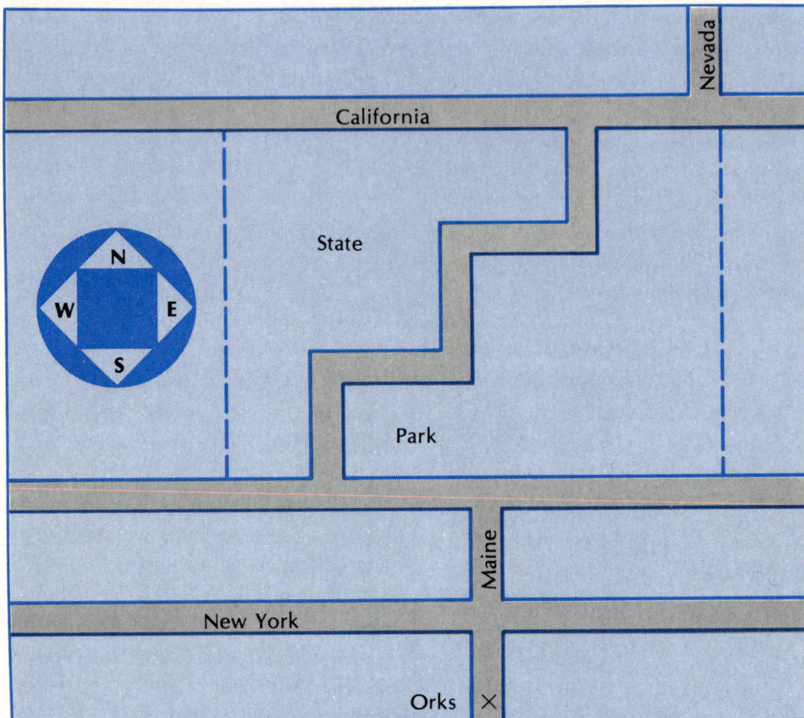

Figure 5.3 Another section of Smallville.

To begin with, you can use the instructions:

```
Go North 2 blocks.
Go West 1 block.
```

to get the Orks to the southwest corner of State Park. Now you must instruct the Orks to reach the northeast corner of the park. You could, of course, use the instructions:

```
Go North 1 block.
Go East 1 block.
Go North 1 block.
Go East 1 block.
Go North 1 block.
Go East 1 block.
```

In doing so, you should recognize a group of instructions that are being performed repeatedly. Specifically, you want the Orks to repeat the two instructions:

```
Go North 1 block. }
Go East 1 block.  } Body of the loop
```

exactly

3 times. } Stopping rule

The body of the loop together with the stopping rule constitute a FOR loop because you know precisely how many times to perform the body of the loop. Putting together the pieces, the desired set of instructions for solving this problem is

```
Go North 2 blocks.
Go West 1 block.
FOR 3 times DO
    Go North 1 block.
    Go East 1 block.
```

In general, pseudocode will be used to write the FOR-loop statement as follows:

```
FOR Expression times DO
    Action
```

This statement will instruct the computer to evaluate the Expression, and to perform the Action exactly Expression times. You should note that the value of the Expression should be a nonnegative integer, and that the Action can be a single statement or a compound statement, just like in the IF/THEN statement (see Section 4.1). Each performance of the Action is called an **iteration of the loop.**

Iteration of a loop One complete execution of the body of a loop.

Comparison of Loops and Procedures

Recall from Section 5.1 that the concept of a procedure refers to a group of instructions that could be performed several times. In contrast, a loop includes not only the group of instructions to be performed (i.e., the body of the loop), but also an associated stopping rule. In essence, a procedure is like the body of a loop. Indeed, in the FOR-loop statement

```
FOR Expression times DO
    Action
```

you can think of the Action as one call to a procedure (that actually performs the Action). The stopping rule then specifies how many times the procedure is to be called, i.e., how many times the Action will be performed.

One of the primary advantages associated with using procedures to perform repetition is that you can call the procedure from many different places in the program. Thus, it is possible to repeat the same action at various different points in the program. In contrast, when using a loop to repeat an action, all of the repetition is done in that one spot.

One of the advantages of a loop, however, is that it has an associated stopping rule, so you can repeat the desired instructions a large number of times by writing those instructions (together with the stopping rule) only once. Using a procedure, on the other hand, would require you to write the procedure name each time you want to perform the associated instructions. Doing so for a large number of times is cumbersome. Using a loop (with a stopping rule) will greatly simplify the task, as you will now see.

Using a `FOR` Loop in Problem Solving

The following example illustrates the use of a `FOR` loop in computer problem solving, together with many of the previous pseudocode statements you have already learned.

Problem: Betty Broker has been using her computer to keep track of her winnings (and losings) on the stock market. For the past 30 days, she has recorded the stock prices of Mega-Corp and is interested in finding the highest price during that period. Since Betty is going to want to do this every 30 days, she has asked you to write a computer program to perform the task.

Algorithm Development. The first step never changes: you must determine how you would solve the problem yourself. Without giving the issue much thought, you might provide the following.

Solution: I simply look down the list of prices and pick out the largest one.

Unfortunately, this solution is not very useful because a computer cannot "see," and so you cannot tell the computer to "look down the list of prices and pick out the largest one." As always, you must think through your solution.

Thinking through Your Solution. In this problem, a new technique will be used to help you think through your solution. Specifically, suppose that the given list is so long that you cannot see all of the numbers at one glance (see Fig. 5.4). Under these circumstances, can you state more precisely how to solve the problem?

After some thought, you might provide the following more refined solution.

Solution: I look at a manageable group of numbers and pick out the largest one in that group. Then I look at a second group of numbers and pick out the largest number for that group. Comparing the largest number for these two groups, I then write down the single largest number. Now I continue working with different groups of numbers, each time picking out the largest number for that group and then keeping track of the single largest number I have found so far. I repeat these operations over and over again until all groups of numbers have been examined.

Perhaps you already recognize the concept of a loop arising in the solution procedure. The fact that in the method used above you "repeat these operations over and over again," is the idea of a loop. Before examining the loop concept more closely, however, you need to consider what you mean by a "manageable" group of numbers. How many numbers are there in a manageable group? You would probably find 5 or 10 numbers manageable, but a computer is designed to read

237	833	145	227
185	140	377	543
433	757	845	782
271	822	690	459
312	630	960	666
845	110	144	392
196	450	327	932
344	788	866	785
121	820	155	644
645	382	222	118

Figure 5.4 A long list of numbers.

only one number at a time. With this fact in mind, you might provide the following steps for solving the problem:

Step 1: Look at the next number on the list.

Step 2: If the number you are currently looking at is larger than the single largest number so far, then the current number becomes the largest number so far.

Step 3: Repeat Step 1 and Step 2 until the entire list of numbers has been examined.

In the above format, the concept of a loop is even more evident. Step 1 and Step 2 constitute the body of the loop while the stopping rule is given in Step 3.

The solution procedure obtained by thinking through your solution will now be refined further. The result will be an algorithm (containing a `FOR` loop) that can be programmed readily in Pascal. To that end, recall the three basic components of a computer program: inputting, processing, and outputting.

Inputting. To determine the inputting phase of the problem, ask yourself what information you will need to be given in order to solve the problem. Certainly, you will need to be given the actual list of numbers. In addition, for the stopping rule of the loop given in Step 3 above, you will need to know when "the entire list of numbers has been examined." Once again, the problem-solving capabilities of human beings differ from those of a computer. You would have no trouble in detecting the end of the given list, but a computer must be "told" how to recognize the end of the list.

One possible method for doing so was described in Section 3.2. There, the use of the end-of-file marker was explained. However, if the precise length of the list is known, as is the case in this problem, then it is also possible to provide that information to the computer. Since the length of the list for this problem is known to be 30 (for 30 days), the latter technique will be used here. Thus the input for this problem will consist of a single integer whose value represents the length of the list—i.e., how many numbers are in the list, together with the individual numbers that constitute the list.

The length of the list, i.e., 30, will be stored in the variable *ListLength* by using the pseudocode statements

```
READ ListLength
WRITE ListLength
```

to read and to echo print that value, respectively.

Now it is necessary to obtain the 30 values that constitute the numbers on the list. If you are thinking about using a `READ` statement to enter those 30 values, then consider that you would need 30 different variables in which to store those values. Surely you do not want to write

```
READ Value1, Value2, ... , Value30
```

because you will eventually have to replace the three dots (. . .) with the actual names of the variables. As you will see below, all of the values in the list can be read by using only one variable.

Processing. The processing portion of this algorithm was described previously by the following `FOR` loop:

Step 1: Look at the next number on the list.

Step 2: If the number you are currently looking at is larger than the single largest number so far, then the current number becomes the largest number so far.

Step 3: Repeat Step 1 and Step 2 *ListLength* times (i.e., in this case, 30 times).

Now, the process of refinement will be used to write the body of the loop (consisting of Step 1 and Step 2 above) with pseudocode. In so doing, you will see how all of the numbers in the list can be read and processed using only one variable.

You can translate Step 1 in the solution procedure above into the following pseudocode statement:

```
READ NextNumber
```

Thus instead of reading all 30 values into 30 variables at one time, the single variable *NextNumber* is used to read and to process each number, in turn.

Look now at Step 2 in the body of the loop as outlined above. Suppose, for example, that the computer has just read the second number in the list, and has stored that value in the variable *NextNumber*. Then the phrase, "the number you are currently looking at," refers to the current value of *NextNumber* (i.e., the second number in the list). However, what variable contains "the single largest number so far?" It would appear that another variable is needed to keep track of that information. So, let *LargestSoFar* be a variable whose value will be that of the largest number examined so far. Using *NextNumber* and *LargestSoFar*, you can translate Step 2 into the following pseudocode `IF/THEN` statement:

```
IF NextNumber > LargestSoFar THEN
   LargestSoFar := NextNumber
```

Finally, according to the stopping rule in Step 3 above, these READ and IF/THEN statements must be repeated *ListLength* times (i.e., however many numbers are in the list). So, putting together what has been done so far, and using the pseudocode FOR-loop statement, the inputting and processing phases are

```
READ ListLength      {The echo-printing and data-verification statements
                      will be omitted temporarily.}
FOR ListLength times DO
     READ NextNumber
     IF NextNumber > LargestSoFar THEN
        LargestSoFar := NextNumber
```

You should note that each time a new value from the list is read and stored in *NextNumber*, the previous value is lost forever (which is all right because that previous value is no longer needed).

Outputting. After the inputting and processing have been performed, it is necessary to display the answer. So, exactly what constitutes the answer? One could, for example, display the original list of numbers, the largest number, and the position of that number in the list. How much information should be displayed is determined by the person for whom the program is being written. Here, only the largest number of the list will be displayed. At the end of the processing, that number will be stored in the variable *LargestSoFar*. Thus you should have the final pseudocode statement

```
WRITE LargestSoFar
```

Putting together the inputting, processing, and outputting phases, temporarily omitting the echo-printing and data-verification statements, and assigning a statement label to each statement for reference purposes during the subsequent discussion of tracing, the algorithm becomes

```
S1:  READ ListLength
S2:  FOR ListLength times DO
S3:       READ NextNumber
```

```
S4:        IF NextNumber > LargestSoFar THEN
              LargestSoFar := NextNumber
S5:   WRITE LargestSoFar
```

Tracing and Debugging

While it is possible to code the above algorithm and "see what happens," you can save time and trouble by tracing the algorithm with a small sample of test data. For example, suppose that the data consists of a short list of the three numbers 4.12, 7.25, and 5.33. The result of the algorithm should be 7.25, or something is wrong. Let us see what happens by tracing the program using these data values.

Begin by executing S1, after which the value of the variable *ListLength* becomes 3. Turning now to S2, that statement instructs the computer to perform the body of the loop, which consists of S3 and S4, *ListLength* times (i.e., three times). In order to keep track of how many times the body of the loop is performed, a **loop-counter variable,** whose name is *Counter*, will be used during the tracing below. Although this variable is not currently part of the algorithm, in Section 5.3, you will see how to incorporate the loop-counter variable into the program. For now, however, the value of this variable will be recorded separately.

Loop-counter variable A variable whose value represents the number of times the body of the loop has been performed. FOR loops automatically have such a variable associated with them; WHILE loops do not.

Tracing the First Iteration of the Loop. In order to trace the body of the loop for the first time, begin by setting the loop-counter variable to 1, so that

```
Counter := 1
```

Now, in tracing, you can perform S3, which provides the value of 4.12 for *NextNumber*. Subsequently, you can trace S4. Accordingly, you should check to see if the appropriate condition in the IF/THEN statement is true, i.e., if *NextNumber* is greater than *Largest-SoFar*. In so doing, you will immediately encounter a problem; although the value of *NextNumber* is 4.12 as seen above, at this point in time, *LargestSoFar* has no value because none was assigned *before* beginning the loop.

In view of this problem, you might ask what value should *LargestSoFar* have been given. To answer the question, think through your solution once again. When you look at the first number on the list, you would surely consider that number to be the largest

number so far (because you have seen no other numbers). Thus in S4 you want the value of *LargestSoFar* to become that of the first number on the list. Looking at S4, one way to accomplish that goal is to assign an initial value for *LargestSoFar* so that during the first iteration of the loop the condition in the IF/THEN statement is true, for then the value of *LargestSoFar* will be replaced by the first number in the list. In other words, you need to think of a value for *LargestSoFar* so that, no matter what data are given, the first number on the list will always be greater than *LargestSoFar*. Can you think of such a number?

To begin with, recall that according to the original problem statement, all numbers in the data will be positive (since those numbers represent dollar values). Thus you could set *LargestSoFar* initially to 0.0 (or to any negative number) and be sure that the first number on the list will always be greater than *LargestSoFar*. Observe that for this particular data set you could also have set the value of *LargestSoFar* initially to 3.0, for example, instead of 0.0, because 3.0 is less than the first number on the list (which, in this case, is 4.12). However, you should not do so because, for other data sets, the initial value of 3.0 for *LargestSoFar* might not be less than the first number in that list.

Initializing a variable The process of assigning an initial value to a variable prior to beginning a loop.

There is a very important lesson to be learned here. Almost always, when working with a loop, you will need to make sure that you have **initialized certain variables,** that is, assigned appropriate values to those variables, prior to performing the loop. In the example above, you discovered the need to initialize the value of *LargestSoFar* to 0.0. As another example of initialization, recall the example of hammering a nail into a piece of wood. At that time, it was assumed that the nail had already penetrated the wood. In fact, the act of making the nail penetrate the wood in the first place is the "initialization" of that loop.

Having initialized *LargestSoFar* with a value of 0.0, and relabeled the statements for reference purposes, the new algorithm becomes

```
S0:  LargestSoFar := 0.0
S1:  READ ListLength
S2:  FOR ListLength times DO
S3:       READ NextNumber
S4:       IF NextNumber > LargestSoFar THEN
            LargestSoFar := NextNumber
S5:  WRITE LargestSoFar
```

With the corrections in place, it is time to retrace the algorithm. Using the previously given data, everything will be the same except that `LargestSoFar` will be assigned a value of 0.0 initially. After performing S1, `ListLength` will have a value of 3. Once again, when S2 is executed, you should set the value of the loop-counter variable to 1, so,

```
Counter := 1
```

Retracing the First Iteration of the Loop. Now S3 must be performed for the first time (since the value of `Counter` is 1). On reading the first number of the list into `NextNumber`, you have

Variable	Value
`LargestSoFar`	0.0
`ListLength`	3
`NextNumber`	4.12

Now it is time to perform S4 for the first time. When you do so, you will see that the condition in the `IF/THEN` statement is true because the value of `NextNumber` is 4.12, which is greater than `LargestSoFar`, whose value is 0.0. Therefore `LargestSoFar` is now assigned the value of `NextNumber`, so you have

Variable	Value
`LargestSoFar`	4.12
`ListLength`	3
`NextNumber`	4.12

The body of the loop has now been completed for the first time.

Tracing the Second Iteration of the Loop. Since the body of the loop must be performed three times, statements S3 and S4 must be repeated again. Before doing so, you should increase the value of the loop-counter variable to 2 to signify the beginning of the second repetition, so

```
Counter := 2
```

Since the value of `Counter` is 2, it is necessary to execute both S3 and S4 again. On performing S3, you have

Variable	Value
`LargestSoFar`	4.12
`ListLength`	3
`NextNumber`	7.25

Note that the previous value of 4.12 for `NextNumber` has been lost, but fortunately, that value is no longer needed. The new value of 7.25 is now stored in `NextNumber`.

Now it is time to perform S4 for the second time. In so doing, the condition in the `IF/THEN` statement is true, and so `LargestSoFar` is now assigned the value of `NextNumber`. Thus you have

Variable	**Value**
`LargestSoFar`	7.25
`ListLength`	3
`NextNumber`	7.25

The body of the loop has now been completed for the second time.

Tracing the Third Iteration of the Loop. Since the loop has not yet been performed the necessary three times, you should increase the value of the loop-counter variable to 3, and the body of the loop is repeated, so

```
Counter := 3
```

On performing S3 for the final time, you have

Variable	**Value**
`LargestSoFar`	7.25
`ListLength`	3
`NextNumber`	5.33

Now it is time to perform S4 for the third time. In so doing, you will see that the condition in the `IF/THEN` statement is false; that is, `NextNumber` is not greater than `LargestSoFar`, and so no action takes place. The body of the loop is now complete, and since the loop-counter variable has reached its final value of 3 (because the value of `ListLength` is 3), the loop is finished.

Finally, S5 is performed, producing the desired result that the largest number is, indeed,

```
7.25
```

It would thus appear that this algorithm is working correctly for this set of data. Although there is no assurance that the algorithm will perform correctly on all sets of data, the next step would be to code the algorithm. First, however, the use of loops will be discussed further in the next section.

Recap

To use a loop in problem solving, you should (1) think through your initial solution so as to identify a sequence of instructions to be repeated over and over again, (2) specify the individual instructions that, when taken together, constitute the body of the loop, and (3) specify a stopping rule to indicate when the body of the loop should no longer be executed.

Exercises for Section 5.2

For each of the following problems, describe, in English, how a loop could be used. Specifically, (a) identify a sequence of operations to be performed repeatedly (i.e., the body of the loop), and (b) indicate an associated stopping rule. Is the loop a `FOR` loop or a `WHILE` loop?

1. Dialing a three-digit area code and a seven-digit telephone number.
2. Adding a row of numbers (whose length is not known) by hand.
3. Given 13 playing cards, determine how many of them are clubs.
4. Dividing two single-digit integers by long-hand division.
5. Given a list of 1000 names (in random order), see how many times the name Smith is on the list.

Trace each of the following program segments. Use the given data to assign values to variables that appear in `READ` statements. Also, use a loop-counter variable when tracing the `FOR`-loop statements.

6.
```
SoMany := 5
Total := 0.0
Repetitions := 0
FOR SoMany times DO
     Repetitions := Repetitions + 1
     Total := Total + Repetitions
WRITE Total
```
How does the value of the loop-counter variable compare with the value of the variable *Repetitions* in the algorithm above?

7.
```
Count := 0
Suit := 'H'
FOR 5 times DO
     READ Card
     IF Card = Suit THEN
          Count := Count + 1
WRITE Count

Given Data: SHHCH
```

8.
```
SoMany := 2
FOR SoMany times DO
     READ Number
     I := 0
     FOR Number / 2 times DO
          I := I + 1
          IF I * I = Number THEN
             WRITE Number, ' = ', I, ' squared'
```

Given data: 4 6

Write pseudocode instructions to perform the following tasks. Assume that the length of each list will be supplied as data for the problem. When done, make the body of each loop into a procedure that you declare. In the loop itself, call the procedure. For example, a FOR loop might appear as

```
FOR 5 times DO
     ComputeCost        {ComputeCost is the name of the procedure
                        whose instructions constitute the body of the
                        loop.}
```

9. Given a list of *N* test scores, display each score and the associated grade according to the following:

Test Score	Grade
90–100	A
80–89	B
70–79	C
60–69	D
below 60	F

10. For each of *M* customers, you will be given the account number, the previous balance, and an amount that is being paid. Compute the new balance together with an interest charge of 1.5% of that amount. Display all appropriate information, including the new amount due. However, when a customer pays more than the original balance due, display an appropriate message to that effect (and be sure that no interest is charged).

11. For the problem of this section, write an algorithm that would enable you to handle any list of numbers—positive, negative, or zero. (*Hint:* Read the first number in the list before entering the loop, and consider it to be the largest number so far.)

5.3 More on FOR Loops

While tracing the FOR loop in the problem of the previous section, the concept of the loop-counter variable, *Counter*, was introduced to keep track of the number of times the body of the loop was performed. In this section you will see a FOR loop that uses the value of the loop-counter variable within the body of the loop. The need to use the value of the loop-counter variable arises so frequently that a new FOR-loop statement will be introduced to allow you to do so. In addition, you will learn about another technique that arises frequently when using loops; namely, using the same variable on both the left and right sides of an assignment statement in the body of a loop.

Incorporating the Loop-Counter Variable

There are so many problems for which the value of the loop-counter variable is needed within the body of the loop that programming languages like Pascal enable you to incorporate that variable directly into the FOR-loop statement itself. Thus from now on, instead of the statement

```
FOR Expression times DO
    Action
```

(which does not explicitly have a loop-counter variable), the equivalent pseudocode statement

```
FOR Variable := 1 TO Expression DO
    Action
```

will be used in this text (and should be used by you from now on). The Variable is the loop-counter variable (e.g., *Counter* in the example of the previous section). In this new statement, each time the Action (i.e., the body of the loop) is performed, the computer will automatically set the value of the Variable to the number of the current repetition. Thus during the first iteration of the loop, the value of the Variable will be 1; during the second iteration of the loop, the value of the Variable will be 2; and so on, until the body of the loop has been repeated Expression times. What is more important, however, is that within the body of the loop you can use the value of the loop-counter variable when performing calculations, as illustrated in the following problem.

Problem Solving

Betty Broker was very pleased when she saw the results of the algorithm of the previous section. Realizing that the computer can do even more for her, she has asked you to make some modification to the program. Here, then, is the new problem.

Problem: In addition to finding the highest selling price of MegaCorp during the past 30 days, identify the number of the day on which that event occurred. Also, compute an average selling price for the stock over the past 30 days.

Algorithm Modification. The algorithm of the previous section will be modified so as to incorporate the desired changes. To that end, using the new pseudocode FOR-loop statement (but omitting the echo-printing and data-verification statements), and using *Counter* as the loop-counter variable, the algorithm of the previous section is

```
READ ListLength
LargestSoFar := 0.0
FOR Counter := 1 TO ListLength DO
     READ NextNumber
     IF NextNumber > LargestSoFar THEN
        LargestSoFar := NextNumber
WRITE LargestSoFar
```

Finding the Position of the Largest Number. According to the current problem, the first additional requirement is to have the computer report the position of the largest number in the list. In order to do so, you can use the value of the loop-counter variable, *Counter*. As usual, however, you must first determine how you would find the desired position yourself. Without too much thought, you might provide the following solution.

Solution: As I search for the largest number in the list, I keep track of the position of each number. Then, when I find the largest number in the list, I will also know the position of that number.

Now, look at the FOR-loop statement in the algorithm above. You will see that the loop-counter variable in that statement will do precisely what you want. That is, the value of *Counter* will "keep track of the position of each number in the list." Each time the body of the loop is performed, the value of the loop-counter variable will be equal to the position of the current number in the list.

The question now becomes how can the value of the loop-counter variable, *Counter*, be saved at the appropriate time so that, "when I find the largest number in the list, I also know the position of that number." The answer is that, whenever the number you are looking at becomes the largest so far, you should store the value of *Counter* in a new variable, say *Position*, in the event that the current number is indeed the largest number in the list. Thus the corrected FOR-loop statement becomes

```
FOR Counter := 1 TO ListLength DO
    IF NextNumber > LargestSoFar THEN
        LargestSoFar := NextNumber
        Position := Counter
```

Note that it is necessary to save the value of *Counter* in a new variable because the current value of *Counter* will be changed at the beginning of the next iteration of the loop. Naturally, after the FOR loop is completed, you must display the value of *Position* in addition to that of *LargestSoFar*.

Computing the Average Price. According to the new instructions of Betty Broker, you must also compute the average stock price for the 30 days. As usual, you will not be able to provide the computer with the appropriate instructions until you understand how you solve the problem yourself. Since you know how to find an average, your initial solution will probably be

Solution: First I compute the total by adding the numbers in the list. Then I divide that total by the length of the list.

The next step is to think through your solution in order to express it in terms that a computer can understand. So how, precisely, do you add a list of numbers? Using a specific example to aid you, you might provide the following more refined solution.

Solution: To add the list of numbers, I first add the digits in the ones column. After carrying the appropriate digit, I do the same for the tens column. Then I repeat those operations until I run out of columns.

You will probably recognize the concept of a loop arising in the above solution (i.e., the repetition of adding individual columns). However, a computer does not add a list of numbers in the same way that you do. Computers read and process one number at a time; not groups of numbers and not parts of numbers. With this in mind, think of the given list of numbers as being displayed in a long row, instead of in a single column. Now can you explain how you would add this row of numbers?

If you have thought through your solution sufficiently, and/or worked through a specific example, then you might provide the answer that, to the first number on the list, you would add the second number. Then, to the total thus obtained, you would add the third number on the list, and so on, until all numbers on the list have been added. When writing these instructions for a computer, remember that the result of adding the next number to the total so far must be stored somewhere. In fact, you want that result to become the new value of the total. Thus using the variable *Total* to keep track of the running total, you want the computer to perform these steps:

Step 1: READ *NextNumber*

Step 2: *Total* := *Total* + *NextNumber* {This will add the next number to the total and store that new value back into the variable *Total*.}

Step 3: Repeat Step 1 and Step 2 *ListLength* times.

Thus the correct FOR-loop statement for obtaining the desired total and for finding the largest number and the corresponding position is

```
FOR Counter := 1 TO ListLength DO
     READ NextNumber
     Total := Total + NextNumber
     IF NextNumber > LargestSoFar THEN
        LargestSoFar := NextNumber
        Position := Counter
```

You should note that the occurrence of a variable (e.g., *Total*) on both sides of a := is typical when using loops. The reason is that the new value of that variable can then be used on the right side of the := during the *next* iteration of the loop. When working with loops, you should learn to think in these terms. The exercises will provide numerous examples for practice.

In writing the above FOR loop, the issue of initializing the variables has been overlooked. In the previous section, you saw that it was necessary to initialize the value of *LargestSoFar* to 0.0. How about the value of *Total*?

To answer the question, trace the first iteration of the loop. In so doing, you will see that the value of *Total* should also be initialized to 0.0 because, when you perform the loop for the first time, no numbers have been added; i.e., the total is zero to begin with. In fact, as a general rule, when using loops, you should initialize all variables whose values will be needed when performing the first iteration of the loop. The value of the variable *Position* in the example above, however, need not be initialized because its value is not needed for performing any of the computations during the first iteration of the loop.

When the FOR-loop statement is completed, the total will have been computed and stored in the variable *Total*. The final step is to have the computer calculate and display the average, which is obtained by dividing the total by the length of the list. Using the new variable *Average*, after the FOR-loop statement, you should have these pseudocode statements:

```
Average := Total / ListLength
WRITE LargestSoFar, Position, Average
```

Putting together all components (except the echo-printing and data-verification statements), the desired algorithm is

```
READ ListLength
Total := 0.0
LargestSoFar := 0.0
FOR Counter := 1 TO ListLength DO
      Read NextNumber
      Total := Total + NextNumber
      IF NextNumber > LargestSoFar THEN
          LargestSoFar := NextNumber
          Position := Counter
Average := Total / ListLength
WRITE LargestSoFar, Position, Average
```

Interpreting the Loop-Counter Variable

As you have seen, the value of the loop-counter variable represents the number of the current repetition in a FOR loop. In addition, when using a FOR loop in problem solving, the loop-counter variable usually has a physical meaning in terms of the problem itself, which you should learn to interpret. For example, suppose that, for each of *N* customers, you were performing some calculations with the statement

```
FOR Customer := 1 TO N DO
     Action
```

During a particular iteration of the loop, you can interpret the meaning of the value of the variable *Customer* as being the number of the customer you are currently working with. Thus, for instance, when the value of the variable *Customer* is 3, the Action that will be performed during that iteration will pertain to the third customer.

It is also helpful to use this way of thinking when developing a FOR loop to solve a problem. For example, suppose that each of four card players had 13 cards. In order to process each card for each player, you could use the statement

```
FOR Player := 1 TO 4 DO
     FOR Card := 1 TO 13 DO
          Action
```

When the value of the variable *Player* is *i* and that of *Card* is *j*, the Action will pertain to card *j* belonging to player *i*. The physical interpretation and meaning of the loop-counter variable will be of great importance in Chapter 6. Also, a FOR loop within a FOR loop (as used above) is called a *nested* FOR loop.

The General FOR-Loop Statement

In the FOR-loop statement of this section, the loop-counter variable started with a value of 1, and progressively increased by 1 at each iteration, until reaching the final value. In Pascal, it is possible to have the loop-counter variable start at any desired value, and increase by 1, until reaching some specified final value. This type of loop will be called an **increasing FOR loop.** Alternatively, the loop-counter variable can be made to decrease by 1, from a large value to a small value. Such a loop will be called a **decreasing FOR loop.** Both of these pseudocode statements will be described now.

Increasing FOR loop A FOR loop in which the loop-counter variable is increased by 1 at each iteration.

Decreasing FOR loop A FOR loop in which the loop-counter variable is decreased by 1 at each iteration.

Increasing FOR Loops. For an increasing FOR loop, the pseudocode statement

```
FOR Variable := SmallValue TO BigValue DO
     Action
```

will be used to instruct the computer to (1) compute the values of the expressions SmallValue and BigValue, (2) set the value of the Variable to the value of SmallValue, and (3) compare the value of the Variable with that of BigValue. If the value of the Variable has not yet exceeded that of BigValue, then the Action is performed, and the value of the Variable is increased, or, in computer terminology, *incremented*, by 1. The actions in the third step are repeated until the value of the Variable becomes greater than that of BigValue. At that time, the computer will proceed to the instruction immediately following the Action. Observe that the Action will be performed precisely (BigValue − SmallValue + 1) times, provided that BigValue is at least as large as SmallValue.

Decreasing FOR **Loops.** The situation for a decreasing FOR loop is analogous to that of an increasing FOR loop. The major difference is that the value of the loop-counter variable begins at the largest value, and successively decreases by 1, until reaching the smallest value. Specifically, the pseudocode statement

```
FOR Variable := BigValue DOWNTO SmallValue DO
    Action
```

will instruct the computer to (1) compute the value of the expressions BigValue and SmallValue, (2) set the value of the Variable to that of BigValue, and (3) compare the value of the Variable with that of SmallValue. If the value of the Variable is not less than that of SmallValue, then the Action is performed, and the value of the Variable is then decreased, or, in computer terminology, *decremented*, by 1. The actions in the third step are repeated until the value of the Variable is less than that of SmallValue. At that time, the computer will proceed to the instruction immediately following the Action.

Some examples of decreasing FOR loops in pseudocode are

Example

```
FOR Discount := 10 DOWNTO 1 DO
    Total := Total - Discount
```

Example

```
FOR Counter := 5 * Last DOWNTO Last DO
    IF Counter > Last + 10 THEN
        Sum := Sum + Counter
        Total := Total + Sum
```

Other issues pertaining to the decreasing FOR loop are completely analogous to those of the increasing FOR loop, and will not be discussed.

In this section you have learned how to write in pseudocode a FOR loop that has a loop-counter variable whose value you can use in the body of the loop. In addition, you have learned about the concept of using the same variable on both the left and right sides of an assignment statement in the body of the loop. In the next section, you will learn how to code procedures and FOR loops in Pascal.

Exercises for Section 5.3

Write complete pseudocode algorithms to perform each of the following tasks. In doing so, think through your solution so as to identify the loop structure. Be sure to initialize all necessary variables before the loop statement. When appropriate, use the same variable on both the left and right side of a := in the body of the loop. Finally, trace your FOR loops to be sure that they are correct. Be sure to write all FOR loops using a loop-counter variable whose value should be used in the body of the loop, whenever possible.

1. Given a list of seven temperature readings, report the number of times the temperature dropped below 0 degrees.
2. Given the value of the positive integer *N*, compute the value of *N*! (*N* factorial), which is given by the formula:

   ```
   N! = 1 * 2 * ... * (N - 1) * N
   ```

3. Given the value of the positive integer *N*, compute the sum of the first *N* odd integers.
4. Given a text consisting of a number of characters, to be denoted by the value of the variable *TotalChars*, and given a special character, count the number of times the special character occurs in the text.
5. The Handy Hardware store wishes to update their inventory records on various parts, the actual number of which is denoted by the value of the variable *TotalParts*. Each part comes in a different, but known, number of sizes. For each part and each size, you will be given the selling price, the previous inventory, the number of units sold from that inventory, and the number of units bought (which are to be added to the previous inventory). Compute and display the new inventory level and the associated dollar value.
6. A class of *K* students has just taken an exam. The test has *N* questions, and each question has *M* parts. For each student, you will be given the scores for each part of each question. Report the total score for each question and the total score for each of the students.

For each of the following problems, indicate the total number of times the Action will be performed. Assume that the value of *Min* is 3 and that of *Max* is 4.

7.
```
FOR Counter := 1 TO Max DO
    Action
FOR NextCounter := 1 TO Min DO
    Action
```

8.
```
FOR Counter := 1 TO Max DO
    FOR NextCounter := 1 TO Min DO
        Action
```

9.
```
FOR Counter := 2 * Min TO Max + 2 DO
    Action
```

10.
```
FOR Counter := Max DOWNTO Min DO
    Action
```

5.4 Coding Procedures and FOR Loops

In this section you will learn the details of how to code procedures and increasing and decreasing FOR loops in Pascal. In addition, you will see that, in Pascal, the loop-counter variable can be a character or boolean variable as well as an integer variable, but never a real variable.

Coding Procedures in Pascal

Recall, from Section 5.1, that a procedure is group of instructions that is given a name when you declare the procedure. You can subsequently instruct the computer to perform the instructions simply by calling (i.e., writing) the name of the procedure. In this section, you will learn the details of how to declare and how to call a procedure in Pascal.

Declaring Procedures (without Parameters). In Pascal, a procedure is part of the declaration section and, in fact, is the last item that must be declared. To understand the details involved in declaring a procedure in Pascal, you should once again think of a procedure as a program within a program. As such, each local variable—that is, each variable that is used only within the procedure—must also be declared explicitly in the procedure. Global variables, in contrast, which appear in the main program as well as in the procedure, should not be declared within the procedure because those variables will have been declared in the main program.

The syntax for declaring a procedure in Pascal, which includes the declaration of local variables, the use of semicolons, and the use of the reserved words BEGIN and END is

```
PROCEDURE Name;
   VAR
      Local Declarations;
   BEGIN
      Statement;
      .
      .
      .
      Statement
   END;
```

Below is an example that uses the actual Pascal syntax introduced above. The declaration is valid for the procedure *ComputeCost* of Section 5.1.

```
PROCEDURE ComputeCost;
   VAR
      Area :REAL;        {Area is a local variable. All other variables
                          are global variables that must be declared
                          separately in the main program.}
   BEGIN
      Area := Length * Width;
      IF Area <= 12 THEN
         Cost := 1.50 * Area
      ELSE
         Cost := 1.50 * 12 + 1.25 * (Area - 12)
   END;     {End of the procedure ComputeCost.}
```

Using Procedures in the Main Program. In Pascal, to use a properly declared procedure in the main program, you can call the procedure simply by referring to the appropriate name as specified in the declaration. Doing so has the effect of making the computer perform the instructions in the procedure declaration. For example, the following executable section of a Pascal program calls the procedure *ComputeCost* twice:

```
BEGIN
   WRITELN('Enter the length and width of the tablecloth.');
   READ(Length, Width);
   WRITELN('Length = ', Length:8:2, ' Width = ',
         Width:8:2);
```

```
    ComputeCost;        {This is a call to the procedure that was declared
                         above.}
    WRITELN('Cost = ', Cost:8:2);
    Length := Length + 2;
    Width := Width + 1;
    WRITELN('New length = ', Length:8:2,
          ' New width = ', Width:8:2);
    ComputeCost;
    WRITELN('Cost = ', Cost:8:2)
END.
```

Using Procedures in Other Procedures. In Pascal, it is also possible for a procedure (as well as the main program) to call another procedure. In that regard, the procedure (or main program) that does the calling is referred to as the *calling program*. Whenever the instructions in a procedure are completed, the computer will return to the calling program and perform the statement immediately following the call to the procedure. Here is such an example that includes a program heading, the declaration of global variables, procedures, and local variables, together with the main program:

```
PROGRAM Test(INPUT, OUTPUT);
VAR
    Length, Width, Cost: REAL;      {Declare global variables.}

PROCEDURE DisplayCost;      {Declare a procedure.}
    BEGIN
        WRITELN('For a tablecloth of size ',
                Length * Width:10:2);
        WRITELN('the cost is :', Cost:10:2)
    END;    {End of the procedure DisplayCost.}

PROCEDURE ComputeCost;
    VAR
        Area :REAL;     {Declare a local variable.}
    BEGIN
        Area := Length * Width;
        IF Area <= 12 THEN
            Cost := 1.50 * Area
        ELSE
            Cost := 1.50 * 12 + 1.25 * (Area -12);
        DisplayCost     {Here, the previous procedure
                         DisplayCost is being called by this
                         procedure.}
    END;    {End of the procedure ComputeCost.}
```

```
{The main program begins here.}
BEGIN
    READ(Length, Width);
    ComputeCost    {When the instructions in this procedure are
                    performed, they, in turn, will call the procedure
                    DisplayCost, which will actually display the
                    results of the computations in the procedure
                    ComputeCost.}
END.
```

Coding Loops

For the remainder of this section, you will learn how to code increasing and decreasing FOR loops in Pascal. As always, you will see the need to pay attention to details, such as the use of semicolons as statement separators, the use of the reserved words BEGIN and END, and more.

Coding Increasing FOR Loops. The syntax for an increasing FOR loop in Pascal is similar to the associated pseudocode statement that you saw in the previous section. The specific Pascal syntax is

```
FOR Variable := SmallValue TO BigValue DO
    Action
```

In this statement, the Variable can be an integer, character, or boolean variable. Consequently, the expressions SmallValue and BigValue should be of the same type as the Variable. Observe that the Variable cannot be a real variable. The reason is that, in the statement

```
FOR Change := 1.5 TO 2.7 DO
    Amount := Amount + Change
```

for example, the computer cannot list all of the real values between 1.5 and 2.7. Thus the computer would not know how many times to perform the body of the loop.

The Action, on the other hand, can be any valid Pascal statement, including another FOR loop. The following are Pascal examples of increasing FOR loops in which the loop-counter variable is an integer variable; the use of a boolean and a character loop-counter variable will be illustrated later in this section.

Example

```
FOR Digit := 0 TO 9 DO
    IF Digit > NextNumber THEN
       NextNumber := NextNumber + 1
```

Example

```
FOR Sum := 2 * First TO UpperLimit DO
    FOR Counter := 1 TO 10 DO
        Total := Total + Sum
```

Only the statement immediately after the word DO will be performed. If more than one such statement is to be performed, then those statements must be surrounded with a BEGIN and END. Also, do not forget to use semicolons as statement separators. In that regard, the entire FOR statement begins with the word FOR and ends at the end of the action that constitutes the body of the loop. These details are illustrated in the following example.

Example

```
Last := 100;
FOR Customer := 1 TO Last DO
    BEGIN    {The body of this loop is the compound statement that ends
              at the second END below.}
       Total := 0.0;
       FOR SalesItem := Lower TO Upper DO
           BEGIN    {The body of this loop is the compound
                     statement that ends at the first END below.}
              READ(Balance);
              Total := Total + Balance
           END;    {End of the SalesItem loop.}
       WRITE('Total for customer', Customer:5);
       WRITELN(' is', Total:8:2)
    END    {End of the Customer loop.}
```

What Happens If . . . ? As is often the case when you learn a new computer instruction, you should ask "What happens if . . . ?" For example, in the Pascal statement

```
FOR Variable := SmallValue TO BigValue DO
    Action
```

what happens if BigValue is less than SmallValue? In Pascal, the computer will not perform the Action even once. However, if SmallValue is less than or equal to BigValue, then the Action will be performed a total of (BigValue − SmallValue + 1) times.

You might also ask what happens when the value of a variable in the expressions SmallValue or BigValue is changed within the body of the loop? Will that change affect the number of times the Action is performed? In Pascal, the answer is no because SmallValue and BigValue are evaluated once (and only once) before the body of the loop is executed for the first time. Thus changing the value of a variable in these expressions within the body of the loop will not affect the number of times the Action is performed.

Example

The body of the following `FOR` loop will be executed 3 times, not 10 times, even though the value of the variable *Last* is changed within the body of the loop.

```
First := 3;
Last := 5;
FOR Counter := First TO Last DO
    BEGIN
       First := 1;
       Last := 10
    END
```

Another question that might arise is what happens if the value of the loop-counter variable is changed within the body of the loop? In Pascal, you are not allowed to do so. In other words, although the loop-counter variable does appear on the left side of a := in the `FOR` statement, that variable must never appear on the left side of an assignment statement within the body of the loop. To illustrate, the following `FOR` loop is in error.

Example

```
FOR Id := 1 TO 10 DO
    BEGIN
```

```
        Box := 2 * Id;      {This statment is valid.}
        Id := Box + 1       {This statement is in error.}
    END
```

Finally, what is the value of the loop-counter variable after the `FOR` loop has been completed? In Pascal, the value of that variable is undefined, and so you should not use the loop-counter variable on the right side of an assignment statement outside the body of the loop. You can, however, redefine the value of the loop-counter variable by assigning it a new value outside of the loop.

Coding Decreasing `FOR` Loops. Recall, from Section 5.3, that a decreasing `FOR` loop is similar to an increasing `FOR` loop with the major exception that the loop-counter variable decreases by one at each iteration, from some large value to some small value. The syntax for a decreasing `FOR` loop in Pascal is

```
FOR Variable := BigValue DOWNTO SmallValue DO
    Action
```

All notes and comments pertaining to the decreasing `FOR` loop are similar to those for the increasing `FOR` loop, so the discussion will not be repeated. However, note that the major difference in a decreasing `FOR` loop is that the Variable is first assigned the value of BigValue (instead of SmallValue). Also, at the end of each iteration of a decreasing `FOR` loop, the value of the Variable is decreased by 1 instead of increased by 1.

Some examples of decreasing `FOR` loops in Pascal are

Example

```
FOR Discount := 10 DOWNTO 1 DO
    Total := Total + Discount
```

Example

```
FOR Counter := 5 * Last DOWNTO Last DO
    BEGIN
        IF Counter > Last + 10 THEN
            Sum := Sum + Counter;
        Total := Total + Sum
    END
```

Coding Character and Boolean FOR Loops. As was mentioned earlier, in Pascal the loop-counter variable can be a character variable, i.e., a variable whose value can be any of the symbols available on your computer. The Pascal syntax for an increasing and decreasing character FOR-loop statement is, respectively,

```
FOR Variable := FirstCharacter TO
    LastCharacter DO
    Action
FOR Variable := LastCharacter DOWNTO
    FirstCharacter DO
    Action
```

You should note that FirstCharacter and LastCharacter must be character expressions. Also, when performing the iterations of a character FOR loop, the Variable will successively be assigned all of the characters between FirstCharacter and LastCharacter according to the collating sequence of the computer you are using (see Appendix D).

The following examples illustrate the syntax introduced above by using character variables as loop-counter variables. Assume that all variables have been declared to be of the appropriate type, and that they have been initialized when necessary.

Example

```
FOR Chart := 'A' TO 'Z' DO
    WRITE(Chart)
```

Example

```
FOR Character := 'e' DOWNTO 'a' DO
    IF CurrentChar = Character THEN
       BEGIN
          CharCounter := CharCounter + 1;
          WRITE(Character)
       END
```

The loop-counter variable can also be a boolean variable, as illustrated in the following examples.

Example

```
FOR Open := FALSE TO TRUE DO
    IF Open THEN
       WRITELN('we are open for business')
    ELSE
       WRITELN('we are not open for business')
```

Example

```
FOR Deposit := TRUE DOWNTO FALSE DO
    Amount := -Amount
```

A Complete Pascal Example

In the next example, you will see a complete Pascal program that includes a program heading, a declaration section, and an executable section containing a `FOR` loop. This example is written for users of an interactive system in which the data are being entered from a terminal. As such, a `WRITE` statement has been included to display a message at the terminal to tell the user when to enter the list of data. However, observe that the `WRITE` statement is placed prior to the loop, and not in the body of the loop, so that the message is displayed only once, instead of each time the loop is performed. Specifically then, the stock problem that was developed at the end of Section 5.3 (excluding echo-printing and data-verification statements) could be coded in Pascal as

```
PROGRAM Stocks(INPUT, OUTPUT);
VAR
   Counter, ListLength, Position                :INTEGER;
   NextNumber, Total, LargestSoFar, Average :REAL;
BEGIN
   WRITE('Enter the number of days of prices and');
   WRITELN(' press return.');
   READ(ListLength);
   LargestSoFar := 0.0;
   Total := 0.0;
   {This next WRITELN statement should not be put inside the body of the
   subsequent FOR loop, for otherwise, its message would be displayed on
   the screen each time the body of the loop is performed.}
   WRITELN('Enter all of the individual prices.');
   FOR Counter := 1 TO ListLength DO
```

```
        BEGIN
           READ(NextNumber);
           Total := Total + NextNumber;
           IF NextNumber > LargestSoFar THEN
              BEGIN
                 LargestSoFar := NextNumber;
                 Position := Counter
              END   {End of the IF/THEN statement.}
        END;   {End of the FOR loop.}
     Average := Total / ListLength;
     WRITELN('The highest stock price is:',
          LargestSoFar:10:2);
     WRITELN('This price occurred on day',
          Position:3);
     WRITE('The average stock price for the past',
        ListLength:3);
     WRITELN(' days is', Average:10:2)
  END.
```

In this section you have learned how to code procedures and increasing and decreasing FOR loops in Pascal. In the next section you will begin to learn about WHILE loops.

Exercises for Section 5.4

Rewrite each of the following program segments so as to correct all of the syntax errors.

1.
```
PROCEDURE Total;
   Cost :REAL;
   FOR Cost := 2.0 TO 5.0 DO
        BEGIN
           Profit := Cost * Units;
           WRITELN(Profit)
        END
```

2.
```
FOR Counter := 2 * Highest DOWN Lowest / 2 DO
     BEGIN
        READ (Amount)
        Sum: = Sum + Amount
     END
```

3.
```
FOR Player = 1 TO Last DO
     BEGIN
        Count := 0
```

```
      FOR I = 1 TO 5 DO
          BEGIN
             READ(Card);
             IF Card = 'H' THEN
                Count := Count + 1
          END;
   END
```

In each of the following exercises you will be given a word problem, an associated Pascal program segment, and some results that have been displayed by the computer. Locate and correct the run-time and logic errors that have occurred.

4. Problem

For each value of *K* between 1 and 3, at the beginning of year *K*, Bob invests 100 * *K* dollars at an annual interest rate of 10%. How much money will Bob have at the end of three years?

Program Segment

```
Interest := 0.10;
Years := 3;
Principal := 0.0;
FOR YearCounter := 1 TO Years DO
   {Add the new deposit for the year.}
   Principal := Principal + 100 * YearCounter;
   {Add the interest earned.}
   Principal := (1.0 + Interest) * Principal;
WRITELN('You will have', Principal:10:2);
WRITELN('at the end of year', YearCounter:3)
```

Computer Output

```
You will have    660.00
*** Undefined variable YearCounter
```

You should realize that the output should have been:

```
You will have    705.10
at the end of year   3
```

5. Problem

A truck having a weight capacity of 1837 kg is to be loaded (in order) with as many items of weight 625, 125, 25, 5, and 1 kg, respectively, as possible. Report the total number of items in the truck.

Program Segment

```
Capacity := 1837;
Weight := 625;
NumberOfItems := 0;
FOR Item := 1 TO 4 DO
   BEGIN
      Number := Capacity DIV Weight;
```

```
        NumberOfItems := NumberOfItems +
                         Number;
        Capacity := Capacity MOD Weight;
        Weight := Weight DIV 5
     END;
  WRITELN('The total number of items is',
        NumberOfItems:3)
```

Computer Output

```
The total number of items is 11
```

```
The answer should have been 13.
```

Code, run, and debug each of the following algorithms that you wrote in Section 5.1 (see page 199) using the given data sets.

6. The algorithm for Exercise 3.
   a) Number of copies = 2000; selling price = \$20.00
   b) Number of copies = 3000; selling price = \$30.00
   c) Number of copies = 5500; selling price = \$ 8.95

7. The algorithm for Exercise 4.
   a) Given word: cab
   b) Given word: bac
   c) Given word: aac

Code, run, and debug each of the following algorithms that you wrote in Section 5.2 (see page 214) using the given data sets.

8. The algorithm for Exercise 9.
   a) *N* = 3; test scores = 75, 88, 92
   b) *N* = 4; test scores = 98, 90, 80, 55
   c) *N* = 5; test scores = 25, 69, 70, 80, 89

9. The algorithm for Exercise 10.
   a) *M* = 1; account number = 21397;
   previous balance = \$300.00; amount being paid = \$275.00
   b) *M* = 2; account number = 18317;
   previous balance = \$250.00; amount being paid = \$275.00;
   account number = 26305; previous balance = \$500.00;
   amount being paid = \$150.00
   c) *M* = 2; account number = 11445;
   previous balance = \$325.00; amount being paid = \$275.00;
   account number = 10163; previous balance = \$200.00;
   amount being paid = \$200.00

Code, run, and debug each of the following algorithms that you wrote in Section 5.3 (see page 222) using the given data sets.

10. The algorithm for Exercise 1.
   a) 10, 0, −3, 12, 18, 5, −1
   b) 20, 15, 18, 5, −5, −3, −2
   c) 5, 10, 12, 18, 22, 30, 35

11. The algorithm for Exercise 2.
   a) 3
   b) 7
   c) −4

12. The algorithm for Exercise 3.
   a) 4
   b) 8
   c) 32

13. The algorithm for Exercise 4.
   a) (For this data, the value of `TotalChars` is 15 and that of the special character is ‘t’.)
   Given data: This is a test.■
   b) (For this data, the value of `TotalChars` is 9 and that of the special character is ‘6’.)
   Given data: 1.2247239■
   c) (For this data, the value of `TotalChars` is 53 and that of the special character is ‘e’.)
   Given data: This is a long sentence■
   that is split over two lines.■

You should recall that, when reading characters in Pascal, you must be very careful in handling the end-of-line marker (see Section 3.2).

14. The algorithm for Exercise 5.
   a) Number of parts = 1; number of sizes = 1;
   selling price = 240.25; previous inventory = 27;
   units sold = 8; units bought = 1
   b) Number of parts = 1; number of sizes = 2;
   For the first size:
   selling price = 29.50; previous inventory = 103;
   units sold = 55; unit bought = 0
   For the second size:
   selling price = 15.00; previous inventory = 78;
   units sold = 75; units bought = 83

15. The algorithm for Exercise 6.
   a) Number of students = 3; number of questions = 3;
   number of parts = 1; the associated scores are

Student	Question	Score
1	1	22
1	2	36
1	3	30
2	1	18
2	2	33
2	3	33
3	1	20
3	2	18
3	3	35

b) Number of students = 2; number of questions = 2; number of parts = 3; the associated scores are

Student	Question	Part	Score
1	1	1	15
1	1	2	10
1	1	3	18
1	2	1	12
1	2	2	15
1	2	3	20
2	1	1	12
2	1	2	18
2	1	3	15
2	2	1	17
2	2	2	19
2	2	3	22

5.5 `WHILE` Loops

You have learned that you can use a `FOR` loop to instruct the computer to repeat an operation any [known] number of times. However, sometimes you will want the computer to repeat an operation an unspecified number of times, so long as some condition is satisfied. `WHILE` loops are used for this purpose, as will be described in this section. In addition, you will see that, unlike a `FOR` loop, a `WHILE` loop does not contain a loop-counter variable.

To illustrate the concept of a `WHILE` loop, recall the Ork problem of Section 5.1. There, you wanted to instruct the Orks on how to go from where they are on Maine Street to the corner of California and Nevada (see Fig. 5.2). After the instructions

```
Go North 2 blocks.
Go West 1 block.
```

the Orks will have reached the southwest corner of State Park. In Section 5.1, the instructions

```
FOR 3 times DO
    Go North 1 block.
    Go East 1 block.
```

were then used to direct the Orks to the northeast corner of State Park. Since you knew that three repetitions of these instructions would accomplish the desired objective, a FOR loop could be used. However, suppose that you were not sure of the correct number of repetitions. In that case, it would have been convenient to use a WHILE loop. For example:

```
WHILE not yet at the northeast corner of State
      Park DO
      Go North 1 block.
      Go East 1 block.
```

Specifically, then, the pseudocode statement

```
WHILE Condition DO
      Action
```

will be used to instruct the computer to (1) determine whether the Condition is true or false, (2) perform the Action if the Condition is true, and (3) repeat (1) and (2) until the Condition is false, at which time the computer proceeds to the instruction immediately following the Action.

The Condition of the WHILE loop should be a boolean expression, just like in an IF/THEN statement. The Action, which can be thought of as one call to a procedure, is any instruction (or group of instructions) that the computer can perform, including another FOR or WHILE loop statement. When the Action is a compound statement, those statements will be indented as a group. Finally, observe that the Condition is evaluated *before* the Action is performed. Thus all variables that are used in the Condition must be initialized prior to entering the loop. More comments regarding the WHILE loop will be made later in this section. Now, however, it is time to see how the WHILE loop is used in problem solving.

Problem Solving with WHILE Loops

Betty Broker has another program for you to write.

Problem: Betty Broker has purchased 200 shares of Mega-Corp stock at $5.50 per share. Since that time, for 30 days she has recorded the daily price. She would like you to write a program to locate the first day that the price decreases from the previous day's price. For each day up until that point, display the daily price, the value of the 200 shares on that day, and the amount of profit that she has earned since the initial purchase of the 200 shares. Thus, if the prices for five days were $5.50, $6.00, $6.50, $6.00, $5.25, respectively, then the output should be

Price	Value	Profit Since Original Purchase
5.50	1100	
6.00	1200	100
6.50	1300	200

The price has now dropped.

Algorithm Development. Knowing that the first step is to determine how you would solve the problem yourself, you might provide the following solution.

Solution: I look down the list of prices until I find the first day on which the price drops below the previous day's price. Then, for each of those days, I calculate the value of the 200 shares of stock and the amount of profit earned since the original purchase.

Observe that, in the solution procedure given above, you must go through some of the prices in the list twice: once to find the point at which the price drops, and a second time to compute some desired values. A more efficient method can be developed. To see how, begin by identifying the inputting, processing, and outputting phases of the problem. In considering what follows, keep in mind that a computer reads only one number at a time.

Inputting. In order to identify the inputting phase of the problem, you need to ask, "What information will I need to be given in order to solve the problem?" After rereading the problem statement, you can see that you will need to be given (1) the number of shares purchased (i.e., 200 shares), (2) the number of prices in the list (i.e., 30), and (3) the list of daily prices since the day of purchase of the 200 shares.

To enter the data for (1) and (2), you should use a READ statement instead of an assignment statement. The READ statement is better in this case because someday the number of shares and/or the number of days for which the price has been recorded might change. The following READ statement will allow for such changes:

```
READ Shares, ListLength
```

As for the list of prices, those data will be entered with some kind of loop statement, since the operation of entering each price will be repeated a number of times. The details are described below in the development of the processing portion of this algoritm.

Processing. At this point, the values of the variables *Shares* and *ListLength* have been entered. Although the actual prices have not yet been read, the question to ask is "What should I do with the values of the variables, and with the values in the list of prices?"

To answer this question, and to help you think through your solution, recall that a computer reads and processes only one number at a time. So, try to think like a computer, keeping in mind that you want the computer to display the daily prices, the corresponding value of the 200 shares, and the profit since the initial purchase.

You would probably begin by looking at the first price in the list. What do you want to do with that number? Well, since the first price on the list represents the original purchase price of each share of the stock, you can use that price to compute the initial value of the 200 shares. In other words, you can multiply the original purchase price by the number of shares (200) to obtain the initial value of those 200 shares. Thus you are led to the pseudocode statements

```
READ OriginalPrice
InitialValue := OriginalPrice * Shares
WRITE OriginalPrice, InitialValue
```

Now you would look at the second price in the list. What should you do with that value? First of all, you should realize that, if the second price on the list is less than the previous one, then the problem is over (and you need only display an appropriate message). On the other hand, if the second price is greater than or equal to the previous price, then you must perform some calculations. Specifically, you must compute the value of the shares at the current price, and the amount of profit earned since the original purchase. After displaying those results, you want to look at the next price in the list, and repeat these operations over and over again.

Once again, the desire to "repeat these operations over and over again" is precisely the concept of a loop. Furthermore, since you do not know beforehand how many times these operations are to be performed, a `WHILE` loop will be used instead of a `FOR` loop.

The following steps summarize the `WHILE` loop in the solution of the problem.

Step 1: Look at the next price in the list.

Step 2: Compute and display the value of the shares at that price, and the profit earned since the initial purchase.

Step 3: Perform Steps 1 and 2 so long as the current price is greater than or equal to the previous day's price.

In the above form, the concept of a loop is even more evident. Steps 1 and 2 constitute the body of the loop. The stopping rule in Step 3 indicates that a WHILE loop should be used, as the number of repetitions cannot be specified. There is, however, one nagging question that must be addressed sooner or later: When should the stopping rule be checked—before the body of the loop is performed, or after?

To answer the question, try each of the two cases and see what happens. For instance, if the stopping rule is checked after the body of the loop is performed, can anything go wrong? Yes! If the price you have just looked at in Step 1 is less than the previous price, then the information in Step 2 will be computed and displayed, which is something you do not want the computer to do.

On the other hand, consider the problem that arises if the stopping rule is checked before the body of the loop is performed. In order to be able to do so, the computer would have to "know" the second day's price in order to check to see if that value is greater than or equal to the previous price. However, the computer will not obtain the value for the second day's price until Step 1 is performed.

Either of these two approaches can, in fact, be used. No matter which method is chosen, the associated problems will have to be resolved. Issues pertaining to the first approach will be addressed in the next section. Here, the second approach will be discussed. Therefore assume that the stopping rule is checked before performing the body of the loop. As mentioned previously, in order to be able to do so, it will be necessary for the computer to know the value of the second price before that test is made. Thus you should instruct the computer to read the second price prior to entering the loop. Assuming you have done so, if the second price is greater than or equal to the previous price, then you will want to perform Step 2 above. Subsequently, you must read the next price, and repeat these operations over and over again. With these modifications, the processing portion of the algorithm becomes

Step 1: Look at the next price in the list.

Step 2: Perform the next three steps so long as the price you are looking at is greater than or equal to the previous price. (This step constitutes the stopping rule.)

Step 3: Compute and display the value of the shares at the current price.

Step 4: Compute and display the profit that has been earned since the original purchase.

Step 5: Look at the next price in the list.

In the previous version, the computer looked at the next price in the beginning of the body of the loop (see Step 1 of that version), and then performed the computations. In this version, however, the computer looks at the next price in Step 1 *before* entering the body of the loop, which consists of Steps 3, 4, and 5. In Steps 3 and 4, computations are being performed with the current price. Then, in Step 5, the computer will look at the next price for the *following* iteration. The process of performing certain operations within the body of the loop to prepare for the following iteration is typical when using loops.

Refinement. Now the process of refinement will be used to write the loop in pseudocode using the `WHILE` statement. Compare each of the following steps with the corresponding one above.

```
Step 1: READ CurrentPrice
Step 2: WHILE CurrentPrice ≥ PreviousPrice DO
Step 3:         Value := Shares * CurrentPrice
                WRITE CurrentPrice, Value
Step 4:         Profit := Value - InitialValue
                WRITE Profit
Step 5:         READ CurrentPrice
```

Initialization. Recall that, when working with any loop structure, you must initialize all variables whose values will be needed when performing the first iteration of the loop. For instance, since the stopping rule in Step 2 is performed before the body of the loop, the variables *CurrentPrice* and *PreviousPrice* must have been given values before Step 2. Indeed, the value of *CurrentPrice* is obtained in Step 1. However, in order to evaluate the condition in Step 2, the value of *PreviousPrice* should also have been initialized (which has not yet been done). By working through this example, you can see that the first value of *PreviousPrice* should be the original purchase price (which was read and stored in the variable *OriginalPrice* during the inputting phase). Thus the statement

```
PreviousPrice := OriginalPrice
```

should be used to initialize the value of *PreviousPrice* prior to performing the loop.

You can easily see that the remaining variables (e.g., *Shares* and *InitialValue*) whose values are needed during the first iteration of the loop have been properly initialized in the inputting phase. The outputting phase is all that remains in developing the algorithm.

Outputting. Much of the outputting has already been performed during the inputting and processing phases. However, once the loop is completed, it is necessary to display a message to the effect that the price has finally dropped. To that end, you can use the statement

```
WRITE 'The price has now dropped.'
```

Putting together what has been done so far, and adding labels for reference purposes, the algorithm is

```
S1:  READ Shares, ListLength, OriginalPrice
S2:  InitialValue := Shares * OriginalPrice
S3:  WRITE OriginalPrice, InitialValue
S4:  PreviousPrice := OriginalPrice
S5:  READ CurrentPrice
S6:  WHILE CurrentPrice ≥ PreviousPrice DO
S7:          Value := Shares * CurrentPrice          ⎫
S8:          Profit := Value - InitialValue          ⎬ Process the current price
S9:          WRITE CurrentPrice, Value, Profit       ⎭
S10:         READ CurrentPrice                       } Prepare for next iteration
S11: WRITE 'The price has now dropped.'
```

Unfortunately, the algorithm is not yet correct. However, through the process of tracing and debugging illustrated below, all of the remaining errors will be located and corrected.

Tracing

In order to trace the above algorithm, appropriate data must be chosen. Additional data will also be needed when the program is tested and debugged. For this problem, you might consider constructing the following test data: (1) The stock prices increase for a period, and then decrease. (This situation might be considered as the "normal," or expected case.) (2) The stock prices increase without ever dropping. (This data will test if the algorithm works properly in the "extreme" case.) (3) The stock prices drop immediately. (This is another "extreme" situation.)

Here, only data of the first (i.e., normal) kind will be used to trace the algorithm. To that end, suppose that for three days, the price of the stock is $5.50, $6.00, and $5.75, respectively. If 200 shares were purchased, then the expected output for this problem is

Price	**Value**	**Profit Since Original Purchase**
5.50	1100	
6.00	1200	100

The price has now dropped. The results of tracing the program will now be given.

After performing statements S1 through S5, the values of the variables are

Variables	**Values**
Shares	200
ListLength	3
OriginalPrice	5.50
InitialValue	1100
PreviousPrice	5.50
CurrentPrice	6.00

You should note that, at this point, the remaining variables (*Value* and *Profit*) have not been assigned values.

In order to perform the WHILE loop beginning in S6, the first step is to evaluate the condition in S6. Given the values of the variables above, the condition is true; that is, the *CurrentPrice* of 6.00 is greater than the *PreviousPrice* of 5.50, so, the computer would perform the body of the loop, which consists of statements S7 through S10. After completing the computations in S7 and S8, the WRITE statement in S9 will produce

```
6.00          1200          100
```

which appears to be correct. On completing the READ statement in S10, the new values of the variables are

Variables	**Values**
Shares	200
ListLength	3
OriginalPrice	5.50
InitialValue	1100
PreviousPrice	5.50

CurrentPrice	5.75
Value	1200
Profit	100

Now, the first iteration of the loop is complete. Accordingly, the condition in S6 must be evaluated again to determine if the body of the WHILE loop (consisting of steps S7 through S10) is to be performed another time. Using the values of the variables as given above, the condition is true (because the value of the *CurrentPrice*, which is 5.75, is greater than that of the *PreviousPrice*, which is 5.50). Consequently, S7 through S10 must be repeated.

After performing the computations in S7 and S8, the WRITE statement in S9 will produce

```
5.75                 1150                 50
```

At this point you should realize that something is wrong. The price has dropped, and yet the program is displaying information as though the price has continued to go up. Can you determine what caused the problem?

The cause of the problem is that after the first iteration of the loop is complete the condition in S6 should have been false, for that would have prevented the body of the loop from being performed again. Specifically, when the condition in S6 is evaluated for the second time, the value of *CurrentPrice* is 5.75 (as it should be), but the value of *PreviousPrice* is still 5.50; here is the problem. According to the given data, when the value of *CurrentPrice* is 5.75, the value of *PreviousPrice* should be 6.00, but it was not. Can you correct this error?

Correcting the Error. Looking carefully at S10, you should realize that, when the computer reads the new value of 5.75 for *CurrentPrice*, that value will be used for the next iteration. However, the value of *PreviousPrice* was incorrectly left at 5.50. To correct this "oversight," after displaying the appropriate values in S9, the value of *PreviousPrice*, which was 5.50, should have become that of *CurrentPrice*, which was 6.00. You can do so with the statement

```
PreviousPrice := CurrentPrice
```

However, a very serious problem would arise if this new statement were placed *after* the READ statement in S10 instead of *before* S10, in which case you would have these two statements

```
READ CurrentPrice
PreviousPrice := CurrentPrice
```

Can you see what that problem is?

The problem is that, after performing these two statements, the value of *CurrentPrice* and *PreviousPrice* would be exactly the same, because the assignment statement sets the value of *PreviousPrice* to that of the [new] *CurrentPrice*. Consequently, when the computer returns to S6, the condition in that statement would always be true, and so the body of the loop would be performed over and over again, forever, no matter what the values of the data are.

The problem described above is called an **infinite loop,** because the body of the loop would, in theory, be repeated forever. However, in such a situation, the computer usually will keep track of how much time (and/or other computer resources) you have used on the machine. After a predetermined point (as specified in the system-command cards that accompanied your job), the computer will automatically terminate your program with an error message of the form:

Infinite loop An error in a WHILE loop that causes the computer to perform the repetition "forever."

```
***Time limit (or page limit) exceeded
```

You will have used a lot of the computer's resources and gotten "nothing for your money." On a microcomputer, such automatic termination might not take place. Rather, you would have to press a certain button (or buttons) on the keyboard to stop the program from running forever.

In order to avoid the serious problem of an infinite loop, you should always check carefully that, within the body of the loop, the values of some variables in the condition of the WHILE statement are being changed in such a way that, eventually, the stopping rule will be satisfied. Thus, for example, the following WHILE statement will cause an infinite loop because the value of the variable *X* is not being changed within the body of the loop:

```
X := 1.0
WHILE X ≥ 0.0 DO
        Counter := Counter + 1
```

In any event, with the proper correction in place, and using a new set of labels for reference purposes, the new algorithm becomes

```
T1: READ Shares, ListLength, OriginalPrice
T2: InitialValue := Shares * OriginalPrice
T3: WRITE OriginalPrice, InitialValue
```

```
PreviousPrice := OriginalPrice
READ CurrentPrice
WHILE CurrentPrice ≥ PreviousPrice DO
      Value := Shares * CurrentPrice          }
      Profit := Value - InitialValue          } Process the current price
      WRITE CurrentPrice, Value, Profit       }
      PreviousPrice := CurrentPrice           } Prepare for
      READ CurrentPrice                       } next iteration
WRITE 'The price has now dropped.'
```

Of course you must now retrace the algorithm with the current data to make sure that the error has been corrected. Those steps will not be demonstrated here.

Debugging

After sufficient tracing, and when you are satisfied that the algorithm is correct, the next step would be to code the algorithm. That process will be illustrated in Section 5.6. Therefore assume that you have done so, and that all of the syntax errors have been removed. Now, the process of locating and correcting the run-time and logic errors begins.

The following data will be used to test whether the program will perform properly when the price of the stock rises continuously. To that end, suppose that 200 shares are purchased at the initial price of $5.50, and that the prices on the following two days are $6.00 and $6.50, respectively.

When the program is run with these data, the results are

Price	Value	Profit Since Original Purchase
5.50	1100	
6.00	1200	100
6.50	1300	200

****End of file encountered*

Now you must follow the steps of locating, understanding, and correcting the run-time error caused by attempting to read past the end-of-file marker. Of course, you could trace the entire program from beginning to end. However, to save time, look carefully at the output and at the program. Can you determine what has happened?

If you cannot see what is causing the error, then find the last point at which the program was working correctly and start tracing from there, if possible. For instance, when the value of *CurrentPrice* is 6.50, that of *PreviousPrice* will be 6.00. Thus at that point the condition in T6 is true, and so the body of the WHILE loop will be performed again. Indeed, the execution of T7 through T10 has been performed (and the results have been displayed correctly). However, when T11 is now performed, there are no more data to read. No wonder the end-of-file condition was encountered.

Correcting the Error. Since the problem is in T11, you might consider instructing the computer to read *CurrentPrice* only if there are more data to read. But how will the computer know if there are more data? One answer is to use the value of the variable *ListLength* which, up until this point, has not been used. This fact should have made you suspicious about the program some time ago.

To correct the problem, a variable, say *NumberProcessed*, should be introduced to count the number of prices that have been processed and, each time a new price is processed, the value of that variable should be increased by 1. Specifically, then, inside the body of the loop, and before the READ statement in T11, you should include the statement

```
NumberProcessed := NumberProcessed + 1
```

Once again, you should recall that all variables whose values are used during the first iteration of a loop (including *NumberProcessed*) must be initialized properly. To that end, note that, up until T5, just prior to performing the loop for the first time, only the original price will have been read and processed. Thus after T5, you should initialize with the statement

```
NumberProcessed := 1
```

Using the value for *NumberProcessed* in the body of the loop, the READ statement in T11 should be performed only if fewer than *ListLength* prices have been processed. Thus after increasing *NumberProcessed*, T11 should be changed to

```
IF NumberProcessed < ListLength THEN
    READ CurrentPrice
```

Furthermore, when the value of *NumberProcessed* reaches that of *ListLength*, not only do you want to avoid reading more data, but you also want the WHILE loop to be finished. One possibility is to alter the condition in the WHILE statement of T6 in such a way that, when the value of *NumberProcessed* is equal to that of *List-*

Length, the body of the loop will not be performed. Specifically, you could write T6 as

```
WHILE (CurrentPrice ≥ PreviousPrice) AND
      (NumberProcessed < ListLength) DO
```

Observe that, with a WHILE loop, there is no loop-counter variable (as there is with a FOR loop). If you need to use a loop-counter variable in the body of a WHILE loop (as was the case in this problem), then you must create that variable yourself, and increase or decrease its value at the appropriate point in the loop. Do not forget to initialize that variable before entering the loop.

With these corrections in place, and with a new set of labels for reference purposes, the new algorithm becomes:

```
 U1: READ Shares, ListLength, OriginalPrice
 U2: InitialValue := Shares * OriginalPrice
 U3: WRITE OriginalPrice, InitialValue
 U4: PreviousPrice := OriginalPrice
 U5: READ CurrentPrice
 U6: NumberProcessed := 1
 U7: WHILE (CurrentPrice ≥ PreviousPrice) AND
           (NumberProcessed < ListLength) DO
 U8:       Value := Shares * CurrentPrice
 U9:       Profit := Value - InitialValue
U10:       WRITE CurrentPrice, Value, Profit
U11:       PreviousPrice := CurrentPrice
U12:       NumberProcessed := NumberProcessed + 1
U13:       IF NumberProcessed < ListLength THEN
              READ CurrentPrice
U14: WRITE 'The price has now dropped.'
```

Retracing. Finally, it is necessary to retrace the new algorithm with the previous set of data. Unfortunately, there is still a small problem that needs to be corrected. For the current data, when the WHILE loop is completed, the WRITE statement in U14 will display a message indicating that the price has dropped when in fact the price has not dropped. To correct for this, U14 should be altered as follows:

```
IF NumberProcessed < ListLength THEN
   WRITE 'The price has now dropped.'
```

Do not forget that you should test the new program with all previous sets of data to make sure that no new error has been introduced by mistake.

In this section, you have learned how the WHILE statement works. Also, you have seen the need to initialize all variables properly, and to perform computations within the body of the loop so as to prepare for the next iteration of the loop. You must take great care not only to avoid computational errors, but also to avoid the possibility of an infinite loop. The next section deals with coding a WHILE loop in Pascal.

Exercises for Section 5.5

Rewrite the following instructions using a WHILE loop. Initialize variables when necessary, and be sure that the body of the WHILE loop is being performed the same number of times as in the original instructions.

1.
```
FOR Number := 1 TO LastNumber DO
      Product := Product * Number
      Sum := Sum + Number
```

2. Perform the following instructions so long as the value of the variable *Amount* is nonnegative, but at most *M* times.

```
READ Amount
Total := Total + Amount
```

Each of the following algorithms is supposed to obtain the sum of the first five integers. Trace each algorithm and correct any mistake you find.

3.
```
LastNumber := 5
Number := 1
Sum := 0
WHILE Number ≤ LastNumber DO
      Number := Number + 1
      Sum := Sum + Number
```

4.
```
LastNumber := 5
Number := 1
Sum := 0
WHILE Number < LastNumber DO
      Sum := Sum + Number
      Number := Number + 1
```

Write complete pseudocode algorithms to perform each of the following tasks. In so doing, think through your solution so as to identify the loop structure. Be sure to initialize all necessary variables before the loop statement. Trace your algorithms with data of your own choosing to be sure that the loop statements are correct and do not result in infinite loops.

5. Find the largest integer whose square is less than some given integer, say, `MaxNumber`.

6. The U.S. National Bank has recorded a list of deposits and withdrawals. The amount of a deposit is indicated by a positive number, while the amount of a withdrawal is indicated by a negative number. Assuming that you will be given the length of the list, determine the transaction number of the first point at which the total amount withdrawn exceeds the total amount deposited, and indicate by how much.

7. Given some text in which the last character (and only the last character) is an asterisk (`*`), and given a special character, determine whether the special character appears in the text. Even if the special character occurs many times, display a message only once.

8. The Fibonacci numbers (named after an Italian mathematician) are the numbers

   1, 1, 2, 3, 5, 8, . . .

   Each successive number (except the first two) is obtained by adding the previous two numbers in the sequence. Thus the next Fibonacci number in the sequence above is 13. Compute and display all Fibonacci numbers that are less than some given integer, say `LastNumber`. (You can assume that the value of `LastNumber` will be greater than 2.)

9. Modify the stock problem of this section so as to determine the first time that the price changes direction (either from up to down, or vice versa). As before, next to each day's price during the "trend," display the amount of profit or loss relative to the original purchase value. You will, of course, be given the number of shares and the length of the price list.

5.6 Coding `WHILE` and `REPEAT` Loops

In this section you will learn how to code `WHILE` loops in Pascal. As usual, you will have to pay attention to the details of syntax, such as the use of `BEGIN` and `END`, semicolons, and special Pascal symbols such as <=. In addition, you will learn about the `REPEAT` loop. This Pascal statement is similar to that of the `WHILE` loop. The one major difference, however, is that the stopping rule for the `REPEAT` loop is checked after the body of the loop is performed.

Coding WHILE Loops

The syntax for a WHILE loop in Pascal is

```
WHILE Condition DO
      Action
```

The Condition is precisely the same as that in an IF/THEN statement, i.e., a Pascal boolean expression. Recall that, when writing a boolean expression in Pascal, you must remember to use parentheses and the symbols <=, >=, and <>, when appropriate. The Action can be any valid Pascal statement, including a compound statement, which would have to be surrounded by the words BEGIN and END. The following example of a WHILE loop in Pascal illustrates these rules.

Example

```
WHILE CurrentNumber >= 0.0 DO
      BEGIN
         Total := Total + CurrentNumber;
         READ(CurrentNumber)
      END
```

You should note, once again, the function of the words BEGIN and END. Without them, only the statement immediately following the word DO in the example above would be performed. Therefore the READ statement would not be part of the loop, and hence, would be performed only after the loop is completed.

The next example illustrates the proper use of semicolons as statement separators. In that regard, the WHILE-loop statement starts with the word WHILE and ends at the end of the action. Consequently, if there is a statement preceding the WHILE-loop statement, you will have to use a semicolon (prior to the word WHILE) to separate those two statements. Similarly, if there is a statement following the action of the WHILE loop, you will have to use a semicolon (after the action) to separate the WHILE-loop statement from the subsequent statement.

Example

(Recall, from Section 3.2, that in standard Pascal EOLN is a boolean variable whose value is TRUE if the next character to be read is the end-of-line marker.)

```
READ(Chart);
NonBlanks := 1;
WHILE (Chart = ' ') AND NOT EOLN DO
   BEGIN
      READ(Chart);
      NonBlanks := NonBlanks + 1
   END;
WRITELN('Number of nonblank characters =',
      NonBlanks:3)
```

A Complete Example of a `WHILE` Loop in Pascal. Now you will see a complete program in Pascal that includes a program heading, a declaration section, and an executable section containing a `WHILE` loop. Indeed, the last version of the stock problem of Section 5.5, in which you had to find the first day that a stock price decreased, could be coded as

```
PROGRAM StockPrice(INPUT, OUTPUT);
VAR
   Shares, ListLength, NumberProcessed        :INTEGER;
   OriginalPrice, InitialValue, PreviousPrice :REAL;
   CurrentPrice, Value, Profit                :REAL;
BEGIN
   WRITELN('Enter the number of shares purchased.');
   WRITELN('Enter the number of days of prices.');
   WRITELN('Enter the list of prices and press return.');
   READ(Shares, ListLength, OriginalPrice);
   WRITELN(Shares:5, ' shares were purchased at',
         OriginalPrice:10:2);
   WRITELN(ListLength:4, ' days of prices were recorded.');
   WRITELN;
   WRITELN('Price':10, 'Value':10, 'Profit Since Purchase':25);
   InitialValue := Shares * OriginalPrice;
   WRITELN(OriginalPrice:10:2, InitialValue:10:2);
   PreviousPrice := OriginalPrice;
   READ(CurrentPrice);
   NumberProcessed := 1;
   WHILE (CurrentPrice >= PreviousPrice) AND
         (NumberProcessed < ListLength) DO
         BEGIN
            Value := Shares * CurrentPrice;
            Profit := Value - InitialValue;
            WRITELN(CurrentPrice:10:2, Value:10:2, Profit:25:2);
            PreviousPrice := CurrentPrice;
```

```
            NumberProcessed := NumberProcessed + 1;
            IF NumberProcessed < ListLength THEN
               READ(CurrentPrice)
         END; {End of WHILE loop}
      WRITELN;
      IF NumberProcessed < ListLength THEN
         WRITELN('The price has now dropped.')
   END.
```

Coding REPEAT Loops

Recall, from Section 5.5, that with the WHILE loop

```
WHILE Conditon DO
      Action
```

the Condition is checked before the Action is performed. Sometimes, however, it is preferable to have the Condition checked after the Action is performed. In Pascal, the REPEAT **loop** is designed to do just that. The syntax for that statement is

REPEAT **loop** A loop that is similar to a WHILE loop except that the stopping rule is checked after the body of the loop is performed.

```
REPEAT Action
UNTIL  Condition
```

Specifically, when the computer encounters a REPEAT statement in the above form, the following steps are performed:

Step 1: The Action is performed.

Step 2: The Condition is evaluated.

Step 3: If the Condition is false, then Steps 1 and 2 are repeated. If the Condition is true, then the loop is over and the computer proceeds to the instruction immediately following the Condition.

With a REPEAT loop, regardless of the value of the Condition, the Action will be performed at least once, whereas with a WHILE loop the Action might not be performed even once because the Condition, which is checked before the Action is performed, might be false. In addition, a REPEAT loop (like a WHILE loop) has no loop-counter variable. Finally, Step 3 of the REPEAT loop significantly contrasts with the WHILE loop. That is, in a WHILE loop, the Action is performed so long as the Condition is true. On the other hand, in a REPEAT loop, the Action is performed so long as the Condition is false. Consequently, in order to avoid an infinite loop in a REPEAT statement, the Condition must contain a variable whose value is changed somewhere within the body of the loop in such a way that, eventually, the Condition becomes true.

The following are examples of REPEAT loops in Pascal. As you read the first example, note that, when the Action is a compound statement, the individual statements need not be surrounded with a BEGIN and END. The reason for this is that all statements between the reserved words REPEAT and UNTIL will (automatically) constitute the Action. If you so choose to, however, you could surround the Action with BEGIN and END.

Example

```
REPEAT
   Counter := Counter + 1;
   Sum := Sum + Counter * Counter
UNTIL Sum >= 1000
```

The next example illustrates the use of semicolons as statement separators. In that regard, the REPEAT statement begins with the word REPEAT and ends at the end of the Condition. Also, you will observe that, since the Condition is checked after the body of the loop is performed, the values of the variables in the Condition (e.g., *CustomerNumber*) can be initialized within the body of the loop.

Example

```
Owing := 0.0;
REPEAT
   BEGIN
      READ(CustomerNumber, Amount);
      Owing := Owing + Amount
   END     {The use of BEGIN and END here is acceptable but not
            necessary.}
UNTIL CustomerNumber > 1001;
WRITELN('Amount owing =', Owing:12:2)
```

There are no hard and fast rules for deciding when to use a WHILE loop and when to use a REPEAT loop. In fact, it is generally true that in a given situation, if care is taken, either of the two loops can be used. Just remember that with a REPEAT loop the body of the loop will be performed at least once, whereas with a WHILE loop, since the stopping rule is checked first, the body of the loop might not be performed at all. The following table presents a comparison of the WHILE and REPEAT loops.

WHILE Loops

1. The Condition is tested before the body of the loop is performed.
2. As a result of (1), the body of the loop might not be performed at all (if the Condition is false).
3. As a result of (1), the variables in the Condition must have been initialized prior to reaching the WHILE statement so that the Condition can be checked.
4. If the Condition is true, the body of the loop will be performed, and looping will continue.
5. To avoid an infinite loop, the Condition must contain a variable whose value is changed somewhere within the body of the loop so that, eventually, the Condition becomes false.

REPEAT Loops

1. The Condition is tested after the body of the loop is performed.
2. As a result of (1), the body of the loop will be performed at least once (no matter what the value of the Condition).
3. As a result of (1), the variables in the Condition need not be initialized before reaching the REPEAT statement. Those variables can be assigned values in the body of the loop, which will be performed before the Condition is checked.
4. If the Condition is true, the body of the loop will have been executed already but looping will stop.
5. To avoid an infinite loop, the Condition must contain a variable whose value is changed somewhere within the body of loop so that, eventually, the Condition becomes true.

A Complete Example of a REPEAT Loop in Pascal. Recall, from Section 5.5, the stock problem of determining the first day that the stock price dropped from the previous day's price. In developing that algorithm, after entering the initial purchase price, the following loop structure was identified.

Step 1: Look at the next price in the list.

Step 2: Compute and display the value of the shares at that price, and the profit earned since the initial purchase.

Step 3: Perform Steps 1 and 2 so long as the current price is greater than or equal to the previous day's price.

If the stopping rule in Step 3 is checked after the body of the loop (consisting of Steps 1 and 2) is performed, as would be the case with a REPEAT loop, then there is a problem. Specifically, if the price you have just looked at in Step 1 is less than the previous price, then the information in Step 2 will be computed and displayed, which is something you do not want the computer to do. One way to correct this problem is to reverse the order of Steps 1 and 2. In so doing, the actions in Step 2 will pertain to the *previous* day's price, while the subsequent instruction to "look at the next price" will pertain to the *following* iteration of the loop.

With this discussion in mind, the following is a Pascal version of the stock problem that contains a REPEAT loop instead of a WHILE loop. Compare the two loop structures and the variables that are being initialized.

```
PROGRAM StockPrice(INPUT, OUTPUT);
VAR
   Shares, ListLength, NumberProcessed           :INTEGER;
   OriginalPrice, InitialValue, PreviousPrice :REAL;
   CurrentPrice, Value, Profit                   :REAL;
BEGIN
   WRITELN('Enter the number of shares purchased.');
   WRITELN('Enter the number of days of prices.');
   WRITELN('Enter the list of prices and press return.');
   READ(Shares, ListLength, OriginalPrice);
   WRITELN(Shares:5, ' shares were purchased at',
         OriginalPrice:10:2);
   WRITELN(ListLength:4, ' days of prices have been recorded.');
   WRITELN;
   WRITELN('Price':10, 'Value':10, 'Profit Since Purchase':25);
   InitialValue := Shares * OriginalPrice;
   CurrentPrice := OriginalPrice;
   NumberProcessed := 0;
   REPEAT
      Value := Shares * CurrentPrice;
      Profit := Value - InitialValue;
      WRITELN(CurrentPrice:10:2, Value:10:2, Profit:25:2);
      PreviousPrice := CurrentPrice;
      NumberProcessed := NumberProcessed + 1;
      IF NumberProcessed < ListLength THEN
         READ(CurrentPrice)
   UNTIL (CurrentPrice < PreviousPrice) OR
         (NumberProcessed >= ListLength);
   WRITELN;
   IF NumberProcessed < ListLength THEN
      WRITELN('The price has now dropped.')
END.
```

In this section, you have learned the details of how to code WHILE and REPEAT loops in Pascal. In addition, you have seen the differences between a WHILE loop, which tests the stopping rule before the body of the loop is performed, and a REPEAT loop, which tests the stopping rule after the body of the loop is performed. In Chapter 6, you will learn a powerful programming structure for storing and for processing large quantities of data.

Exercises for Section 5.6

Rewrite the following program segments so as to correct all of the syntax errors in the following Pascal statements.

1.
```
WHILE Card = 'H' DO
          Count := Count + 1;
          READ(Card)
     END
```

2.
```
UNTIL Sum ≥ 1000 REPEAT
     BEGIN
          Counter := Counter + 1;
          Sum := Sum + Counter * Counter
     END
WRITELN('Sum =', Sum:10:2)
```

Rewrite each of the following program segments using a REPEAT statement. Initialize all variables appropriately. Also, be sure that the body of the loop is being performed the same number of times as in the original instructions.

3.
```
Product := 1;
Number := 1;
WHILE Product <= N DO
          BEGIN
               Number := Number + 1;
               Product := Product * Number
          END;
WRITELN(Product:10, Number:3)
```

4.
```
Freezing := 0;
Sum := 0.0;
FOR Days := 1 TO NumberOfDays DO
     BEGIN
          READ(Temp);
          IF Temp < 0.0 THEN
               BEGIN
                    Freezing := Freezing + 1;
                    Sum := Sum + Temp
               END
     END;
WRITELN((Sum / Freezing):12)
```

Code, run, and debug each of the following algorithms that you wrote in Section 5.5 (see page 250) using the given data.

5. The algorithm for Exercise 5.
   a) Given integer: 20
   b) Given integer: 1
   c) Given integer: 345

6. The algorithm for Exercise 6.
   a) (the length of this list is 4)
   25.50, 18.00, −45.25, 22.30
   b) (the length of this list is 5)
   20.25, −10.50, 13.75, −22.50, −5.00
   c) (the length of this list is 4)
   18.75, 12.25, −10.00, 15.50

7. The algorithm for Exercise 7.
   a) Special character: '.'
   Given text: This is a sentence.*■
   b) Special character: '!'
   Given text: There is no exclamation point.*■
   c) Special character; 'e'
   Given text: Not now.■
   Later you will find the letter.*■

8. The algorithm for Exercise 8.
   a) Given integer: 7
   b) Given integer: 45
   c) Given integer: 130

9. The algorithm for Exercise 9.
   a) Number of shares = 25; original price = 5.00; number of days of prices = 4; the actual prices are: 5.00, 5.50, 6.00, 5.75
   b) Number of shares = 50; original price = 20.00; number of days of prices = 5; the actual prices are: 20.00, 19.50, 19.25, 19.75, 21.00
   c) Number of shares = 50; original price = 120.25; number of days of prices = 4; the actual prices are: 120.25, 119.50, 118.75, 118.25

5.7 Summary

For computer problem solving, the concept of repetition can be described as the process of performing a group of instructions a certain number of times, while having to write those instructions only once. Sometimes, the specific group of instructions to be repeated is obvious. At other times, when solving a problem, you must consciously look for and identify some instructions to be repeated. In any event, the two major methods for performing repetition are procedures and loops.

A procedure, which can be thought of as a "program within a program" (i.e., a subprogram), refers to a group of specific instructions that has been given a name. The act of specifying the actual instructions is called declaring the procedure, during which you will most likely use three types of variables, namely (1) input variables (which are global variables, declared in the main program, and whose values will be computed and stored in the main program); (2) local variables (which are declared in the procedure and whose values will be computed and used only within the procedure); and (3) output variables (which are global variables whose values will be computed in the procedure, but used in the main program).

Subsequently, by simply referring to the procedure name in the program, the computer can be made to perform all of the instructions in the procedure declaration at any point in the program. The act of doing so is referred to as calling (or invoking) the procedure. Each time you want the computer to perform the instructions in the procedure, you have to write the procedure name.

A loop, in contrast, contains not only the statements to be repeated (i.e., the body of the loop), but also an associated stopping rule. The stopping rule is used to specify that the repetition is to be performed either a known number of times, or so long as a boolean condition is true. The former stopping rule gives rise to a `FOR` loop; the latter to a `WHILE` loop. You can also use a `REPEAT` loop to perform an action an unknown number of times. The primary differences between a `WHILE` and a `REPEAT` loop are (1) in a `REPEAT` loop the condition is checked after the action is performed, whereas in a `WHILE` loop the condition is checked before the action is performed; and (2) in a `REPEAT` loop, if the condition is true, then the loop is over, whereas in a `WHILE` loop, if the condition is true, then the loop is not over.

Key Terms

Repetition 190
Procedure 190
Declaring a procedure 191
Calling a procedure 191
Procedure name 191
Body of a procedure 191
Global variables 196
Local variables 196
Loop 200
Body of a loop 201
Stopping rule 201
`FOR` **loop 201**
`WHILE` **loop 201**
Iteration of a loop 203
Loop-counter variable 209
Initializing a variable 210
Increasing `FOR` **loop 220**
Decreasing `FOR` **loop 220**
Infinite loop 245
`REPEAT` **loop 253**

The ENIAC (Electronic Numerical Integrator and Calculator), the first large-scale digital computer, weighed 50 tons, operated on 18,000 vacuum tubes, and sprawled across a thirty- by fifty-foot space. Its creators, Dr. John W. Mauchly (at right foreground) and J. Presper Eckert, Jr. (at left), joined forces to create a machine that could perform mathematical calculations one thousand times faster than any previous machine. Although the ENIAC was in use only until 1955, it is part of a revolution that appears to have no end. (UPI/BETTMANN NEWSPHOTOS)

6

ARRAYS

In Chapter 5 you saw that sometimes an entire list of numbers could be read and processed using a single variable. However, what would you do if, for some reason, it was necessary to store all of the numbers on the list? If the list was long, then you probably would not want to create (and to declare) a separate variable for each number. Instead, as you will learn in this chapter, you can use an *array*, which is a convenient method for storing (and manipulating) such data.

6.1 What Is an Array?

Array A collection of variables that is used for storing and processing a list of data.

An **array** is a collection of variables that you can use to store large quantities of data. Suppose, for example, that you want to read and to store the values of 26 numbers in a list. You could, of course, create 26 different variables, and then use the pseudocode statement

```
READ A, B, ..., Z
```

Since a computer cannot understand those three dots (...), you would actually have to write out the 26 variable names in the above list when you code the program in Pascal. Fortunately, you can avoid having to do so by using an array, as will be illustrated below.

Array name The common name that is given to each variable of an array.

Array subscript An integer value following the array name that is used to distinguish one array variable from the next.

Looking at the READ statement above, you will notice that each variable has an entirely different name. With an array, the idea is to provide only one name, called the **array name,** that is common to all of the variables. For the example above, you might choose the array name *List*. However, in order to distinguish one variable from the next, the common name is then followed by a number, called the **array subscript,** that is used to identify each individual variable. In this book, the array name will be separated from the subscript by enclosing the latter in brackets. Thus the 26 variables above would be referenced by the 26 names *List*[1] (pronounced "List sub 1"), *List*[2] (pronounced "List sub 2"), ..., *List*[26] (pronounced "List sub 26").

Element of an array One specific array variable consisting of the array name followed by the subscript of that variable.

In essence, an array should be thought of as a collection of variables, each of which is called an **element of the array.** The array consists of a single array name that is common to all of the variables. However, in order to distinguish one variable from the next, a subscripting integer is placed in brackets immediately following the array name. Figure 6.1 provides a convenient method for picturing an array and its values.

Array Name	Subscript	Value	
List	[1]	3.14	(first element)
List	[2]	−1.13	(second element)
.			
.			
.			
List	[N]	6.66	(Nth element)

Figure 6.1 An array and its elements.

When thinking about an array, an appropriate analogy is that of houses on a street. The entire street has one common name (e.g., Maple Street), which is common to all of the variables just like the array name *List* above. To refer to one specific house on the street, you would place the number of the house just before the street name; e.g.,

```
24 Maple
```

To refer to one specific variable in the array, i.e., to one array element, you put the number of that variable in brackets just to the right of the array name; e.g.,

```
Maple[24]
```

Returning to the array *List*, you can now use each of these 26 variables, *List*[1], *List*[2], ..., *List*[26], in your algorithm, just as you would use any other variables. For instance, you could write the pseudocode assignment statements

```
List[1] := 250
List[2] := List[1] + 1
```

In fact, you could write the original pseudocode READ statement above as

```
READ List[1], List[2], ..., List[26]
```

So far, the problem of having to replace the three dots with the actual variable names has not yet been overcome. However, below you will see how to exploit the fact that each variable has a common name, *List*, so as to perform the above READ statement without having to list all of the variables explicitly.

Using the Subscript of an Array

Until now, the subscript of an array, i.e., the item in brackets that follows the array name, has been a specific integer. However, you will now learn that the quantity that appears in brackets can also be an integer variable, whose value can be made to change. It is this fact that will enable you to perform the above READ statement without having to list all of the variables.

To understand the use of a variable as a subscript, suppose for the moment that after the array name *List* you were allowed to put a variable, such as *I* (instead of a number), to refer to one specific variable in the list. Thus, for example, if the value of the variable *I* is 7, then

```
List[I]
```

will refer to the variable

```
List[7]
```

Similarly, if the value of *I* is 23, then

```
List[I]
```

will refer to the variable

```
List[23]
```

The variable *I* above is called a *subscripting variable*. With the use of the subscripting variable *I*, it is possible to perform the desired READ statement without listing all of the variables. To see how, think of the instruction

```
READ List[1], List[2], ..., List[26]
```

as wanting to repeat the statement

```
READ List[I]
```

for each value of *I* from 1 to 26. Thus, for example, by recalling the concept of a FOR loop from Section 5.4, you can read the entire list of numbers by using the pseudocode instruction

```
FOR I := 1 TO 26 DO
    READ List[I]
```

According to the way in which a FOR loop is performed, the value of *I* will first be set to 1. Then the body of the loop will be performed, so the computer will read the value of the variable List[1]. Subsequently, the value of *I* is set to 2, and the body of the loop will then instruct the computer to read the value for List[2]. This process will be repeated until the value of List[26] is read.

You have just seen the concept (and power) of an array; namely, the ability to store and to process large quantities of data by using one common array name (e.g., List), together with a subscripting variable (e.g., *I*), whose value is used to identify one specific variable (e.g., List[I]). The power of an array lies in the ability to change the value of the subscripting variable (often within a FOR or a WHILE loop, as was done above).

Interpreting the Array Subscript and the Array Element. Your ability to use an array effectively depends on your ability to use the subscripting variable properly. In order to do so, the first step is to understand, in the context of the specific problem, the meaning and interpretation of (1) the array subscript, and (2) the corresponding array element (which consists of the array name together with the subscript). You can interpret the meaning of the array subscript and the corresponding array element by following these three steps:

Step 1: Choose (arbitrarily) a specific integer subscript, and write the corresponding array element consisting of the array name followed by the subscript. Then, by looking *only* at the specific subscript, interpret the meaning of that number.

Step 2: Looking at the *entire* array element (including both the array name and the subscript), interpret the meaning of the value of that variable.

Step 3: Replace the specific integer subscript with a variable name (of your choosing). Then repeat Steps 1 and 2 so as to interpret the meaning of both the subscripting variable and the corresponding array element.

These three steps will be illustrated in the following examples.

Example

Suppose that the values of the 100 elements of the array `Amount` are to contain the amounts of money owed by 100 customers.

In accordance with Step 1, begin by choosing an arbitrary, but specific, array subscript, say 5, for which the corresponding array element is `Amount[5]`. Now, looking only at the subscript value 5, you can interpret the meaning of 5 as referring to the *fifth* customer.

In accordance with Step 2, you should look at the entire array element, namely, `Amount[5]`, and interpret the meaning of the value of that variable. In this case, the value of `Amount[5]` is the *amount of money* owed by the fifth customer.

Finally, in accordance with Step 3, you should replace the specific subscript 5 above with a variable, say `Customer`, and write the corresponding array element, `Amount[Customer]`. Looking only at the subscript in brackets, you can interpret the meaning of the value of `Customer` as referring to the *number* of the customer under consideration. Finally, you can interpret the meaning of the entire array element, `Amount[Customer]`, as the amount of money owed by the customer whose number is the value of the variable `Customer`.

Example

Suppose that the values of the 26 elements of the array `Frequency` are to contain the number of times each letter of the alphabet occurs in a given paragraph of text.

In accordance with Step 1, begin by choosing an arbitary, but specific, array subscript, say 3, for which the corresponding array element is `Frequency[3]`. Now, looking only at the subscript value 3, you can interpret the meaning of 3 as referring to the *third* letter of the alphabet (i.e., to the letter "c").

In accordance with Step 2, you should look at the entire array element, namely, `Frequency[3]`, and interpret the meaning of the value of that variable. In this case, the value of `Frequency[3]` is the *number of times* the letter "c" has occurred in the paragraph of text.

Finally, in accordance with Step 3, you should replace the specific subscript 3 above with a variable, say `Letter`, and write the corresponding array element, `Frequency[Letter]`. Looking only at the subscript in brackets, you can interpret the meaning of the value of `Letter` as referring to the position of a letter in the alphabet (i.e., a value of 1 for `Letter` corresponds to the letter "a", 2 to the letter "b", and so on). Finally, you can interpret the meaning of the entire array element, *Frequency*[*Letter*], as the number of times the corresponding letter occurs in the paragraph.

In the examples above, you should note that there is a big difference between the meaning of the subscript (i.e., the quantity in brackets) and the meaning of the corresponding array element, which is the variable that consists of the array name together with the subscript.

Subscript Expressions. After understanding the meaning of a subscript (and the corresponding array element), the next step is to learn how to use the subscript to perform appropriate computations with the array. In that regard, you have already seen that a subscript can be an integer constant or an integer variable. Now you will see that a subscript can also be an integer *expression*. In the illustrative examples that follow, assume that appropriate values have been stored into each element. Also, keep in mind the fact that each array element is, itself, a variable, and can be used as such. In each FOR loop, observe how the loop-counter variable is being used to form an appropriate subscript expression. Finally, you should trace each of these pseudocode statements carefully. In so doing, you will find it useful to keep track of the array subscript and the values of the array elements by making a list as in Fig. 6.1.

Example

Suppose that the array *Frequency* contains the number of times each letter of the alphabet occurs in a given paragraph of text. The following FOR loop displays the frequencies of the "even" (i.e., the second, fourth, sixth, and so on) letters:

```
FOR NextEven := 1 TO 13 DO
    WRITE Frequency[2 * NextEven]
```

Example

The following FOR loop shifts the value of each of the *N* elements of the array *Count* up one position.

```
FOR Position := 2 TO N DO
    Count[Position - 1] := Count[Position]
```

If you have traced this FOR loop correctly, then you will discover that, indeed, the value of each element has been shifted up one position, except that the original value of *Count*[*N*] remains unchanged, while that of *Count*[1] is lost forever.

Declaring Arrays

When you are developing an algorithm using pseudocode, you can simply use an array. However, when you code the algorithm into Pascal, for example, you will have to declare the array. Specifically, in the declaration section of the program, you will have to provide the computer with the following information.

The Array Name. The array name is just like any other variable name and should be treated as such.

The Type of the Array. As you have seen, each element of an array is itself a variable. Thus into each element of an array you can store an integer, real, character, or boolean value by using an assignment statement. However, all elements of the array must contain the same type of value. You cannot, for example, store an integer value in one element of the array, and a character value in another element of the array. Thus when you declare an array you will have to specify the type of the array, i.e., the type of values that are to be stored in each element of the array (e.g., integer, real, etc.).

The Allowable Range for the Subscript. If an array, say *List*, is to contain 10 elements, then it is natural to assume that the first element is *List*[1], the second is *List*[2], and the last is *List*[10]. Thus if you were using the subscripting variable *Number* to reference *List*[*Number*], then clearly the value of *Number* should be between 1 and 10. However, in Pascal it is possible to have an array of 10 elements in which, for example, the first is *List*[−5], the second is *List*[−4], and the last is *List*[4]. In this case, the value of the subscripting variable *Number* should be between −5 and 4. In other words, you can have an array in which the subscript can be a negative integer. In general, it is necessary to specify in the declaration section the allowable range for the subscript, i.e., the first and last possible values of a subscript. Thus, for example, in pseudocode you might write

Declaration	**Meaning**
List[−5..4]	{The subscript must be between −5 and 4.}
Count[0..20]	{The subscript must be between 0 and 20.}
A[101..200]	{The subscript must be between 101 and 200.}

In the event that the value of a subscript is either less than the smallest allowable value or greater than the largest allowable value, a run-time error will occur, as you will see in Section 6.2.

When you declare an array, the computer will automatically create one variable for each element of the array. For example, if you declare an array whose smallest allowable subscript is the integer *M*, and whose largest allowable subscript is the integer *N*, then the array will contain *N* − *M* + 1 elements, and the computer will create that many variables. For example, the three arrays above will contain 10, 21, and 100 elements, respectively. Since each computer has a different limit on the total number of variables that can be used in a program, you must be careful when declaring arrays so as not to exceed the memory capacity of the computer. Microcomputers are particularly limited in their available storage space.

Recap

As you have seen, an array is a powerful method for storing and manipulating data. An array is a collection of variables each of which consists of a common array name followed by a subscript that is used to distinguish one variable from the next. The subscript can be an integer constant, an integer variable, or an integer expression. The power of an array lies in your ability to use a subscripting variable (whose value can be made to change using a loop, for example) so as to process the various array elements. When you code an algorithm, you have to declare the array, which consists of telling the computer the array name, the type of values that will be stored into each element of the array, and the allowable range for a subscripting variable. Section 6.2 shows how an array is used in the problem-solving process.

Exercises for Section 6.1

In the following exercises, assume that *Price* is a real array of five elements, the first of which is *Price*[0]. Trace each of the following pseudocode instructions. Use a table similar to the one in Fig. 6.1 to keep track of the array values. Clearly indicate when you encounter an error.

1.
```
Price[1] := 25.45
Price[2] := 48.55
```

```
Price[3] := 56.28
Price[4] := 89.72
Sum := Price[1] + Price[2] + Price[3] +
       Price[4]
IF Sum < 200 THEN
   Price[0] := Sum
ELSE
   Price[0] := '*'
```

2.
```
FOR Item := 1 TO 5 DO
    Price[4 - Item] := 3 + Item
```

3.
```
Price[2] := 2
Item := 2
WHILE Price[Item] < 10 DO
      Price[Item + 1] := 2 * Price[Item]
      Item := Item + 1
```

After reading each of the following program segments, create declaration statements for the arrays; include (1) the array name, (2) the type of the array, and (3) the allowable range for the subscript. How many elements does each array have?

4.
```
FOR Frame := 1 TO 12 DO
    READ Ball1, Ball2
    Spare[Frame] := Ball1 + Ball2 = 10
```

5.
```
FOR I := 1 TO 100 DO
    X[4 - I] := -I
```

6.
```
Position := 1
WHILE Position < 10 DO
      READ Ch
      Position := Position + 1
      IF Ch ≠ '.' THEN
         String[Position] := Ch
```

Using the loop-counter variable, replace the question marks in each of the following program segments with appropriate subscript expressions that would accomplish the given word instructions. Check your results by tracing.

7. Given an array *Scores* of 11 elements in which the subscripting variable can be between −3 and 7, obtain the total sum of all the elements.

```
Sum := 0
FOR Student := 1 TO 11 DO
    Sum := Sum + Scores[?]
```

8. Given an array *X* having *N* elements, display the values of all the odd elements, i.e., X[1], X[3], etc. Then display the value of all the elements, but in reverse order, i.e., X[N], X[N - 1], ..., X[1].

```
NumberOfOdds := (N + 1) / 2     {drop any remainder}
FOR NextOdd := 1 TO NumberOfOdds DO
    WRITE X[?]
FOR J := 1 TO N DO
    WRITE X[?]
```

9. Given an array *Perm* of *N* elements, shift the value of each element down one position (see Fig. 6.1). The original value of the last element of *Perm* should, at the end, become the value of the first element of *Perm*. (*Hint:* Work from bottom to top in the array.)

```
Temp := Perm[?]
FOR Location := 1 TO N - 1 DO
    Perm[?] := Perm[?]
Perm[?] := Temp
```

6.2 Using an Array in Problem Solving

In Section 6.1, you learned that an array, together with the subscripting variable, can be a useful way to store and manipulate a group of data. In this section, you will see how an array is used in the problem-solving process.

When to Use an Array

In Chapter 5, you saw that it was sometimes possible to process a list of information by using only one variable. You might therefore ask why it is necessary to use an array, or when should an array be used? An array can be used as a matter of convenience, simply to group and to store a collection of related information. However, you *must* use an array when you need to save a group of data for later, or repeated, use in a program. For example, suppose that in a given problem you need to find the largest number in a list. That task could be accomplished by using only one variable (see Section 5.3). However, if, in addition to finding the largest number, you needed to compute the amount by which each number in the list differs from the largest one, then you would need an array to store all of the numbers. In other words, you need to store these numbers in an array so that, after finding the largest number, you could go back through the list again and compute the differences.

An Example of Using an Array

As an example of using an array in the problem-solving process, imagine that you have just been employed in the data-processing division of the College of Computing. Your supervisor, Mary Martin, presented you with the following problem.

Problem: Given a list of student-identification numbers that correspond to those students who have not yet paid their tuition, display the original list, and then display the list in increasing order of student-identification number. (The length of the list is not known beforehand.)

Mary has researched several different methods for sorting information, and she would like you to use the following one in developing your algorithm.

Solution: Look down the list. Whenever you find two consecutive numbers that are not in the proper sequence, interchange the position of those two numbers. Continue these operations as long as necessary until you can no longer find two numbers out of sequence, at which time the list will be sorted.

Algorithm Development. In the spirit of top-down programming, you might begin by identifying the following major tasks to be accomplished:

Step 1: Read the original list of numbers.

Step 2: Display the original list of numbers.

Step 3: Sort the list in increasing order of student-identification number.

Step 4: Display the sorted list.

Observe that in Steps 2 and 4, the list of numbers must be displayed. Recalling from Section 5.1 that a procedure can be used to perform that task twice (while only having to write the instructions once), you should indeed create such a procedure, whose name, say, is `DisplayIds`. You will also need to create a procedure, say `ReadIds`, to accomplish the task in Step 1. Likewise, a procedure, say `SortIds`, can be created to perform Step 3. Putting this discussion together, the main program would consist of the following procedure calls (corresponding to the four steps above):

```
ReadIds
DisplayIds
SortIds
DisplayIds
```

All that remains is to fill in the details that constitute the body of each procedure, which will be done below.

Declaring the Procedure *ReadIds*. The objective of this procedure is to accomplish the inputting phase of this problem, i.e., Step 1 above. To that end, reread the solution to the problem that was presented above. Note that you will have to look at the list of numbers several times in order to search for two consecutive numbers that are out of sequence. It is this fact that makes it necessary to create an array, say *Id*, to store the list.

Before proceeding further, be sure that you understand the meaning of the subscript of this array and the meaning of the value of the corresponding array element. For example, when working with the array element *Id*[7], the subscript 7 refers to the *seventh* student in the list, whereas the value of the corresponding array element, *Id*[7], is the actual identification number of the seventh student. Now repeat this interpretation process by replacing the specific subscript 7 with a variable. For example, when working with the array element *Id*[*Student*], the value of the subscripting variable *Student* refers to the position of the student in the given list (i.e., first, fifth, etc.), whereas the value of the array element *Id*[*Student*] refers to the identification number of that student. With this understanding, you can now address the inputting phase.

Using the array name *Id*, it would indeed be convenient if the data for this problem could be read with the pseudocode instruction

```
FOR Student := 1 TO NumberOfStudents DO
    READ Id[Student]
```

Unfortunately, you do not know the value of *NumberOfStudents* because, as was mentioned in the original problem statement, the length of the list is unknown. You will therefore need a different strategy. That is, in order to read the entire list, you will want to repeat the statement

```
READ Id[Student]
```

an unknown number of times. Thus you should think of using a WHILE loop instead of a FOR loop (see Section 5.6). Specifically, you might try the instruction

```
WHILE <there are more identification numbers
        on the list> DO
      READ Id[Student]
```

Recalling that a WHILE loop does not have a loop-counter variable, it is necessary for you to change the value of the subscripting variable *Student* within the body of the loop. Thus you should include the statement

```
Student := Student + 1
```

within the body of the loop; but should this statement come before or after the READ statement? With appropriate care, either approach can be used. Here, the former will be adopted, leading to

```
WHILE <there are more identification numbers
        on the list> DO
      Student := Student + 1
      READ Id[Student]
```

Now, through the refinement process, you must replace the English expression in angle brackets with an appropriate boolean expression. So, how will the computer know if "there are more identification numbers in the list"? That is, how will the computer know where the end of the list is? One solution is to use the end-of-file marker (together with the Pascal variable EOF). A second solution is to count the number of students in the list, and to supply that information to the computer as data *before* the list of numbers is read. Here, a third solution will be used. Specifically, a "special" number (that cannot possibly be taken as an identification number) will be placed at the very end of the data. Then, when that special number is read, you can instruct the computer to stop reading student-identification numbers, because the list is over.

With regard to choosing this special number, the primary concern is that the number be distinguishable from all other identification numbers in the list. For example, since all student-identification numbers are positive, the special number could be any negative number, say −9999. Using this special number, the WHILE loop above becomes

```
WHILE Id[Student] ≠ -9999 DO
      Student := Student + 1
      READ Id[Student]
```

Finally, recall that the variables whose values are used in the first iteration of the loop must be initialized prior to performing the loop.

In this case, those variables are *Student* and *Id*[*Student*]. The former should be initialized to 1, and thus *Id*[1] must also be initialized (by reading the first value on the list). The data will be echo printed after all the student-identification numbers have been read by calling the procedure *DisplayIds*. In any event, the procedure declaration for *ReadIds* in pseudocode is

```
PROCEDURE ReadIds
    Student := 1
    READ Id[1]
    WHILE Id[Student] ≠ -9999 DO
            Student := Student + 1
            READ Id[Student]
```

Note that *Student* should be a local variable because its value is used only in this procedure. In contrast, *Id* should be a global array because its values will be used outside of this procedure.

Declaring the Array. Normally, in the context of using pseudocode, there would be no need to worry at this time about the issue of declaring the array. Nonetheless, to illustrate a problem that often arises when declaring an array, that topic will be discussed here briefly.

Recall that, in order to declare the above array, you would have to identify the following three components: (1) the array name (in this case, *Id*); (2) the type of the array (in this case, integer, because all values, i.e., student-identification numbers, will be integers); and (3) the allowable range for the subscript (in this case, 1 to an undetermined number, and here is where the problem lies). Indeed, the problem is that you must declare the array *before* you know how many elements there will be in the array. Thus you do not know the largest possible value of the subscript, which you *must* specify in the array declaration. What should you do?

The solution is that for the upper limit on the array subscript you should use a number that is the largest possible number of student-identification numbers that could ever be encountered. How many is that? Perhaps you should ask the supervisor, Mary Martin, for she is the person who gave you the problem in the first place.

As you learned in Section 6.1, it is not possible for a subscript to be outside the allowable range specified in the array declaration. However, it is always possible for the computer to have elements of an array that are not used in the program. Thus if you do not know the precise number of elements that will be in an array, always declare the array to have enough elements to handle the largest possible case, provided, of course, that in so doing, you do not exceed the available memory capacity of the computer.

Declaring the Procedure *DisplayIds*. The list of student identification numbers (i.e., the values of the array *Id*) will have to be displayed twice—once to echo print the data (see Step 2), and once to display the list after it has been sorted (see Step 4). In order to display the values of the array *Id*, it would be convenient to use the following FOR loop:

```
FOR Student := 1 TO ??? DO
     WRITE Id[Student]
```

The question marks must now be replaced by the exact length of the list. During the inputting phase described above, the length of the list was not known. However, *after* reading the entire list, you will know the exact length. Specifically, in the procedure *ReadIds* above, the value of the local variable *Student* was increased by 1 each time a new number on the list was read. Thus at the end of the procedure *ReadIds*, the length of the list will be stored in the variable *Student*. Unfortunately, the variable *Student* is a local variable, and so its value cannot be used outside of the procedure *ReadIds*. Can you resolve this problem?

One possible solution is to create a new global variable, say *NumberOfStudent*, whose value is to be the number of students in the list. Then the assignment statement

```
NumberOfStudents := Student
```

should be placed at the very end of the procedure *ReadIds*, because it is the very last value of *Student* that represents the number of students in the list. In so doing, you can now use the (global) variable *NumberOfStudents* in the procedure *DisplayIds*. Specifically, the procedure *DisplayIds* is

```
PROCEDURE DisplayIds
     FOR Student := 1 TO NumberOfStudents DO
          WRITE Id[Student]
```

Observe that here, *Student* is a local variable that is different from the local variable *Student* used in the procedure *ReadIds*, even though both variables have the same name. On the other hand, *NumberOfStudents* and *Id* were chosen to be global variables so that their values could be used outside of the individual procedures.

Declaring the Procedure *SortIds*. All that remains is to specify the instructions that constitute the procedure *SortIds* in Step 3. To do so, recall the solution recommended by Mary Martin:

> Look down the list. Whenever you find two consecutive numbers that are not in the proper sequence, interchange the position of those two numbers. Continue these operations as long as necessary until you can no longer find two numbers that are out of sequence.

Since you want to "continue these operations as long as necessary," you should realize immediately that some form of loop structure is going to be used. Your next task is to think through the solution offered by the above instructions, which you can accomplish by working through a specific example. For instance, do so for the specific list: 10, 14, 8, 12, 11. In following the above instructions, you will see that 10 and 14 are in the correct order. However, you will want to interchange the two consecutive numbers 14 and 8 since they are out of order. The result is the new list: 10, 8, 14, 12, 11. From here, you might wonder which numbers should be interchanged next: 10 and 8, 14 and 12, or 12 and 11. When solving this problem by hand, it obviously does not matter which of these pairs of consecutive numbers are interchanged next; however, in order to develop a computer program, a *systematic* method, using a specific rule, must be developed. Hence, one might conceive of the following possible rules:

Rule 1: After interchanging two numbers, go back to the beginning of the list and start over again looking for two consecutive numbers that are not in order. (For the example above, this rule means that 10 and 8 would be interchanged next.)

Rule 2: After interchanging two numbers, continue looking down the list from the current point onward. When you reach the bottom of the list, start again at the top. (For the example above, this rule means that 14 and 12 would be interchanged next.)

The specific algorithm you develop will depend entirely on which rule you select. Other rules are, of course, possible. However, some rules might be easier to program, while other rules might require less "work" for the computer. These concerns will be addressed in greater detail in Section 6.3.

For illustration purposes, the second rule given above will be used here. Applying that rule to the original list, the following sequence of interchanges would be produced (the column immediately to the right of a set of arrows indicates the new list obtained by interchanging those numbers with arrows):

Column	**1**	**2**	**3**	**4**	**5**	**6**
	10	10	10	↗10↘	8	8
	↗14↘	8	8	↖8↙	10	10
	↖8↙	↗14↘	12	12	↗12↘	11
	12	↖12↙	↗14↘	11	↖11↙	12
	11	11	↖11↙	14	14	14

Note that in columns 1, 4, and 6, you begin looking down the list from the top. In columns 2, 3, and 5, you continue looking down the list from where you left off (in the previous column).

Refinement. The time has come to specify the body of the procedure *SortIds*. To that end, the original processing instructions will be written using a progressively more "limited" pseudocode. (This is the refinement process.) Thus as a first step, the original English instructions might be rewritten as

```
<Look down the entire list of numbers>
IF <two consecutive numbers are out of order>
    THEN
      <Interchange the position of those two
      numbers>
<Repeat all of the above instructions until
 you can no longer find two consecutive numbers
 that are out of order>
```

Recall that, because of Rule 2 above, after finding two numbers to interchange, you should continue looking down the list from where you left off. With this in mind, each of the above concepts in angle brackets (< >) will be expressed in a pseudocode that is more closely related to Pascal.

To begin refining the first instruction

```
<Look down the entire list of numbers>
```

recall that the list of numbers was stored into the array *Id* during the inputting phase. Therefore, in order to "look down the entire list," you must instruct the computer to look at each element in the array *Id*. This task can be accomplished by using the FOR-loop statement

```
FOR Student := 1 TO NumberOfStudents DO ...
```

Thus for each specific value of `Student` the computer can be made to "look" at the corresponding element in the list by referencing `Id [Student]` in the body of the loop, as will be illustrated during the refinement of the next English instruction

```
IF <two consecutive numbers are out of order>
     THEN ...
```

The English statement in angle brackets must be replaced with a pseudocode boolean expression that has the same meaning. In order to instruct the computer to check whether two consecutive numbers are out of order, you can use the loop-counter variable `Student` as a subscripting variable for the array `Id`. So, for a specific value of `Student`, two consecutive numbers in the list are `Id[Student]` and `Id[Student + 1]`. Thus to check whether `Id[Student]` and `Id[Student + 1]` are "out of order," you must check whether `Id[Student] > Id[Student + 1]`. Consequently, the desired expression becomes

```
IF Id[Student] > Id[Student + 1] THEN ...
```

In the event that these two consecutive numbers are out of order (i.e., `Id[Student] > Id[Student + 1]`), then you must instruct the computer to

```
<Interchange the position of these two
  numbers>
```

In essence, you want the value of `Id[Student]` to become that of `Id[Student + 1]`, and vice versa. To accomplish the task, recall from Chapter 2 that you will need yet another variable, say `Temp`, to store the original value of `Id[Student]` temporarily. Thus the correct assignment statements are

```
Temp := Id[Student]
Id[Student] := Id[Student + 1]
Id[Student + 1] := Temp
```

Putting together the entire `FOR`-loop statement that has been developed, you have

```
FOR Student := 1 TO NumberOfStudents DO
     IF Id[Student] > Id[Student + 1] THEN
         Temp := Id[Student]
         Id[Student] := Id[Student + 1]
         Id[Student + 1] := Temp
```

After the computer interchanges the position of *Id[Student]* and *Id[Student + 1]*, the next iteration of the FOR loop will be performed. Thus the value of *Student* will be increased by 1, the body of the loop will be executed again, and the computer will continue looking down the list from this point onward. The FOR loop continues through the value of *Student* = *NumberOfStudents*.

Finally, you must apply refinement to the last instruction:

```
<Repeat all of the above instructions until
 you can no longer find two consecutive numbers
 out of order>
```

You must first realize that "all of the above instructions" refers to the entire FOR loop. Then you should recognize that the desire to "repeat" will manifest itself in the form of another loop. Finally, because you do not know beforehand how many times to perform the repetition, a WHILE loop is needed. Thus you are led to the instructions

```
WHILE <the list is not ordered> DO
      FOR Student := 1 TO NumberOfStudents DO
          IF Id[Student] > Id[Student + 1] THEN
             Temp := Id[Student]
             Id[Student] := Id[Student + 1]
             Id[Student + 1] := Temp
```

All that remains is to replace the above English statement

"the list is not ordered"

with an appropriate boolean expression in pseudocode. After some thought, you might discover that writing the appropriate boolean expression is not as easy as it first seemed. The reason is that the desired expression is quite complicated and lengthy. For example, you might have tried to write

```
WHILE NOT(Id[1] ≤ Id[2] ≤ ...
           ≤ Id[NumberOfStudents]) DO ...
```

The problem is that the three dots will have to be replaced with the entire list of array elements when the algorithm is coded into Pascal.

To overcome this difficulty, you could, for example, replace this long boolean expression with a single boolean variable, say *NotOrdered*, whose value will be TRUE if the list is not ordered, and FALSE if the list is ordered. Thus the WHILE statement becomes

```
WHILE NotOrdered DO ...
```

You should note, however, that the value for *NotOrdered* must be computed both prior to entering the WHILE loop as well as within the body of the WHILE loop, as will now be illustrated.

Initializing the Value of *NotOrdered*. Prior to performing the WHILE loop, the value of *NotOrdered* must be properly initialized. You could do so in one of two ways. For example, you could attempt to look down the list (immediately after reading those values), and compute the value of *NotOrdered* accordingly. A second (and more simple) alternative is to initialize the value of *NotOrdered* to TRUE so that the body of the WHILE loop is performed the first time. Thus, prior to the WHILE loop, the statement

```
NotOrdered := TRUE
```

should be incorporated.

Computing the Value of *NotOrdered* within the Body of the Loop. As a result of initialization, upon entering the WHILE-loop statement the value of *NotOrdered* is TRUE. Consequently, the body of the WHILE loop will be performed, i.e., the FOR loop will be executed. However, before performing the *next* iteration of the WHILE loop, the new value of *NotOrdered* must be computed. Thus you should ask yourself how you will know if the list is ordered or not after you have performed the FOR loop.

In fact, the list will be ordered if the FOR loop is completed without ever interchanging two of the numbers, i.e., if the condition *Id*[*Student*] > *Id*[*Student* + 1] is never true as the computer processes the list of numbers with the FOR loop.

The issue now is how to incorporate the above answer into the algorithm because, unfortunately, there is no single pseudocode instruction that will accomplish this task. Instead, you must somehow compute the value of *NotOrdered* so that if, in fact, the condition *Id*[*Student*] > *Id*[*Student* + 1] is never true during the FOR loop, the value of *NotOrdered* is FALSE; otherwise, the value of *NotOrdered* should be TRUE. Doing so requires some creativity.

One approach is to set the value of *NotOrdered* to FALSE as the first instruction in the body of the WHILE loop, just prior to performing the FOR loop. In so doing, you are assuming (prior to performing the FOR loop) that the list is ordered. However, as you perform the FOR loop, if you discover that your assumption was incorrect and that the list was in fact not ordered, then at that time you can change the value of `NotOrdered` to `TRUE`. Indeed, when performing the `FOR` loop, you will be able to tell if the list is not ordered when the condition in the `IF/THEN` statement (i.e., `Id[Student] > Id[Student + 1]`) is true. If so, then the action following the word `THEN` will be performed, and you should set the value of `NotOrdered` to `TRUE` at that time.

In view of the above discussion, the entire `WHILE` loop becomes

```
WHILE NotOrdered DO
        NotOrdered := FALSE
        FOR Student := 1 TO NumberOfStudents DO
              IF Id[Student] > Id[Student + 1] THEN
                  Temp := Id[Student]
                  Id[Student] := Id[Student + 1]
                  Id[Student + 1] := Temp
                  NotOrdered := TRUE
```

Putting together the three procedures and the main program, the pseudocode algorithm becomes

```
PROCEDURE ReadIds
    Student := 1
    READ Id[1]
    WHILE Id[Student] ≠ -9999 DO
            Student := Student + 1
            READ Id[Student]
    NumberOfStudents := Student

PROCEDURE DisplayIds
    FOR Student := 1 TO NumberOfStudents DO
         WRITE Id[Student]

PROCEDURE SortIds
    NotOrdered := TRUE
    WHILE NotOrdered DO
            NotOrdered := FALSE
            FOR Student := 1 TO NumberOfStudents
                 DO
                 IF Id[Student] > Id[Student + 1]
                     THEN
                     Temp := Id[Student]
                     Id[Student] := Id[Student + 1]
                     Id[Student + 1] := Temp
                     NotOrdered := TRUE
```

{The above portion of the algorithm consists of the three procedure declarations; the main program begins here.}

```
ReadIds
DisplayIds
SortIds
DisplayIds
```

In the next section, this algorithm will be traced and debugged.

Exercises for Section 6.2

Modify or rewrite the procedure *SortIds* of this section so as to sort the list of identity numbers according to the following instructions.

1. Instead of the variable *NotOrdered*, use a variable *Ordered*, whose value is TRUE if the list is ordered, and FALSE otherwise.
2. After interchanging two numbers in the list, go back to the top of the list to search for two consecutive numbers that are not in sequence; do not continue looking down the list from where you left off. (*Hint:* Replace the first FOR loop with an appropriate WHILE loop in which you control the value of *Student*.)

Write pseudocode algorithms to perform the following tasks. Use an array only where necessary and explain the meaning of the subscript and of the corresponding value of the array element. Be sure to think through your solution by working through a specific example.

3. The National Testing Service has just given an examination to *N* students. The company has asked you to perform some computations on the list of scores. Specifically, they want you to compute and to display
   a) The average score (i.e., the sum of all the scores divided by *N*).
   b) The number of points by which each score differs from the average.
   c) The variance of the scores (to do so, square the difference of each score from the average, add all of the resulting numbers, and divide the total thus obtained by $N - 1$).
4. Gary Gambler has been recording the results of a roulette wheel in which a ball can fall into a hole whose number is between 0 and 36, and also 00. Given *M* different integers between 0 and 37 (37 corresponds to 00), each of which represents one result of the roulette wheel, report the number of times the ball fell into each of the following categories: 0, 1 to 6, 7 to 12, 13 to 18, 19 to 24, 25 to 30, 31 to 36, or 00. (*Hint:* Create a variable, say *Group*, whose value is 0, 1, ..., 7 depending on which of the eight ranges the actual result belongs to. Use assignment statements, if possible, to compute the value of *Group*. Then use *Group* as the subscript of an array.)
5. You will be given a "code" that associates with each integer between 1 and 27 a unique letter of the alphabet, or the blank space. In addition, you will be given a coded English message that consists of a list of inte-

gers obtained by replacing each letter of the message with its corresponding integer in the code. Read the list of integers in the coded message, and display the associated English text. For example, if the given code associates the integer 3 to "a", 5 to "b", and 13 to "c", then the coded message 13, 3, 5 should be displayed as the word "cab." (You will recognize the end of the coded message when you encounter the integer 28.)

6.3 Tracing and Debugging

As a general rule, you should trace your program before running it on the computer. However, doing so for the program of the previous section can be quite time consuming due to the complex loop structures. Therefore why not let the computer help in this tracing process? To do so, you can include several additional `WRITE` statements in the program. Those new `WRITE` statements should be placed judiciously so as to provide enough useful information so that, if an error occurs, you will then be able to locate the error and to trace the program by hand. They should also be placed so as to avoid displaying so much information that you would be unable to follow the output. Of course, the specific choice is up to you. The pseudocode algorithm of the previous section is displayed below once again. This time, however, several new `WRITE` statements have been added.

```
PROCEDURE ReadIds
   Student := 1
   READ Id[1]
   WHILE Id[Student] ≠ -9999 DO
         Student := Student + 1
         READ Id[Student]
   NumberOfStudents := Student

PROCEDURE DisplayIds
   FOR Student := 1 TO NumberOfStudents DO
       WRITE Id[Student]

PROCEDURE SortIds
   NotOrdered := TRUE
   WHILE NotOrdered DO
         NotOrdered := FALSE
         FOR Student := 1 TO NumberOfStudents DO
             IF Id[Student] > Id[Student + 1] THEN
             Temp := Id[Student]
             Id[Student] := Id[Student + 1]
```

```
                Id[Student + 1] := Temp
                NotOrdered := TRUE
          IF Debug THEN    {This statement is new.}
             DisplayIds
{The procedure declarations are given above; the main program begins here.}
   Debug := TRUE
   ReadIds
   IF Debug THEN    {This statement is new.}
      WRITE NumberOfStudents
   DisplayIds
   SortIds
   DisplayIds
```

Notice that the boolean variable *Debug* has been used with each new WRITE statement. At the beginning of the program, you simply set the value of *Debug* to TRUE if you want the new WRITE statements to display information, and FALSE otherwise. In this way, when the debugging process is completed, you need not remove all of these statements. Rather, you need only set the value of *Debug* to FALSE.

Now suppose that the above main program is run with the five student-identification numbers of Section 6.2, so the input file is

10 14 8 12 11 −9999■

Assuming that the array *Id* was declared in such a way that the value of the subscripting variable could be an integer between 1 and 5 (because there are five student-identification numbers in the above list), the computer would provide the following results:

```
***Error—subscript out of range for array Id
```

Locating the Error

Your first step is to locate the cause of the error. Looking at the main program, did this error occur during the call to the procedure *ReadIds*, *DisplayIds*, or *SortIds*? To answer the question, you should scan the main program and the output to see which WRITE statements have and have not been performed. Evidently, since no output has been displayed by the computer, the new statement in the main program

```
   IF Debug THEN
      WRITE NumberOfStudents
```

has not been performed. Thus the error must have occurred prior to this statement, i.e., during the call to the procedure *ReadIds*, for otherwise you would have seen some displayed output corresponding to the above WRITE statement.

Now you should trace the WHILE loop in the procedure *ReadIds* to locate the cause of the error. In so doing, you will discover that when the value of *Student* is 5, the body of the WHILE loop will still be performed because *Id*[5] is not equal to −9999. The first instruction in the body of the loop will then increase the value of *Student* to 6. Subsequently, when the computer attempts to perform the statement

```
READ Id[Student]
```

an error will occur because the computer cannot read *Id*[6]. The reason for this is that the value of the subscripting variable was only allowed to go up to 5 in the declaration of the array.

Correcting the Error

The problem is caused by the fact that while there are only five numbers in the list, one additional position in the array is needed to store the number −9999. One solution to this problem is to change the declaration of the array, thus allowing the subscripting variable to have a value between 1 and 6. Suppose that this alteration has been made.

Running the Program Again

On rerunning the program with the same data, the following results would be displayed:

```
    6   (= NumberOfStudents)
   10   (= Id[1])
   14   (= Id[2])
    8   (= Id[3])
   12   (= Id[4])
   11   (= Id[5])
-9999   (= Id[6])
***Error—subscript out of range for array Id
```

Locating the Error Again

Once again, you can use the WRITE statements in the program, together with the computer output, to find the approximate location of the error. Looking at the main program, this time you can be sure that the call to the procedure *ReadIds* has been completed because the statement

```
IF Debug THEN
   WRITE NumberOfStudent
```

has been performed. So has the first call to the procedure *DisplayIds*. However, the second call to that procedure in the main program has not been performed. Thus the error must have occurred when calling the procedure *SortIds*. Indeed, on examining that procedure, you can see that the call to the procedure *DisplayIds* in the body of the WHILE loop at the very end of the procedure has not been performed. Evidently, then, this subscripting error occurred during the first iteration of the WHILE loop in the procedure *SortIds*.

To identify the exact location of the error, trace the body of the WHILE loop. The first instruction of that loop is to set the value of *NotOrdered* to FALSE, after which, the body of the FOR loop will be executed six times (because the value of *NumberOfStudents* is 6). By tracing the FOR loop, you will discover a problem when the value of the loop-counter variable *Student* is 6. Specifically, when you evaluate the condition in the statement

```
IF Id[Student] > Id[Student + 1] THEN ...
```

you will discover an error because, when the value of *Student* is 6, you must verify if *Id*[6] > *Id*[7], and this will not be possible because *Id*[7] does not exist. It is no wonder that the subscript (namely, 7) is out of range.

Correcting the Error Again

The problem above is caused by the fact that the data value −9999, which is not a student-identification number, is being read and stored by the procedure *ReadIds* in the array element *Id*[6]. At the same time, the value of *NumberOfStudents* is being computed as 6, instead of 5. Thus the FOR loop in the procedure *SortIds* is being performed one too many times, resulting in the subscripting error. If you have understood this discussion, then you should realize that in order to correct the error this time, you should *not* increase the size of the array *Id*. Rather, you should replace the statement

```
NumberOfStudents := Student
```

with

```
NumberOfStudents := Student - 1
```

in the procedure *ReadIds*.

Returning to the FOR loop in the procedure *SortIds*, careful tracing will show that even after this correction you do not want the value of the loop-counter variable *Student* to go from 1 to *NumberOfStudents*, but rather from 1 to *NumberOfStudents* − 1. The reason for this is that when the value of *Student* is equal to *NumberOfStudents* (i.e., 5 in this case), you will be comparing *Id*[5] to *Id*[6]. You should not do so because the value of *Id*[6] is −9999 and, again, that number is not really part of the list. The corrected FOR statement should be

```
FOR Student := 1 TO NumberOfStudents - 1 DO ...
```

Check that this statement is indeed correct. In fact, the program should now be rerun and, on so doing, the desired solution consisting of the sorted list would be obtained.

The next step would be to code the algorithm into Pascal, and to test the program with various different sets of data. When you are satisfied that the program is working properly, do not forget to set the value of *Debug* to FALSE at the beginning of the program so as to prevent the WRITE statements that were inserted for debugging purposes from displaying information when the program is used by someone else.

On Computational Efficiency

Until now, your sole concern has been to develop a correct and working program for solving a given problem. Imagine, for the moment, that you have mastered the art. Good computer programmers not only solve problems correctly, but they also try to do so with programs that are as efficient as possible. Thus you must eventually concern yourself with the issue of what constitutes an efficient program. For instance, in the corrected procedure *SortIds* above, the body of the FOR loop will always be performed (*NumberOfStudents* − 1) times. However, the same results can be obtained by doing fewer repetitions. To see how, you might notice that, when the entire FOR-loop statement is completed for the first time, the largest number in the list will have moved to the bottom position (try an example to see for yourself). As a result, when the whole FOR-loop statement is performed for the second time, the last number in the list need not be compared (because that last number is the largest one and will never be moved again). Indeed, after performing the entire FOR-loop statement for the second time, the second largest number will be located just above the largest number. In the exercises below, you will be asked to rewrite the program so as to take advantage of this observation by reducing the number of times the body of the FOR loop has to be performed each time.

In Sections 6.2 and 6.3 you have seen how to use an array in problem solving. You have also learned of the care that must be taken in order to avoid the error that arises when the value of an array subscript is outside the allowable range. In Section 6.4 you will learn about arrays that have more than one subscripting variable.

Exercises for Section 6.3

Rewrite the final program of this section so as to incorporate each of the changes given in the following instructions. Trace the new programs using the data of this section.

1. Rewrite the procedure *ReadIds* so that the number −9999 is not stored in the array *Id*. (You will not know, or be given, the length of the list.)
2. Recall that, after the entire FOR-loop statement is completed for the first time, the largest number in the list will be located in the last position. Using this fact, rewrite the procedure *SortIds* in such a way that (a) the WHILE loop is replaced with a FOR loop, and (b) the body of the original FOR loop is performed fewer times. (*Hint:* Replace the WHILE loop with a FOR loop in which the value of the loop-counter variable *J* represents the process of locating and moving the *J*th largest number to the bottom of the list. Use the value of *J* to alter the upper limit for *Student* in the original FOR loop.)
3. Explain what error would occur (and why), had the procedure *SortIds* been

```
NotOrdered := TRUE
WHILE NotOrdered DO
        NotOrdered := FALSE
        FOR Student := 1 TO NumberOfStudents - 1
             DO
             IF Id[Student] > Id[Student + 1] THEN
                 Temp := Id[Student]
                 Id[Student] := Id[Student + 1]
                 Id[Student + 1] := Temp
             NotOrdered := TRUE     {This statement is
                                     different from the
                                     previous one.}
```

For each of the following algorithms that you wrote in Section 6.2 (see page 283), check (by tracing) the first and last iteration of all loops. Be especially careful to watch for subscripting errors.

4. The algorithm for Exercise 3.
5. The algorithm for Exercise 4.
6. The algorithm for Exercise 5.

6.4 Multidimensional Arrays

Multidimensional array An array in which each element can be referenced by more than one subscript.

So far, you have learned that an array can be a useful way of storing and manipulating a list of information. Sometimes, however, the data for a problem is given as a rectangular table of information, or in some other special form. A **multidimensional array** can often be used to store and manipulate such information conveniently, as you will learn in this section.

What Is a Multidimensional Array?

Imagine that you are a teacher with a small class of five students, and that each student has taken three examinations. The results for each student are

	Exam 1	Exam 2	Exam 3
Student 1	75	80	83
Student 2	88	85	84
Student 3	57	62	75
Student 4	92	83	90
Student 5	84	77	88

Suppose that you want to read and to store this information in the computer. One approach is to use 15 different variables for these 15 values. By now, however, you know that there is a better way. That is, you could create an array, say `Score`, that has 15 elements. One problem with doing so, however, is that when you work with `Score[7]`, for example, you would not easily know to which student and to which exam `Score[7]` refers. To overcome this difficulty, a multidimensional array can be used.

As with the previous concept of an array, a multidimensional array also consists of a single array name, say `Score`, for all of the data. Previously, you learned to use a single subscript to distinguish one variable from the next. With a multidimensional array, you will use more than one subscript to reference each individual variable. For the example above, two subscripts will be used together with an array name to create a *two-dimensional array*, sometimes called a *matrix*, meaning that two subscripts are to be used in conjunction with the array name. Such an array should be pictured in your mind as a rectangular table of information. The first subscript always refers to a row number; the second subscript always refers to a column number.

As before, each subscript, as well as the corresponding array element consisting of the array name together with the subscripts, will have a physical interpretation and meaning in the context of the specific problem that you should learn to identify. To illustrate how you do so for the example above, observe that the collection of test scores consists of five rows of students and three columns of exams. The value of the first subscript will refer to a specific student number; the second subscript will refer to an exam number. For example, when working with the variable `Score[4, 3]` (which is read as "`Score` sub 4 comma 3," or simply, "`Score` sub 4 3"), the first subscript, 4, refers to the *fourth* student; the second subscript, 3, refers to the *third* exam. Finally, the value of the entire variable `Score[4, 3]` is the *score* of the fourth student on the third exam. You should note that, as before, the subscripts are separated from the array name by enclosing the former in brackets. Moreover, the subscripts themselves are separated from each other by commas.

Just as with simple arrays, each subscript of a multidimensional array can be any one of the following: (1) an integer constant (e.g., `Score[2, 3]`); (2) an integer variable (e.g., `Score[1, Exam]` or `Score[Student, Exam]`); or (3) an integer expression (e.g., `Score[2 * Student - 3, Exam + 1]`).

Using the Subscripts of a Multidimensional Array

You must learn to use the subscripts of a multidimensional array correctly. For instance, suppose that you want to read the 15 values for `Score` corresponding to the test results above from the input file:

```
75    80    83■
88    85    84■
57    62    75■
92    83    90■
84    77    88■
□
```

Recalling the concept of repetition from Chapter 5, you might specify these pseudocode instructions for entering the data:

```
FOR <each of the five rows> DO
    READ <the three numbers in that row and
          store the results in the
          corresponding array elements>
```

Using a loop-counter variable, say *Student*, the FOR loop becomes:

```
FOR Student := 1 TO 5 DO
    READ <the three exam scores for that
          student and store the results in the
          corresponding array elements>
```

Looking at the READ statement above, for a fixed value of the variable *Student*, the "corresponding array elements" are *Score*[*Student*, 1], *Score*[*Student*, 2], and *Score*[*Student*, 3], respectively. Thus the correct statements are

```
FOR Student := 1 TO 5 DO
    READ Score[Student, 1], Score[Student, 2],
        Score[Student, 3]
```

In fact, looking carefully at the READ statement above, you might again notice that repetition is involved, since you want to repeat the process of reading each of the three exam scores for a particular student. Using another loop-counter variable, say *Exam*, you can write the above instructions as

```
FOR Student := 1 TO 5 DO
    FOR Exam := 1 TO 3 DO
        READ Score[Student, Exam]
```

For each value of *Student* (corresponding to a row number) the *Exam*-loop will read the three scores for that student and store those values into *Score*[*Student*, 1], *Score*[*Student*, 2], and *Score*[*Student*, 3], respectively. This operation is repeated five times—once for each value of *Student*.

Look now at the input file as given above. It is important to realize that the following pseudocode instructions would *not* assign the 15 values to the appropriate array elements:

```
FOR <each of the three columns> DO
    READ <the five numbers in that column and
          store the results in the
          corresponding array elements>
```

The reason is that, while a human can read down a column of an input file, a computer reads only from left to right across a row. Therefore the pseudocode instructions

```
FOR Exam := 1 TO 3 DO
    FOR Student := 1 TO 5 DO
        READ Score[Student, Exam]
```

would not assign the values in the input file to the proper array elements. Be sure to trace these statements to see which values of the input file are assigned to which array elements.

As is often the case, processing of arrays is done with FOR (or WHILE) loops—generally one loop for each subscript. The key is to learn how to use the loop-counter variables to create appropriate subscript expressions for the array. Here, then, are some examples of how to use the subscripts of a multidimensional array. These first pseudocode instructions compute and display the sums of each row of the array *Score*.

Example

```
FOR Student := 1 TO 5 DO
    Sum := Score[Student, 1] +
           Score[Student, 2] + Score[Student, 3]
    WRITE Student, Sum
```

Equivalently, using a second FOR loop (and a corresponding loop-counter variable), you can perform the desired addition with these instructions:

```
FOR Student := 1 TO 5 DO
    Sum := 0
    FOR Exam := 1 TO 3 DO
        Sum := Sum + Score[Student, Exam]
    WRITE Student, Sum
```

As another example of using subscripts, suppose that *J* is a variable whose value represents one of the exams. Thus the value of *J* might be 1, 2, or 3. Similarly, suppose that *K* is a second such variable. The following instructions could be used to interchange columns *J* and *K* of the array *Score*.

Example

```
FOR Student := 1 TO 5 DO
    Temp := Score[Student, J]
```

```
Score[Student, J] := Score [Student, K]
Score[Student, K] := Temp
```

Higher Dimensional Arrays

It is possible (and often useful) to create arrays with more than two subscripts. For example, suppose that you had a number of customers, and that each customer has been paying you an amount of money each month from January 1980 to December 1984. To store the various amounts paid by each customer, you could, for instance, use a *three-dimensional array*, say `Payment`. The first subscript of the array `Payment` might refer to the number of the customer; the second subscript might refer to the month of the payment; and the third subscript would refer to the year of the payment. Thus the value of the variable

```
Payment[25, 11, 1982]
```

would correspond to the amount of money paid by customer number 25 in month 11 of year 1982.

Declaring Multidimensional Arrays. As with one-dimensional arrays, multidimensional arrays must be created in the declaration section of a program when you code the algorithm into Pascal. At that time, you will have to provide the computer with (1) the array name, (2) the type of the array (recall that all elements of an array must contain the same type of value, e.g., integer, character, real, etc.), and (3) the allowable range (i.e., the first and last possible values) for each subscript. For example:

Declaration	Meaning
`Cost[1..100, 1..100]`	Each subscript must be between 1 and 100.
`Payment[0..50, 1..12, 1980..1984]`	The first subscript must be between 0 and 50, the second subscript must be between 1 and 12, and the third subscript must be between 1980 and 1984.

As with simple arrays, in the event that the value of any subscript is either less than the smallest allowable value or greater than the largest allowable value, a run-time error will occur. In this case, either you have made a logic error, or else you must change the allowable range of the subscripting variable in the array declaration.

How to Save Computer Storage

When declaring multidimensional arrays, the number of individual elements thus created might be larger than the memory capacity of the computer. For instance, the declaration

```
Customer[1..100, 1..100, 1..100]
```

has created an array with 100 × 100 × 100 = 1,000,000 elements, which requires more storage space than many computers have available. In this event, a syntax error will occur. In the the remainder of this section, you are presented with several methods for economizing on the storage requirements of a program.

Multiple Use of an Array. It sometimes happens that a program requires two (or more) arrays of the same type and the same number of dimensions. If, by fortunate circumstances, the second array is needed only after the first array is completely processed, then it is possible to use a single array for both purposes. Thus you need only declare one array instead of two, and so the computer will create only enough variables for that one array.

In so doing, however, remember that when you use the array for the second task, the array will still contain values that were used during the first task. All of these old values should be changed accordingly, prior to or during the second task.

Overlaying. Sometimes, with very large arrays, it is possible to perform the desired computations by working sequentially with smaller portions of the array, until all of the data are processed. If this is possible, then you could read and store part of the data into a smaller array, process that information, and then read the next portion of the data and store that information into the *same* array. The old values in the array are thus *overlaid* (i.e., replaced) with the new values. When overlaying, it is often possible to store the old values of the array on a disk or tape for later use so those values are not lost.

Packing the Information. Normally, one piece of information (corresponding to the value of an element of an array) is stored in each memory location of the computer. However, when the values in the array are integers or characters, it is possible to store more than one such value in a single memory location. The details for doing so in Pascal will be described in Section 6.6. For now, you should note that the act of squeezing as much information into a memory location as possible is called *packing the information*.

When an array is stored in packed form, the computer will automatically be able to select and to retrieve the correct value from the memory location when you use the subscript of the array. However, because several values are stored in the same memory location, extra time will be needed for the computer to determine and to retrieve the desired value. Thus when working with packed information you are gaining storage space at the expense of computer time.

In this section, you have learned about the concept of a multidimensional array. Once the array has been declared properly, you can then use each element of the array as a variable. In so doing, you must learn how to use the subscripts effectively. The process of using a multidimensional array in problem solving will be demonstrated in Section 6.5.

Exercises for Section 6.4

For each of the following word problems, determine which arrays you would need in order to solve the problem. (You need not actually solve the problem). Explain, in English, the physical meaning of each subscript, and of the corresponding array element; then prepare declaration statements that include (1) the array name, (2) the type of the array, and (3) the range of allowable values for each subscript. (Use the fewest number of arrays, and make them as small as possible.)

1. Given a tic-tac-toe board with Xs, Os, and blank spaces, determine if there is a tic-tac-toe or not.
2. Each of 52 states has kept a total of the number of votes cast for each of three different parties during each year from 1960 through 1980. Determine the percentage of total votes cast for each party in each year.
3. For (at most) 100 cities, you will be given the cost of going from each city to each other city. Once you have entered that data, you will also be given a list of an unknown number of "tours." Each tour consists of a sequence of (at most) 100 integers, each of which represents a city in that tour. You will want to compute the total cost of going from the first city in each tour to the last city in the tour; and then select the tour with the smallest total cost.
4. The score for each of the two balls in each of (at most) 12 frames of a bowling game have been recorded for four players. For later processing purposes, determine, for each frame of each player, whether the total score in that frame constitutes a "spare" or not. A spare occurs in a frame if the total of the two balls in the frame is 10 and the second ball is not 0.

5. You will be given as data the entire text of a 320-page book (80 characters per line, 32 lines per page). Given a list of key words (each containing at most 20 characters), search the text for each key word, reporting the page and line number of the first occurrence of the word. You do not know how many key words there will be.

Replace each of the following question marks with an appropriate subscript expression that would accomplish the given word instructions.

6. Given a two-dimensional array *First* with *M* rows and *N* columns, create a two-dimensional array *Second* with *N* rows and *M* columns in which each row *I* of *First* becomes column *I* of *Second*.

```
FOR Row:= 1 TO N DO
    FOR Column := 1 TO M DO
        Second[?, ?] := First[?, ?]
```

7. Suppose that *Ascii* is a two-dimensional array whose values are the ASCII characters as given in Appendix D. Also, the *M* rows of the two-dimensional arrays *LeftDigit* and *RightDigit* each contain *N* integers corresponding to the *N* left and right digits of some ASCII characters. Display these *M* sequences of *N* characters.

```
FOR Row := 1 TO M DO
    FOR Column := 1 TO N DO
        WRITE Ascii[LeftDigit[?, ?], ?]
```

8. Given a two-dimensional array *Numbers* with *N* rows and *N* columns, the (2*N* + 2) elements of the one-dimensional array *Total* should contain in order the sum of each row, then the sum of each column, and finally the sum of the two diagonals of *Numbers*. (Be sure that each of the 2*N* + 2 values are stored in different elements of the array *Total*.)

```
{This portion computes the row sums.}
FOR Row := 1 TO N DO
    Sum := 0
    FOR Column := 1 TO N DO
        Sum := Sum + Numbers[?, ?]
    Total[?] := Sum
{This portion computes the column sums.}
FOR Column := 1 TO N DO
    Sum := 0
    FOR Row := 1 TO N DO
        Sum := Sum + Numbers[?, ?]
    Total[?] := Sum
{This portion computes the two diagonal sums.}
Sum1 := 0
Sum2 := 0
FOR I := 1 TO N DO
    Sum1 := Sum1 + Numbers[?, ?]
    Sum2 := Sum2 + Numbers[?, ?]
```

```
Total[?] := Sum1
Total[?] := Sum2
```

For each of the following word instructions, prepare pseudocode statements to accomplish the given task. You need not be concerned with declarations or inputting. However, trace your statements for the first and last values of all loop-counter variables to be sure that all array subscripts are within the proper range.

9. Each card of a deck is represented by an integer from 1 to 52. Four players have been dealt 13 cards each, and the value of the variable `Card[I, J]` of the two-dimensional array `Card` is card *J* belonging to player *I* (the value of *I* is between 1 and 4, and that of *J* is between 1 and 13). Construct a one-dimensional array `Deck` in which the value of `Deck[K]` is the number of the player holding the card whose number is *K* (the value of *K* is between 1 and 52).
10. Given the three-dimensional array `Book` of *P* pages, *L* lines per page, and *C* characters per line, and given a one-dimensional array `Ch` of *N* characters, report the page, line, and column of each occurrence of each of the *N* characters.
11. Perform the instructions in Exercise 4 above, storing the results in the appropriate array whose name is `Spare`.

6.5 Using Multidimensional Arrays in Problem Solving

In this section, you will see how to use multidimensional arrays in solving a particular problem. Suppose that you are part of a programming team that is developing a program to play the game of chess. A chess board consists of 64 squares arranged in 8 rows, each of which contains 8 columns. On various squares of this board you will find certain pieces—some white and some black. After applying top-down programming to this complex problem, the leader of the programming team has identified two procedures for you to write. Here then is your problem.

Problem: Given a list of pieces together with their colors and location on the board, write a procedure called `ReadBoard` to read and to store the current board position in appropriate two-dimensional arrays. Then, write a procedure called `DisplayBoard` to display the board with all of the pieces, their colors, and their position on the board.

The data for each piece will consist of one letter, "B" or "W," to indicate the color of the piece; one letter to indicate the type of piece, e.g.,"Q" to represent the piece known as the queen; and two integers that represent the row and column of the square on which the piece is located. Also, each line of the input file will contain the data corresponding to one, and only one, piece.

Analysis of Data Structures

Before specifying the details of the procedures *ReadBoard* and *DisplayBoard*, you should understand how and in what form you will store the data. Since a chess board consists of a rectangular table of information, it seems reasonable to create a two-dimensional array whose name is *Piece* and whose values are the pieces on the chess board. The value of *Piece*[2, 5], for example, is the piece that is located on the square in row 2 and column 5 of the chess board. In other words, when working with the variable *Piece*[*Row*, *Column*], the first subscript refers to the row number of the chess board; the second subscript refers to the column number. Finally, the value of the array element *Piece*[*Row*, *Column*] is the character corresponding to the piece that is on the associated square of the board. But, what if there is no piece on that square? In this case, the value of *Piece*[*Row*, *Column*] will be set to a blank space.

In view of this discussion, when the array *Piece* is declared, you would have to provide the computer with (1) the array name—in this case, *Piece*; (2) the type of information stored in each element of the array—in this case, character (because each array element will contain a character corresponding to the piece on that square); and (3) the allowable range for each of the two subscripts—in this case, 1 to 8 (corresponding to the eight rows and columns).

In addition, you must also read and store the color of each piece. Thus, you will need yet another two-dimensional array, say *Color*. The value of *Color*[*Row*, *Column*] will be the character ('B' or 'W') representing the color of the piece located on the associated square. Once again, if there is no piece on that square, then the value of *Color*[*Row*, *Column*] should be set to a blank space.

Declaring the Procedure *ReadBoard*

Now it is time to develop the details that constitute the procedure *ReadBoard*. Without giving the issue too much thought, you might provide the following solution.

Solution: I read the data for each piece on the board and store that information in the appropriate array elements.

Now, think through your solution by working through a specific example. If you have done so, then you should be able to identify the following repetition, which constitutes the procedure `ReadBoard`:

Step 1: Read the data for one piece.

Step 2: Store the data in the appropriate array elements.

Step 3: Repeat these two steps so long as there are pieces to be read.

Since, for each chess piece, there are four data values (the piece's color, name, row, and column), four variables are needed to enter these four values. With regard to the piece's color and name, you might be tempted to read those values into the appropriate elements of the arrays `Piece` and `Color`, respectively. However, in order to do so, when writing the `READ` statement, you would have to specify the correct subscripts for these two arrays (i.e., the row and column number of the piece that is being read). Unfortunately, according to the order in which the data values are given for each piece, you will not know the row and column until *after* you have read the piece's color and name. Consequently, you will need two new variables, say `PieceColor` and `PieceName`, to store those given data values temporarily. After you have read the corresponding row and column number of the piece into the variables `Row` and `Column`, say, you will then be able to store the value of `PieceColor` and `PieceName` into the appropriate array elements. Thus in order to accomplish Step 1 above you are led to the pseudocode instruction

```
READ PieceColor, PieceName, Row, Column
```

The next step (Step 2), is to store the color and name of the piece into the appropriate elements of the arrays `Color` and `Piece`, respectively. Indeed, the values of `Row` and `Column` that were just read can now be used as subscripts for these arrays to specify the "appropriate" array elements. Thus the desired assignment statements are

```
Piece[Row, Column] := PieceName
Color[Row, Column] := PieceColor
```

Finally, Step 3 indicates that a `WHILE` loop should be used to perform the repetition because you do not know how many pieces will be given to you in the data. Thus in pseudocode you might write

```
WHILE <there is more data> DO ...
```

However, you will need to refine this solution to take into account the fact that you cannot count the number of pieces beforehand. Assuming that no "special" data will be included at the end of the input file to signal the last piece of data (as was done with the list of student-identification numbers in the problem of Section 6.2), the only alternative is to use the end-of-file variable, `EOF` (see Section 3.2). In so doing, the procedure declaration would appear to be

```
PROCEDURE ReadBoard
    WHILE NOT EOF DO
            READ PieceName, PieceColor, Row, Column
            Piece[Row, Column] := PieceName
            Color[Row, Column] := PieceColor
```

Declaring the Procedure *DisplayBoard*

In order to declare the procedure *DisplayBoard*, which is your final task according to the stated problem, all that needs to be done is to display the values of the 64 elements in each of the arrays *Piece* and *Color*. Since both of these arrays contain eight rows and eight columns, you can use the following `FOR` loops to accomplish the task:

```
PROCEDURE DisplayBoard
    FOR Row := 1 TO 8 DO
        FOR Column := 1 TO 8 DO
            WRITE Color[Row, Column], Piece[Row,
                  Column]
```

Careful attention to detail will be required when coding these instructions in Pascal to make sure that the results are displayed in a readable manner that is consistent with the way a chess board actually looks. You will see how to do so in Section 6.6.

Debugging

In order to test the two procedures above, you will need to write a main program that calls each of these procedures. To help trace the flow of the program, it is advisable to put an additional `WRITE` statement after the call to the procedure *ReadBoard* but before the call to the procedure *DisplayBoard*. Thus the main program might consist of

```
ReadBoard
WRITE 'The data has been read'
DisplayBoard
```

If you were now to run this program with the following data (in which the "K" represents the piece known as a "king"):

B K 1 7
W K 8 2

you would obtain the following results from the computer:

```
The data has been read
*** A variable has not been assigned a value
```

Locating the Error

Looking at the main program and at the output, evidently the procedure *ReadBoard* has been completed, and the subsequent `WRITE` statement has been performed. Consequently the error must be in the procedure *DisplayBoard*. Tracing the `FOR` loops when the values of the variables *Row* and *Column* are both 1, you should encounter the error, for where has the variable `Piece[1, 1]` been assigned a value? If you think that the answer is in *ReadBoard*, look at that procedure again, and trace it with the given data. You will see that nowhere was `Piece[1, 1]` assigned a value.

Correcting the Error

The problem is that the instructions in *ReadBoard* assign values only to those elements of the array *Piece* (and *Color*) that have pieces on the squares corresponding to the list of given data values. To correct the error, all remaining values of the elements of *Piece* and *Color* should be set to a blank space, i.e., ' '. However, how will you know which squares do (and do not) have pieces on them?

One simple approach to resolving this problem is to initialize *all* of the elements of *Piece* and *Color* to ' ' *before* the data values are read. For example:

```
FOR Row := 1 TO 8 DO
    FOR Column := 1 TO 8 DO
        Piece[Row, Column] := ' '
        Color[Row, Column] := ' '
```

Then when the data are read, the values of the appropriate elements in *Piece* and *Color* corresponding to the given pieces will be changed; however, all other elements of those arrays will have the value ' ' as they should.

The final and correct procedure declarations in pseudocode are

```
PROCEDURE ReadBoard
   FOR Row := 1 TO 8 DO
       FOR Column := 1 TO 8 DO
           Piece[Row, Column] := ' '
           Color[Row, Column] := ' '
       WHILE NOT EOF DO
             READ PieceColor, PieceName, Row, Column
             Piece[Row, Column] := PieceName
             Color[Row, Column] := PieceColor

PROCEDURE DisplayBoard
   FOR Row := 1 TO 8 DO
       FOR Column := 1 TO 8 DO
           WRITE Color[Row, Column], Piece[Row,
                 Column]
```

In this section you have learned to use multidimensional arrays in problem solving. In Section 6.6, you will learn how to code and how to declare arrays in Pascal.

Exercises for Section 6.5

Prepare complete pseudocode algorithms to perform each of the following tasks. Use the technique of top-down programming. Also, be sure to think through your solution. Include appropriate data-verification statements.

1. Given a tic-tac-toe board with Xs, Os, and blank spaces, determine if there is a tic-tac-toe or not, and indicate the appropriate row, column, or diagonal.
2. A board for playing the game of checkers consists of 64 squares arranged in eight rows of eight squares each. Pieces, whose color is either black or red, are located on certain squares. You will be given the number of pieces, and a list of those pieces and their respective positions on the board. The data for each such piece consists of one letter ("B" or "R") to indicate the color of the piece, and two integers that represent the row and column of the square on which the piece is located, respectively.

   A red piece can conceivably capture and remove a black piece that is diagonally one square in front of the red piece. (By "front" is meant that the row number of the black piece is one less than that of the red piece.) To capture the black piece, the red piece moves over the black piece (in the diagonal direction) landing on the square diagonally in front of the black piece, provided that that square is on the board and has no piece on it; otherwise, the red piece cannot capture the black piece.

   For the very last piece in the data list (which will be a red piece), display the board that would be obtained after the given red piece captures one (and only one) black piece in each of the two possible directions, or indicate that the red piece cannot capture a black piece at all.

3. Write a program to score a bowling game. Specifically, you will be given the individual scores of each of two balls for each of 12 frames. (The sum of the scores of the two balls in a given frame should never exceed 10.) The total score in a particular frame is then obtained by adding the scores of the individual balls in that frame. However, if the score of the first ball of that frame is 10 (called a strike), then the total score for the current frame is 10 plus the score of the two balls in the next frame (unless those two scores are 10 and 0, respectively, in which case you also add the score of the first ball in the following frame). Finally, if the score of the first ball in a frame is not 10, but the sum of the scores of the two balls is 10 (called a spare), then the score of that frame is 10 plus the score of the first ball in the next frame. Obtain, for each of the first ten frames, the total cumulative score of all frames up to and including that frame.

6.6 Coding Arrays

In this section you will learn how to use an array in Pascal. As usual, you will learn the details of Pascal syntax, including how to declare an array. In addition, you will see that Pascal allows great flexibility in forming the subscript expression.

Types of Array Subscripts in Pascal

Up to this point, you have seen examples of array subscripts that are integer constants, integer variables, or integer expressions. In Pascal, however, a subscript can be any type of expression, except real.

Example

The subscript of the following one-dimensional array is a character:

```
Letter['a']
```

Example

The first subscript of the following three-dimensional array is an integer value, the second is a boolean value, and the third is a character value:

```
Worker[3, TRUE, 'b']
```

Example

The following subscript of the array *Time* is in error because a subscript cannot be a real number:

```
Time[1 / 3]
```

The flexibility of being able to use a subscript other than an integer can be very useful. For example, imagine that you want to count the number of times the letter "e" occurs in a book. If the value of the variable *CurrentLetter* is the letter in the text that you are currently looking at, then in Pascal the following statement is valid (provided, of course, that the array *Letter* has been declared properly):

```
IF CurrentLetter := 'e' THEN
    Letter['e'] := Letter['e'] + 1
```

In this example, the subscript of the array *Letter* is the character 'e', but the value of the element *Letter['e']* is an integer (representing the number of times the letter "e" has been encountered).

Declaring One-Dimensional Arrays

When you wish to use an array in solving a problem, you must create the array. In Pascal, you do so in the variable-declaration section. Recall that in so doing you must provide the computer with the name of the array, the allowable range of values for the subscript, and the type of values to be stored in each element of the array. The syntax for accomplishing this task with a VAR declaration for a one-dimensional array is

```
VAR
    ArrayName :ARRAY[Range] OF ArrayType;
```

The words ARRAY and OF are reserved words in Pascal that you should not use as variable names.

Range. You must replace the Range above with the allowable range of values for the subscript. The following examples are valid for Range:

`-1..9` {The subscript must be an integer expression whose value is between −1 and 9. The array will contain 10 elements.}

`'a'..'z'` {The subscript must be a character between 'a' and 'z', i.e., a character whose corresponding integer in the collating sequence is between that of 'a' and 'z'. The array will contain

26 elements if your computer uses the ASCII collating sequence (see Appendix D).}

`CHAR` {The subscript must be a character expression whose value is any valid character on your computer. The number of elements in the array will vary, depending on the number of characters available on your computer.}

`BOOLEAN` {The subscript must be a boolean expression whose value is either `TRUE` or `FALSE`. The array will contain two elements.}

You should note that it is incorrect to use 1..*N* for the Range, unless *N* has been defined previously as a constant in a `CONST` declaration. In other words, the declaration 1..Variable is not allowed. If you do not know exactly how many elements will be in the array, then declare the array to have more elements than you will ever use, but less than the available memory capacity of the computer.

ArrayType. You must replace the ArrayType in the declaration above with the type of values that will be stored in each element of the array. Any of the following are valid for ArrayType: `INTEGER`, `REAL`, `CHAR`, `BOOLEAN`.

The following are examples of one-dimensional array declarations. In the first example, the subscript of the array *Prices* must be an integer between 0 and 100; each element of the array will contain a real value.

Example

```
VAR
    Prices :ARRAY[0..100] OF REAL;
```

In the next example, the subscript of the array *Paragraph* must be an integer between 1 and 500; each element of the array will contain a character value.

Example

```
VAR
    TextArray :ARRAY[1..500] OF CHAR;
```

In the next example, the subscript of the array *Symbol* must be a valid character on your computer; each element of the array will contain an integer value.

Example

```
VAR
    Symbol :ARRAY[CHAR] OF INTEGER;
```

The TYPE Declaration

When you want to create many arrays of the same type and that have the same subscript range you can either list the array names, separated by commas, in the VAR declaration or you can use a TYPE declaration in conjunction with a VAR declaration, as you will now learn.

With the TYPE declaration, you will associate a name (of your choosing) to the collection of *all* arrays of a specific type that have the same subscript range. The Pascal syntax for doing so is

```
TYPE
    TypeName = ARRAY[Range] OF ArrayType;
```

You must replace the TypeName with the name you choose to associate with the collection of all those arrays. For example, if you were going to create several arrays containing real values in which the allowable subscript range was to be between 1 and 50, you could use the following TYPE declaration to associate the name *ManyArrays* with the collection of all such arrays:

```
TYPE
    ManyArrays = ARRAY[1..50] OF REAL;
```

When using the TYPE declaration, you should realize that you have not yet created any specific array variables. Rather, you have given a name to the collection of all such arrays that will be used in your program. Consequently, if you then wish to create specific arrays, you would use the following VAR declaration in which the following TypeName refers to the same TypeName you used in the TYPE declaration:

```
VAR
    ArrayName, ArrayName, ..., ArrayName
    :TypeName;
```

For example, to create three arrays, say *First*, *Second*, and *Third*, whose elements will contain real values and whose subscript will be an integer between 1 and 50, you would follow the TYPE declaration above with the following VAR declaration:

```
VAR
    First, Second, Third :ManyArrays;
```

As was stated in Section 3.1, all TYPE declarations should immediately follow the CONST declarations and precede the VAR declarations.

You might very well ask why you need the TYPE declaration. You will learn the answer to this question in Chapters 7 and 8. The TYPE and VAR declarations will be used from now on when declaring arrays to accustom you to that process.

Declaring Multidimensional and Packed Arrays

The syntax for declaring a multidimensional array is the same as that of a one-dimensional array except that you must supply a range for each subscript. Thus using the TYPE and VAR declarations, the syntax is

```
TYPE
    TypeName  =  ARRAY[Range, ..., Range] OF
                 ArrayType;
VAR
    ArrayName :TypeName;
```

These declarations are illustrated in the following examples. The first example shows how to declare a two-dimensional array in which each subscript is an integer between 1 and 100, and each element of the array will contain a real value.

Example

```
TYPE
    RealArrays  =  ARRAY[1..100, 1..100] OF REAL;
VAR
    Cost :RealArrays;
```

The next example is the declaration for a two-dimensional array in which the first subscript is an integer between 1 and 4, and the second subscript is any valid character. Each element of the array will contain a boolean value (TRUE or FALSE).

Example

```
TYPE
    BooleanArray  =  ARRAY[1..4, CHAR] OF BOOLEAN;
```

```
VAR
    Book :BooleanArray;
```

Although there is no limit to the number of subscripts that an array can have in Pascal, you must be careful that the total number of elements in the array does not exceed the storage capacity of the computer. If you wish to save storage space, Pascal allows you to use packed arrays (see Section 6.4). The syntax for declaring a multidimensional packed array with a TYPE declaration is

```
TYPE
    TypeName = PACKED ARRAY[Range, ..., Range] OF
               ArrayType;
```

Some Complete Examples

The (corrected) algorithms that were developed in Sections 6.2 and 6.5 will now be coded in Pascal. These examples contain a program heading, a declaration section (including CONST, TYPE, and VAR declarations), as well as an executable section. In addition, you will notice the use of semicolons, BEGIN and END, and other details pertaining to Pascal syntax.

Example

Example from Section 6.2:

```
PROGRAM SortStudents(INPUT, OUTPUT);
    {This program reads a list of student-identification numbers in which the last
    number is -9999. After displaying the data, that list is sorted into
    increasing order, and the new sorted list is displayed.}
CONST
    Max = 500;      {Assume at most 500 students.}
TYPE
    Lists = ARRAY[1..Max] OF INTEGER;
VAR
    NumberOfStudents  :INTEGER;
    Id                :Lists;

PROCEDURE ReadIds;
    {This procedure reads the given list of student-identification numbers and
    stores those values in the global array Id. At the same time, this procedure
    computes the total number of students on this list and stores that value into
    the global variable NumberOfStudents.}
```

```
    VAR
       Student  :INTEGER;       {Declare a local variable.}
    BEGIN
       Student  := 1;
       {Observe that the next two WRITELN statements are not in the
       body of the loop.}
       WRITELN('Enter the list of student identity numbers');
       WRITELN('followed by the number -9999');
       READ(Id[1]);
       WHILE Id[Student] <> -9999 DO
             BEGIN
               Student := Student + 1;
               READ(Id[Student])
             END;    {End of WHILE loop.}
       NumberOfStudents := Student - 1
    END;    {End of procedure ReadIds.}

PROCEDURE DisplayIds;
    {This procedure displays the list of student-identification numbers contained
    in the global array Id, whose subscripting variable can be between 1 and
    NumberOfStudents, which is a global variable.}
    VAR
       Student  :INTEGER;       {Declare a local variable.}
    BEGIN
       WRITELN('The list of student identity numbers is:');
       FOR Student := 1 TO NumberOfStudents DO
            WRITELN('Student', Student:4, ' has an ',
                    'identity number of', Id[Student]:7)
    END;    {End of procedure DisplayIds.}

PROCEDURE SortIds;
    {This procedure will sort the global array Id into ascending order. The
    algorithm will continually look down the list of identification numbers,
    interchanging two consecutive values that are not in sequence. The resulting
    sorted list will be stored back into the global array Id.}
    VAR
       Student, Temp  :INTEGER; {Declare local variables.}
       NotOrdered     :BOOLEAN;

    BEGIN
       NotOrdered := TRUE;
       WHILE NotOrdered DO
             BEGIN
               NotOrdered := FALSE;
               {See if two consecutive elements are out of order.}
```

```
            FOR Student := 1 TO
                NumberOfStudents - 1 DO
                IF Id[Student] > Id[Student + 1] THEN
                    BEGIN
                        {Switch those two elements.}
                        Temp := Id[Student];
                        Id[Student] := Id[Student + 1];
                        Id[Student + 1] := Temp;
                        NotOrdered := TRUE
                    END  {End of IF/THEN.}
          END  {End of WHILE loop.}
    END;  {End of procedure SortIds.}
{The main program begins here.}
BEGIN
    ReadIds;
    DisplayIds;
    SortIds;
    WRITELN('The list has now been sorted');
    DisplayIds
END.  {End of program.}
```

Example

Example from Section 6.5:

```
PROGRAM ChessBoard(INPUT, OUTPUT);
    {This program reads the location, name, and color of a number of chess
    pieces, and displays the resulting board in the form of an 8-by-8 rectangular
    table.}
TYPE
    Boards = ARRAY[1..8, 1..8] OF CHAR;
VAR
    Color, Piece :Boards;

PROCEDURE ReadBoard;
    {This procedure sets all values of the global arrays Color and Piece to
    a blank space. Then a list of the locations, names, and colors of various
    pieces are read and stored in the appropriate elements of the arrays.}
    VAR
        Row, Column              :INTEGER;   {Declare local
                                              variables.}
        PieceName, PieceColor :CHAR;
    BEGIN
```

```
    FOR Row := 1 TO 8 DO
        FOR Column := 1 TO 8 DO
            BEGIN
                Piece[Row, Column] := ' ';
                Color[Row, Column] := ' '
          END;     {End of FOR loops.}
    WRITELN('For each piece, enter one character');
    WRITELN('for its color, one character for its');
    WRITELN('name, and two integers to represent');
    WRITELN('the row and column of the square.');
    WRITELN('Then press return and enter the data');
    WRITELN('for the next piece.');
    WRITELN('When done, type an end-of-file marker.');
    WHILE NOT EOF DO
          BEGIN
              READLN(PieceColor, PieceName, Row, Column);
              Piece[Row, Column] := PieceName;
              Color[Row, Column] := PieceColor
          END     {End of WHILE loop.}
  END;     {End of procedure ReadBoard.}

PROCEDURE DisplayBoard;
  {This procedure displays the 8-by-8 chess board together with the color and name of each
  piece displayed on the appropriate square of the board. Those data are stored in the global arrays
  Piece and Color.}
  VAR
     Row, Column :INTEGER;     {Declare local variables.}
  BEGIN
     WRITELN('The current chess board is:');
     WRITE(' ':5);
     FOR Column := 1 TO 8 DO
         WRITE(Column:5);
     WRITELN;
     FOR Row := 1 TO 8 DO
         BEGIN
           WRITELN;
           WRITE(Row:5);
           FOR Column := 1 TO 8 DO
               WRITE(Color[Row, Column]:4,
                     Piece[Row, Column]:1);
           WRITELN; WRITELN
         END     {End of FOR loop.}
  END;     {End of procedure DisplayBoard.}
```

```
{The main program begins here.}
BEGIN
   ReadBoard;
   DisplayBoard
END.     {End of program.}
```

In this chapter you have learned how to use and how to code arrays. In Chapter 7 you will learn an extension of the concept of procedures that provides greater programming flexibility.

Exercises for Section 6.6

Code, run, and debug each of the following algorithms that you wrote in Section 6.2 (see page 283). Use the given sets of data values.

1. The algorithm for Exercise 3.

a) Number of students: 5
   Test scores: 680, 550, 497, 575, 660

b) Number of students: 7
   Test scores: 83, 79, 85, 93, 98, 82, 75

c) Number of students: 10
   Test scores: 5, 9, 14, 3, 10, 8, 8, 7, 12, 10

2. The algorithm for Exercise 4.

a) Number of spins: 4
   Results of the spins: 30, 37, 4, 38

b) Number of spins: 8
   Results of the spins: 13, 25, 0, 31, 11, 19, 1, 7

c) Number of spins: 10
   Results of the spins: 6, 12, 18, 0, 24, 37, 36, 3, 19, 11

3. The algorithm for Exercise 5.

a)

Integers:	1	2	3	4	5	6	7	8	9	10	11	12	13	14	15	16	17	18	19	20
Letters:	c	d	z	x		b	g	m	p	q	e	i	k	l	a	w	r	f	h	t

Integers:	21	22	23	24	25	26	27
Letters:	y	u	s	j	n	v	o

Message: 20, 19, 12, 23, 5, 9, 17, 27, 7, 17, 15, 8, 5, 16, 27, 17, 13, 23

b)

Integers:	1	2	3	4	5	6	7	8	9	10	11	12	13	14	15	16	17	18	19	20
Letters:	p	e	r	x	m	w	i	b	o		n	f	j	l	s	a	y	z	c	q

Integers:	21	22	23	24	25	26	27
Letters:	d	u	t	h	k	g	v

Message: 17, 9, 22, 10, 16, 3, 2, 10, 5, 17, 10,
12, 3, 7, 2, 11, 21

c)

Integers:	1	2	3	4	5	6	7	8	9	10	11	12	13	14	15	16	17	18	19	20
Letters:	q	b	s		e	r	x	n	c	o	h	j	a	i	t	z	p	d	y	v

Integers:	21	22	23	24	25	26	27
Letters:	l	w	f	m	g	k	u

Message: 15, 11, 14, 3, 4, 14, 3, 4, 15, 11, 5, 4,
21, 13, 3, 15, 4, 24, 5, 3, 3, 13, 25, 5

Code, run, and debug each of the algorithms you wrote in Section 6.5 (see page 303). Use the given set of data values.

4. The algorithm for Exercise 1.

a)

X		O
O	X	
O	X	O

b)

O		X
O	X	O
X	O	

c)

O	O	O
X	X	X
O	X	X

5. The algorithm for Exercise 2.

a) Number of pieces: 2
The pieces: B 3 5
R 4 8

b) Number of pieces: 3
The pieces: B 2 5
B 6 4
R 3 6

c) Number of pieces: 4
The pieces: B 2 1
B 2 3
R 6 6
R 3 2

6. The algorithm for Exercise 3.

a)

Frame:	1	2	3	4	5	6	7	8	9	10	11	12
Ball 1:	4	3	4	0	3	7	8	2	3	5	0	0
Ball 2:	2	3	5	2	4	1	0	0	5	4	0	0

b)

Frame:	1	2	3	4	5	6	7	8	9	10	11	12
Ball 1:	3	6	8	10	3	2	5	6	10	8	5	0
Ball 2:	5	4	1	0	6	8	4	2	0	2	3	0

c)

Frame:	1	2	3	4	5	6	7	8	9	10	11	12
Ball 1:	3	8	9	10	10	10	6	9	10	10	7	0
Ball 2:	6	2	1	0	0	0	3	1	0	0	2	0

6.7 Summary

In this chapter you learned that an array is a useful method for storing and processing data. The idea is to create many variables by using one common variable name (the array name) together with one or more subscripts so as to distinguish one variable from another. Each individual variable of the array is called an element, and the number of subscripts is referred to as the dimension of the array.

When creating or using an array, learn to give a physical meaning and interpretation to the subscripting variable. Be sure to distinguish the meaning of the subscript from the value that will be stored in the corresponding element of the array.

Before using an array in a program, you must declare that array to the computer by supplying the computer with the array name, the allowable range for each subscript, and the type of the array. In Pascal, when you do not know the last value for the allowable range of a subscript, a variable is not permitted. Thus, for example, for the one-dimensional array *List*, you cannot declare the subscript range to be from 1 to *N*. Instead, you must provide a specific integer constant (instead of *N*) whose value is larger than you will actually need.

When using arrays, the following issues will arise. First, if a subscript is not within the allowable range as specified in the declaration, a run-time error will occur. Therefore great care should be taken to keep the array subscripts within the bounds specified in the declaration. Second, if the type of value that is being stored into an array element does not agree with the array type as specified in the declaration statement, a syntax error will occur. Finally, if an array requires more storage locations than are available on the computer, then, again, a syntax error will occur. When this problem arises, you might consider the following possible solutions: multiple use of an array (i.e., using one array for more than one purpose); overlaying (i.e., breaking the array into smaller portions, and then working with each portion individually); or packing the information so that you can store more than one piece of information in each memory location of the computer.

Key Terms

Array 262
Array name 262
Array subscript 262
Element of an array 262
Multidimensional array 290

While writing an article on hang-gliding, pilot and engineer Paul McCready became fascinated with the flying abilities of large, soaring birds. McCready and his team quickly devised the *Gossamer Condor*—an unconventional aircraft with a wingspan of nearly 100 feet, supported by an intricate web of wire bracing and powered by pedaling. Aviation history was made in August 1977 when the *Condor* captured the coveted Kremer Prize of £50,000, offered for the first human-powered flight around a figure-eight course. (THE SMITHSONIAN INSTITUTION)

7

PROCEDURES (WITH PARAMETERS) AND FUNCTIONS

In Section 5.1, you saw that a procedure could be used to perform the same set of instructions at various places in a program without having to write those instructions each time. In this chapter, you will learn several ways to provide added programming flexibility to the original concept of procedures.

7.1 Procedures with Parameters

Parameter A programming concept used with a procedure, which enables the computer to perform a group of instructions using different values and/or variables each time the procedure is called. There are two major types of parameters: *actual parameters* and *dummy parameters*.

In Section 5.1, you learned that one way to pass information to and from a procedure is by using a global variable. A **parameter** is a second and more powerful method for accomplishing the same goal, as you will now see. To illustrate the concept of parameters, consider the following instructions for finding the largest value in an array *A* having *N* elements:

```
Max := A[1]
FOR I := 2 TO N DO
    IF A[I] > Max THEN
        Max := A[I]
```

Imagine that, in a particular program, you need to find the largest value not only of the array *A*, but also of the arrays *B*, *C*, and *D* at various places in the program. You could, of course, accomplish the task by rewriting the above instructions, each time replacing the array *A* with *B*, *C*, or *D* whenever appropriate. However, a procedure with parameters can be used to simplify this task by allowing you to write the above instructions only once. Therefore consider how you would write the corresponding procedure declaration in pseudocode. For instance, you might write

```
PROCEDURE FindMax
    Max = ?[1]
    FOR I := 2 TO N DO
        IF ?[I] > Max THEN
            Max := ?[I]
```

The issue is how to make the question mark represent a different array at different points in time. For instance, when you need to find the largest value of the array *A*, the question mark should be replaced everywhere by the symbol *A*; when you need to find the largest value of the array *B*, the question mark should be replaced everywhere by the symbol *B*. In other words, you would like to have the flexibility of changing the question mark to different symbols each time the procedure is called. The concept of a parameter allows you to do precisely that.

You inform the computer that the question mark is going to be replaced with different symbols at different times when you declare the procedure. Specifically, in the pseudocode declaration of the procedure, you first replace the question mark everywhere by any name you choose. That name is called the *parameter* of the procedure, and should be different from all other names used in the procedure declaration. Then, you must put the parameter name you just chose, enclosed in parentheses, immediately after the procedure name (*FindMax*, in the example above).

Example

Replacing the question mark in the above procedure declaration with the parameter *ArrayName*, the new pseudocode declaration becomes

```
PROCEDURE FindMax(ArrayName)
    Max := ArrayName[1]
    FOR I := 2 TO N DO
          IF ArrayName[I] > Max THEN
              Max := ArrayName[I]
```

In the above example, you could have used any name in place of *ArrayName* except *FindMax*, *Max*, *I*, and *N*. Also, the fact that the parameter appears in parentheses next to the procedure name tells the computer that this particular name can be changed when the procedure is called. How you do so will be explained momentarily.

Multiple Parameters

Recall that the above procedure declaration was designed to enable you to find the largest element in the arrays *A* and *B*, each of which has the same number of elements, namely, *N*. However, what would happen if *A* and *B* had a different number of elements? For example, what if *A* had *N* elements and *B* had *M* elements?

The FOR-loop statement in the body of the procedure

```
FOR I := 2 TO N DO
    IF ArrayName[I] > Max THEN
        Max := ArrayName[I]
```

would work perfectly when the parameter *ArrayName* is replaced by *A*. However, when *ArrayName* is replaced by *B*, you need the variable *N* to be replaced by *M*. To accomplish this goal, in place of *N* you should also use a parameter (whose name can change each time you call the procedure). Thus, using the name *ArraySize* for this parameter, the new procedure declaration in pseudocode becomes

```
PROCEDURE FindMax(ArrayName, ArraySize)
   Max := ArrayName[1]
   FOR I := 2 TO ArraySize DO
        IF ArrayName[I] > Max THEN
           Max := ArrayName[I]
```

As illustrated in the example above, a procedure can have more than one parameter, in which case you simply list the parameters, separated by commas and enclosed in parentheses, next to the procedure name. The order in which you list the parameters in the procedure declaration does not matter. Also, note that the parameters in the declaration of a procedure are neither local variables nor global variables. Rather, they are items whose specific names and values will be determined when the procedure is called.

Choosing Parameters

Careful consideration should be given to the issue of deciding what the parameters for a procedure should be. Recall that a procedure is often used when a sequence of instructions will be repeated several times in a program. To determine the parameters for a procedure, look carefully at the instructions that are to be repeated, and ask yourself which items (i.e., variables, arrays, etc.) change each time the instructions are to be performed. Generally, those items constitute the parameters, and they should be treated as such when writing the procedure declaration.

In Chapter 5, you learned that when working with a procedure, there is input information and output information. For the procedure *FindMax* above, the specific array whose maximum is sought and the number of elements in that array constitute the input information; the value of the largest element of that array constitutes the output information. In general, when identifying parameters, you should think of them as being input parameters or output parameters (although no formal distinction between these two is made in the pseudocode procedure declaration). An *input* parameter is one whose value will have to be supplied by the main program to the procedure. An *output* parameter is one whose value will be computed and stored by the procedure, and then returned to the main program. A parameter can also serve as both an input and an output parameter. In this case, the main program must provide a value for that [input] parameter. Then, when the procedure is called, the value of that same [output] parameter will be changed within the procedure and returned to the main program for further processing.

Identifying the input parameters to a procedure is similar to identifying the inputting phase of a main program. Likewise, identifying the output parameters to a procedure is similar to identifying the outputting phase of a main program. Perhaps the following problem will clarify how to identify the parameters of a procedure.

Problem: Given a list of the names of a number of people (denoted by the variable *NumberOfPeople*), together with their phone numbers, ZIP codes, and social security numbers, display the names of the people after sorting them first by phone number, then by ZIP code, and finally by social security number.

Identifying the Procedures and Their Parameters. The objective here is to show you how to identify the various procedures and the associated parameters that can be used to solve this problem. Therefore, to focus on those aspects, the specific instructions that constitute each procedure will not be developed here. Before identifying the procedures and their parameters, however, you should think about how the data for this problem will be stored.

The name of each person consists of a sequence of characters that could be stored in an array. However, since there are many different people, a two-dimensional array, say *Name*, should be used to store that information. Each row of the array will contain the characters in the name of one person. For example, the first two rows of the array might contain the following data:

(Column)	1	2	3	4	5	6	7	8	9	10	11
Row 1	T	o	m	m	y		S	m	i	t	h
Row 2	H	a	r	r	y		J	o	n	e	s

Since each phone number consists of a single integer, a one-dimensional array, say *PhoneNumber*, will be used to store the list of phone numbers for each person. The one-dimensional arrays *ZipCode* and *SocialSecurity* will contain similar information.

Now it is time to tackle the problem itself. By using top-down programming you might identify the following subproblems:

Read the data.
Sort the array *PhoneNumber*.
Display the names according to that ordering.
Sort the array *ZipCode*.
Display the names according to that ordering.
Sort the array *SocialSecurity*.
Display the names according to that ordering.

Evidently, you need to repeat the sorting and displaying of information three times. It is therefore reasonable to construct two procedures, say *Sort* and *Display*, for performing those tasks.

To determine the input and output parameters for the procedure *Sort*, begin by asking yourself which items vary each time you want to perform the sorting instructions. One item that will change each time is the specific array of information you wish to sort (e.g., *PhoneNumber*, *ZipCode*, etc.). Thus one input parameter to the procedure *Sort* should be the array to be sorted. That input parameter will be denoted by the name *List*, which will represent the list of phone numbers, ZIP Codes, and social security numbers.

A second possible parameter to the procedure *Sort* is the length of the list to be sorted. In this problem, the length is always the same, namely, the number of people, which is denoted by the global variable *NumberOfPeople*. Although you could use this global variable in the procedure, for readability purposes, it is better to create a second parameter (say, *ListLength*) to represent the length of the list to be sorted.

Well, so much for the input parameters, but what about the output parameters? What exactly is the output of the procedure *Sort*? At first glance, you might think that the output is the sorted list, which also could be stored in the parameter *List*. However, not only do you need to have the sorted list of phone numbers, but you also need to know which person corresponds to each phone number in the sorted list so that you can display their names in that order. Thus the output parameter of the procedure *Sort* is the *order* in which the names of the people should be displayed. But what form does that ordering take?

One way to represent the order is to have a one-dimensional array, say *Order*, having as many elements as the global variable *NumberOfPeople*, in which the value of *Order[1]* would be the row number of the array *Name* corresponding to the first person's name to be displayed, the value of `Order[2]` would be the row number of the array `Name` corresponding to the second person's name to be displayed, and so on. In view of this, the declaration for the procedure `Sort` in pseudocode would be

```
PROCEDURE Sort(List, Order, ListLength)
    {List is the input parameter that represents the array to be sorted;
    Order is the output parameter that represents the array containing the
    order in which the names will subsequently be displayed; ListLength
    is the input parameter that represents the length of these two arrays.}

    {In here would go the specific instructions for using the input values of
    List and ListLength to compute the output values of Order.}
```

Now, the input and output parameters of the procedure `Display` must be identified. To determine the input parameters, ask yourself, once again, which items change each time you wish to display information. Obviously, it is not the names of the individuals that change. Therefore that information can be passed to the procedure `Display` through the global array `Name` instead of as a parameter. What does change each time is the *order* in which the names are to be displayed. Thus the array `Order`, together with its length (i.e., `ListLength`), become the input parameters to the procedure `Display`.

You should note that the array `Order` is an *output* parameter of the procedure `Sort` and, at the same time, that array is an *input* parameter to the procedure `Display`. The reason is that the values of the array `Order` will be computed and stored by the procedure `Sort`, whereas the values of the array `Order` must be supplied to the procedure `Display`.

Finally, what are the output parameters for the procedure `Display`? It appears that no output parameters are necessary because this procedure will actually display the output. Thus the declaration for the procedure `Display` in pseudocode would be

```
PROCEDURE Display(Order, ListLength)
    {Order is the input parameter that represents the array containing the
    order in which the names will be displayed. The values for this parameter
    are computed by the procedure Sort.}

    {In here would go the specific instructions for displaying the names of the
    people according to the order specified in the parameter Order. Those
    names will be obtained from the global array Name.}
```

Although the same names, `Order` and `ListLength`, were used for the parameters of both the procedures `Sort` and `Display`, it was not necessary to do so. You could have used one set of names for the parameters in *Sort*, and a different set of names in *Display*.

Calling a Procedure with Parameters

After properly declaring a procedure and its associated parameters, you are finally in a position to be able to use that procedure. In Section 5.1, you learned to call a procedure by writing the name of that procedure in the main program whenever you wanted to perform those instructions. When a procedure has parameters, more care must be taken.

Recall that the reason for using parameters is to enable you to use different names for those parameters each time the procedure is called. For the example above, each time you call the procedure *Sort*, you will want the computer to replace the parameter *List* with the actual array to be sorted, i.e., *PhoneNumber*, *ZipCode*, and *SocialSecurity*. Thus each time you call the procedure from the main program, you must provide not only the name of the procedure (*Sort*, in this case), but also a list of the actual names of the variables (e.g., *PhoneNumber*) to be used in place of the parameter names (e.g., *List*). The actual names that are provided when calling the procedure are referred to as **actual parameters**. In contrast, the parameters in the procedure declaration are called **dummy** (or *formal*) **parameters**.

Actual parameters The specific names and/or values that are specified when a procedure is called. Those names and/or values will replace the corresponding parameters in the procedure declaration.

Dummy parameters The parameters that appear in the procedure declaration. Those parameters will be replaced by the actual parameters when the procedure is called.

In summary, to instruct the computer to replace the dummy parameters in the procedure declaration with the actual parameter names, and to perform the statements in the body of the procedure, you simply place those actual parameters, separated by commas, in parentheses following the procedure name. Thus to call a procedure from the main program in pseudocode, you would write

```
ProcedureName(ActualParameter, ...,
              ActualParameter)
```

It is possible for an actual parameter to have precisely the same name as the dummy parameter. In this event, be careful to distinguish, in your mind, the actual parameter (which is a global variable in the main program) from the dummy parameter in the procedure (which is simply a "place holder" that will be replaced with the name of the actual parameter when the procedure is called).

As an example of calling a procedure, recall from the beginning of this section the procedure declaration for finding the maximum of an array in which the dummy parameters are *ArrayName* and *ArraySize*:

```
PROCEDURE FindMax(ArrayName, ArraySize)
    Max := ArrayName[1]
    FOR I := 2 TO ArraySize DO
          IF ArrayName[I] > Max THEN
              Max := ArrayName[I]
```

Suppose that in the main program, you want to find the largest element of an array *A* of *N* elements. To do so, you would write

```
FindMax(A, N)
```

This would cause the computer to perform the instructions in the body of the procedure *FindMax*, using *A* in place of *ArrayName* and *N* in place of *ArraySize*. On completing the instructions in *FindMax*, the value of the largest element of the array would be stored in the global variable *Max*. In this example, *A* and *N* are the actual parameters.

If you subsequently want to find the largest value of an array *Cost* that has 200 elements, you would then write

```
FindMax(Cost, 200)
```

This would cause the computer to perform the instructions in the body of the procedure *FindMax* using *Cost* in place of *ArrayName* and 200 in place of *ArraySize*. On completing the instructions in *FindMax*, the largest value of the array *Cost* would be stored in the global variable *Max* (destroying any previous value of *Max*, if any). In this example, *Cost* and 200 were the actual parameters.

Notice that when a procedure is called, the actual parameters are listed in precisely the same order as the dummy parameters in the procedure declaration. For the example above, this means that, when calling the procedure *FindMax*, the array name should be listed first, followed by the number of elements in that array. Also, the type of each actual parameter must match precisely that of its corresponding dummy parameter. Thus it would not be acceptable to use a real variable as an actual parameter when its corresponding dummy parameter in the procedure declaration is supposed to be an integer.

Finally, recall the READ and WRITE statements. In reality, those statements are calls to procedures (that are already built in to the computer). The list of variables to be read or displayed is precisely the list of actual parameters to those procedures.

How Information Is Transferred to Parameters

When the computer encounters a call to a procedure in the main program, the computer first "matches up" the actual parameters to the dummy parameters according to the order in which those parameters are listed. This raises an important issue that you should be aware of.

Recall the analogy of the computer memory as being a large book in which each variable corresponds to a page number. Now, when the computer matches up the actual parameters with the dummy parameters, the computer can replace the dummy parameter with either the *name* of the actual parameter, i.e., the page number of the book corresponding to the actual parameter (from which the value of that variable can then be obtained), or directly with the *value* of the actual parameter. With regard to the dummy parameters, the former case is referred to as a **call-by-variable parameter**; the latter is referred to as a **call-by-value parameter**. There is a significant difference between these two types of dummy parameters, each with its inherent advantages and disadvantages, as will now be discussed.

Call-by-variable parameter A dummy parameter that will be replaced with the *name* of the corresponding actual parameter when the procedure is called.

Call-by-value parameter A dummy parameter that will be replaced with the *value* of the corresponding actual parameter when the procedure is called.

Call-by-Variable Parameters. To understand the concept of a call-by-variable parameter, suppose you have prepared the following procedure declaration:

```
PROCEDURE Change(X, Y)     {X and Y are the (real) dummy
                            parameters.}
    X := Y
```

Then, assuming that *X* and *Y* are call-by-variable parameters, a number of steps are performed when the computer encounters the following call to the procedure *Change* in the main program:

```
A := 1.0
B := 2.0
Change(A, B) {A and B are global real variables.}
WRITE 'A = ', A, ' B = ', B
```

First, the computer matches the actual parameters to the corresponding dummy parameters in the order listed. In this case, *A* is matched to *X* and *B* is matched to *Y*. Second, the computer replaces each dummy parameter with the corresponding *name* of the actual parameter everywhere in the procedure declaration. For this example, on replacing *X* by *A* and *Y* by *B* everywhere in the procedure declaration above, one obtains the "new" declaration

```
PROCEDURE Change(A, B)
    A := B
```

Then, all of the instructions in the new procedure declaration are performed. In this example, the above assignment statement is performed, and so the value of *A* is changed to that of *B*. Finally, when completed, the computer returns to the main program and executes the instruction immediately following the call to the procedure. In this example, the WRITE statement is performed producing the results

```
A = 2.0    B = 2.0
```

In essence, with call-by-variable parameters, the computer will pass the *name* of each actual parameter from the main program to the corresponding dummy parameter in the procedure declaration.

In view of this discussion, you should realize that with call-by-variable parameters, the values of the actual parameters from the main program can be permanently changed when the instructions in the body of the procedure are performed. This feature has both advantages and disadvantages. One advantage is that a call-by-variable parameter can be used as an output parameter for a procedure. This is because the value of the actual parameter from the main program can be altered permanently within the procedure. Thus when the call to the procedure is completed, the new value of the actual parameter serves as the output of the procedure.

One disadvantage of call-by-variable parameters also stems from the fact that the value of an actual parameter can be changed. Specifically, there is a greater danger of accidentally (and incorrectly) changing the value of an actual parameter within the procedure. Such logic errors can be difficult to locate.

There is yet another disadvantage to using a call-by-variable parameter. To illustrate, consider, once again, the procedure declaration from above:

```
PROCEDURE Change(X, Y)
   X := Y
```

Suppose that from the main program you want to pass the value of 5 * *B* / 2 to *Y* when you call the procedure. Assuming that *X* and *Y* are call-by-variable parameters, the statement

```
Change(A, 5 * B / 2)
```

would cause a problem. The reason is that, since *Y* is a call-by-variable parameter, the computer is expecting to replace *Y* with a variable *name* at the time the procedure is called. In this example, however, when the procedure is called, a *value* for *Y* (namely, 5 * *B* / 2) is being provided instead of a variable name. The concept of a call-by-value parameter allows for the ability to pass a value from the main program to the procedure, as will now be described.

Call-by-Value Parameters. In contrast to call-by-variable parameters, with call-by-value parameters the *values* (instead of the variable names) of the actual parameters are transferred to the dummy parameters when the procedure is called. As an example, recall the procedure declaration

```
PROCEDURE Change(X, Y)      {X and Y are the (real) dummy
                             parameters.}
    X := Y
```

Then, assuming that *X* and *Y* are call-by-value parameters, a number of steps are performed when the computer encounters the following call to the procedure *Change* in the main program:

```
A := 1.0
B := 2.0
Change(A, B)
WRITE 'A = ', A, ' B = ', B
```

First, the computer matches the actual parameters to the corresponding dummy parameters in the order listed. In this case, *A* is matched to *X* and *B* is matched to *Y*. Next, the computer converts each dummy parameter into a [local] variable and initializes the values of these variables to those of the corresponding actual parameters. In this example, the value of *X* is initialized to that of *A* (i.e., 1.0) and the value of *Y* is initialized to that of *B* (i.e., 2.0). Then, all of the instructions in the body of the procedure are performed *using the new local variables*, not the actual parameters. In this example, the assignment statement

```
X := Y
```

is performed with the local variables *X* and *Y*, not *A* and *B*. Thus the value of *X* now becomes 2.0 (observe that the value of *A* does not change). Finally, when completed, the computer returns to the main program and executes the instruction immediately following the call to the procedure. In this example, the WRITE statement is performed, producing the results

```
A = 1.0    B = 2.0
```

(Note that the values of *A* and *B* have not been changed by the procedure call.) In essence, with call-by-value parameters, the computer passes the *values*, not the names, of the actual parameters from the main program to the dummy parameters in the procedure.

In view of this discussion, you should realize that with call-by-value parameters, the values of the variables corresponding to the actual parameters in the main program cannot be changed when the instructions in the body of the procedure are performed. This feature has precisely the reverse advantages and disadvantages of the call-by-variable parameters. One disadvantage arises because a procedure cannot change the value of a variable corresponding to an actual parameter. Therefore a call-by-value parameter cannot be used as an output parameter, but only as an input parameter.

One advantage of a call-by-value parameter is that there is no danger of accidentally altering the value of a variable corresponding to an actual parameter when performing the instructions in the body of the procedure. This is because the procedure does not know the names of the actual parameters, only their values.

There is another advantage to using call-by-value parameters. When the procedure is called, the actual parameter can be a specific value, a variable, or even an expression, as illustrated in the following example.

Example

For the procedure declaration

```
PROCEDURE Change(X, Y)
    X := Y
```

the following procedure calls are all valid, assuming that *X* and *Y* are call-by-value parameters:

```
Change(A, 2.0)
Change(A, B)
Change(A - B, A + B)
```

In a given procedure declaration, it is possible to have some parameters that are call-by-variable and others that are call-by-value. Indeed, in Pascal it is the programmer who specifies (in the procedure declaration) which dummy parameters are call-by-variable and which are call-by-value. The details for doing so will be described in Section 7.5. You need not be concerned with this issue when working in pseudocode.

Recap

To summarize, with call-by-variable parameters, when a procedure is called from the main program, the dummy parameters are literally replaced by the names of the variables corresponding to the actual parameters. With call-by-value parameters, the dummy parameters are converted into [local] variables whose values are initialized to those of the corresponding actual parameters. As a result, it is advisable to use call-by-variable parameters for output parameters and call-by-value parameters for input parameters. If a parameter is to be used for both input and output, use a call-by-variable parameter; otherwise, the value of the actual parameter cannot be changed in the body of the procedure and returned to the main program for further processing.

In this section you have learned the concept of using procedures with parameters. You have also seen how information is transferred between the main program and the procedure. In Section 7.2, the process of using a procedure with parameters in problem solving is demonstrated.

Exercises for Section 7.1

Suppose that you declared the

```
PROCEDURE Proc(I, C, R, B)
```

in which *I* is an integer input parameter, *C* is a character input parameter, *R* is a real output parameter, and *B* is a boolean output parameter. Under each of the following assumptions on these dummy parameters, what, if anything, is wrong with the given procedure call in the main programs? Where possible, write a correct procedure call. (In each problem, all variables are global variables.)

1. {Assume that all dummy parameters are call-by-variable.}
```
N := 1
Ch := 'A'
A := 0.0
T := 2
Proc(N, Ch, A, T)
```
2. {Assume that all dummy parameters are call-by-variable.}
```
B := TRUE
R := 1.0
N := 2
Proc(N, 'M', R, B)
```

3. {Assume that *I* and *C* are call-by-value; *R* and *B* are call-by-variable.}

```
J := 1
Ch := 'A'
B := FALSE
R := 1.0
Proc(J, Ch, B, R)
```

4. {Assume that *I* and *C* are call-by-value; *R* and *B* are call-by-variable.}

```
I := 1
B := 0.0
R := TRUE
Proc(3 * I - 1, 'A', B, R)
```

You will be working with the following procedure in which the dummy parameters *X* and *Y* are one-dimensional (real) arrays of *N* elements, and *Z* is a real variable:

```
PROCEDURE DotProduct(X, Y, Z, N)
    Z := 0.0
    FOR I := 1 TO N DO {I is a local variable.}
        Z := Z + (X[I] * Y[I])
```

What will the WRITE statements in the following main programs produce under the given assumptions regarding the above dummy parameters? (In each problem, all variables are global variables.)

5. {Assume that all dummy parameters are call-by-variable.}

```
C := 1.0
N := 2
FOR I := 1 TO N DO
    A[I] := I
    B[I] := I * I
DotProduct(A, B, C, N)
WRITE C
```

6. {Assume that all dummy parameters are call-by-variable.}

```
I := 2
FOR J := 1 TO I DO
    W[J] := 2 + J
    X[J] := -J
DotProduct(W, X, Y, I)
WRITE Y
```

7. {Assume that the dummy parameters *X* and *Y* are call-by-variable, while *Z* and *N* are call-by-value.}

```
Z := 2.0
I := 1
FOR J := 1 TO 3 DO
    U[J] := 3 - J
    V[J] := J - 1
DotProduct(U, V, Z, 2 * I)
WRITE Z
```

Each of the following word instructions is to be made into a single procedure that uses no global variables, and which, when called from the main program, should return the stated solution. Prepare the appropriate procedure declarations including: (1) the procedure name, (2) the dummy parameters to the procedure, (3) an indication of the type (e.g., integer, real, array, etc.) and purpose (i.e., input or output) of each parameter, and (4) an explanation of whether the dummy parameters should be call-by-variable or call-by-value. You need not provide the instructions that constitute the body of the procedure.

8. This procedure should compute and save all of the integers greater than 1 and less than a given positive integer that evenly divide the given integer.

9. For a hand consisting of a given number of playing cards, each of which is represented by an integer between 1 and 52, this procedure should extract (and save) from the hand all cards of a given suit. The desired suit will be denoted by one of the following characters: 'C', 'D', 'H', or 'S'.

10. The main program is going to display a calendar for each month of a year. Therefore the current procedure should display the calendar for one given month. For example, the output of the procedure might be

```
                               January
Sun     Mon     Tue     Wed     Thu     Fri     Sat
                          1       2       3       4
  5       6       7       8       9      10      11
 12      13      14      15      16      17      18
 19      20      21      22      23      24      25
 26      27      28      29      30      31
```

(*Hint:* How will the procedure know on which day of the week to begin the current and the next month?)

7.2 Using Procedures in Problem Solving

Now that you know what constitutes a procedure with parameters and how to declare one, it is time to see how this tool is used in the problem-solving process. In the analysis that follows, pay particular attention to the use of top-down programming.

Recall from the chess problem of Section 6.5 that a chess board consists of 64 squares arranged in eight rows of eight columns each. On various squares of this board will be found certain pieces—some white and some black. Each piece can move from its current square according to some specific rules. For the problem of this section, special attention is given to the piece known as the bishop.

The bishop can move from its current square in any diagonal direction (forward or backward) until it reaches a square where there is another piece (or until reaching the end of the board). Only if the color of the piece encountered is different from that of the bishop can the bishop move to that square, removing (or "capturing") the other piece from the board. In this event, no further movement in this direction is possible.

With these rules in mind, as part of a programming team, you have been asked to write a program to solve the following problem.

Problem: Given a chess board together with a number of pieces on various specified squares, display the current board. Then, given a particular bishop, display all of the pieces that could be removed; i.e., captured by the given bishop from the original starting position. Also, display all of the resulting boards.

By design, the data for each piece will consist of one letter ('B' or 'W') to indicate the color of the piece, one letter to indicate the type of piece (e.g., 'B' represents a bishop), and two integers that represent the row and column of the square on which the piece is located. The last piece of data will be the bishop of interest.

Algorithm Development

Begin by providing a rough word description of how you would solve the problem yourself.

Solution: First read, display, and store the position and color of all of the given pieces. Then, from the original square on which the given bishop is located, look in each of the four diagonal directions and take the appropriate action.

In refining the solution given above, you might begin by using the technique of top-down programming to identify the following tasks to be performed:

Step 1: Read the data consisting of the locations and colors of the pieces.

Step 2: Display the current board (and pieces).

Step 3: For each of the four diagonal directions, start at the original location of the bishop of interest and look in that direction, taking appropriate action when necessary.

Recalling that procedures can be used in conjunction with top-down programming, the first two steps above can be accomplished by calling the following two procedures, respectively:

```
ReadBoard
DisplayBoard
```

The details of these procedures were developed in Section 6.5. At that time, the two-dimensional arrays *Piece* and *Color* were created. Recall that the values of *Piece*[*Row*, *Column*] and *Color*[*Row*, *Column*] are characters that represent the type and the color of the piece that is located in that row and column of the board, respectively. If there is no piece on that square, the value of these variables is the blank space. Later in this section, you will see that the procedure *ReadBoard* will need a minor modificiation.

Looking now at Step 3, your first inclination might be to use a FOR loop to accomplish the desired repetition associated with each direction. Thus you might be tempted to write

```
FOR Direction := 1 TO 4 DO . . .
```

While it is possible to proceed with this line of reasoning (as you will be asked to do in the exercises), further reflection should indicate some difficulties. For instance, when the value of the loop-counter variable *Direction* is 1, which actual direction are you dealing with?

For now, recall that a procedure can also be used to perform a group of instructions repeatedly. In Step 3, you want to repeat the operation of searching in a given direction and taking the appropriate action. So, using the procedure whose name is *Search* to perform these instructions, Step 3 can be rewritten as

Step 3: Choose one of the diagonal directions, and then *Search* (in that direction).

Choose a second diagonal direction, and then *Search* (in that direction).

Choose a third diagonal direction, and then *Search* (in that direction).

Choose the fourth diagonal direction, and then *Search* (in that direction).

What remains now is to fill in the details that constitute the body of the procedure *Search*. After this procedure has been declared, the main program (which consists primarily of the calls to these procedures) must be written carefully.

Declaring the Procedure *Search*

The first step in developing this procedure is to determine its parameters. To that end, begin by asking yourself what items change each time the procedure is to be performed. If you have read the new version of Step 3 carefully, you will see that it is the direction of movement that changes each time the procedure is called. Thus one input parameter to the procedure *Search* is the direction of movement.

The next issue is how (i.e., by what variables) that direction will be represented in the algorithm. To determine how to represent a particular diagonal direction, suppose that the bishop is currently located on square *IJ* (i.e., the square whose row number is *I* and whose column number is *J*). Once you have chosen one of the four diagonal directions, how will movement in that direction affect the values of *I* and *J*?

Observe that in one diagonal direction, both the row number and the column number will increase by one each time a move of one square is made in that direction. Similarly, in each of the other directions, the row number will either increase by one or decrease by one, as will the column number. Thus each of the diagonal directions can be thought of as a pair of integer values for the parameters *RowDirection* and *ColumnDirection*, hereafter abbreviated as *RowDir* and *ColDir*. Specifically, the four directions can be represented by the four pairs of values (+1, +1), (+1, −1), (−1, +1), and (−1, −1) for *RowDir* and *ColDir*, respectively. Note that the parameters *RowDir* and *ColDir* are input parameters because their values will be supplied by the main program.

Perhaps there are other input parameters that are needed. To find out, ask yourself what other information will be needed in order to accomplish the objectives of the procedure. Recall that, for a given direction, you will have to search from the square on which the bishop is located. Therefore you will need to know the row and column number representing the current position of the bishop. Thus it is reasonable to create two more input parameters, say *BishopRow* and *BishopCol*, whose values represent respectively the row and column of the square on which the bishop is originally located. The specific values for these parameters will have to be provided by the main program, or, more appropriately, by the procedure *ReadBoard*. In the exercises following this section, you will be asked to change that procedure accordingly.

Finally, it is necessary to determine if the procedure *Search* has any output parameters. To do so, ask yourself what are the results that will be obtained after the instructions in the body of the procedure have been performed. Again, recall that the objectives of this procedure dictate that either the procedure should display the board obtained after the bishop captures a piece, or else the procedure should do nothing. Given, then, that the output consists solely of displayed information, it would appear that at this point no output parameters are needed.

In summary, the procedure *Search* has the following four input parameters:

BishopRow—An integer variable whose value will be the row number of the square on which the bishop is initially located.

BishopCol—An integer variable whose value will be the column number of the square on which the bishop is initially located.

RowDir —An integer variable whose value of +1 or −1 will indicate a diagonal direction of movement.

ColDir —An integer variable whose value of +1 or −1 will indicate a diagonal direction of movement.

Putting these observations together, the pseudocode procedure heading is

```
PROCEDURE Search(BishopRow, BishopCol, RowDir,
                 ColDir)
```

In Section 7.3, you will learn which of these parameters should be call-by-variable and which should be call-by-value. You will also see how important this issue really is.

Declaring the Body of the Procedure *Search*

In the spirit of top-down programming, it is time to fill in the details that constitute the body of the procedure *Search*. To that end, you should proceed in much the same way as you would if you were developing the processing portion of a program. Specifically, you should ask yourself what computations should be done with the input parameters (assuming that the main program has provided appropriate values for those variables).

In rereading Step 3, you can see that the computer is asked to search from the initial square on which the bishop is located in each of the four different directions and, in each case, to take the "appropriate action." Now it is necessary to provide pseudocode instructions for accomplishing this task. Recalling what the "appropriate action" is, the above answer can be written as

Step 3(a): See how far the bishop can be moved (from its current position) in the direction specified by the values of `RowDir` and `ColDir`.

Step 3(b): If a piece of the opposite color is encountered, then (1) move the bishop to that square, and (2) display the resulting board (and the captured piece).

Through the process of refinement, these two steps will be restated using a pseudocode that is closer to Pascal.

Refining Step 3(a). In order to accomplish the task described in Step 3(a), you need to understand more precisely the way in which you determine how far the bishop can be moved in the given direction. To do so, look for an operation that will be repeated. By thinking through your solution, you will see that moving in the specified direction can be accomplished by repeating the instruction

> Look at the next square in the given direction a certain (unknown) number of times.

Thus you should consider using a `WHILE` loop. However, you will also need to specify the associated stopping rule. After reviewing the rules that describe how the bishop moves, you should realize that you want to continue looking at the next square so long as that square is still on the board, and so long as there is no other piece on that square. Thus you are led to refine Step 3(a) into the instruction

```
WHILE <still on the board> AND NOT <found a
      piece> DO
      <look at the next square>
```

Further refinement is necessary so as to express the items in angle brackets (< >) using pseudocode, as will now be illustrated.

Staying on the Board. One approach to determining if the bishop is still on the board is to replace this English concept with an appropriate boolean expression (in terms of the parameters to the procedure, and other local and global variables). A second approach (which is the one that will be used here) is to create a boolean variable, say *OnBoard*, whose value is TRUE when the square you are currently looking at is still on the board, and FALSE otherwise.

The value of the boolean variable *OnBoard* must be computed both before entering the WHILE loop and also within the body of that loop. Obviously, the initial value for *OnBoard* should be TRUE, because the first square you are looking at (i.e., the original position of the bishop) is indeed on the board. Then, somewhere in the body of the loop, it will be necessary to compute the new value of *OnBoard* each time you look at the next square in the given direction. So, how will you know if that square is still on the board?

By thinking through your solution, perhaps you realize that you will need to know the row and column number of the square you are currently looking at. As long as each of those integers is between 1 and 8, the square you are looking at is indeed on the board.

Thus you are led to the conclusion that it is necessary to have two variables whose values represent the current square you are looking at. To that end, you could use the parameters *BishopRow* and *BishopCol*. Each time you want to look at the next square, the values of these parameters must be changed accordingly to reflect the new row and column number of that square. With the use of these variables, and recalling that a chess board has eight rows and columns, it is possible to compute the value of *OnBoard* as follows:

```
OnBoard := 1 ≤ BishopRow ≤ 8 AND 1
              ≤ BishopCol ≤ 8
```

This instruction must be put in the body of the loop *after* looking at the next square, not before, because you are preparing the value of *OnBoard* for the *next* iteration of the loop.

Finding a Piece. Now you must be able to determine when you have encountered a piece on the board, as you look in the given direction. Again, rather than attempt to write an appropriate expression, create a boolean variable, say *FoundPiece*, whose value will be TRUE if you have encountered a piece, and FALSE otherwise.

As before, the value of *FoundPiece* must be initialized before entering the WHILE loop. That initial value is FALSE because when you start from the position of the given bishop you have not yet encountered another piece.

Finally, it is necessary to compute the new value of *FoundPiece* somewhere within the body of the WHILE loop each time you look at the next square. So, how will you know if the square you are currently looking at has a piece on it?

The answer is that you simply look at the board and see if there is a piece. Unfortunately, the computer cannot "look" at the board, as you can. Yet, recall that during the inputting phase, the two-dimensional array *Piece* was created. At that time the value of *Piece[I, J]* was set to a blank space (' ') when there was no piece on square *IJ*. Thus you will encounter a piece on the current square if the value of *Piece[BishopRow, BishopCol]* is *not* equal to ' '. Therefore, the correct pseudocode statement for computing the value of *FoundPiece* is

```
FoundPiece := Piece[BishopRow, BishopCol]
                ≠ ' '
```

The above instruction must be placed in the body of the WHILE loop after looking at the next square, not before, because the value of *FoundPiece* is being computed for the *next* iteration of the loop.

You should also note that the values of the array *Piece* must have been properly computed and stored by the procedure *ReadBoard*. Furthermore, in order to be able to use the values of *Piece* in the procedure *Search*, this array must be a global one since *Piece* was not passed as a parameter to the procedure *Search*.

Looking at the Next Square. In order to complete the body of the WHILE loop, you must express the instruction

```
<Look at the next square>
```

in pseudocode, using the values of the variables and the parameters. Can you do this?

Recall that the values of the parameters *BishopRow* and *BishopCol* are supposed to contain the row and column numbers, respectively, of the square you are currently looking at. So, to "look" at the next square in the direction specified by the values of *RowDir* and *ColDir*, you must perform the assignment statements

```
BishopRow := BishopRow + RowDir
BishopCol := BishopCol + ColDir
```

Putting together all of the instructions so far, the act of "seeing how far the bishop can be moved from its current position in the given direction" can now be expressed in pseudocode. As you read this pseudocode (and throughout the rest of this chapter), comments appearing in { } pertain to the statement(s) immediately following the comments.

```
OnBoard := TRUE
FoundPiece := FALSE
WHILE OnBoard AND NOT FoundPiece DO
        {Look at the next square.}
        BishopRow := BishopRow + RowDir
        BishopCol := BishopCol + ColDir
        {See if that square is still on the board.}
        OnBoard := 1 ≤ BishopRow ≤ 8 AND
                   1 ≤ BishopCol ≤ 8
        {Check if a piece has been found.}
        FoundPiece := Piece[BishopRow,
                        BishopCol] ≠ ' '
```

To complete the body of the procedure *Search*, the refinement process will be applied to Step 3(b), which was described previously in this section.

Refining Step 3(b). By thinking through your solution, the instructions in Step 3(b) can be refined to the following:

```
IF <a piece of the opposite color is found>
   THEN
   <move the bishop to that square>
   <display the captured piece and the
   resulting board>
```

As you will now see, each of the expressions in angle brackets (< >) can be refined using pseudocode.

Determining If a Piece of the Opposite Color Is Found. The objective here is to replace the English expression

```
<a piece of the opposite color is found>
```

in the IF/THEN statement above with a boolean expression that will indicate whether or not a piece of the opposite color has been encountered. First of all, recall that in the WHILE loop that was created above the boolean variable *FoundPiece* was used to determine whether or not any piece had been encountered by the bishop. Suppose, for the moment, that indeed the value of *FoundPiece* is TRUE. How will you know what the color of that piece is?

Recall that the colors of the pieces were supplied in the given data. Therefore those values will have been read and stored by the procedure *ReadBoard* in the two-dimensional array *Color*. Thus if the value of *FoundPiece* is TRUE, then the color of the piece that has been encountered is contained in the variable *Color* [*BishopRow*, *BishopCol*], but what about the color of the bishop itself?

That color is contained in the variable *Color*[<*the original row of the bishop*>, <*the original column of the bishop*>]. Unfortunately, the values of those two subscripts are no longer available in the procedure because the values of *BishopRow* and *BishopCol* (which originally contained this information) have been altered by the WHILE loop above. Here are three possible solutions to this difficulty.

First, in the WHILE loop, you could use two new [local] variables, say *CurrentRow* and *CurrentCol*, in place of the variables *BishopRow* and *BishopCol*. These new variables would have to be initialized to the values of *BishopRow* and *BishopCol*, respectively, prior to performing the loop. Then, the color of the piece encountered by the bishop would be contained in the variable *Color* [*CurrentRow*, *CurrentCol*]; the color of the bishop would be contained in the variable *Color*[*BishopRow*, *BishopCol*].

A second solution is to create a global variable, say *BishopColor*, whose value contains the color of the bishop of interest. The value of that variable should be stored either in the main program or in the procedure *ReadBoard*. (The variable *BishopColor* could also become a parameter to the procedure *Search*.)

As a final solution, at the very beginning of the body of the procedure *Search* you could save the original values of *BishopRow* and *BishopCol* in two new (local) variables, say *OrigRow* and *OrigCol*, for later use.

Assuming, for the sake of argument, that this last solution is used here, the desired boolean expression for the IF/THEN statement would be

```
IF FoundPiece AND Color[BishopRow, BishopCol] ≠
   Color[OrigRow, OrigCol] THEN . . .
```

Moving the Bishop to Capture the Piece. To accomplish this task, ask yourself how, precisely, you capture a piece with the bishop. By thinking through your solution, you might realize that, first, you lift the bishop from its original square, then you move the bishop to the new square. In other words, before you can place a bishop on the new square, you must remove that bishop from its original square. Doing so requires that you know the square on which the bishop started. Fortunately, that information was saved in the variables *OrigRow* and *OrigCol*, as just described. Thus you can remove the bishop (and its color) from its original square with the assignment statements

```
Piece[OrigRow, OrigCol] := ' '
Color[OrigRow, OrigCol] := ' '
```

Then, you can move the bishop (and its color) to the current square by using the assignment statements

```
Piece[BishopRow, BishopCol] := 'B'
Color[BishopRow, BishopCol] := Color[OrigRow,
                                OrigCol]
```

Indeed, when the computer assigns the value of 'B' to the array element *Piece[BishopRow, BishopCol]*, the previous value of that element (i.e., the piece that was on that square) will be "destroyed" (i.e., captured).

Displaying the Captured Piece and the Resulting Board. Recall that the procedure *DisplayBoard* was already created to display the original board. It is indeed convenient that this procedure can also be used here to display the current board. To do so from within the procedure *Search*, you need only write the instruction

```
DisplayBoard
```

Note that this procedure, *DisplayBoard*, is being called from within another procedure, *Search*; this is perfectly acceptable. After the new board has been displayed, the computer will return to the procedure *Search* and continue performing instructions from that point on. This is a good example of the power of a procedure; namely, the ability to perform the same set of instructions from different places in a program, while only having to write those instructions once.

All that remains is to display the captured piece (and its color). Unfortunately, by having used the assignment statements

```
Piece[BishopRow, BishopCol] := 'B'
Color[BishopRow, BishopCol] := Color[OrigRow,
                                OrigCol]
```

to move the bishop to the new square, you have lost the knowledge of the piece that was on this square previously. Can you correct this problem?

One solution is to save those values in the two new local variables, say *CapturedPiece* and *CapturedColor*, before the assignment statements that "removed" the captured piece. The entire IF/THEN statement would then become

```
IF FoundPiece AND Color[BishopRow, BishopCol]
    ≠ Color[OrigRow, OrigCol] THEN
    {Save the captured piece.}
    CapturedPiece := Piece[BishopRow,  BishopCol]
    CapturedColor := Color[BishowRow,  BishopCol]
    {Move the bishop to the new square.}
    Piece[BishopRow, BishopCol] := 'B'
    Color[BishopRow, BishopCol] := Color
          [OrigRow, OrigCol]
    {Remove the bishop from the old square.}
    Piece[OrigRow, OrigCol] := ' '
    Color[OrigRow, OrigCol] := ' '
    {Display the captured piece.}
    WRITE CapturedColor
    WRITE CapturedPiece
    {Display the resulting board.}
    DisplayBoard
```

This section has demonstrated the use of procedures in the problem-solving process. In the exercises that follow you will be asked to write the main program for solving this problem. Section 7.3 will then take you through the tracing and debugging phases.

Exercises for Section 7.2

With regard to the chess problem of this section, perform each of the following instructions.

1. For each variable that appears in the procedure *Search*, indicate (1) the type of the variable (e.g., integer, array, etc.), (2) whether the variable is local, global, or a parameter, (3) where (i.e., in what part of the algorithm) the variable obtains its value, and (4) for each parameter, whether that parameter should be call-by-variable or call-by-value.
2. Change the procedure *ReadBoard* of Section 6.5 so that, in addition to reading the data, the appropriate values of the variables *BishopRow* and *BishopCol* are stored. (*Hint:* Make *BishopRow* and *BishopCol* into parameters for the procedure *ReadBoard*. Remem-

ber that the information pertaining to the bishop will be provided as the last piece of the given data.)

3. Prepare a main program that calls all of the procedures with the actual parameters.
4. Prepare a different main program that replaces all of the calls to the procedure *Search* with a FOR loop that will accomplish the same results. The procedure *Search* should not be used at all. (*Hint:* You might want to create an array whose values represent the four diagonal directions of movement.)

Develop pseudocode algorithms that use procedures for solving each of the following problems. Think carefully about the parameters for the procedures.

5. Given a hand of *N* playing cards, each of which is represented by an integer between 1 and 52, compute and display the number of cards in each suit of the hand (card values of 1 to 13 are clubs; 14 to 26 are diamonds; 27 to 39 are hearts; 40 to 52 are spades). Then, you will be given *M* new cards together with the position of *M* old cards in the hand. Compute and display the number of cards in each suit of the hand that is obtained by replacing the *M* old cards with the *M* new ones. (All WRITE statements should be done in the main program.)
6. This program should display a calendar for each of the 12 months of a particular year given the day on which January 1 falls (see Exercise 10 of Section 7.1 on page 332).

7.3 Tracing and Debugging

In the previous section an algorithm (using procedures with parameters) was developed for solving a particular problem involving the game of chess. In this section, you will see how to trace and debug that algorithm. Special attention will be given to the difference of call-by-variable and call-by-value parameters. Here, then, is the pseudocode algorithm that was developed in the previous section.

```
PROCEDURE ReadBoard(BishopRow, BishopCol)
    {This procedure reads and stores the data into the global arrays Piece
    and Color, and into the parameters BishopRow and
    BishopCol. The details can be found in Section 6.5 together with the
    changes specified in Exercise 2 of Section 7.2.}

PROCEDURE DisplayBoard
    {This procedure will display the current board by using the values of the
    global arrays Piece and Color. The details can be found in Section
    6.5.}

PROCEDURE Search(BishopRow, BishopCol, RowDir,
                 ColDir)
```

```
{The next two instructions save the original position of the bishop.}
OrigRow := BishopRow
OrigCol := BishopCol
OnBoard := TRUE
FoundPiece := FALSE
{See how far the bishop can move.}
WHILE OnBoard AND NOT FoundPiece DO
        {Move to the next square.}
        BishopRow := BishopRow + RowDir
        BishopCol := BishopCol + ColDir
        {Check if the square is still on the board.}
        OnBoard := 1 ≤ BishopRow ≤ 8 AND
                   1 ≤ BishopCol ≤ 8
        {Check if a piece has been found.}
        FoundPiece := Piece[BishopRow,
                            BishopCol] ≠ ' '
{Check if the bishop can capture a piece.}
IF FoundPiece AND Color[BishopRow, BishopCol ≠
    Color[OrigRow, OrigCol] THEN
    {Save the captured piece.}
    CapturedPiece := Piece[BishopRow, BishopCol]
    CapturedColor := Color[BishopRow, BishopCol]
    {Move the bishop to the new square.}
    Piece[BishopRow, BishopCol] := 'B'
    Color[BishopRow, BishopCol] := Color[OrigRow,
                                          OrigCol]
   {Remove the bishop from its original square.}
   Piece[OrigRow, OrigCol] := ' '
   Color[OrigRow, OrigCol] := ' '
   {Display the captured piece.}
   WRITE CapturedColor
   WRITE CapturedPiece
   {Display the resulting board.}
   DisplayBoard

{The main program begins here. The variables BishopRow and
BishopCol used below are global variables whose names happen to be
precisely the same as the dummy parameters in the procedure declaration
above.}

ReadBoard(BishopRow, BishopCol)
DisplayBoard
Search(BishopRow, BishopCol, +1, +1)
Search(BishopRow, BishopCol, +1, -1)
Search(BishopRow, BishopCol, -1, +1)
Search(BishopRow, BishopCol, -1, -1)
```

Now it is time to trace this algorithm in an attempt to locate errors. In so doing, it will be assumed that the procedures *ReadBoard* and *DisplayBoard* are working correctly.

Tracing

Since this program is complex, tracing will be done only on the simplest of examples. To that end, suppose that the data consists of one and only one piece, namely the (white) bishop of interest. In this case, there is no piece that the bishop can capture. Nonetheless, suppose that the bishop is located in row 8, column 5, of the board. Therefore the values of the associated variables that would have been stored by the procedure *Readboard* when called from the main program are

Variable	Value
Piece[8, 5]	'B' (all other values of *Piece* are ' ')
Color[8, 5]	'W' (all other values of *Color* are ' ')
BishopRow	8
BishopCol	5

Subsequently, when the procedure *DisplayBoard* is called from the main program, the computer would display the board with the bishop being located in row 8, column 5. Now you are ready to trace the first call to the procedure *Search*. In so doing, assume that all of the dummy parameters in the declaration of that procedure are call-by-value; that is, those dummy parameters will be replaced by the *values* of the actual parameters that appear in the call to the procedure *Search* in the main program.

After performing the first four instructions in the procedure *Search*, the values of the variables are

Variable	Value
BishopRow	8
BishopCol	5
RowDir	1
ColDir	1
OrigRow	8
OrigCol	5
OnBoard	TRUE
FoundPiece	FALSE

Now trace the next part of the procedure, which consists of the WHILE loop. On performing the instructions in the body of that loop for the first time, you will discover that the values of the variables become

Variable	**Value**
BishopRow	9
BishopCol	6
OnBoard	FALSE (This is correct since the value of *BishopRow* is now 9.)
FoundPiece	****Error—subscript out of range*

Indeed, the value of *FoundPiece* cannot be computed because the subscript *BishopRow* of the array *Piece* in that assignment statement will have a value of 9, which is outside the allowable range. Can you correct this problem?

Correcting the Error. To correct this error, you should realize that the value of *FoundPiece* should be computed (in the body of the WHILE loop) only if you are still on the board. Thus the correct instruction is

```
IF OnBoard THEN
   FoundPiece := Piece[BishopRow, BishopCol] ≠
                 ' '
```

Tracing the IF/THEN Statement

With this correction in place, everything will be as before except that, after the first iteration of the WHILE loop, the value of *FoundPiece* will remain at FALSE because the bishop is no longer on the board. Now it is time to evaluate the stopping rule in the WHILE statement to see if the body of the loop should be performed again. However, since the value of *OnBoard* is FALSE, the WHILE loop is over.

The next step is to perform the IF/THEN statement that follows the WHILE loop; namely,

```
IF FoundPiece AND Color[OrigRow, OrigCol] ≠
   Color[OrigRow, OrigCol] THEN . . .
```

However, you will (or should) discover a difficulty in evaluating the boolean condition. Note that, even though the value of *FoundPiece* is FALSE, you will encounter a problem with the rest of the boolean expression

```
Color[BishopRow, BishopCol] ≠ Color[OrigRow,
OrigCol]
```

That is, you will detect that a subscript is out of range, because the value of *BishopRow* is still 9. Can you correct this problem?

Correcting the Error. Here you should realize that the above comparison should be performed only if a piece has been found, i.e., only if the value of *FoundPiece* is TRUE. Hence, you will need to replace the AND with another IF/THEN statement, leading to the following:

```
IF FoundPiece THEN
   IF Color[BishopRow, BishopCol] ≠
      Color[OrigRow, OrigCol] THEN . . .
```

Retracing

If you now retrace the IF/THEN statement, you will see that the procedure preforms correctly in the first direction; that is, the procedure does nothing. In fact, when you trace the body of the procedure using each of the other three directions, each time the procedure will correctly do nothing because there is no piece for the bishop to capture. Then, in the main program, when the last procedure call has been performed, the program will terminate. Note that no information other than the original board will be displayed.

While it is true that in this example the bishop cannot capture any piece, it would be better to display a message to that effect. Can you alter the program to do so?

In order to accomplish this task, you will have to know if in any of the four calls to the procedure *Search* a piece has been captured. At first, you might think that the value of the variable *FoundPiece* can be used. However, recall that that variable is a local variable, and hence its value cannot be used in the main program. Moreover, even if you were to make *FoundPiece* a global variable, there would still be a problem; namely, each time the procedure is called, the value of *FoundPiece* might change.

The solution is to construct a new global boolean variable, say *Captured*, whose value is TRUE if the bishop ever captures a piece, and FALSE otherwise. In the main program, prior to the first call to the procedure *Search*, the value of *Captured* should be set to FALSE (because at that point, the bishop has not captured another piece). Then, in the body of the procedure *Search*, the value of *Captured* should be set to TRUE if the bishop does indeed capture a piece. Finally, in the main program, after the last call to the procedure *Search*, if the value of *Captured* is still FALSE, then an appropriate message should be displayed.

With all these corrections in place, and adding a WRITE statement for debugging purposes, the new algorithm becomes:

```
PROCEDURE ReadBoard(BishopRow, BishopCol)

PROCEDURE DisplayBoard

PROCEDURE Search(BishopRow, BishopCol, RowDir,
                 ColDir)
   {Save the original position of the bishop.}
   OrigRow := BishopRow
   OrigCol := BishopCol
   OnBoard := TRUE
   FoundPiece := FALSE
   {See how far the bishop can move.}
   WHILE OnBoard AND NOT FoundPiece DO
         {Move to the next square.}
         BishopRow := BishopRow + RowDir
         BishopCol := BishopCol + ColDir
         {Check if the square is still on the board.}
         OnBoard := 1 ≤ BishopRow ≤ 8 AND
                    1 ≤ BishopCol ≤ 8
         {If the square is on the board, then check if a piece has been
         found.}
         IF OnBoard THEN
            FoundPiece := Piece[BishopRow,
                                BishopCol] ≠ ' '
   {See if the bishop can capture a piece.}
   IF FoundPiece THEN
      IF Color[BishopRow, BishopCol] ≠
         Color[OrigRow, OrigCol] THEN
         Captured := TRUE
         {Save the captured piece.}
         CapturedPiece := Piece[BishopRow,
                                BishopCol]
         CapturedColor := Color[BishopRow,
                                BishopCol]
         {Move the bishop to the new square.}
         Piece[BishopRow, BishopCol] := 'B'
         Color[BishopRow, BishopCol] :=
               Color[OrigRow, OrigCol]
         {Remove the bishop from its original square.}
```

```
            Piece[OrigRow, OrigCol] := ' '
            Color[OrigRow, OrigCol] := ' '
            {Display the captured piece.}
            WRITE CapturedColor
            WRITE CapturedPiece
            {Display the resulting board.}
            DisplayBoard
    IF Debug THEN
        WRITE OnBoard, FoundPiece, BishopRow,
              BishopCol, Captured
```

{The main program begins here. The variables *BishopRow* and *BishopCol* used below are global variables whose names, by choice, happen to be precisely the same as the dummy parameters in the procedure declaration above.}

```
Debug := TRUE
ReadBoard(BishopRow, BishopCol)
DisplayBoard
Captured := FALSE
Search(BishopRow, BishopCol, +1, +1)
Search(BishopRow, BishopCol, +1, -1)
Search(BishopRow, BishopCol, -1, +1)
Search(BishopRow, BishopCol, -1, -1)
IF NOT Captured THEN
    WRITE 'No piece can be captured by the bishop.'
```

Debugging

Assuming that this algorithm has been coded properly, the next step would be to locate and correct the run-time and logic errors. To show you some of the subtle types of errors that can arise when using procedures, assume that the first two dummy parameters of the procedure *Search* are call-by-variable, and that the last two parameters are call-by-value. Recall that with call-by-variable parameters the names of the dummy parameters in the procedure declaration will be replaced with the names of the actual parameters when the procedure is called from the main program.

For illustration purposes, suppose that after the calls to *ReadBoard* and *DisplayBoard*, the following results have been obtained. Note that the first letter displayed is the color of the piece; the second letter is the type of piece. Also, the (white) bishop of interest is located in row 2, column 5.

	1	2	3	4	5	6	7	8
1							BK	
2					WB			
3						BN		
4			BP					
5								BP
6								
7			WP					WP
8	WK							

Before proceeding, you should anticipate the desired results using the above data. Specifically, in the direction corresponding to (+1, +1), the bishop should capture the black piece that is in row 3, column 6. Then, in the direction corresponding to (+1, −1), the bishop should capture the black piece that is in row 4, column 3. In the remaining two directions, nothing should happen since the bishop will encounter the end of the board in those directions.

After the first call to the procedure *Search*, the computer will correctly display the following information:

	1	2	3	4	5	6	7	8
1							BK	
2								
3						WB		
4			BP					
5								BP
6								
7			WP					WP
8	WK							

```
The captured piece is BN
OnBoard = TRUE    FoundPiece = TRUE
BishopRow = 3   BishopCol = 6
Captured = TRUE
```

However, after the second, third, and fourth calls to the procedure *Search*, the computer will display, respectively:

```
OnBoard = TRUE    FoundPiece = TRUE
BishopRow = 8   BishopCol = 1
Captured = TRUE
```

```
OnBoard = TRUE   FoundPiece = TRUE
BishopRow = 3   BishopCol = 6
Captured = TRUE
OnBoard = FALSE   FoundPiece = FALSE
BishopRow = 0   BishopCol = 3
Captured = TRUE
```

After the second call to the procedure *Search*, you can see that there is an error because the values of *BishopRow* and *BishopCol* are 8 and 1, respectively. Since the bishop should have captured the black piece in row 4, column 3, those numbers should have been the respective values of *BishopRow* and *BishopCol*. Can you determine what is causing the error?

The answer is that, on performing the body of the procedure *Search* associated with the second call, the initial values of *BishopRow* and *BishopCol* are 3 and 6, respectively, instead of 2 and 5 as they should have been. Consequently, as the bishop is moved in the second direction of (+1, −1), as specified in the second call to the procedure *Search*, the values of *BishopRow* and *BishopCol* will increase and decrease by 1, respectively, until the bishop encounters the piece located in row 8, column 1. Can you explain why, when the procedure *Search* is called for the second time, the initial values of *BishopRow* and *BishopCol* are 3 and 6, respectively, instead of 2 and 5?

The reason is that the dummy parameters *BishopRow* and *BishopCol* are call-by-variable parameters. As a result, at the end of the first call to the procedure *Search*, the values of 3 and 6 will be *permanently* stored in the global variables *BishopRow* and *BishopCol* and returned to the main program. Consequently, it is these values for *BishopRow* and *BishopCol* that will be used at the beginning of the second call, and not the original values of 2 and 5, respectively.

One simple solution to this problem is to make sure that when the algorithm is coded into Pascal, these dummy parameters are call-by-value, and not call-by-variable. Then, the procedure *Search* would not be able to change the original values of the global variables *BishopRow* and *BishopCol*. In the exercises, you will be asked to correct this problem without changing the fact that these two dummy parameters are call-by-variable.

More Debugging

In view of the above discussion, suppose that all dummy parameters of the procedure *Search* are call-by-value. This time, the result of the first call to the procedure *Search* would be identical to the previous one. However, the second call would produce

	1	2	3	4	5	6	7	8
1							BK	
2								
3						WB		
4			B					
5								BP
6								
7			WP					WP
8	WK							

```
The captured piece is BP
OnBoard = TRUE    FoundPiece = TRUE
BishopRow = 4   BishopCol = 3
Captured = TRUE
```

If you carefully compare the original board set up as previously on page 351 to the current one, you should notice that the black piece that was in row 3, column 6, is now (incorrectly) missing, and instead, a (colorless) bishop is (incorrectly) there. How did this happen?

Recall that during the first call to the procedure *Search*, the bishop did indeed capture the black piece that was in row 3, column 6. Unfortunately, after that board was displayed, there were no instructions to restore the captured piece (and its color) to its original position. You can correct this error by placing these needed instructions in the procedure *Search* just after the call to the procedure *DisplayBoard*:

```
Piece[OrigRow, OrigCol] := 'B'
Color[OrigRow, OrigCol] := Color[BishopRow,
                                 BishopCol]
Piece[BishopRow, BishopCol] := CapturedPiece
Color[BishopRow, BishopCol] := CapturedColor
```

The first two instructions restore the bishop to its original row and column; the second two instructions replace the captured piece in its original row and column.

This section has shown you some of the difficulties that can be encountered when working with procedures, especially the differences between call-by-value and call-by-variable parameters. As usual, careful tracing and debugging techniques will always enable you to locate and correct errors when they arise. In the next section, you will learn a new programming concept that is very similar to a procedure.

Exercises for Section 7.3

Implement each of the following changes to the procedure `Search`. Always start with the final version obtained in this section.

1. Assume that the first two parameters are call-by-variable. Correct the problem that would be caused by the fact that the values of the global variables `BishopRow` and `BishopCol` are permanently altered in the procedure.
2. Rewrite the body of the procedure, eliminating the local variables `OrigRow` and `OrigCol` altogether. Instead, use two new local variables `CurrentRow` and `CurrentCol` in the `WHILE` loop instead of the parameters `BishopRow` and `BishopCol`.

Trace and correct the algorithms that you developed in Section 7.2 (see page 344) for solving each of the following problems.

3. The algorithm for Exercise 5.
4. The algorithm for Exercise 6.

7.4 Functions

Function A programming tool, like a procedure, that enables you to perform a group of instructions many times while having to write those instructions only once. However, the primary output of a function is a single value that is stored into the function name itself.

You have already seen that a procedure can be used to save time and effort by allowing you to perform a group of instructions many times while having to write those instructions only once. In this section you will learn that a **function** can be used in a similar manner. In fact, a function is, in many respects, exactly like a procedure. The major difference is that the primary output of a function is one single value, which will be called the *value of the function*. This difference manifests itself by the fact that a function will generally have input parameters, but usually not have output parameters. Rather, the value of the function will be returned to the main program in a very special way. A comparison of the similarities and differences between functions and procedures will be helpful.

Similarities between Functions and Procedures

One similarity between procedures and functions is that both can be used to perform a set of instructions at various places in a program, while having to code those instructions only once. A second similarity is that both procedures and functions can have parameters. However, as mentioned above, all parameters to a function are usually input parameters, whereas generally a procedure will also have output parameters. A third similarity is that a function, like a procedure, must also be declared. To do so in pseudocode, you would write

```
FUNCTION Name(Parameter, ... , Parameter)
    Statement
    .
    .                   body of the function
    .
    Statement
```

A fourth similarity is that within the bodies of both functions and procedures you can use local and global variables as well as the parameters. Also, each parameter can be call-by-value or call-by-variable. Finally, a function, like a procedure, is called from a main program; however, the way in which you do so is slightly different from that of a procedure, as will be described below.

Differences between Functions and Procedures

As mentioned previously, the major difference between functions and procedures is that a function generally has only one output value. Thus you might ask, "If a function does not have an output parameter, how and where will the value of the function be stored so that the main program can use that information?" The answer is that the very Name of the function that is used in the declaration (see above) serves that purpose. Specifically, think of the function name as being an ordinary variable name. Within the body of the function, you can (and must) compute and store into the function name the single value that constitutes the output of the function.

Example

The following function declaration is designed to take, as input, the value of a real number *R* and return, as output, the value of *R* cubed:

```
FUNCTION Cube(R)
    Cube := R * R * R
```

The fact that the (output) value of a function (*R* * *R* * *R*, in the example above) is stored in the function name (*Cube*, in the example above) causes several other differences between functions and procedures. For example, when declaring a function in Pascal, you will have to specify the type of the function (e.g., integer, real, etc.); that is, the type of value that will be stored into the name of the function. When working in pseudocode, however, you need not be concerned about this detail. Also, to call a function from a main program, you do not simply put the name of the function on a line by itself as you did with a procedure. Instead, recalling that the function name is a variable, you should place the function name (together with the actual parameters) anywhere that a variable (of the same type) could appear. The following is an example of how the function *Cube* (that was declared above) could be used in a main program.

Example

```
T := Cube(S) + 3 * Cube(U)
IF Cube(A) < 100 THEN
   WRITE Cube(A)
```

Built-in Functions

Built-in functions Functions that already exist in the computer and that you can use in your program without having to declare them.

From experience, the need to perform several specific types of computations often arises in programs. For this reason, most programming languages including Pascal have a large number of functions that are immediately available for your use. These functions are called **built-in functions** and to use them you need only provide the actual parameters at the time you call those functions; you need not declare those functions. The specific list of built-in functions that are available in Pascal, their various parameters, and the type of value that will be stored in the function name, are given in Appendix B. You should study this appendix because knowing which built-in functions are available to you (and how they work) can greatly simplify your programming task.

One example of a built-in function is that of finding the absolute value of a variable, say *X*. You could, of course, do so with the instructions

```
IF X ≥ 0 THEN
   Y := X
ELSE
   Y := -X
```

However, using the built-in function ABS, you could more easily write the instruction:

```
Y := ABS(X)
```

There are generally many built-in functions for accomplishing simple tasks such as computing the square root of a number, and many other special computations including logarithms and trigonometric functions. In addition, there are often functions for converting one type of value into another; e.g., in Pascal it is possible to convert an integer into the corresponding character in the collating sequence (and vice versa) by using an appropriate built-in function; also, a real number can be converted into an integer by using a built-in function that removes the decimal point and all subsequent digits.

Using a Function in Problem Solving

Because of the similarity between functions and procedures, their use in problem solving is almost identical. When considering the possibility of using a function in a problem, look for a particular type of computation whose (single) value must be computed at various times. This process will now be illustrated with the following problem.

Problem: Gary Gambler has discovered a new lottery game. In this game, you can choose up to a maximum of 15 out of 80 different numbers and, depending on which specific group of 20 numbers are later chosen by the computer, you can win different amounts of money if you have selected enough of the same numbers as the computer. Eventually, Gary Gambler wants to calculate his odds of winning. As a first step in that direction, he has asked you to write a program that will determine how many different ways you can choose K out of N numbers.

The resulting number of combinations, called "N choose K," can be computed by the formula below, in which the number $N!$ (N factorial) is the product of all of the integers between 1 and N:

$$\frac{N!}{K!\,(N-K)!}$$

where

$$N! = (1)(2)\;.\;.\;.\;(N-1)(N)$$

Identifying the Function. This particular problem is very straightforward, and so the primary focus will be on the issue of using a function rather than on the entire problem-solving process. First, the inputting, processing, and outputting phases of the program will be identified. The inputting phase consists of entering the values for the integers *K* and *N*. The processing phase consists of using the values of *K* and *N* from the inputting phase in order to compute the value of *N* choose *K*. Finally, the outputting phase consists of displaying the value computed in the processing phase. It is in the processing phase that a function can be used. Specifically, in computing *N* choose *K*, can you identify a computation whose value must be calculated several times?

On looking at the formula for computing *N* choose *K*, which is

$$\frac{N!}{K!\,(N-K)!}$$

you see that the factorial of a number must be computed three times. Specifically, you must compute *N* factorial, *K* factorial, and (*N* − *K*) factorial. Since the result of computing the factorial of a number is a single value, it is indeed appropriate to use a function instead of a procedure.

The next step is to identify the input parameter(s) to the function. To do so, ask yourself what values change each time the function is to be used. The answer is that the specific integer whose factorial is to be computed will change each time. Therefore in declaring the function, the integer whose factorial is to be computed will be denoted by the parameter *Number*. Thus the first part of the function declaration in pseudocode might be

```
FUNCTION Factorial(Number)
```

The next step is to specify the body of the function, which consists of computing the product of all of the integers between 1 and *Number*, that is,

```
(1)(2) . . . (Number − 1) (Number)
```

One set of instructions for performing this computation is

```
Product := 1
FOR NextNumber := 1 TO Number DO
      Product := Product * NextNumber
```

However, a final statement must be added to the above instructions so that the value of the function is stored into the function name; that is,

```
Factorial := Product
```

Thus the function declaration in pseudocode is

```
FUNCTION Factorial(Number)
    Product := 1
    FOR NextNumber := 1 TO Number DO
        Product := Product * NextNumber
    Factorial := Product
```

Now that the function declaration is completed, all that remains is to write the main program that calls the function. Such a main program might consist of the pseudocode instructions

```
READ N, K
WRITE N, K
Combinations := Factorial(N) / (Factorial(K) *
                Factorial(N - K))
WRITE Combinations
```

The tracing and debugging issues will not be addressed because the main program and the function are correct.

In this section you have learned the concept of a function. This programming feature is similar in many respects to a procedure. The major difference is that the output of a function is one single value that must be stored into the function name. You have learned that to use a function in the main program, you put the function name, followed by the actual parameters, anywhere that a variable of the same type as the function could be used. In the next section you will learn to code procedures and functions into Pascal.

Exercises for Section 7.4

For each of the following word problems, look for a value that will be computed several times. In so doing, identify one or more functions that could be used in solving the problem. Prepare complete function declarations for accomplishing those tasks. Be sure to include: (1) the function name, (2) a list of the input parameters, (3) the type of the function and the parameters, (4) the body of the function, and (5) an identification of each variable in the function as being local, global, or a parameter. Finally, prepare the main program and the associated function calls.

1. Given a tic-tac-toe board consisting of Xs, Os, and blank spaces, write a program to determine if and where there is a tic-tac-toe. The board will be represented by a two-dimensional array. (*Hint*: Look at the form of the boolean expressions in all of the `IF/THEN` statements. Can you see how a function might be useful?)
2. You will be given an amount of money that was invested at the beginning of the year, together with a real number that represents the annual percentage rate. Then you will be given two dates during that year (in the form month, day, year). For the first date, compute the number of days since the first of the year (watch out for leap years). Then compute the interest earned for those days and add that to the original amount of money to obtain a new balance. Then, for the second date, compute the number of days since the first date and obtain the interest on the new balance together with the final resulting balance. Interest is to be compounded daily from the first day of the year.

   Hint 1: With regard to the first date, to compute the number of days since the first of the year, create an array that, for each month, contains the number of days in that month. Also, pertaining to a leap year, you can use the operator `MOD` if you wish.

   Hint 2: With regard to the second date, if you knew how many days that date was since the first of the year, then you could easily compute the number of days since the first date by a simple subtraction. Work through a specific example to understand this hint.

   Hint 3: After reading the first two hints, do you see an appropriate function that might be useful? How about a function for handling the amounts of interest?

7.5 Coding Procedures and Functions

In this section, you will learn how to code procedures and functions in Pascal. As always, you will have to follow the rules of syntax, which include the use of semicolons and other punctuation, as well as the use of reserved words such as `BEGIN` and `END`, and special symbols such as <=. You will also see how to declare local variables, and how to specify whether a dummy parameter in the declarations is call-by-variable or call-by-value.

Procedures With Prameters

As you learned in Section 5.5, in Pascal a procedure is part of the declaration section. It is, in fact, the last item (together with functions) that must be declared. To understand the details involved in declaring a procedure with parameters, think of a procedure as a program by itself. As such, each local variable and each parameter must be declared. In contrast, recall that global variables should not be declared within a procedure because those variables will have been declared in the main program.

The parameters of a procedure are declared directly in the procedure heading. Observe the use of semicolons, instead of commas, to separate the parameters in the following declaration, which illustrates the correct Pascal syntax.

```
PROCEDURE Name(Parameter :Type; . . . Parameter
               :Type);
```

The Type of the parameter can be any of the four standard types (REAL, INTEGER, CHAR, and BOOLEAN).

In the above procedure declaration, all parameters are assumed to be call-by-value parameters. In the event that you wish a particular parameter to be call-by-variable, you must precede that parameter in the list above with the word VAR.

Example

The first and second parameters below are call-by-value; the third parameter is call-by-variable.

```
PROCEDURE Save(First :INTEGER; Second :INTEGER;
               VAR Success :BOOLEAN);
```

If a parameter is an array, then special care is needed. Specifically, prior to the procedure declaration, you should create the appropriate array using a TYPE declaration in which you provide a type name (see Section 6.6). It is this type name that should appear in the subsequent procedure heading as is illustrated in the following example.

Example

In this example, the first parameter is an array (note the required preceding TYPE declaration). Only the fourth parameter is call-by-variable.

```
TYPE Words = ARRAY[1..50] OF CHAR;
PROCEDURE Find(List :Words; Length :INTEGER;
               Letter :CHAR; VAR Found
               :BOOLEAN);
```

You should declare all local variables immediately following the procedure heading. You do so with the VAR declaration in precisely the same way you would in the main program.

Example

```
PROCEDURE Save(First :INTEGER; Second :INTEGER;
                    VAR Success :BOOLEAN);
   VAR    {The following are all local variables.}
      R      :REAL;
      I, J   :INTEGER;
      B      :BOOLEAN;
      C      :CHAR;
      Test   :ARRAY[1..20] OF INTEGER;
```

Finally, the body of the procedure can be declared. To indicate the beginning and end of those instructions, you must precede the first such statement with a BEGIN and follow the last one with an END.

Example

```
TYPE Prices = ARRAY[1..50] OF REAL;
PROCEDURE FindMax(A :Prices; Length :INTEGER;
                       VAR Largest :REAL; VAR
                       Subscript :INTEGER);
   VAR
      I :INTEGER;
   BEGIN
      Largest := A[1];
      Subscript := 1;
      FOR I := 1 TO Length DO
          IF A[I] > Largest THEN
            BEGIN
               Largest := A[I];
               Subscript := I
            END
   END;    {End of the procedure.}
```

Calling a Procedure in Pascal

To call a procedure from a main program (or from another procedure), you need only use the procedure name together with a list of the actual parameters (separated by commas, not semicolons). In so doing, keep in mind that if a parameter in the procedure declaration is call-by-variable, then the actual parameter must be a variable (of the same type); specific values and/or expressions are not allowed. Also, if a parameter in the procedure declaration is call-by-value, then the actual parameter can be a specific value, variable, or expression (of the same type as the dummy parameter in the declaration).

Example

Assuming that the array *Cost* has been declared of type *Prices* (see above), the following calls to the procedure *FindMax* above are all valid:

```
FindMax(Cost, N, Biggest, Index);

FindMax(Cost, 2 * I + 1, Large, Final)
```

On the other hand, the following calls are invalid:

```
FindMax(Cost, N, Biggest, 20);      {The fourth parameter
                                     must be a variable; not a value.}

FindMax(Cost, 20, 2 / 3, Index);    {The third parameter
                                     must be a variable; not an expression.}
```

Functions

A function declaration is similar to that of a procedure with the exception that you must also specify the type of the function itself. That is to say, you must indicate what type of value will be stored in the function name. This information is provided in the declaration just after the last parameter of the function is given. Thus the syntax for a function declaration is

```
FUNCTION Name(Parameter :Type; ... Parameter
              :Type): FunctionType;
   VAR
      {Local variables are declared here.}
```

```
BEGIN
   Statement;
   .
   .
   .
   Statement
END;
```

In the above declaration, the Type of each Parameter is the same as in the procedure declaration. Also, the FunctionType can be any of INTEGER, REAL, CHAR, or BOOLEAN, and indicates the type of value that will be stored into the function Name. Furthermore, all parameters are assumed to be call-by-value. If a call-by-variable parameter is desired, that parameter must be preceded with the word VAR, just as in a procedure declaration. Finally, somewhere within the body of the function, the function Name must be assigned a value corresponding to FunctionType. In the following example, observe that all parameters are call-by-value.

Example

```
FUNCTION Power(R :REAL; N :INTEGER) :REAL;
   VAR
      I          :INTEGER;
      Product    :REAL;
   BEGIN
      Product := R;
      FOR I := 2 TO N DO
           Product := Product * R;
      Power := Product
   END;
```

Example

```
FUNCTION TicTacToe(A :CHAR; B :CHAR; C :CHAR)
                          :BOOLEAN;
   BEGIN
      TicTacToe := (A = B) AND (B = C) AND
                   (A <> ' ')
   END;
```

Calling a Function

Recall that the function name can be thought of as an ordinary variable. Thus to call a function in a main program, you need only place the function name together with the actual parameters (separated by commas, not semicolons) anywhere that a variable of the same type as the function could appear.

Example

Assuming that all of the following actual parameters have been declared to be of the appropriate type and given some initial values, the following calls to the function *Power* and *TicTacToe* (see above) are valid:

```
S := 5.0 * Power(3.0, 2) + 2.0 * Power(T, 4);
IF TicTacToe(Board[1, 1], Board[2, 2],
             Board[3,3]) THEN
   WRITELN('TicTacToe on a diagonal')
```

Recall, from Chapter 3, the Pascal "variables" EOLN(FileName) and EOF(FileName). In reality, EOLN and EOF are boolean functions, and not variables. The FileName is the parameter of the function; the type of value that will be stored in the function name is boolean.

Recursion

Pascal has the added feature of allowing a procedure or function to call itself. The process of doing so is called **recursion.** A study of recursion is beyond the scope of this book; however, because of recursion, you should not use the function name on the right side of a := in the declaration of a function, but only on the left side.

Recursion The process of having a procedure or function call itself.

Complete Examples

As an example of a Pascal program that uses procedures, the chess algorithm at the end of Section 7.3 could be coded as

```
PROGRAM Chess(INPUT, OUTPUT);
TYPE
   Board = ARRAY[1..8, 1..8] OF CHAR;
VAR      {These are the global variables.}
```

```
    Debug, Captured          :BOOLEAN;
    BishopRow, BishopCol     :INTEGER;
    Piece, Color             :Board;

PROCEDURE ReadBoard(VAR BishopRow, BishopCol
                    :INTEGER);
    {The details of this procedure will not be given here.}

PROCEDURE DisplayBoard;
    {The details of this procedure will not be given here.}

PROCEDURE Search(BishopRow, BishopCol, RowDir,
                 ColDir :INTEGER);    {Note the comma
                 between all of these call-by-value, integer
                 parameters.}
    VAR    {Declare local variables.}
        OrigRow, OrigCol                :INTEGER;
        CapturedPiece, CapturedColor    :CHAR;
        OnBoard, FoundPiece             :BOOLEAN;
    BEGIN
        {Save the original position of the bishop.}
        OrigRow := BishopRow;
        OrigCol := BishopCol;
        OnBoard := TRUE;
        FoundPiece := FALSE;
        {See how far the bishop can move.}
        WHILE OnBoard AND NOT FoundPiece DO
            BEGIN
                {Move to the next square.}
                BishopRow := BishopRow + RowDir;
                BishopCol := BishopCol + ColDir;
                {Check if the square is still on the board.}
                OnBoard := (1 <= BishopRow) AND
                           (BishopRow <= 8) AND
                           (1 <= BishopCol) AND
                           (BishopCol <= 8);
                {If the square is on the board, then check if a piece has been
                found.}
                IF OnBoard THEN
                    FoundPiece := Piece[BishopRow,
                                  BishopCol] <> ' '
            END;    {End of WHILE loop.}
        {See if the bishop can capture a piece.}
        IF FoundPiece THEN
            IF Color[BishopRow, BishopCol] <>
```

```
        Color[OrigRow, OrigCol] THEN
        BEGIN
          Captured := TRUE;
          {Save the captured piece.}
          CapturedPiece := Piece[BishopRow,
                                 BishopCol];
          CapturedColor := Color[BishopRow,
                                 BishopCol];
          {Move the bishop to the new square.}
          Piece[BishopRow, BishopCol] := 'B';
          Color[BishopRow, BishopCol] :=
                Color[OrigRow, OrigCol];
          {Remove the bishop from its original square.}
          Piece[OrigRow, OrigCol] := ' ';
          Color[OrigRow, OrigCol] := ' ';
          {Display the captured piece.}
          WRITE('The captured piece is: ');
          WRITELN(CapturedColor,
                  CapturedPiece);
          {Display the resulting board.}
          DisplayBoard;
          {Restore the original board.}
          Piece[OrigRow, OrigCol] := 'B';
          Color[OrigRow, OrigCol] :=
               Color[BishopRow, BishopCol];
          Piece[BishopRow, BishopCol] :=
                CapturedPiece;
          Color[BishopRow, BishopCol] :=
                CapturedColor
      END;  {End of IF/THEN statement.}
    IF Debug THEN
      BEGIN
        WRITELN('OnBoard = ', OnBoard:5,
                ' FoundPiece = ',
                FoundPiece:5,
                ' BishopRow = ',
                BishopRow:5);
        WRITELN(' BishopCol = ',
                BishopCol:5,
                ' Captured = ', Captured:5)
      END  {End of IF/THEN statement.}
  END;  {End of procedure Search.}

{The main program begins here.}
```

```
BEGIN
   Debug := TRUE;
   ReadBoard(BishopRow, BishopCol);
   DisplayBoard;
   Captured := FALSE;
   Search(BishopRow, BishopCol, +1, +1);
   Search(BishopRow, BishopCol, +1, -1);
   Search(BishopRow, BishopCol, -1, +1);
   Search(BishopRow, BishopCol, -1, -1);
   IF NOT Captured THEN
      WRITELN('No piece can be captured '
              'by the bishop.')
   END.
```

In this second example, a function is declared and used in the main program. Specifically, the program of Section 7.4 could be coded in Pascal as

```
PROGRAM Combo(INPUT, OUTPUT);
VAR     {The following variables are global.}
   N, K, Combinations :INTEGER;

FUNCTION Factorial(Number :INTEGER) :INTEGER;
   VAR     {The following variables are local ones.}
      NextNumber, Product :INTEGER;
   BEGIN
      Product := 1;
      FOR NextNumber := 2 TO Number DO
           Product := Product * NextNumber;
      Factorial := Product
   END;     {End of function Factorial.}

{The main program begins here.}

BEGIN
   WRITELN('Enter a value for the ',
           'integers N and K');
   READ(N, K);
   WRITELN('N =', N:5, ' K =', K:5);
   Combinations := Factorial(N) DIV
                   (Factorial(K) *
                   Factorial(N - K));
   WRITELN('N choose K =', Combinations:5)
END.
```

In this chapter you have learned how to use and how to code procedures and functions in Pascal. In Chapter 8, you will begin to learn about the special types of data structures that are available in Pascal.

Exercises for Section 7.5

Code, run, and debug each of the following algorithms you wrote in Section 7.3 (see page 354), using the given data values.

1. The algorithm for Exercise 3.
   a) Number of cards: 3
      Given cards: 28, 3, 5
      Number of new cards: 1
      New card: 8
      Position of old card to be replaced: 1
   b) Number of cards: 5
      Given cards: 11, 24, 8, 15, 33
      Number of new cards: 2
      New cards: 37, 5
      Positions of old cards to be replaced: 4, 5
   c) Number of cards: 7
      Given cards: 3, 14, 22, 23, 30, 41, 50
      Number of new cards: 3
      New cards: 16, 48, 20
      Positions of old cards to be replaced: 1, 5, 6

2. The algorithm for Exercise 4.
   a) 1983 begins on a Saturday.
   b) 1984 begins on a Sunday.
   c) 1985 begins on a Tuesday.

Code, run, and debug each of the following algorithms you wrote in Section 7.4 (see page 360), using the given data values.

3. The algorithm for Exercise 1.

a)
```
X   O
  X
  O
```
b)
```
O   X
  X
    X
```
c)
```
O   X
O X X
O   X
```

4. The algorithm for Exercise 2.
   a) Amount of money: 100.00
      Interest rate: 0.09

First date: 3 23 1983
Second date: 9 23 1983

b) Amount of money: 2500.00
Interest rate: 0.11
First date: 6 30 1985
Second date: 12 31 1985

c) Amount of money: 3000.00
Interest rate: 0.125
First date: 4 20 1984
Second date: 7 19 1984

7.6 Summary

A procedure is a programming device that will enable you to perform a group of instructions many different times within a program while having to write those instructions only once. A procedure can also be used in conjunction with the problem-solving technique of top-down programming, or simply to improve the readability of a program.

The process of specifying the instructions that constitute the procedure is called declaring the procedure, which is done only once in the declaration section of a Pascal program. The process of instructing the computer to execute the procedure from within a program is referred to as calling, or invoking, the procedure. A procedure, being a small program in its own right, is often called a subprogram while the actual program itself is called the main program.

When performing the instructions in the procedure, the three types of variables that can be used are local variables, global variables, and parameters. Each parameter is either an input or an output parameter. Generally, you can identify what the parameters of a procedure should be by asking yourself what items are going to be different each time the procedure is called.

When declaring a procedure, you can choose any names you wish for the parameters, provided that those names are distinct from all other names used in the procedure declaration. The parameters in the procedure declaration are sometimes called dummy, or formal parameters to distinguish them from the actual parameters that are used at the time the procedure is called from the main program.

In the main program, when you want to call the procedure, you simply write the name of the procedure followed by the list of actual parameters whose names and/or values will be used in place of the dummy parameters. In that regard, you should always be concerned with whether it is the name or the value of the actual parameter that will be used in place of the dummy parameters, for these are two entirely different types of parameters. Specifically, when you declare a procedure, each dummy parameter can be either a call-by-variable parameter or a call-by-value parameter. As a general rule, use call-by-value parameters for input parameters; use call-by-variable parameters for output parameters.

When you call a procedure from a main program, several steps are performed. First, the list of actual parameters is matched to the list of dummy parameters, as they appear from left to right. Second, the names or values of the actual parameters are substituted for the corresponding dummy parameters, depending on whether the dummy parameter is call-by-variable or call-by-value, respectively. Third, the individual instructions that constitute the body of the procedure are performed. Finally, when finished, the computer returns to the calling program and performs the instruction immediately following the call to the procedure.

A function is similar, in many respects, to a procedure. The biggest difference is that the primary output of a function is a single value, which is referred to as the value of the function. Generally speaking, the parameters to a function are input parameters (and, as such, should be call-by-value). The single value that constitutes the value of the function must be stored into the function name used in the declaration. This assignment should be done somewhere within the body of the function.

To use a function, think of the function name as being an ordinary variable name. Thus to call a function from a main program, you simply put the name, followed by the actual parameters, anywhere that a variable of that type would normally be placed. In all other respects, a function behaves like a procedure.

Key Terms

Parameter 318

Actual parameters 324

Dummy parameters 324

Call-by-variable parameter 326

Call-by-value parameter 326

Function 354

Built-in functions 356

Recursion 365

After the 1969 Apollo moon landing, NASA's Space Transportation System—more familiar to the public as the Space Shuttle—began with the launch of the reusable spaceship *Columbia*. With the shuttle launch, the United States' space program soared to new heights. The imaginations of people in business and science soared with it: visions of orbiting factories and medical or military research in germ-free, weightless environments approached reality. NASA calls the next logical step a permanent, manned space station, where earthlings would live in three- to six-month shifts and experiment on space-age methods of chemical, drug, and alloy production. (NASA)

8

ADVANCED DATA STRUCTURES—PART I

You have already learned of four standard types of values: integer, real, character, and boolean. Also, in Chapter 6, you learned about the array data structure. In some programming languages, these are the only types of variables you can work with. In this chapter, however, you will learn that Pascal has several other powerful data types that can be useful in solving problems.

8.1 User-Defined and Subrange Data Types

In addition to the four standard types of values, for some problems, it is convenient to "design" your own special values for certain purposes (such as improving the readability of your program). In this section you will learn two special types of values and variables that you can create in Pascal.

User-Defined Values and Variables

To illustrate a situation in which you might wish to create your own values, imagine that you are solving a problem involving a deck of playing cards. In so doing, you might find it useful to work with the different suits, whose "values" are clubs, diamonds, hearts, and spades. You could, of course, work with the four integers 1, 2, 3, and 4 for the corresponding suit. However, to another person who reads your program, the assignment statement

```
CardSuit := 3
```

would be more understandable if you could write

```
CardSuit := Hearts
```

User-defined values
Names chosen by you that can be used in your program as values.

User-defined values enable you to use names as values instead of numbers.

Declaring User-Defined Values. In order to create the four suits as "values," in Pascal, you must associate a single name of your choosing to these four suits, say *Suits*. Then, you should use a TYPE declaration (see Section 6.6) to declare these values. Specifically, in the declaration section of your Pascal program you would write

```
TYPE
   Suits = (Clubs, Diamonds, Hearts, Spades);
```

The symbol = is used instead of := to make you aware that the process of creating a group of user-defined values is different from assigning a value to a variable. Also, note that the specific values (i.e., the names of the four suits in the example above) are listed in parentheses and separated by commas to the right of the = sign, whereas the single name that is given to the collection of values as a whole (*Suits*, in the example above) is listed to the left of the = sign.

More generally, the syntax for creating your own user-defined values with the TYPE declaration is

```
TYPE
   TypeName = (Value, Value, ..., Value);
```

Example

```
TYPE
   Days = (Sunday, Monday, Tuesday, Wednesday,
           Thursday, Friday, Saturday);
   Friends = (Bob, Carol, Ted, Alice);
```

You should think of the TypeName in the same sense as you think of the words integer, real, character, and boolean. For instance, just as the number 3 is one example of an integer value, so the value *Sunday* is one example of a "*Days*" value. As another example, recall that the two possible boolean values are TRUE and FALSE. Similarly, the four possible "*Friends*" values from the example above are *Bob*, *Carol*, *Ted*, and *Alice*.

For reasons that will soon become clear, a user-defined value can appear in only one TYPE declaration. Thus the following would be incorrect because the values *Clubs* and *Spades* appear in two TYPE declarations:

```
TYPE
   Suits = (Clubs, Diamonds, Hearts, Spades);
   BlackSuits = (Spades, Clubs);
```

Declaring User-Defined Variables. In Pascal, if you want a variable to be used for storing an integer value, then you must declare that variable to be an integer variable with the VAR declaration. In a similar sense, if you want a variable to be used for storing suit values, for example, then you must declare that variable to be a "*Suits*" variable. You do so with the VAR declaration. For example,

```
VAR
    CardSuit, Trump  :Suits;
    Day              :Days;
    Person           :Friends;
```

Note that the variable name appears to the left of the colon; the type of variable (from the TYPE declaration) appears to the right of the colon.

Using User-Defined Values and Variables. Once you have created user-defined values with the TYPE declaration and user-defined variables with the VAR declaration, you can then use those values and variables in your program much like you use any other values. For example, using the declarations above, you could write the Pascal assignment statements

```
CardSuit := Hearts;
Day := Sunday;
Person := Carol
```

There are, however, some operations that you cannot perform with user-defined data types. For example, you cannot perform arithmetic computations, for what would the expression *Sunday* + *Monday* mean? As another example, in current versions of Pascal, it is not possible to read or write the values of user-defined variables. If you need to do so, then you must use some form of coding scheme. For example, the following instructions read the first letter of the suit of a card into the character variable *Ch*, and then set the value of the user-defined variable *CardSuit* accordingly:

```
READ (Ch);
CASE Ch OF
      'C' : CardSuit := Clubs;
      'D' : CardSuit := Diamonds;
      'H' : CardSuit := Hearts;
      'S' : CardSuit := Spades
END
```

In Chapter 4 you learned that you can compare any two values (or variables) of the same type using the Pascal operators <, >, =, <=, >=, <>. In a similar sense, you can compare two user-defined values (or variables) using these same operators. The user-defined values are ordered according to the way they are listed in the TYPE declaration. For example, suppose you have the declaration

```
TYPE
    Suits = (Clubs, Diamonds, Hearts, Spades);
```

Looking at the value *Diamonds*, for instance, all values to the left of this value are "less than" *Diamonds* (e.g., *Clubs* is less than *Diamonds*). Correspondingly, all values to the right of *Diamonds* (i.e., *Hearts* and *Spades* in the example above) are "greater than" *Diamonds*. Thus the value of the following comparisons are all TRUE:

```
Clubs < Hearts
Spades > Diamonds
Spades >= Hearts
```

From the example above, you can see that if a user-defined value appeared in more than one TYPE declaration, then the computer would not know which of the two declarations to use in performing the comparison. It is for this reason that a user-defined value can appear in only one TYPE declaration.

You can also use user-defined variables as loop-counter variables in FOR loops, and even as subscripts of an array. In the next example, suppose that you have made the following declarations:

```
TYPE
    Players = (One, Two, Three, Four);
    Suits = (Clubs, Diamonds, Hearts, Spades);
    CardArray = ARRAY[One..Four, 1..13] OF
                   Suits;
VAR
    Card, HeartCount  :INTEGER;
    Player            :Players;
    Suit              :Suits;
    Hand              :CardArray;
```

Example

These next instructions would count the number of hearts in the array *Hand*:

```
FOR Player := One TO Four DO
    FOR Card := 1 TO 13 DO
        IF Hand[Player, Card] = Hearts THEN
            HeartCount := HeartCount + 1
```

In summary, user-defined values and variables improve the readability of your program by allowing you to use values whose names are representative of their meaning. The major disadvantage is that current versions of Pascal will not allow you to read or to write the values of user-defined variables.

Subrange Data Types

When solving a problem, you might sometimes find it necessary (or convenient) to work with a specific portion of an existing set of values. For instance, instead of working with all of the characters on your computer, you might want to reference only the characters corresponding to the digits 0 to 9. In Pascal, you can create the desired set of values, called a **subrange of values,** by using the following TYPE declaration:

Subrange of values A specific portion of an existing set of values.

```
TYPE
   Digits = '0' .. '9';
```

In general, the Pascal syntax for a declaration of subrange values is

```
TYPE
   TypeName = FirstValue .. LastValue;
```

Example

```
TYPE
   PhoneNumbers = 1000000 . . 9999999;
                                  {A subrange of integer values.}
   Letters = 'a' .. 'z';          {A subrange of character values.}
   Weekdays = Monday .. Friday;
               {A subrange of the user-defined values Days (see above).}
```

You should note that it is not possible to have a subrange of real values because it is not possible to list all of the real numbers between two given real numbers. Indeed, it is for this same reason that a loop-counter variable in a FOR-loop statement cannot be a real variable.

With regard to subrange values, you might very well ask, "Why create a subrange? Why not work with the entire set of values?" One reason for using subrange values is to improve the readability of a program. For instance, a positive integer variable can be assigned any value between 1 and MAXINT—a very wide range. However, if that same variable is declared to be of type *PhoneNumbers* (see above), for example, then that variable is known to be a seven-digit number between 1000000 and 9999999.

A second possible reason for using subrange values is to help debug a program. For example, if *Card* is an array whose subscript is supposed to be between 1 and 52, then you might consider creating a subrange of the integers between 1 and 52. For instance,

```
TYPE
    Deck = 1 .. 52;
```

Subsequently, any variable that will be used as a subscript for the array *Card* should be declared of type *Deck* (instead of INTEGER). For example,

```
VAR
    Position :Deck;
```

Now, whenever the variable *Position* is assigned a value that is not between 1 and 52, the computer can be instructed to display an appropriate error message, thus preventing you from using an incorrect value of *Position* as a subscript for the array *Card*.

In this section you have learned to create and to use user-defined and subrange values to improve the readability of a program, and to help in the debugging process. In Section 8.2 you will learn about a new data structure that will allow you to store many different values into a single variable.

Exercises for Section 8.1

Create appropriate TYPE and VAR declarations for each of the following problems.

1. The variable *Car* can be any of the following models: Chevrolet, Ford, Toyota, Datsun, or Fiat.
2. The variable *Ball* can be any of the following colors: red, yellow, orange, blue, green, brown, or black.
3. The value of a variable *Month* is to represent one of the 12 months (by name); the variable *Season* is to be the name of a season according to the value of *Month* as follows:

Winter—January, February, March
Spring—April, May, June
Summer—July, August, September
Fall—October, November, December

4. The variable *Fruit* can be any one of: banana, apple, orange, grapefruit, melon, or pear. The value of the variable *Citrus* can be either orange or grapefruit.

Rewrite each of the following program segments eliminating all of the syntax errors you can find.

5.
```
PROGRAM First(INPUT, OUTPUT);
VAR
   Ch, Blank  :CHAR;
   Date       :Month;
TYPE
   Month  =  (Jan, Feb, Mar);
```

6.
```
PROGRAM Test(INPUT, OUTPUT);
TYPE
   Animals  =  (Bats, Cats, Dogs, Cows);
   Farm     =  (Chickens, Horses, Cows, Pigs);
   Costs    =  8.00 .. 15.00;
VAR
   Pet     :Animals;
   Amount  :Costs;
CONST
   Workdays  =  5;
```

8.2 Records

Record A Pascal data structure that allows you to store more than one type of value in each variable.

Fields of a record The various individual values that are stored in a record.

In the previous section, you learned how to use user-defined and subrange values for solving certain problems. Nonetheless, you are still restricted by the fact that into each variable you can store only one type of value (e.g., user-defined, integer, or real). Even with an array, each element must contain the same type of value. In this section, you will learn about a **record,** which is a Pascal data structure that will allow you to store more than one type of value in each such variable. The individual values of a record are called the **fields of a record.**

As an example of the need for a record, imagine that you are keeping the accounts for a list of students who have not yet paid all their fees. The information associated with each student might consist of the student's name, which could be stored in an array of 30 characters; the student's identification number, which consists of a single integer; and the amount of money the student owes, which consists of a single real number.

In Pascal, you will be able to store all three of these different types of values into a single record variable that has only one name, called the **record name.** However, it will be necessary to distinguish between the three different values mentioned above that are stored in this one variable. Each of the three values is, in fact, a field of the record.

Record name The single name given to the record variable as a whole.

In Chapter 6, you learned to distinguish the individual elements of an array by using a subscript (enclosed in brackets) following the array name. The process of distinguishing the individual elements of a record, however, is slightly different. You will, of course, have to use the record name. However, in addition, you will have to associate another name, called a **field name,** with each field of the record. To identify one specific field of a record, you will need to follow the record name with a period (.), and then the associated field name.

Field names The various names given to the individual fields of a record.

Example

Suppose that, for the student example above, the chosen record name is *Student*, and the three chosen field names are *Name*, *Number*, and *Amount*. Using these names, you could then refer to the following three variables. The first, *Student.Name*, is an array consisting of 30 characters whose values represent the letters in the name of the student. The second variable, *Student.Number*, is an integer variable whose value is the student-identification number. The last variable, *Student.Amount*, is a real variable whose value represents the amount of money owed by that student.

Note that the individual values of the variable *Student.Name* in the example above would be referenced by using a subscript because that variable is an array. Thus the individual elements of the array are *Student.Name[1]*, . . . , Student.Name[30].

Perhaps another example will clarify the concept of a record and its fields. Imagine that you are keeping medical records on patients and, for each one, the following information will be retained:

1. Name
2. Sex
3. Marital status
4. Social security number

5. Whether the patient is insured or not
6. The amount of money owed

Each of these six items should be thought of as a field of the record. The record itself needs a name, say *Patient*. The next step in creating the record is to select individual names for each of the six fields described above, and to identify the type of value that will be stored in each one. For instance:

1. *Name* — An array of 30 characters whose values are the letters in the name of the patient.
2. *Sex* — A user-defined variable whose value will be either *Male* or *Female*.
3. *MaritalStatus* — A character variable whose value will indicate whether the patient is single, married, divorced, or widowed.
4. *SocSecNum* — An integer variable whose value is the patient's social security number.
5. *Insured* — A boolean variable whose value is TRUE if the patient is insured and FALSE otherwise.
6. *Amount* — A real variable whose value is the amount of money owed by the patient.

Now, to refer to each of these six fields respectively, you would use the variable whose name consists of the record name *Patient*, followed by a period, followed by the specific field name:

```
Patient.Name
Patient.Sex
Patient.MaritalStatus
Patient.SocSecNum
Patient.Insured
Patient.Amount
```

The variable *Patient.Name* above is an array. In order to refer to one element of that array, you would have to follow the array name *Patient.Name* by a subscript, e.g., *Patient.Name*[1].

Each of the above names can now be used as an ordinary variable of the appropriate type. Thus, for example, the following statement is valid:

```
Patient.Insured := FALSE
```

The Pascal Syntax for Records

As with any other data structure, in Pascal, you can use the TYPE declaration to create a record type. The associated Pascal syntax for this declaration is

```
TYPE
   TypeName  =  RECORD
                   FieldName  :Type;
                   .
                   .
                   .
                   FieldName  :Type
                END;
```

The TypeName and FieldNames should be thought of as ordinary variable names and treated as such. Also, the Type can be any valid type that is available in Pascal, including INTEGER, REAL, CHAR, BOOLEAN, user-defined, subrange, and ARRAY. Finally, observe the use of the reserved word END to end the record definition. Note, however, that there is no corresponding use of the word BEGIN.

When you use the syntax given above, you will have created a record type, but you will not yet have created a variable of that type. To do so, you would have to follow the TYPE declaration above with the VAR declaration

```
VAR
   RecordName  :TypeName;
```

The TypeName in the VAR declaration is precisely the same TypeName that you used in the corresponding TYPE declaration. Subsequently, to access a particular field of the variable RecordName, you would write

```
RecordName.FieldName
```

Example

For the medical record-keeping problem described above, you might use the following Pascal syntax:

```
TYPE
   Medical  =  RECORD
      Name              :ARRAY[1 .. 30] OF CHAR;
      Sex               :(Male, Female);
```

```
            MaritalStatus  :CHAR;
            SocSecNum      :INTEGER;
            Insured        :BOOLEAN;
            Amount         :REAL
        END;
    VAR
        Patient :Medical;
```

Now, the individual fields would be referenced by following the variable name `Patient` with a period and then the field name. Thus, for example, the following Pascal statements would all be valid:

```
Patient.Insured := FALSE;
Patient.Sex := Female;
FOR I := 1 TO 30 DO
    READ(Patient.Name[I]);
Patient.Amount := Patient.Amount + 22.50;
READ(Patient.SocSecNum);
Patient.MaritalStatus := 'S'
```

Processing Records

In the example above, each time you wanted to reference a specific field, you had to include the record name (i.e., `Patient`) together with the specific field name. Doing so can be quite burdensome and repetitive. The `WITH` **statement** is designed to ease this process by allowing you to specify only the field name, and not the record name, within the body of the `WITH` statement. The syntax for the `WITH` statement is

`WITH` **statement** A Pascal statement that enables you to refer to the fields of a record without having to specify the record name in the body of the statement.

```
WITH RecordName DO
     BEGIN
        Statement;
        .
        .
        .
        Statement
     END
```

Example

For the processing of the patient record given above, you could use the following `WITH` statement to eliminate the need to repeat the record name, `Patient`, with each specific field name:

```
WITH Patient DO
      BEGIN
          Insured := FALSE;
          Sex := Female;
          FOR I := 1 TO 30 DO
               READ(Name[I]);
          Amount := Amount + 22.50;
          READ(SocSecNum);
          MaritalStatus := 'S'
      END
```

Solving a Problem with Records

To illustrate the process of using records in problem solving, imagine that you are working for the Peter Pan Publishing Company, which maintains records on various books that the company sells. For each book, the company knows the author's name, the book-identification number, the selling price, the number of copies in inventory, and whether or not copies of the book are being reprinted. Here, then, is your problem.

Problem: The programming division of the company wants you to write a procedure that will take this given information for one book together with the number of copies of the book that has been ordered by a customer, and perform the following computations. If the amount ordered can be met from the current inventory, then reduce the inventory on hand by the amount ordered and display the income that the company will receive from this sale. On the other hand, if the amount ordered exceeds the number of copies in inventory, then display a message to that effect and "request the print shop to print additional copies" by setting the value of the appropriate variable to TRUE.

Analysis of Data Structures. Before getting into the details of solving this problem, it is worth your while to think first about how the data will be stored and used in the program. For instance, on rereading the information pertaining to each book, perhaps you recognize that the data can (and should) be stored into a record variable that could be created in the main program as follows:

```
TYPE
   Publication = RECORD
                      Author       :ARRAY[1..30]
                                    OF CHAR;
```

```
                    BookNumber  :INTEGER;
                    SalesPrice  :REAL;
                    Inventory   :INTEGER;
                    ReOrder     :BOOLEAN
                END;
VAR
    Book :Publication;
```

Algorithm Development. Returning, now, to the details of algorithm development, the first step in developing this (or any other) procedure is to identify the parameters. In fact, since a procedure is itself a subprogram, you can proceed by identifying the inputting, processing, and outputting phases of the procedure, as will now be done.

Inputting. As usual, identify the inputting phase by asking yourself what information you will be given in order to solve this problem. In rereading the problem, you see that the company will give you certain information pertaining to the book (e.g., the author's name, the selling price), as well as the number of books that has been ordered.

As discussed previously, the various data pertaining to the book can be thought of as the fields of a record (such as the one that was created above). The number of books ordered is a separate variable altogether, which will be represented by the parameter *OrderQuantity* in the procedure below. Indeed, since the specific data for each book and the number of books ordered will vary each time the procedure is used, these two items are the [input] parameters to the procedure.

In creating the desired procedure, it is necessary to choose a procedure name as well as the names of the [dummy] parameters; for instance,

```
PROCEDURE Sales(BookInfo :Publication;
                OrderQuantity :INTEGER);
```

BookInfo is a dummy parameter that represents a record whose field names will be precisely those of the record as specified in the previous TYPE declaration for *Publication* given above. Also, note that both of these parameters are call-by-value since they are input parameters. At this time, there are no output parameters; however, that fact might have to change when the outputting phase of the procedure is addressed.

Processing. Given the values of the input parameters above, the processing portion of the procedure can be determined by asking yourself what computations should be done with the values of the input parameters. Rereading the problem statement, an English answer might be

Solution: Determine whether or not the current order can be met with the available inventory, and take the appropriate action in either case.

By thinking through your solution, and by working through a specific example, if necessary, you will probably decide that an `IF/THEN` statement is appropriate for this problem. You might then provide the following more refined answer in pseudocode:

```
IF <the order quantity is ≤ inventory amount>
   THEN
   <reduce the inventory by the order
   quantity>
   <compute and display the total sales
   figure>
ELSE
   WRITE 'Unable to meet this order'
   <indicate that a new order must be placed
   with the print shop>
```

The next step is to replace each of the English expressions in angle brackets with pseudocode statements using the appropriate variable and/or parameter names. For instance, "the order quantity" is precisely the value of the parameter *OrderQuantity*; "inventory amount" is the value of the record field *BookInfo.Inventory* (see the record declaration). Using the appropriate variable names and incorporating correct Pascal syntax, the above instructions become

```
IF OrderQuantity <= BookInfo.Inventory THEN
   BEGIN
      BookInfo.Inventory := BookInfo.Inventory
                            - Orderquantity;
      WRITELN('Income from this sale =',
               OrderQuantity *
               BookInfo.SalesPrice:10:2)
```

```
      END
   ELSE
      BEGIN
         WRITELN('Sorry, there are not enough books in ',
                 'inventory to meet this order.');
         BookInfo.ReOrder := TRUE
      END
```

You could write these instructions more simply using the `WITH` statement as follows:

```
WITH BookInfo DO
   IF OrderQuantity <= Inventory THEN
      BEGIN
         Inventory := Inventory - OrderQuantity;
         WRITELN('Income from this sale =',
                 OrderQuantity * SalesPrice:10:2)
      END
   ELSE
      BEGIN
         WRITELN('Sorry, there are not enough books in ',
                 'inventory to meet this order.');
         ReOrder := TRUE
      END
```

Outputting. The outputting phase of this problem has been incorporated into the processing portion above. Specifically, the output of this procedure consists of the two `WRITE` statements above together with the new values of the variables *BookInfo.Inventory* and *BookInfo.ReOrder*, which must be returned to the main program for further processing. Thus you should realize that the parameter *BookInfo*, together with its fields, constitutes an output parameter as well as an input parameter. As such, this parameter should be changed to call-by-variable instead of call-by-value.

Putting together all that has been done so far, the procedure could be coded in Pascal as

```
PROCEDURE Sales(VAR BookInfo :Publication;
                    OrderQuantity :INTEGER);
```

```
BEGIN
   WITH BookInfo DO
         IF OrderQuantity <= Inventory THEN
            BEGIN
               Inventory := Inventory -
                              OrderQuantity;
            WRITELN('Income from this sale = ',
                     OrderQuantity *
                     SalesPrice:10:2)
            END
         ELSE
            BEGIN
               WRITELN('Sorry, there are not enough ',
                        'books in inventory to meet ',
                        'this order.');
               ReOrder := TRUE
            END
END;           {End of procedure Sales.}
```

Since the procedure above is correct, the process of tracing and debugging will not be illustrated.

Advanced Record Structures

In the examples so far, the fields of a record have been integer, real, boolean, user-defined, and array types. In fact, more complicated data structures can be developed. For instance, the fields of a particular record can themselves be records, as the following example shows.

```
TYPE
   Client = RECORD
      Name     :RECORD
                   Last     :ARRAY[1..20] OF CHAR;
                   First    :ARRAY[1..20] OF CHAR;
                   Middle   :CHAR
                END;  {End of Name record.}
     Address   :RECORD
                   Street   :ARRAY[1..50] OF CHAR;
                   City     :ARRAY[1..20] OF CHAR;
                   State    :ARRAY[1..2] OF CHAR;
```

```
                  ZipCode  :INTEGER
               END;        {End of Address record.}
      Property  :RECORD
                  Description    :ARRAY[1..50]
                                  OF CHAR;
                  Quantity       :INTEGER;
                  PurchasePrice  :REAL;
                  CurrentPrice   :REAL;
                  CurrentValue   :REAL
               END    {End of Property record.}
         END;    {End of Client record.}
VAR
   Investor :Client;
```

The variable *Investor* is a record of type *Client*, and has three fields as specified in the TYPE declaration, each of which is itself a record having three, four, and five fields, respectively. To reference the particular field of the record variable *Investor*, you would follow the name *Investor* with a period and the appropriate subfield name (either *Name*, *Address*, or *Property*), followed by another period and the final subfield name. In other words, the following variables could be used:

```
Investor.Name.Last[I]     (I = 1, ..., 20)
Investor.Name.First[I]    (I = 1, ..., 20)
Investor.Name.Middle
Investor.Address.Street[I]  (I = 1, ..., 50)
Investor.Address.City[I]    (I = 1, ..., 20)
Investor.Address.State[I]   (I = 1, 2)
Investor.Address.ZipCode
Investor.Property.Description[I]  (I = 1, ..., 50)
Investor.Property.Quantity
Investor.Property.PurchasePrice
Investor.Property.CurrentPrice
Investor.Property.CurrentValue
```

You could use the WITH statement to facilitate the referencing of these variables. In this situation you would write, for example,

```
WITH Investor.Name, Investor.Property DO
     BEGIN
```

```
        Statement;
        .
        .
        .
        Statement
    END
```

In each Statement, the appropriate variable in the record would be referenced only by its final field name (e.g., *Last*, *ZipCode*, *Description*[*I*], etc.).

Continuing further with this idea of complex data structures, imagine that, instead of working with a single investor, you had to keep information for a collection of investors, each of which is described in the TYPE declaration above. To do so, you can use the concept of an array to create a collection of record variables. In this case, each element of the array would be a record of type *Client* as described above. Specifically, the following would serve to declare the array:

```
TYPE
   ClientArray = ARRAY[1..100] OF Client;
VAR
   InvestorList :ClientArray;
```

Each element of the array must be referenced by a subscript following the array name *InvestorList*. Then each such element, being itself a record, must be followed by the appropriate field names; for example,

```
InvestorList[10]        {This is a record variable corresponding to the
                         tenth investor.}

InvestorList[2].Name.Last[1]     {This is the first character in
                                  the last name of the second
                                  investor.}

InvestorList[3].Property.CurrentValue     {This is the
                 current value of the investment of the third investor.}
```

From these examples, you can see that it is possible to create data structures to suit almost any situation. For instance, you can have arrays whose elements are themselves records, or records whose fields are arrays or other records, and so on.

In this section you have learned about the concept of a record, which enables you to store many different types of values into a single variable. In Section 8.3 you will learn about another type of data structure available in Pascal—the set.

Exercises for Section 8.2

Develop Pascal procedures for solving each of the following problems. In so doing, use records, arrays, user-defined values, and other appropriate data structures for storing and manipulating the given information. Prepare appropriate `TYPE` and `VAR` declarations for the main program; however, you need not write the main program, only the procedure itself.

1. For each part-time employee of a company, the following information is known: name (30 characters), social security number, an hourly wage rate, and a tax withholding percentage. In addition, it will be necessary to compute and to store the gross wages earned in a week, the amount of taxes to be withheld, and the net resulting pay. You will also be given a list of *N* social security numbers and the associated number of hours worked by that person (this information will be stored in two one-dimensional arrays, say *Numbers* and *Pay*). Write a procedure that will take the given information pertaining to an employee, together with the two arrays, and, if the employee's social security number is on the list, will compute and store the gross wages, the taxes withheld, and the net pay. Otherwise, display a message that the employee's social security number is not on the list, and set all wages and taxes withheld to 0.
2. You will be given a (shuffled) deck of 52 playing cards. Each card is to be thought of as a record consisting of an integer from 1 to 13 that represents the face value of the card (an ace is 1, a jack is 11, a queen is 12, and a king is 13), and a suit whose [user-defined] value is either clubs, diamonds, hearts, or spades. First, write a procedure that will "deal" the given deck into four hands, each containing 13 cards (use a two-dimensional array). Then write a procedure that will take the four hands and count the total points in each hand as follows:

   Ace—4 points
   King—3 points
   Queen—2 points
   Jack—1 point

   The total for each hand should be stored for later use.
3. The Gambling Game Company has 200 different games on which to keep records. Each game has a name, an inventor (who has a last name of up to 20 characters, a first name of up to 20 characters, and a middle initial), an order number (consisting of a department code number, a version number, and a sales code), a selling price, and a royalty percentage for the inventor. Given a particular order number of a game and the number of units sold, search through the 200 games until you find the one with the given order number. Then, display the name of the game, the total gross income the company receives from this sale, the inventor's name (in the form: last name, first name, middle initial), the royalty due to the author, and the net income the company receives.

8.3 Sets

In this section you will learn of yet another Pascal data type called a **set.** A set, like an array, consists of a collection of individual elements of the same type. The primary advantage of a set is that instead of working with each individual element (as you would do with an array), you can work with the entire set at once. The major drawback of a set is that you cannot easily access each individual element, which you can do with an array by using the subscript.

Set A collection of individual values of the same type, referenced by a single name, that can be processed as a whole by using appropriate operators.

From mathematics, you probably remember that a set is a collection of (related) items called the *elements of the set*. To write the set, in mathematics, you enclose the list of the individual elements, separated by commas, in braces. For example, the set consisting of the elements 1, 4, and 7 would be written mathematically as

$$\{1, 4, 7\}$$

Since the symbols { and } are used in Pascal to indicate a comment in a program, some other symbol must be used for sets. Those symbols are [and], respectively. Thus the above set would be written in Pascal as

```
[1, 4, 7]
```

Like an array, each element of a set must be of the same type. Thus assuming that *I* and *J* are integer variables, each of the following is a valid set except the last one.

```
[1, 3, 5, 7, 9]                {A set of integers.}
['a', 'e', 'i', 'o', 'u']      {A set of characters.}
[Red, White, Blue]             {A set of user-defined values.}
[I, J]                         {A set of two integers.}
[ ]                            {A set with no elements. This set
                                is called the empty set.}
[1, 'b']                       {This is not a set because the
                                integer 1 and the character 'b'
                                cannot belong to the same set.}
```

As with any other data type, in Pascal you can create a "set" variable. One way to do so is to use a `TYPE` declaration followed by a `VAR` declaration. In the `TYPE` declaration you will provide not only a type name (as usual), but also a description of the type of values that will constitute the actual elements of the sets themselves. The appropriate syntax is

```
TYPE
   TypeName = SET OF SetType;
VAR
   VariableName :TypeName;
```

Example

To create a set variable *Vowels*, whose values are to be the vowels, you could use the following declarations:

```
TYPE
   Letters = SET OF CHAR;
VAR
   Vowels :Letters;
```

Subsequently, it would be valid to write

```
Vowels := ['a', 'e', 'i', 'o', 'u']
```

Example

To create a set variable, say *OddIntegers*, whose values are to be some of the odd integers between 1 and 20, you could use the following declarations:

```
TYPE
   Numbers = SET OF 1..20;
VAR
   OddIntegers :Numbers;
```

Subsequently, it would be valid to write

```
OddIntegers := [1, 3, 5, 7, 9]
```

Example

To create a set variable, say *Cube*, whose elements are to be some of the user-defined values *Red*, *Yellow*, *Green*, *White*, *Orange*, and *Blue*, you could use the following declarations:

```
TYPE
   Colors = (Red, Yellow, Green, White,
             Orange, Blue);
```

```
    ColorSet = SET OF Colors;
VAR
    Cube :Colorset;
```

Subsequently, it would be valid to write

```
Cube := [Red, White, Blue]
```

When using the TYPE declaration

```
TYPE
    TypeName = SET OF SetType;
```

there are several concerns and limitations on SetType that you must be aware of. First, the SetType must include all values that could conceivably become elements of the set variable. That is why in the examples above the SetType always included more values than those contained in the specific assignment statements. Second, the SetType must be one of: INTEGER, CHAR, BOOLEAN, user-defined values (that have previously been declared in a TYPE declaration), or a subrange of one of these. Current versions of Pascal will not allow you to create a set of real numbers. Also, you cannot have a set in which each element is an array. However, it is possible to create an array, each of whose elements is a set. Finally, the total number of different values in *SetType* cannot exceed that allowed by the specific computer system with which you are working. Often, that number can be extremely small, thus ruling out the use of INTEGER and/or CHAR for *SetType* because a set consisting of all of the integers, for example, would be too "big" for the computer to store. In such cases, your sets will not be able to contain many elements.

Pros and Cons of Working with Sets

There are certain advantages and disadvantages of working with sets as opposed to other data structures such as arrays. The two major advantages of a set are as follows: First, it is possible to perform certain operations on the entire set with one instruction rather than having to work with each element individually (as you would have to do with an array). Second, the number of elements in a particular set can vary at different points in the program; yet, you need not keep track of that number. What is more, you need not explicitly declare a "maximum number of elements" that a set can have (as you would have to do with an array). That number is provided implicitly in the TYPE declaration, i.e., the number of elements in SetType.

On the other hand, there are certain difficulties associated with processing sets. Specifically, you cannot easily access an individual element of a set. If you were working with an array, for example, to refer to one specific element, you would simply follow the array name with the appropriate subscript. In contrast, if *X* is a set, then you cannot refer to the first element by writing `X[1]`; you can refer only to the entire set *X*. Second, as with user-defined variables, you cannot read or write set variables. This restriction is due in part to the fact that the number of elements of a set is not known, and to the fact that you cannot refer to one specific element of the set.

While it is usually possible to overcome these restrictions, doing so can sometimes be quite cumbersome. Therefore when deciding whether to use sets in solving a problem, you must give careful consideration as to what operations will be performed with those sets.

Operations on Sets

So far, you have learned how to create sets and set variables, and how to perform assignment statements. There are other powerful operations that can be performed with sets, which are often needed in problem solving. For example, the following three *set operators* can be used to combine two sets, say *A* and *B*, to create a third set as follows:

Operator Symbol	Operator Name	Resulting Set
+	Union	*A* + *B* is the set whose elements are in either *A* or *B*, or both.
−	Difference	*A* − *B* is the set whose elements are in *A* but not in *B*.
*	Intersection	*A* * *B* is the set whose elements are in both *A* and *B* simultaneously.

When working with these operators, you need not be concerned with the number of elements in the resulting set. Also, the precedence of these operators is the same as that of the corresponding arithmetic operators as given in Appendix B.

To illustrate these various operations, assume that the following set variables have been declared and assigned the indicated values:

```
Vowels := ['a', 'e', 'i', 'o', 'u'];
FiveLetters := ['a', 'b', 'c', 'd', 'e'];
Ch := [ ]   {The empty set of characters.}
```

The use of the above operators would result in the indicated sets:

Assignment Statement	Value of *Ch*
Ch := *Vowels* + *FiveLetters*	['a', 'b', 'c', 'd', 'e', 'i', 'o', 'u'] {Note that the letters 'a' and 'e' appear only once in *Ch* even though those letters appear in both *Vowels* and *FiveLetters*.}
Ch := *Vowels* – *FiveLetters*	['i', 'o', 'u']
Ch := *FiveLetters* – *Vowels*	['b', 'c', 'd']
Ch := *Vowels* * *FiveLetters*	['a', 'e']
Ch := (*Vowels* * *FiveLetters*) – ['a', 'e']	[ ] {The empty set.}

You have previously learned that certain types of variables can be compared using the relational operators <, >, =, <=, >=, and <>. Some of these operators can be used to compare two sets, say *A* and *B*. The result will be a boolean value of either TRUE or FALSE, as explained below.

Operator Symbol	Operator Name	Resulting Boolean Value
<=	Subset	The value of *A* <= *B* is TRUE if each element of *A* is also in *B*. Otherwise, the value of *A* <= *B* is FALSE.
=	Equal	The value of *A* = *B* is TRUE if each element of *A* is in *B*, and each element of *B* is also in *A*. Otherwise, the value of *A* = *B* is FALSE. In other words, the value of *A* = *B* is the same as (*A* <= *B*) and (*B* <= *A*).
<>	Not equal	The value of *A* <> *B* is TRUE if the value of *A* = *B* is FALSE, and vice versa. In other words, the value of *A* <> *B* is the same as NOT(*A* = *B*).

The following comparisons illustrate these three operators.

Comparison	Value	
[1, 3] <= [1, 2, 3]	TRUE	
[2, 4] <= [1, 2, 3]	FALSE	
[ ] <= [1, 2, 3]	TRUE	{The empty set is a subset of every set.}
[1, 2, 3] = [3, 1, 2]	TRUE	{Observe that the order in which the elements are listed in a set is completely irrelevant.}
[1, 2, 3] <> [1, 2, 4]	TRUE	

There is one final and important operation that can be performed on a set; namely, IN. This operator checks if a particular value is an element of a given set. Unlike all of the previous operators that work with two sets, the operator IN works with a set and a particular value, say *A* and *Value*, respectively, as follows:

Operator	Resulting Value
IN	The value of (*Value* IN *A*) is TRUE if the *Value* is in the set *A*, and FALSE otherwise.

To illustrate the use of the operator IN, recall the set *Vowels* whose elements are the vowels of the alphabet. The following results would be obtained using the operator IN.

Operation	Resulting Value
'e' IN *Vowels*	TRUE
'b' IN *Vowels*	FALSE

You can also use the operator IN to check if a variable whose value has been assigned is an element of a given set. For example, if *Ch* is a character variable that has been assigned a value, then the following is valid:

```
Ch IN Vowels
```

However, it would be incorrect to write

```
['b'] IN Vowels
```

because ['b'] is a set, not a specific value.

The use of the operator IN is extremely important because, while it is not possible to refer to a specific element of a set directly, it is possible (using the operator IN) to check if a particular value is one of the elements of the set. If so, then you can use that value—for example, you can display it.

To conclude, you can use any of the set operators <=, =, <>, and IN to create a boolean expression that can then be used in an IF/THEN or a WHILE statement, for example.

Problem Solving with Sets

To illustrate the use of sets in problem solving, imagine that you have the following problem.

Problem: The Bountiful Beauty Company has kept separate records on the various products sold during each of the past two months.

Each product has a product number between 1 and 100. Given the two lists of products sold during each month, the company would like a combined list of all products sold during those months (with duplicate numbers not printed). Also, they want a list of those common products that were sold both in the first and in the second month. In the data, each month's list of product codes ends with the number 0.

Analysis of Data Structures. As you have already learned in this chapter, it is well worth your while to give some thought to data structures prior to beginning the problem-solving process. For example, without giving the issue much thought, you might be tempted to use two arrays to store the two lists of product numbers. If you do so, however, you will find the processing portion of the problem to be fairly complicated and involved because you would have to process the two arrays, element by element, to create the combined list, and the common products sold.

On the other hand, if you take a moment to consider various alternatives, you can save yourself a great deal of time and effort later. For instance, if you think of the two lists of product numbers as sets whose names are *FirstMonth* and *SecondMonth*, say, then to solve the problem, the two desired output lists can be obtained by taking the union and the intersection of *FirstMonth* and *LastMonth*.

Having made this choice of data structures, you must now go through the usual problem-solving process. To that end, the inputting, processing, and outputting phases will be identified and developed using pseudocode.

Inputting. Obviously, the data for this problem consists of the list of product numbers that constitute the elements of the two sets *FirstMonth* and *SecondMonth*. Rereading the last sentence in the problem statement that describes the form in which the data will be given, you might be inclined to use a `WHILE` loop to read the values. In fact, using the variable *ProductNumber* to represent the current product number in the list, you might write

```
WHILE <ProductNumber is not 0> DO
      <Store the ProductNumber as an element
      of the set FirstMonth>
      <Read the next value of ProductNumber>
```

Looking at the problem of storing the value of *ProductNumber* in the set *FirstMonth*, how will you refer to that element of *FirstMonth*? You cannot write the instruction

```
FirstMonth[?] := ProductNumber
```

because *FirstMonth* is a set, not an array, and so you cannot refer to a particular element of the set. Can you solve this problem?

The solution is to "add" that product number to the set *FirstMonth* using the set operator +. However, there is a serious problem with doing so because the variable *FirstMonth* is a set, while the variable *ProductNumber* is an integer, and you cannot "add" a set to an integer. You can, however, "add" a set to a set. Thus you should create from the integer *ProductNumber* a set whose only element is the value of *ProductNumber*. To do so, you need only surround the variable *ProductNumber* with square brackets. Thus the correct WHILE loop in pseudocode becomes

```
WHILE ProductNumber ≠ 0 DO
        FirstMonth := FirstMonth +
                          [ProductNumber]
        READ ProductNumber
```

Recalling that all necessary variables must be initialized prior to the loop, it is not difficult to see that the value of *ProductNumber* can be initialized by using a READ statement, but what should the value of *FirstMonth* be initialized to?

To answer this question, you should perform the first iteration of the loop yourself. As you do so, you might realize that, on the first iteration, the set *FirstMonth* should have no elements. Thus you should use the pseudocode instruction

```
FirstMonth := [ ]    {The empty set.}
```

to initialize the value of *FirstMonth*.

Since a similar set of instructions is necessary for entering the values of the set *SecondMonth*, the inputting phase consists of the pseudocode instructions

```
FirstMonth := [ ]
READ ProductNumber
WHILE ProductNumber ≠ 0 DO
        FirstMonth := FirstMonth +
                          [ProductNumber]
        READ ProductNumber
SecondMonth := [ ]
READ ProductNumber
```

```
WHILE ProductNumber ≠ 0 DO
      SecondMonth := SecondMonth +
                     [ProductNumber]
      READ ProductNumber
```

At this point, an astute reader might recognize that the process of reading a list of product numbers is being repeated twice, first with the variable *FirstMonth*, and then with the variable *SecondMonth*. A good programmer would realize that a procedure could (and should) be used. The parameter of the procedure is the specific set whose values are to be read. The procedure could be written in pseudocode as

```
PROCEDURE ReadSet(List)     {List is the dummy parameter
                             representing the set whose values
                             are to be read.}
   List := [ ]
   READ Element       {Element is a local variable that plays the
                       same role as ProductNumber above.}
   WHILE Element ≠ 0 DO
         List := List + [Element]
         READ Element
```

Then, to call the procedure, in the main program you would write the instructions

```
ReadSet(FirstMonth)      {FirstMonth is the actual parameter.}
ReadSet(SecondMonth)     {SecondMonth is the actual
                          parameter.}
```

Observe that nowhere is the number of elements in these sets being counted or stored. Had you used arrays instead of sets, you would have to be concerned about the subscripts of those arrays.

Processing. As was mentioned in the beginning of the problem-solving discussion, the desired computations can be performed by taking the union and intersection of the two sets *FirstMonth* and *SecondMonth*. Creating two new set variables for these purposes, the processing portion of this program in pseudocode is

```
TotalProducts := FirstMonth + SecondMonth
CommonProducts := FirstMonth * SecondMonth
```

Observe, once again, that you need not be concerned with the number of elements in the two new sets, *TotalProducts* and *CommonProducts*. In fact, you do not know how many elements there are in those sets. In addition, you can see that the power of working with sets is that you can perform the entire computation with a single instruction; you do not have to work with the individual elements of the sets *FirstMonth* and *SecondMonth*.

Outputting. The solution to the original problem is the list of elements in the two sets *TotalProducts* and *CommonProducts*. While it would, indeed, be convenient to write the pseudocode instructions

```
WRITE TotalProducts, CommonProducts
```

recall that it is not possible to display the values of set variables. As with reading the elements of a set, you need to be clever in order to accomplish the desired task. The details of doing so will be left to the exercises. At this point, however, you should at least recognize that you will want to use a procedure to enable you to display the values of both the sets *TotalProducts* and *CommonProducts*, while only having to write those instructions once.

Coding. In Pascal, the above pseudocode algorithm could be coded as

```
PROGRAM Products(INPUT, OUTPUT);
CONST
   Max = 100;
TYPE
   Codes = SET OF 1..Max;        {On some computers this range
                                  might be too large.}
VAR
   FirstMonth, SecondMonth       :Codes;
   TotalProducts, CommonProducts :Codes;

PROCEDURE ReadSet(VAR List :Codes);     {Since List
            is an output parameter, the VAR is needed.}
   VAR
      Element :INTEGER;     {A local variable.}
   BEGIN
      List := [ ];
      READ (Element);
      WHILE Element <> 0 DO
            BEGIN
               List := List + [Element];
               READ(Element)
            END    {End of WHILE loop.}
   END;    {End of procedure ReadSet.}

PROCEDURE WriteSet(List :Codes);
   {The details of this procedure are left to the exercises. The main program
   follows.}
```

```
BEGIN
   ReadSet(FirstMonth);
   ReadSet(SecondMonth);
   TotalProducts := FirstMonth + SecondMonth;
   CommonProducts := FirstMonth * SecondMonth;
   WriteSet(TotalProducts);
   WriteSet(CommonProducts)
END.
```

Since the program above is correct, the details of tracing and debugging will not be given here.

In this section you have learned about the data structure known as a set, which, like an array, allows you to work with a collection of values of the same type by referring to the set name. In addition, you have learned about the operators that you can use with sets, and you have seen how sets are used in the problem-solving process. In Chapter 9 you will learn yet other data structures that are useful for storing and processing data. In any event, by now you should realize the importance of thinking carefully about the choice of data structures prior to solving a problem.

Exercises for Section 8.3

Suppose that the following assignments have been made:

```
Vowels := ['a', 'e', 'i', 'o', 'u'];
Worked := ['w', 'o', 'r', 'k', 'e', 'd'];
SomeVowels := ['a', 'i', 'u'];
Letter := 'i'    {Letter is a character variable.}
```

What is the result of performing the following computations with the given set operators?

1. `Vowels * Worked`
2. `Vowels <= SomeVowels`
3. `SomeVowels <= Vowels`
4. `Letter IN Worked`
5. `Vowels - Worked`
6. `Worked - Vowels`
7. `Vowels + SomeVowels`
8. `([Letter] + ['a', 'u']) = SomeVowels`
9. `Letter IN SomeVowels`
10. `(SomeVowels + 'e' + 'o') = Vowels`

Assume that, as in the final program of this section, you have made the declaration

```
TYPE
    Codes = SET OF 1..100;
```

In each of the following problems, suppose that, in the main program, you will be working with a set of type `Codes`. Write Pascal procedures or functions to accomplish each of the following tasks.

11. Display the individual elements of a given set. You do not know specifically how many elements there are in the set. (*Hint*: Use a `FOR` loop to go through all 100 possible values using the operator `IN` to check which values are elements of the set.)

12. Write a function that counts (and returns to the main program) the number of elements in a set.

13. Write a procedure that uses the elements of a set to create an array whose elements are precisely those of the set. The number of elements of the array should also be returned to the main program.

14. Write a procedure that returns the first element of a set whose value is between the given integers `First` and `Last`. In addition, that element should be removed from the set. Be careful to handle the case where the original set is the empty set.

Write Pascal programs to perform each of the following instructions.

15. Someone has created an input file that is supposed to contain real numbers. Thinking of the input file as a list of characters, write a program to check that each character in the file is a valid character belonging to a real number, or a blank space. Display an appropriate message when an invalid character is encountered.

16. Given a paragraph of text, count the number of letters in the paragraph. Do not include punctuation, blank spaces, or any other symbols. (*Hint*: Create a set containing the valid letters.)

8.4 Summary

In this chapter, you have learned three different data structures that are available in Pascal. You have seen how these concepts are used in problem solving. In particular, you have learned the importance of selecting the most appropriate data structures for your problem, because careful forethought can greatly reduce the subsequent programming effort. A brief summary of these data structures together with their advantages and disadvantages will be given here.

The concept of user-defined values allows you to create your own special values consisting of names of your choosing. The main advantage of user-defined values is that, since you can choose the names for those values, the resulting program will be easier for you (and others) to read and understand. After you have created user-defined values, you can then declare and use corresponding variables in solving your problem. The primary disadvantage of user-defined values is that you can neither read nor write these values directly.

When solving a problem, you often need to work with a portion of an existing set of values. You could, of course, choose to work with the entire collection of values; however, the concept of subrange values allows you to create and to work with only that portion in which you are interested.

A record is a variable in which you can store more than one piece of information, each of which is called a field of the record. Each field can contain an integer, array, or other type of value (even another record). One primary advantage of using a record variable is that you can collect many different types of related information into one variable whose single name (together with the individual field names) can be used to access each value. It is possible to have an array in which each element is itself a record. Alternatively, it is possible to have a record in which a particular field is an array.

A set, like an array, is a collection of items of the same type. One primary advantage of a set is that it is possible to perform certain operations on the entire set rather than having to use a loop to process each individual element. As a result, because a set is generally considered as a whole, you do not need to know, to specify, or to keep track of the number of elements in a set.

There are some disadvantages to working with sets; the primary disadvantage is that it is not possible to access directly an individual element of the set. In contrast, with an array you can refer to one particular element simply by using the appropriate subscript. Also, in most versions of Pascal, there are severe limitations on the maximum number of elements that a set can have.

Key Terms

User-defined values 374
Subrange of values 378
Record 380
Fields of a record 380
Record name 381
Field names 381
`WITH` **statement 384**
Set 393

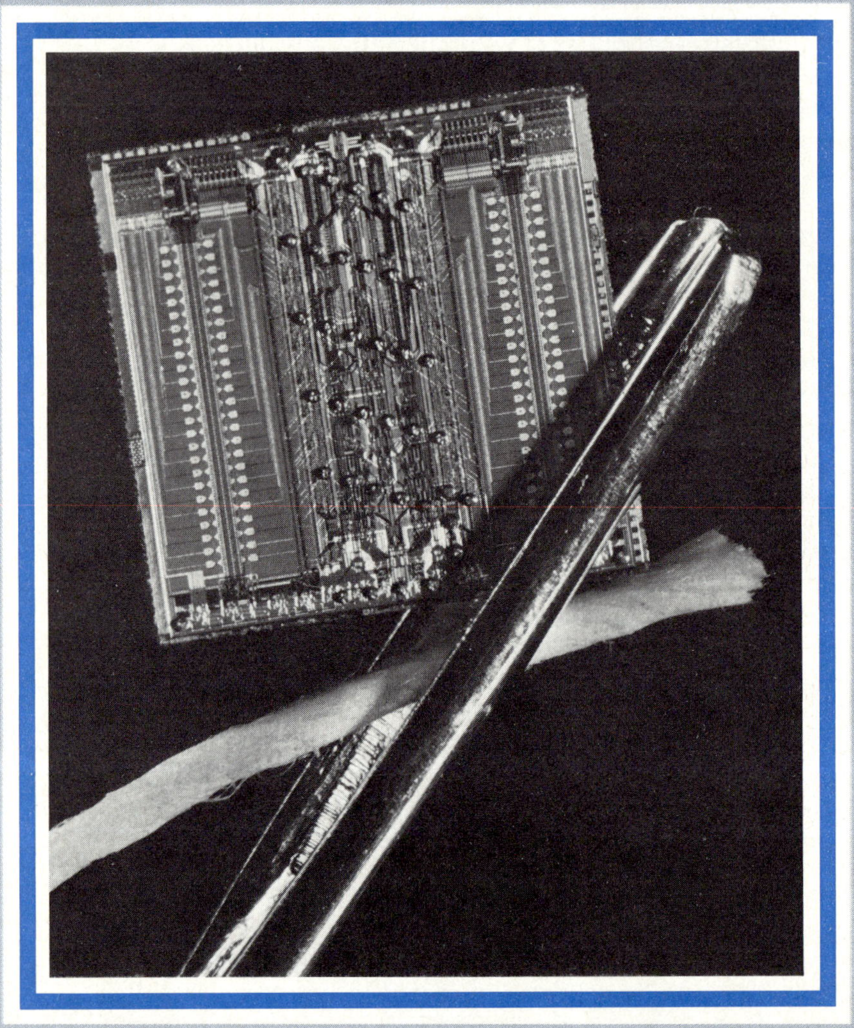

The silicon chip—a thin wafer containing hundreds of thousands of transistors—is the heart of the computer. These tiny wonders even help us use our credit cards, keep track of time on our watches, and entertain us with video games. The million-bit chip shown here, developed by IBM, is so minute it can slip through the eye of a needle with room to spare for the thread. And to think that silicon is the second most abundant element on earth, next to oxygen. (COURTESY OF IBM)

9

ADVANCED DATA STRUCTURES—PART II

In this chapter you will learn two additional data structures, one of which is called a **file.** One advantage of a file is that extremely large quantities of data can be stored in it. In addition, the computer can save the values in a file for future use even after the program is finished running. The primary advantage of the second data structure you will learn is that new elements can be inserted (and old elements deleted) very easily.

File A collection of values of the same type that is stored, as a unit, in some part of the computer, such as on a tape or disk.

9.1 Files

In Chapter 3 you were exposed briefly to the concept of a file, which at that time was described as a collection of information that is stored, as a unit, in some part of the computer. In this section you will learn how to work with files in Pascal.

To be a bit more precise, a file is a collection of information, each element of which must be of the same type. In this sense, a file is much like an array. However, there are several major differences between a file and an array. In Pascal, the number of elements of an array must be known at the time the array is declared. In contrast, when a file is declared, you need not know how many elements are in the file, nor do you need to keep track of that information in the program.

As another comparison, with an array, the values of the individual elements will be stored directly in the memory of the computer, as are those of a **local file.** In contrast, the values of the elements of an **external file** can be located on a magnetic tape, disk, or other storage device. This fact reveals one of the most important and valuable features of an external file. Normally, when the computer finishes running a program, the values of all variables (including arrays and local files) are lost forever. However, since the values of the elements of an external file can be stored on a disk or tape, those values will still be there when the program is finished running. Hence, they can be used again at a later date, or even transported and used on another computer.

Local file A file whose values are stored in the primary memory of the computer just like those of an array. Those values are lost after the program is finished running.

External file A file whose values are stored outside the primary memory of the computer; for example, on a disk or tape. Those values are saved even after the program is finished running.

There is another advantage to the fact that the values of the elements of an external file are not stored in the memory of the computer, for if they were, the number of elements in the file would be limited by the size of the available computer memory (as is an array). However, since the values of the elements of an external file are stored on a magnetic tape or disk, the size of the file is restricted only by the amount of information that can be stored on such a device (which greatly exceeds the available memory capacity of a computer). For instance, on some tapes it is possible to store 20 million pieces of information (or more). Just try to declare an array of that size on your computer!

There is yet another difference between an array and a file (whether local or external). With an array, you can access each and every element simply by following the array name with an appropriate subscript (e.g., *Test*[1] or *Test*[200]). However, with a file, only one element is immediately available. That current element is called the **window of the file,** and is depicted in Fig. 9.1. In order to access an element that is somewhere to the *right* of the window, it is necessary to instruct the computer to read (and to "ignore"), in sequence, each element of the file to the right of the window until the desired element becomes the window. Only then can you process that element. You should note that in Pascal it is not possible to read to the left of the window, only to the right.

Window of a file The one (and only) element of a file whose value is currently available for processing.

The type of file that was just described is called a **sequential file** because, in order to find one particular element, it is necessary to scan all elements sequentially to the right of the window. This situation is analogous to a music tape in which you must search sequentially from the current position in order to reach a desired song. In this chapter, it will be assumed that all files are sequential files of the type illustrated in Fig. 9.1.

Sequential file A file in which the only way to find a particular element is to scan all elements sequentially to the right of the window.

With regard to sequential files, you should realize that, although you have a very large storage capacity, the "price" you pay for this

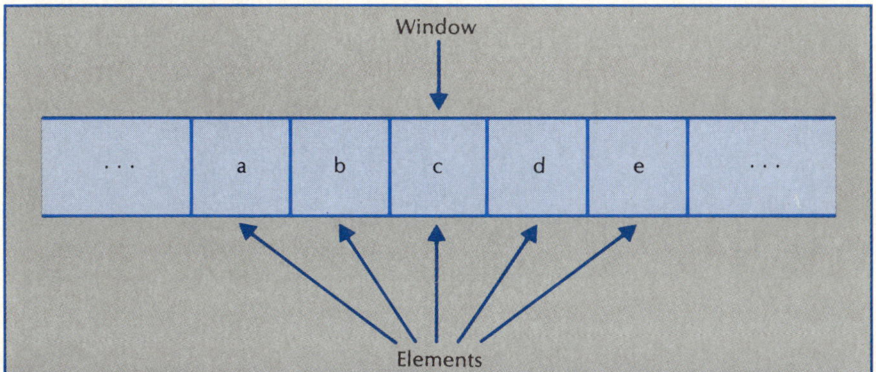

Figure 9.1 A sequential file.

feature is that the computer might require a lot of processing time to search through the file looking for a particular element. Thus there is a trade-off between the amount of storage space and the amount of computer time needed for processing. A similar type of situation arose with regard to packed arrays (see Section 6.6).

Declaring and Processing Files

In Pascal, you declare a file data type in much the same way as you would a user-defined, record, or array type: namely, with the TYPE declaration. The specific syntax for a sequential file declaration is

```
TYPE
   TypeName = FILE OF FileType;
```

The FileType represents the type of value of each element in the file. The FileType can be any Pascal data type except another file (e.g., REAL, ARRAY, RECORD, etc.).

Example

The following is a file type in which each element is going to be a real number:

```
TYPE
   RealFile = FILE OF REAL;
```

Example

The following is a file type in which each element is going to be an array consisting of 50 elements (each of which is a character):

```
TYPE
   ArrayFile = FILE OF ARRAY[1..50] OF CHAR;
```

Example

The following is a file type in which each element is going to be a record with five fields:

```
TYPE
   RecordFile = FILE OF RECORD
                          Author       :ARRAY[1..30] OF
                                         CHAR;
```

```
        BookNumber  :INTEGER;
        SalesPrice  :REAL;
        Inventory   :INTEGER;
        ReOrder     :BOOLEAN
    END;
```

As usual, once a TYPE declaration has been made, it is then possible to create variables of that type by using the VAR declaration. For each of the three TYPE declarations in the examples above, you could create variables of that type as follows:

```
VAR
   R       :RealFile;
   Names   :ArrayFile;
   Book    :RecordFile;
```

When these variables are declared, Pascal will simultaneously create a window variable associated with each file variable. The window variable is often called the **buffer variable.** You can use each of the buffer variables in your program just as you would any other variable. The buffer variable is written by following the name of the file variable (which appears in the VAR declaration) with the symbol ↑ (or some other symbol, depending on your computer). Thus for the three file variables in the VAR declaration above, the respective buffer variables would be

Buffer variable A variable associated with each file, whose value is precisely that of the window of the file.

R↑ {whose value is a real number.}

Names↑ {which is an array of characters, the elements of which would be referenced by *Names*↑[1], . . ., *Names*↑[50].}

Book↑ {which is a record with five fields.}

The five fields of the record variable *Book*↑ would be referenced as

```
Book↑.Author[1], . . ., Book↑.Author[30]
Book↑.BookNumber
Book↑.SalesPrice
Book↑.Inventory
Book↑.ReOrder
```

The value of the buffer variable should be thought of as the element of the file that is currently in the window. The value of the buffer variable is available for use in the program. If, however, you need to use the value of an element that is not currently in the window, then you must instruct the computer to move, element by element, to the right until the desired element is found. Remember, you cannot move to the left of the window.

In addition to declaring files with the TYPE and VAR declarations, you must specify which files are external. You do so in the PROGRAM heading, which, as you learned in Chapter 3, has the following form:

```
PROGRAM Name(FileName, ..., FileName);
```

Indeed, the FileNames in this declaration are precisely those variable names appearing in the VAR declaration that are used for external files (e.g., *R*, *Names*, and *Book* from above, assuming that those files are external files). The special files INPUT and OUTPUT, being external files, also appear in the PROGRAM heading. On the other hand, the names of local files need not appear in the PROGRAM heading; only external file names must be listed there.

Ultimately, you must also tell the computer on which tape, disk, or other storage device each external file is located. Your instructor will have to provide the specific details that pertain to your computer system. In all other regards, local and external files are the same, and so, throughout the rest of this section, no further distinction will be made between these two types of files.

Operations on Files

In standard Pascal, there are five operations that can be performed on a file. Each will be discussed and illustrated using a file whose name is *F*. The form of these procedures, however, may not be correct in nonstandard versions of Pascal (e.g., Turbo or UCSD). Check with your instructor.

EOF(*F*)

This is a boolean function whose value is TRUE if the window is at the end-of-file marker, and FALSE otherwise. The parameter of this function is the name of the file.

RESET(*F*)

This procedure prepares a file for reading by setting the value of the buffer variable *F*↑ to the value of the very first (i.e., leftmost) element in the file. If the file is not empty, then EOF(*F*) is simultaneously set to FALSE. If the file is empty, then EOF(*F*) is set to TRUE, and the value of *F*↑ is undefined. All files (other than INPUT) must be reset before being read for the first time. For example,

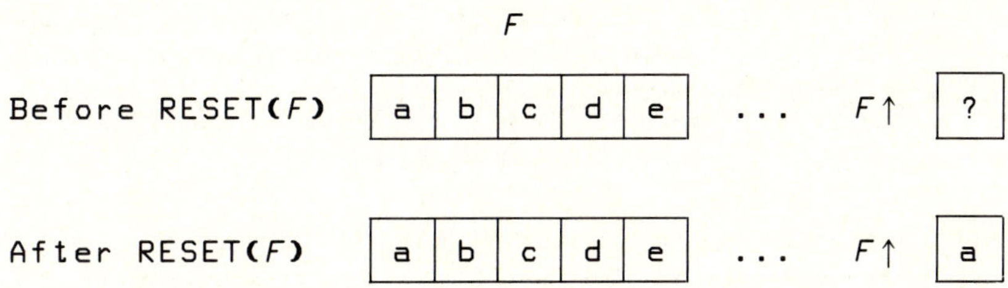

REWRITE(F)

This procedure prepares a file for writing by setting the window to the very first element of the file. The value of EOF(F) is also set to TRUE. All files (other than OUTPUT) must be prepared with this instruction prior to being written on for the first time. For example,

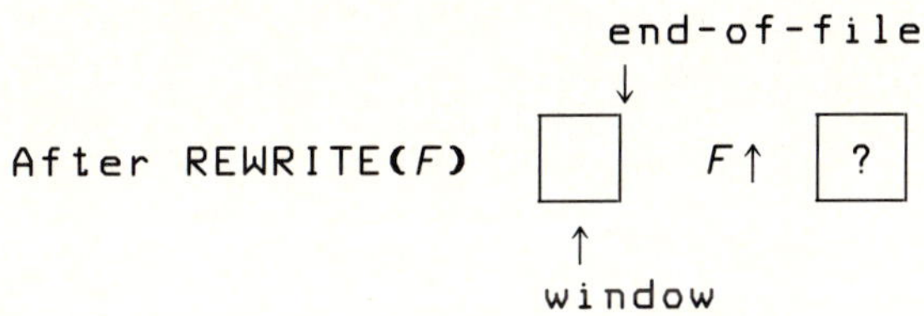

GET(F)

This procedure moves the window one element to the right of the current position. At the same time, the value of the buffer variable F↑ is set to that of the new window in the file. The value of EOF(F) is also set accordingly. If, however, the value of EOF(F) is TRUE before the GET instruction, then this instruction is undefined. For example,

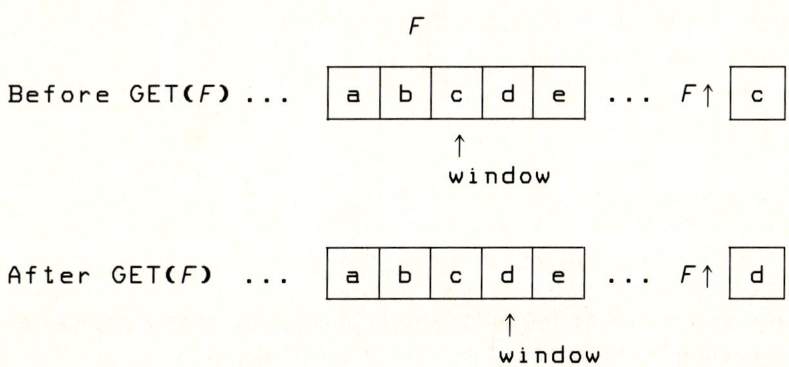

PUT(*F*)

This procedure writes (but does not change) the current value of the buffer variable *F*↑ onto the file in the current window position. The value of EOF(*F*) remains TRUE. For example,

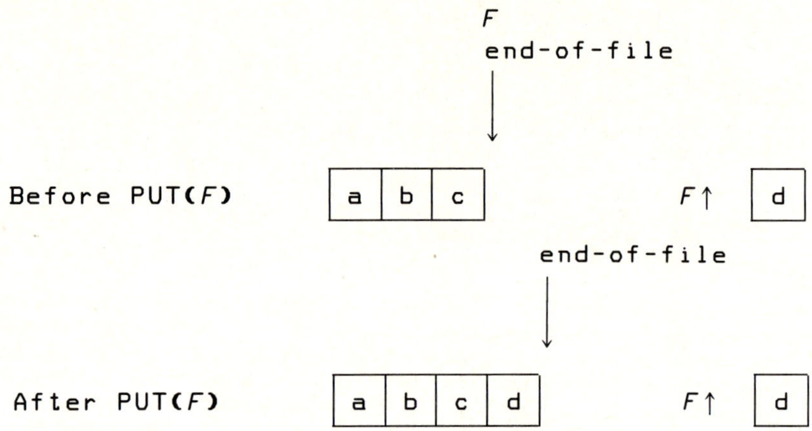

Solving a Problem Using Files

As an example of using files, suppose that Gary Gambler has created a file of trading information on silver. Each element of the file was created originally with the following declaration:

```
TYPE
   Silver = RECORD
              Date    :RECORD
                          Day   :INTEGER;
                          Month :INTEGER;
                          Year  :INTEGER
                       END;   {End of Date record.}
              Price   :RECORD
                          High  :REAL;
                          Low   :REAL;
                          Close :REAL
                       END;   {End of Price record.}
              Volume :INTEGER
            END;   {End of Silver record.}
```

Gary is concerned that at the time the file was created, typing mistakes might have been made on the prices. So he would like you to write a program that reads each element of the given file and creates a new file consisting only of those elements in which the value of *High* is greater than or equal to that of *Low*, and the value of *Close* is between that of *High* and *Low*. In addition, when a "bad" value is found, that record should be displayed as output but not written on the new file. Finally, count and report the number of elements in both the original and the new file.

Instead of going through the details of the problem-solving process, only the completed standard Pascal program will be presented here. This will give you the opportunity to learn to read another person's program. Perhaps then you will appreciate the need to comment and to document your own work. Here, then, is the Pascal program, appropriately commented, for solving Gary Gambler's problem:

```
PROGRAM TestData(InData, OutData, OUTPUT);
   {InData is the original input file; OutData is the new file to be
   created; OUTPUT is for displaying information.}
TYPE
   Silver = RECORD
                Date    :RECORD
                           Day    :INTEGER;
                           Month  :INTEGER;
                           Year   :INTEGER
                         END;       {End of Date record.}
                Price   :RECORD
                           High   :REAL;
                           Low    :REAL;
                           Close  :REAL
                         END;      {End of Price record.}
                Volume  :INTEGER
            END;     {End of Silver record.}
   DataFile = FILE OF Silver;
VAR
   InData          :DataFile;     {The original file of data.}
   OutData         :DataFile;     {The new file of clean data.}
   SizeIn          :INTEGER;
   SizeOut         :INTEGER;

{The main program begins here.}

BEGIN
   RESET(InData);        {Prepare the file for reading, and read the first
                          record.}
   SizeIn := 0;        {No record has been processed.}
```

```
    REWRITE(OutData);      {Prepare the file for writing.}
    SizeOut := 0;      {No records have been written.}
    WHILE NOT EOF(InData) DO
          BEGIN
             WITH InData↑.Date, InData↑.Price DO
                  IF (High >= Close) AND (Close >= Low) THEN
                     BEGIN      {The record is good.}
                        OutData↑ := InData↑;
                        {Write this good record to the file.}
                        PUT(OutData);
                        SizeOut := SizeOut + 1
                     END
                  ELSE      {Display the bad record.}
                     BEGIN
                        WRITELN;
                        WRITELN('The following record has bad ',
                               'price information:');
                        WRITE('Date: ', Month:2);
                        WRITE('/', Day:2, '/');
                        WRITELN(Year:2);
                        WRITELN('High  = ', High:10:2);
                        WRITELN('Close = ', Close:10:2);
                        WRITELN('Low   = ', Low:10:2);
                        WRITELN('Volume = ',
                               InData↑.Volume:5)
                     END;     {End IF/THEN/ELSE and WITH.}
             GET(InData);     {Read the next record.}
             SizeIn := SizeIn + 1
          END;     {End of WHILE loop.}
    WRITELN;
    WRITELN('The original file has',
             SizeIn:5, ' records');
    WRITELN('The new file has',
             SizeOut:5, ' records')
END.    {End of program.}
```

Textfiles

Textfile A file that consists solely of printable characters, end-of-line markers, and a closing end-of-file marker.

There is one type of file that requires special mention: the **textfile**. A textfile is a file that consists of printable characters together with end-of-line markers, denoted in this book by the symbol ■. Of course, there will be an end-of-file marker at the end of the file. For example, the standard files `INPUT` and `OUTPUT` are actually textfiles. In fact, the keyboard, punch cards, and displayed output (on a screen or printer) are all viewed by Pascal as textfiles.

A textfile, being just like any other file, can be processed by using the five standard procedures that were described previously in this section. However, there are five other procedures that you can use exclusively for textfiles: `EOLN`, `READ`, `READLN`, `WRITE`, and `WRITELN`. You have already used these five procedures for the special textfiles whose names are `INPUT` and `OUTPUT`. In fact, these five procedures can be used instead of the procedures `GET`, `PUT`, etc., to process any textile. For example, if *F* is a textfile and *Ch* is a character variable, then the Pascal statement

```
READ(F, Ch)
```

instructs the computer to go to the textfile whose name is *F* and to set the value of *Ch* to that of the buffer variable *F*↑. Having then read the current buffer variable, the computer will move the window of *F* to the right one element, thus changing the value of the buffer variable to the next element in the file. In other words, the `READ` statement above is equivalent to the instructions

```
Ch := F↑;
GET(F)
```

In fact, all five of the procedures `EOLN`, `READ`, `READLN`, `WRITE`, and `WRITELN` can be explained in terms of the equivalent file operators `GET` and `PUT`, as will now be done. In what follows, suppose that *F* is a textfile and *Ch* is a character variable.

Procedure	**Equivalent Instructions**
`EOLN(F)`	The value of `EOLN(F)` is `TRUE` if the value of the buffer variable *F*↑ is the end-of-line marker, and `FALSE` otherwise, i.e., `EOLN(F) := F↑ = '■'`
`READ(F, Ch)`	`Ch := F↑;` `GET(F)`
`READ(F, Ch)`	`Ch := F↑;` `GET(F)`

```
READLN(F, Ch)        Ch := F↑;
                     WHILE NOT EOLN(F) DO
                           GET(F);
                     GET(F)     {This instruction moves the
                                window just past the
                                end-of-line marker.}
WRITE(F)             F↑ := Ch;
                     PUT(F)
WRITELN(F, Ch)       F↑ := Ch;
                     PUT(F);
                     F↑ := '■';
                     PUT(F)
```

Note that, technically, EOLN is a function, not a procedure. Also, when using these procedures, if you omit the file name (e.g., *F* above), the computer will automatically assume that the file name to be used is INPUT or OUTPUT, whichever is appropriate. You can, of course, use these names explicitly. Finally, it is also worth noting that in Turbo and UCSD Pascal (and some other nonstandard versions), when working at a terminal, the value of EOLN(INPUT) is TRUE if the value of the character that has *just been read* is the end-of-file marker; not if the *next* character to be read is the end-of-file marker. In other words, in Turbo and UCSD Pascal, the computer does not "look ahead" when the input file is the terminal.

In this section you have learned how Pascal allows you to work with the data structure known as a [sequential] file. The primary advantage of a file is that, because a file can be located on a magnetic tape or disk, for example, the information stored in that file will be saved (and can be used again) after the program is finished running. In addition, the amount of information that can be stored in a file is very large, and greatly exceeds the memory capacity of the computer. However, each time you want to retrieve information from a file, time will be needed for the computer to go to the appropriate input or output device to obtain the desired values.

Exercises for Section 9.1

Use TYPE and VAR declarations to create file data types and variables according to the following specifications.

1. A student file is to contain elements consisting of

student name	(50 characters)
student number	(integer)
courses	(an array whose values are the [integer] course numbers in which the student is enrolled)

2. The input file will be a textfile (as described in this section). The output file will be a file of characters in which each "line" will contain precisely 81 characters, the last of which will be the end-of-line marker.
3. A file of employee information is to consist of records, each of which contains the following five fields:

last name	(20 characters)
first name	(20 characters)
middle initial	(one character)
social security number	(a nine-digit integer)
pay rate	(a real number)

Assume that you are reading from a file *F* and writing onto a file *G*, and that the current status of each file is

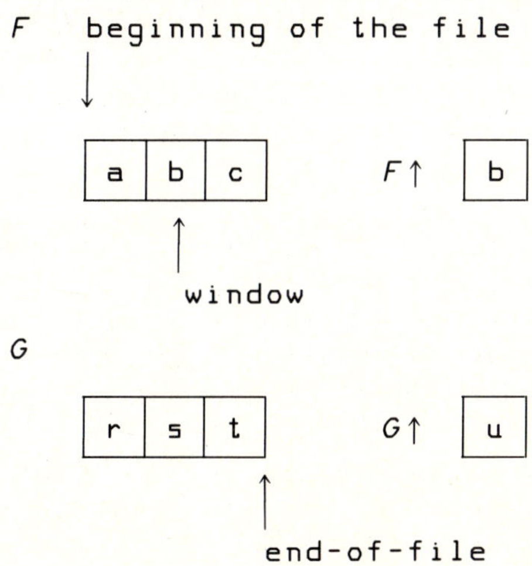

For each exercise, indicate what the new file and value of the buffer variable would be after all of the given instructions in that exercise have been performed using standard Pascal. For each exercise, always start with the files in the position given above.

4. `RESET(F); REWRITE(G)`
5. `GET(F); PUT(G); G↑ := F↑`
6. `REWRITE(G); G↑ := F↑; PUT(G)`

Prepare Pascal programs for accomplishing each of the following tasks.

7. Given an input textfile as described in Exercise 2 above, create an output textfile in which each "line" contains exactly 81 characters, the last of which will be the end-of-line marker. Each input line will have no more than 81 characters, and should be filled (i.e., augmented) with as many blank spaces as necessary to produce an output line of exactly 81 characters.
8. After running the program that was given in this section, Gary Gambler obtained the file of "clean" data (whose name was *OutData*) together with a list of the "bad" price data. He has now obtained all of the correct price information for those records and will supply that data to you (in increasing order of date). Write a program that will take this information, together with the file *OutData*, and will merge the corrected price information into the appropriate position of *OutData*, creating a new file, say *CleanData*, which then has valid price information for every day of trading. (You can assume that the records of *OutData* are in increasing order according to the date.)
9. Given a student file as described in Exercise 1 above, and given a specific course number, write a program that counts and displays the names of all students enrolled in the given course. The output should be displayed as

```
CourseNumber : ____
Number of Students Enrolled : ____
Name
.
.
.
```

(*Hint:* Use a local file to store all the names in this course as you simultaneously count the number of students. After the count is complete, display all names that were stored in the local file.)

9.2 Pointers

Pointer-type data structure A data structure in which each element contains a value together with information that specifies the preceding, the succeeding, or any other related elements.

In this section you will learn about another useful data structure. This **pointer-type data structure**, like an array, consists of a collection of individual elements of the same type. To understand one of the primary advantages of a pointer-type data structure, imagine that you have created an array that currently has 10 elements. As you are processing this array, suppose that you need to insert a new element in the array between the (already existing) fifth and sixth elements. In the absence of pointer-type data structures, you would have to move each element (from the sixth one on) down one position so that there is "room" for the new element in the array. Pointer-type data structures provide a more efficient means of maintaining a list in a sequential order when adding and deleting elements. That is, with a pointer-type data structure, you will be able to insert a new element directly into the "middle" of the structure.

To understand pointer-type data structures, recall from Chapter 2 the analogy of the computer's memory as being like a book. On each page of the book you will find a page number together with a particular value that has been written on that page. In Chapter 2 you learned to use variable names instead of page numbers because names were easier to remember. With pointer-type data structures, the approach is slightly different.

A pointer-type data structure can be thought of as a collection of these individual pages. However, there is no variable name associated with each page. Rather, these pages (which need not be consecutive within the book) are "linked" together in a very special way. On each page you will find not only a page number and a specific value that is written on the page, but also, at the bottom of the page, you will find a "pointer." The **pointer** consists of the page number of the "next" element in this list (which the computer can then use to "turn" to that page). This concept is illustrated in Fig. 9.2.

Pointer The information associated with a specific element of a pointer-type data structure that specifies the preceding, the succeeding, or any other related elements.

Fortunately, you do not have to be concerned with which element is on which page; the computer will automatically maintain that in-

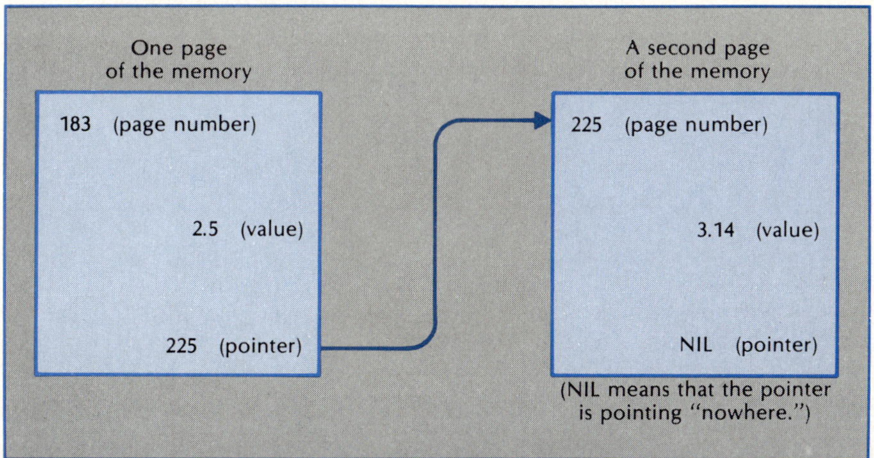

Figure 9.2 Pointers.

formation for you. Rather, you will be working with a "current" element in the list. When you are finished processing that element, you can then process the "next" element in the list by instructing the computer to proceed to the page number that is located in the pointer at the bottom of the current page.

The concept of working with only one element at a time of a pointer-type list is very similar to the way in which a file is processed using only the buffer variable to store the current value in the file. Thus another advantage of a pointer-type data structure is that you need not specify (or keep track of) the number of elements in the list. The number of elements is limited only by the available memory capacity of the computer.

In view of this discussion, perhaps you can see how a new element would be inserted into the middle of the list. For instance, suppose that you want to insert a new element between the two (already existing) elements in Fig. 9.2. After "creating" the new page with its value, you simply "break" the link between the two original pages. Specifically, the pointer of the first element in Fig. 9.2 must be made to point to the page number of the new element; the pointer of the new element must then be made to point to the page number of the second element. The result is illustrated in Fig. 9.3.

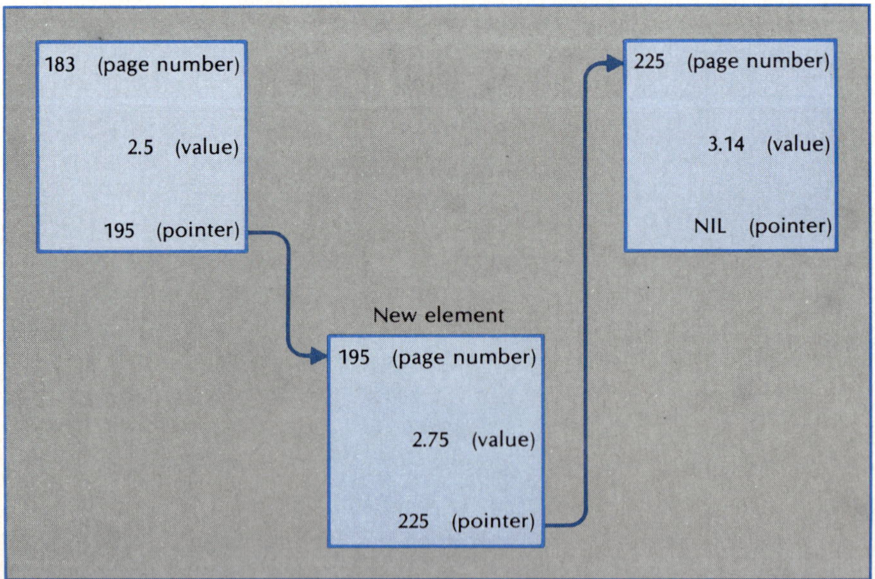

Figure 9.3 Inserting an element into a list.

Creating a Pointer-Type Data Structure

A pointer-type data structure consists of a collection of elements. Each element will contain at least two pieces of information—the first is the value; the second is the pointer (which "points" to the next element). Because each element is to contain more than one piece of information, a record is used to store the various data. Thus a pointer-type data structure in Pascal consists of a collection of records.

To create such a collection of records linked together with pointers, you could, for example, use the following TYPE and VAR declarations:

```
TYPE
    List = ↑Element;          {The ↑ indicates that List is a pointer-
                               type data structure.}
    Element = RECORD
          Value   :REAL;        {This is the value that will be stored
                                 on one page.}
          Pointer :List       {This is the pointer whose value will be
                               the page number of the next record in
                               the list.}
          END;
VAR
    First, Middle, Last :List;    {These are variables of
                                   type List whose values
                                   will be those of three
                                   elements of the list.}
```

The variable *First* above can now be used to create the very first element of the list in Fig. 9.2. To do so, you would use the Pascal statement

```
NEW(First)
```

which instructs the computer to create a page of memory for the first element. Subsequently, you can use the record variable

```
First↑
```

(of type *Element* described above) to store information. The two fields of this record (whose values have not yet been assigned) would be referenced by the names

```
First↑.Value      {whose value will be a real number.}
First↑.Pointer    {whose value will be the page number of the next
                   element in the list.}
```

In addition, when the computer performs the instruction

```
NEW(First)
```

the computer will store the page number of the record `First↑` (that was just created) into the variable

```
First
```

(which has no up arrow). The value of the variable `First` could, for example, be assigned to the pointer of another variable of type `List`.

Now that the first element has been created, you can store a value on that page; for instance, you could write the instruction

```
First↑.Value := 2.5
```

On the other hand, the value of the variable `First↑.Pointer` should be that of the page number of the *next* element in the list. However, since that element has not yet been created, you cannot know the page number of that element at this time. For the moment, the pointer of the current element should point nowhere. The concept of "nowhere" can be made explicit by using the Pascal reserved word `NIL`. Specifically, you could write

```
First↑.Pointer := NIL
```

Now, the second element of the list in Fig. 9.2 can be created. After you do so, you will want to set the pointer of the first element (i.e., the value of the variable `First↑.Pointer` above) to the page number of the new element. Thus you cannot reuse the variable `First` to create the new element because if you now used the instruction

```
NEW(First)
```

to create the new element, the value of the variable `First↑.Pointer` would refer to the value of the pointer at the bottom of the new page, and not at the bottom of the first page. Consequently, you need another variable, say `Last`, to create the next element in the list. Thus you would now use the instruction

```
NEW(Last)
```

which creates a page for this new element as well as the variables `Last↑` and `Last`. Subsequently, you could store a value on that page with the instruction

```
Last↑.Value := 3.14
```

Now, recall that you want the pointer of the first element to point to the page number of this new element. The page number of the new element was stored in the variable `Last` at the time that element was created. Thus you are led to the instruction

```
First↑.Pointer := Last
```

Finally, the pointer of the new element should be set to NIL:

```
Last↑.Pointer := NIL
```

The result of these instructions is the list of the two elements depicted in Fig. 9.2

Now suppose that you want to insert a new element between the two elements that were just created, as shown in Fig. 9.3. To do so, you must first create the new element; but should you use the variable *First*, the variable *Last*, or is yet another variable needed?

To answer the question, consider what must be done once the new element has been created. Of course you will store a value on that page, but subsequently you will have to set the pointer of the new element to the page number that is currently contained in the variable *Last*. Also, you must set the pointer of the first element (denoted by the variable *First↑.Pointer*) to the page number of the new element. Evidently, both of the variables *First↑.Pointer* and *Last* are still needed. Thus a new variable, say *Middle*, must be used to create this third element.

In order to insert the new element in the proper position, you must first create the page for that element with the instruction

```
NEW(Middle)
```

Then you can store the desired value on that page with the instruction

```
Middle↑.Value := 2.75
```

Finally, it is necessary to set the pointers of the first and the new elements appropriately. To have the first element point to the new element, you could use the instruction

```
First↑.Pointer := Middle
```

Similarly, to set the pointer of the new element to that of the element *Last*, you would write

```
Middle↑.Pointer := Last
```

The result is the list of the three elements in Fig. 9.3.

In summary, the Pascal syntax for creating a pointer-type data structure is

```
TYPE
    ListName   = ↑RecordName;
    RecordName = RECORD
                     FieldName :Type;
```

```
        .
        .
        .
        FieldName :Type;
        PointerName :ListName
    END;
```

The symbol ↑ in front of the RecordName tells the computer that ListName is to be a pointer-type data structure. Also, observe that the field specified by PointerName is the pointer of this record. The computer will distinguish this field from the others when you follow the colon in the declaration above with the ListName, which is precisely the same name you gave to the entire data structure.

Removing Elements from the List

Until now, our primary concern has been with creating and inserting new elements in the list. However, it is also possible to remove elements from the list. Suppose, for example, that you want to remove the second element, *Middle*, in Fig. 9.3. In order to do so, the first step would be to set the pointer of the first element, *First↑.Pointer*, to the page number of the third element, which is stored in the variable *Middle↑.Pointer*. Thus you can use the assignment statement

```
First↑.Pointer := Middle↑.Pointer
```

Now, the second element can be removed. To "release" that page (for later use, if necessary), you would use the Pascal statement

```
DISPOSE(Middle)
```

After performing this instruction, the variables *Middle↑* and *Middle* have lost their original values.

As you have seen in this and the previous examples, whenever you wish to add an element to or delete an element from a pointer-type data structure, you must be sure to adjust the pointers accordingly.

Processing Pointer-Type Lists

In the examples given so far, you have used a new variable for each and every element of the list. If that were always necessary, you would need 1,000 variables to process 1,000 elements in a list. Fortunately, a more efficient approach is available.

To understand the idea, recall, from Chapter 5, that it is often possible to process an entire list of numbers with a single variable, whose value is that of the current number with which you are working. In a similar manner, it is possible to proceed through an existing pointer-type list by using only one variable.

To see how to process a pointer-type list, imagine that you have already created a list of elements of type *Element* described above, and suppose that the variable *Next* (also of type *Element*) currently refers to the first element in the list. Thus the value of *Next↑.Value* is the value on the page corresponding to the first element in the list; the value of *Next↑.Pointer* is the page number of the second element in the list.

To "move" to the second element in the list, you could use the assignment statement

```
Next := Next↑.Pointer
```

Now, the value of *Next↑.Value* is the value on the page corresponding to the second element; the value of *Next↑.Pointer* is the page number of the *third* element in the list.

If you subsequently want to "move" *N* more elements down the list, you would write

```
FOR Move := 1 TO N DO
    Next := Next↑.Pointer
```

Using Pointer-Type Data Structures in Problem Solving

To illustrate the use of these new data structures, imagine that you are faced with the problem below.

Problem: The Clean Cosmetic Company has created a [pointer-type] list of its employees, using the following declarations:

```
TYPE
   NameArray = ARRAY[1..30] OF CHAR;
   List = ↑Employee;
   Employee = RECORD
                 Name      :NameArray;
                 SocSecNum :INTEGER;
                 PayRate   :REAL;
                 Pointer   :List
              END;
```

The list is currently sorted in order of increasing social security numbers. Given the list of existing employees, and given a new employee's name, social security number, and pay rate, write a procedure to insert that employee in the proper location so that the list remains sorted by social security numbers.

As you have learned, the first step in developing a procedure is to specify the parameters. To do so, you should identify the inputting, processing, and outputting phases of the procedure.

Inputting. Ask yourself what information you will be given to solve this problem (i.e., what information changes each time the procedure is called). You should come up with this answer: You will be given the list of existing employees together with the name of a new employee and his or her social security number and pay rate.

The data pertaining to the new employee will be transferred from the main program to the procedure as input parameters whose names, say, are

```
NewName        {which is an array of 30
                characters}
NewSocSecNum   {which is an integer}
NewPayRate     {which is a real number}
```

However, what about the list of existing employees?

As a general rule, a pointer-type data structure is global to the entire program, and so you will be able to access those elements directly in the procedure. However, you will need one variable whose value corresponds to the first element in the list. Then, by using the pointers, you can proceed from one element to the next until the entire list is processed. In view of this, the name of the final input parameter is

```
First    {which is a variable of type List declared above, and whose
          values correspond to the first element in the list.}
```

Putting together these observations, the procedure declaration might begin with the heading

```
PROCEDURE Insert(NewName :NameArray;
                 NewSocSecNum :INTEGER;
                 NewPayRate :REAL; First :List);
```

At this point, all parameters, being input parameters, are call-by-value. However, that fact might have to change when the output parameters are identified.

Processing. As usual, to identify the processing phase, you must ask yourself what it is you want to do with the variables once you know their values. Evidently, from the original description of the problem, you will want to insert the new employee into the correct position in the existing list.

Now it is necessary to use stepwise refinement to express this answer in more precise terms. In fact, you can use the technique of top-down programming to identify the following tasks to be performed:

Step 1: Locate the position at which the new employee information will be inserted (Fig. 9.4).

Step 2: Create an element for this new employee.

Step 3: Insert this new element into the list (Fig. 9.5).

In order to convert these steps into a sequence of Pascal statements, you will need to think through your solution using stepwise refinement. By doing so, you might provide the following more refined solution for Step 1.

Step 1: Look at the social security number of the first element in the list. If that number is less than the social security number of the new employee, then move to the next element in the list. Repeat these instructions until the social security number of the element you are looking at exceeds that of the new employee.

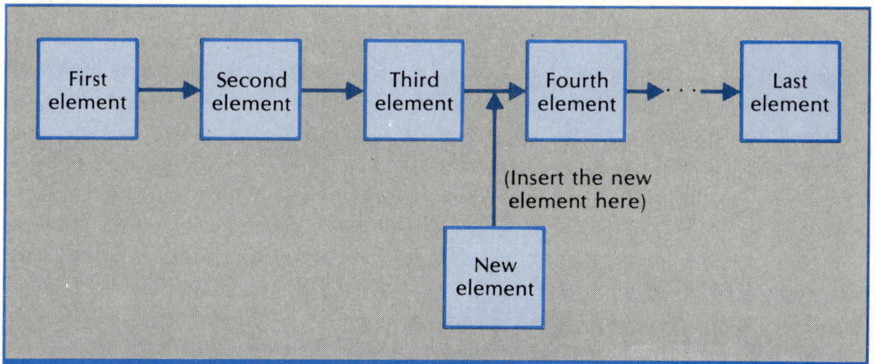

Figure 9.4 Locating where to insert the new element.

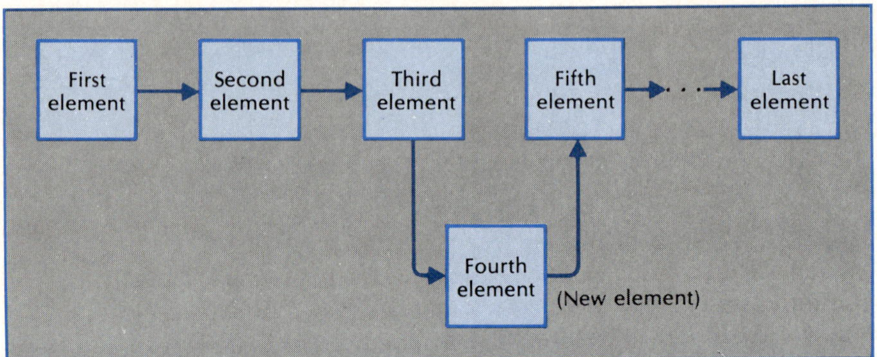

Figure 9.5 Inserting the new element.

Obviously there is a need for repetition; at the same time, however, you do not know how many times to repeat the operation. You might therefore be led to the following pseudocode `WHILE` loop:

```
WHILE <the current social security number is
      less than the new social security
      number> DO
      <Look at the next element in the list>
```

Replacing the expressions in angle brackets with appropriate Pascal statements using the local variable *Current* (of type *List*) for the current element in the list, the loop becomes

```
WHILE Current↑.SocSecNum < NewSocSecNum DO
      Current := Current↑.Pointer
```

Note that when this loop is completed, the variable *Current* will correspond to the element in the list *before* which the new element should be inserted. Also, the value of *Current* should be initialized to the very first element of the list using the input parameter *First*. The correct assignment statement is

```
Current := First
```

In order to refine Step 2 above, which is, to "create an element for this new employee," you will need another local variable of type *List*, say *NewPerson*. Thus the appropriate Pascal statement is

```
NEW(NewPerson)
```

The various data for that person can now be stored in the record variable *NewPerson↑* as follows:

```
NewPerson↑.SocSecNum := NewSocSecNum;
NewPerson↑.PayRate := NewPayRate;
FOR I := 1 TO 30 DO
    NewPerson↑.Name[I] := NewName[I]
```

All that remains, then, is to refine Step 3, which requires the computer to insert the new element into the list. As mentioned above, the new element should be inserted before the element represented by the variable *Current*. Thus, as you will see below, the pointer of the new element must be set to the page number of *Current*:

```
NewPerson↑.Pointer := Current
```

However, which element in the list should point to the page number of the *new* element? The answer is the element that immediately preceded *Current* in the original list should point to the page number of the new element. Unfortunately, you do not have a variable that corresponds to that element!

To resolve this problem, return to the body of the WHILE loop and save the current element in the list *before* you move to the next one. In that way, when the WHILE loop is over, you will have the two elements between which the new element will be inserted. Using yet another local variable of type *List*, say *Previous*, the WHILE loop becomes

```
WHILE Current↑.SocSecNum < NewSocSecNum DO
      BEGIN
         Previous := Current;
         Current := Current↑.Pointer
      END
```

When the WHILE loop is completed, you will be able to insert the new element between *Previous* and *Current*; however, there is still one problem. If the new social security number is less than that of the first employee on the list, then the body of the WHILE loop will not be performed at all, and hence, the variable *Previous* will not have been assigned a value. Consequently, prior to the WHILE loop, you should initialize the value of *Previous* to that of the first element on the list with the statement

```
Previous := First
```

Now, when the `WHILE` loop is completed you can insert the new element between *Previous* and *Current* (provided that they are not the same) by setting the pointer for *Previous* to the page number of the new element with the instruction

```
IF Previous <> Current THEN
   Previous↑.Pointer := NewPerson
```

It would appear that the processing portion is completed until the tracing and debugging phases indicate otherwise.

Outputting. Here you must ask yourself what variables constitute the solution to the original problem. Evidently, the new list is the answer; but how do you return that list to the main program?

As mentioned previously, in Pascal there is no single variable that represents the entire list of a pointer-type data structure. Rather, that data structure is considered to be global to the entire program. Thus the new list that was created by the procedure, being a global data structure, constitutes the output of the procedure. However, what will happen when the procedure is finished and control returns to the main program? How will the main program know where the beginning of the list is?

The answer is that at the point at which this procedure was called there will be an actual parameter whose value corresponds to the first element in the original list. That actual parameter will be used in place of the dummy parameter *First*. However, there is still a small issue that needs to be addressed. Since *First* is a call-by-value parameter, the value of the actual parameter will not be changed by performing the instructions in the procedure. In other words, when the procedure is finished, and control is returned to the main program, the actual parameter corresponding to the dummy parameter *First* will still contain information pertaining to the first element in the original list. However, what if the new element inserted in the list becomes the new first element? How will the main program know that fact?

To address this problem, the dummy parameter *First* should be made a call-by-variable parameter so that the value of the corresponding actual parameter can be changed permanently (in the procedure) in the event that the new element becomes the first element of the list. You will recognize the need to do so if, after the `WHILE` loop is completed, the value of *Current* is still that of *First*.

Putting together the pieces, the procedure would appear to be

```
PROCEDURE Insert (NewName :NameArray;
                  NewSocSecNum :INTEGER;
                  NewPayRate :REAL;
                  VAR First :List);
    {This procedure scans a list of employees whose first element is the
    parameter First, and inserts a new element in the list according to
    increasing social security number. The output of the procedure is the new
    first element in the list.}
VAR
    Previous, Current, NewPerson  :List;
    I                             :INTEGER;
BEGIN
    Previous := First;
    Current := First;
    {Find out where the new element should be inserted.}
    WHILE Current↑.SocSecNum < NewSocSecNum DO
          BEGIN
             Previous := Current;
             Current := Current↑.Pointer
          END;
    {Create the new element.}
    NEW (NewPerson);
    NewPerson↑.SocSecNum := NewSocSecNum;
    NewPerson↑.PayRate := NewPayRate;
    FOR I := 1 TO 30 DO
        NewPerson↑.Name[I] := NewName[I];
    {Adjust all pointers.}
    NewPerson↑.Pointer := Current;
    IF Previous <> Current THEN
       Previous↑.Pointer := NewPerson;
    IF Current = First THEN
       First := NewPerson
END;   {End of procedure Insert.}
```

Tracing and Debugging

In choosing data with which to trace and/or test this procedure, you should probably consider cases where the new employee is to be inserted in the middle of the list, at the beginning of the list, and at the end of the list. For the first and second type of data, you will encounter no problem; however, for data of the third type, can you see where an error will arise? In fact, the stopping condition in the `WHILE` loop will never be true because, indeed, the social security number of the new person will never be less than that of the current person in the existing list.

One solution to the problem is to change the condition in the WHILE statement so that the body of the loop will no longer be performed when the end of the list is encountered. You can detect the end of the list when the value of *Current↑.Pointer* is NIL. Thus the condition in the WHILE statement becomes

```
WHILE (Current↑.Pointer <> NIL) AND
      (Current↑.SocSecNum < NewSocSecNum)
      DO ...
```

Furthermore, if after the WHILE loop is completed the value of *Current↑.Pointer* is NIL, then the last employee's social security number has not been compared to that of the new employee. Thus, after the loop, you should have the instructions

```
IF Current↑.Pointer = NIL THEN
   IF Current↑.SocSecNum < NewSocSecNum THEN
      BEGIN
         Previous := Current;
         Current := NIL
      END
```

Finally, these statements, together with the WHILE loop should be performed only if the list is not empty (i.e., if *First* <> NIL). With all these changes in place, the final and correct procedure declaration in Pascal is

```
PROCEDURE Insert(NewName :NameArray;
                 NewSocSecNum :INTEGER;
                 NewPayRate :REAL;
                 VAR First :List);
   {This procedure scans a list of employees whose first element is the
   parameter First, and inserts a new element in the list according to
   increasing social security numbers. The output of the procedure is the new
   first element in the list.}
   VAR
      Previous, Current, Person :List;
      I                         :INTEGER;
   BEGIN
      Previous := First;
      Current := First;
      {Find out where the new element should be inserted.}
      IF First <> NIL THEN
         BEGIN
```

```
        WHILE (Current↑.Pointer <> NIL) AND
              (Current↑.SocSecNum < NewSocSecNum) DO
              BEGIN
                 Previous := Current;
                 Current := Current↑.Pointer
              END
        IF Current↑.Pointer = NIL THEN
           IF Current↑.SocSecNum < NewSocSecNum THEN
              BEGIN
                 Previous := Current;
                 Current := NIL
              END
           END;
   {Create the new element.}
   NEW(NewPerson);
   NewPerson↑.SocSecNum := NewSocSecNum;
   NewPerson↑.PayRate := NewPayRate;
   FOR I := 1 TO 30 DO
      NewPerson↑.Name[I] := NewName[I];
   {Adjust all pointers.}
   NewPerson↑.Pointer := Current;
   IF Previous <> Current THEN
      Previous↑.Pointer := NewPerson;
   IF Current = First THEN
      First := NewPerson
END;    {End of procedure Insert.}
```

Complex Pointer-Type Data Structures

In the previous examples of this section, each element in the list had one pointer variable that pointed to the "next" element in the list. However, it is often necessary to create list structures in which each element can point to more than one other element. For instance, it is possible to create a list in which each element has two pointers—one that points to the next element, and one that points to the previous element. Such a list is called a *doubly linked list*, in contrast to the data structure of the previous employee example, which is referred to as a *singly linked list*. With a singly linked list, each element has one pointer that points to the next element in the list; with a doubly linked list, each element has two pointers—one that points to the next element, and one that points to the preceding element.

In general, each element of a list can have any number of pointers, thus allowing you to create data structures in which the elements are linked together in a rather complex manner. Some typical such data structures are depicted in Fig. 9.6. To create these collections of elements (each of which, say, is a record), you must have one extra field for each pointer that is needed. For example, to create a doubly linked list of employees as described in the previous example, you could use the following declaration:

```
TYPE
   NameArray = ARRAY[1..30] OF CHAR;
   List = ↑Element;
   Element = RECORD
                  Name              :NameArray;
                  SocSecNum         :INTEGER;
                  PayRate           :REAL;
                  ForwardPointer    :List;
                  BackwardPointer   :List
             END;
VAR
   Person :List;
```

As before, you can create a new element by using the instruction

```
NEW(Person)
```

Then you can work with all of the fields of the record variable `Person↑`, including the two pointer fields. The value of the variable `Person` is the page number of the record variable that was just created. A further study of pointer variables is beyond the scope of this book.

In this section you have learned how to create and how to work with pointer-type data structures. Their primary advantage is that it is easy to insert and to remove elements in the list without having to "move" all of the other elements in order to make the necessary room. Also, with pointer-type data structures, there is no restriction on the number of elements in the list (other than the available memory capacity of the computer). In addition, you need not specify or keep track of the number of elements in the list. You need only be careful to maintain the pointers of each element correctly.

Conclusion

You have now acquired all the basic tools you need to solve problems by computer. You have learned the problem-solving techniques of Chapter 1, and seen them used throughout the book. You have also

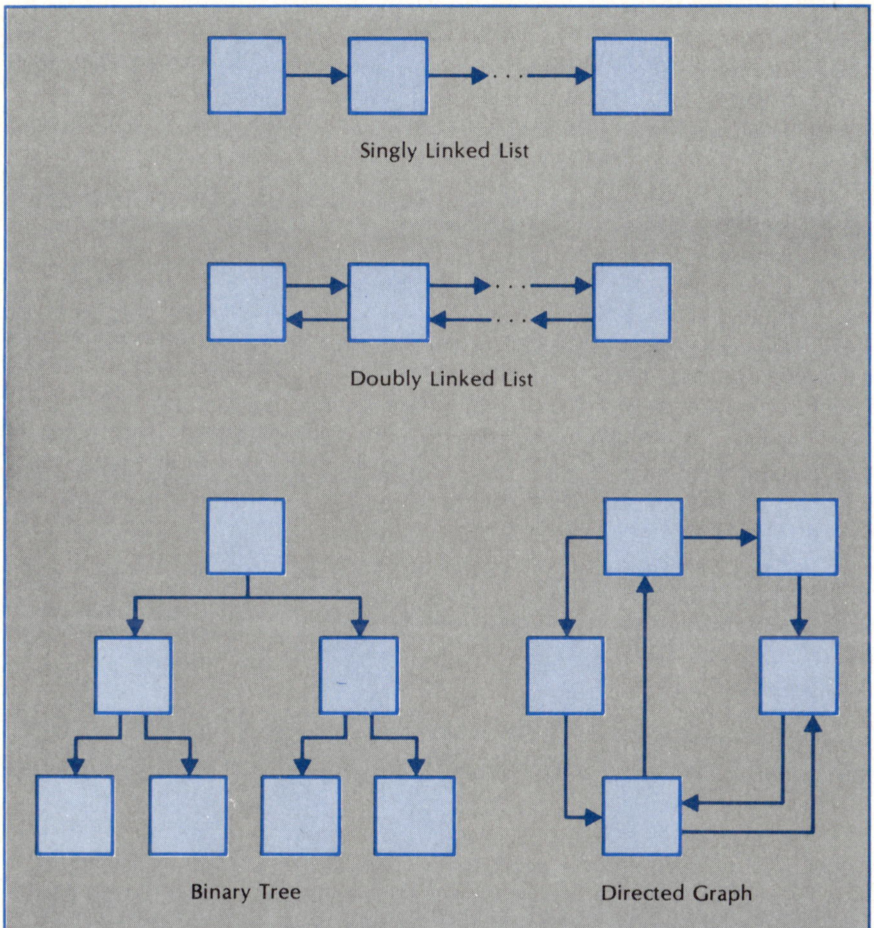

Figure 9.6 Various pointer-type data structures.

learned many types of programming statements that constitute the "language" of the computer, and how to code those statements in Pascal. In addition, you have seen various data structures and the importance of carefully selecting the right one for your problem. Finally, you have learned the debugging process, which enables you to locate and to correct any error that arises. By using the techniques of Chapter 1, you should now be able to translate the way in which you solve a problem into a sequence of Pascal statements that a computer can perform. In other words, you have learned how to program a computer!

Exercises for Section 9.2

Prepare TYPE declarations to create each of the following pointer-type data structures.

1. Create a list of the names of cities to be visited (in order) by a traveling salesman.
2. Create a schedule of patients to be seen by a doctor at a hospital. For each patient, you will have the name (consisting of 30 characters), a room number, and a time (in hours and minutes) at which the patient is to be visited.
3. A family tree is to be constructed in the form of a binary tree (see Fig. 9.6). Each person in the tree will have a name (consisting of 30 characters) and a birth date. The two people that each person is "connected" to are that person's parents.

Prepare Pascal instructions to accomplish each of the following changes to the list in Fig. 9.3. Assume that the three elements in that figure have been created using the three variables *First*, *Middle*, and *Last*, respectively, each of type *List* as described previously in this section. In so doing, use *only* these three variables in your statements—do not create any new variables. For each exercise, start with the three elements as given in Fig. 9.3

4. Add a fourth element, of value 4.3, to the end of the list.
5. Add a new element, of value 0.75, to the beginning of the list.
6. Remove the first element of the list.
7. Remove the last element of the list.

Write a Pascal procedure to perform the following task on the same employee list that was used in the problem of this section.

8. Given a social security number, see if there is an employee on the list with that social security number. If so, then remove that employee from the list. Otherwise, display an appropriate message and return a value of FALSE for a boolean variable to the main program.

9.3 Summary

In this chapter you have learned two different data structures that are available in Pascal, and you have seen how these concepts are used in problem solving. In particular, you have learned the importance of selecting the most appropriate data structures for your problem because careful forethought can greatly reduce your subsequent programming efforts. A brief summary of these structures, together with their advantages and disadvantages, will be given here.

A file, like an array, is a collection of items of the same type. One major difference is that, unlike an array, the values of the elements of a file need not be stored in the computer's memory. Rather, those values can be located on an input or output device, such as a magnetic tape or disk. This fact provides a file with two distinct advantages. First, the values of a file can be saved for use after the program is finished. The values can, for example, be read by another program at a later date, or even transported for use on another computer. In contrast, the values of an array are lost forever once the program ends. Second, the number of elements in a file is limited only by the memory capacity of the device on which the values are being stored. This number can be extremely large. In contrast, the number of elements in an array is restricted by the memory capacity of the computer.

One of the disadvantages of processing a file is that you can access and use only one element of the file at a time. That value is stored in what is called the buffer variable of the file. If you want to process some other element, you will have to instruct the computer to proceed sequentially through the file, one element at a time, looking for the desired element. In contrast, with an array, you can access any element immediately simply by using the appropriate subscript.

Another concern regarding the use of a file is that, when the values are not stored in the computer's memory, extra time will be needed to retrieve the value from the memory device. Nonetheless, a file is a good data structure to use when processing a large quantity of data.

A pointer-type data structure is also a collection of items of the same type, usually records. Each record is stored on one page of the computer's memory, and these pages are linked together in a special way through the use of a pointer. A pointer is a field of the record whose value is the page number of another record in the list. You can instruct the computer to move from one record to the "next" by using the value of the pointer of the record you are currently processing. In fact, as with a file, you will be accessing only one element of a pointer-type data structure at a time. After processing that element, you instruct the computer to move to the next one by using the pointer.

Pointer-type data structures are particularly useful when you have a sorted list of information and you want to insert (or to remove) a particular element in the list. To do so, you need only find the appropriate place in the list, and then adjust the pointers of the affected elements accordingly.

A second major advantage of pointer-type data structures is that you need not be concerned with, or keep track of, the precise number of elements in the list. The list can expand and contract in size throughout the program. The size of the list is limited only by the available amount of the computer's memory.

Key Terms

File 408

Local file 408

External file 408

Window of a file 409

Sequential file 409

Buffer variable 411

Textfile 417

Pointer-type data structure 420

Pointer 421

APPENDIX A

A SUMMARY OF PASCAL SYNTAX

A **syntax diagram** is a precise method for summarizing and for illustrating the syntax of a programming language, as will be explained in this appendix. For example, you might recall from Chapter 2 that an identifier is a name that you use for some purpose in your program (e.g., a variable name, a procedure name, etc.). The syntax diagram below will enable you to determine which sequences of characters constitute a valid identifier in Pascal, and which do not. To understand this syntax diagram, recall that a digit is any one of the numbers 0, 1, . . . , 9. Using this already known concept of a digit, and that of a letter, the syntax diagram for an identifier consisting of letters and digits in Pascal is

Syntax diagram A precise method for summarizing and for illustrating the syntax of a program language.

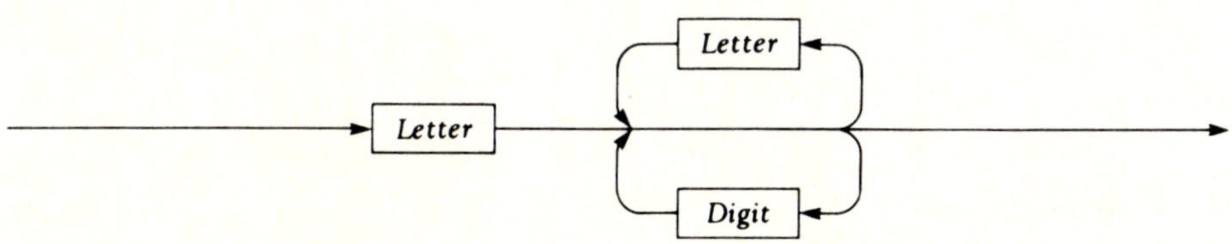

According to this diagram, a valid Pascal identifier is a sequence of characters that can be obtained by starting at the left of the diagram, following *any* sequence of arrows (in the indicated direction), and exiting to the right of the diagram. If you can do so, the particular sequence of characters is an identifier; otherwise, that sequence is not an identifier. According to this syntax diagram, then, the following are identifiers:

A {Start at the left of the diagram. Follow the arrow to obtain the letter A; then follow the center arrow and exit to the right.}

A2B {Start at the left of the diagram. Follow the arrow to obtain the letter A; then follow the bottom arrow to obtain the digit 2; then follow the center arrow to the right leading to the top arrow to obtain the letter B. Now exit to the right.}

The sequence of characters A − B, however, is not an identifier because there is no sequence of arrows that can be followed in the above syntax diagram to obtain the minus sign.

In general, you might find the following symbols used in syntax diagrams:

{which contains a reserved word, such as DIV, or a special symbol, such as +.}

{which contains an item whose specific value is provided by you or by another syntax diagram.}

Here, then, are the syntax diagrams for the Pascal language.*

UnsignedInteger

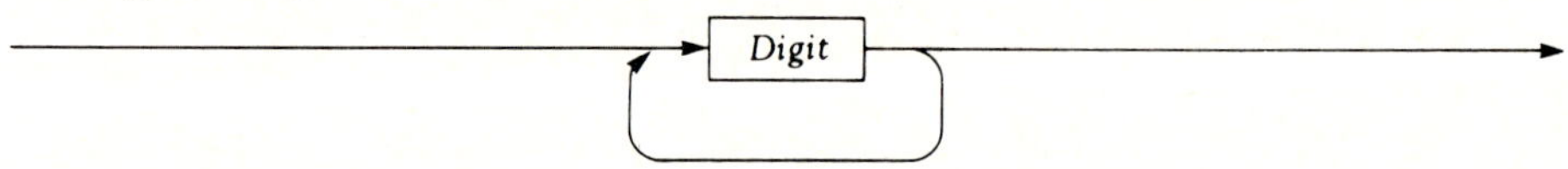

UnsignedNumber

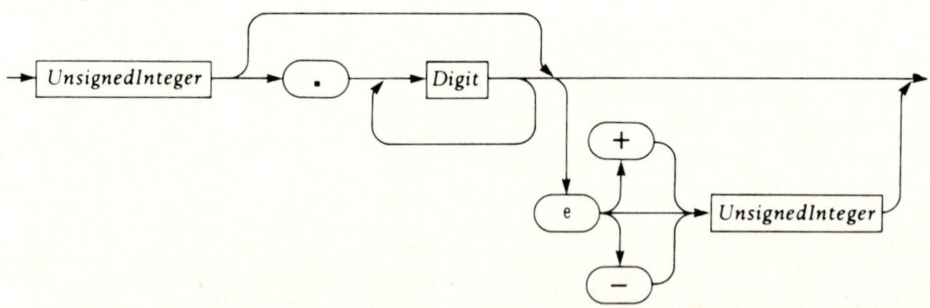

*The syntax diagrams of this appendix are taken from Jensen and Wirth: *Pascal User Manual and Report*, 3rd ed. New York: Springer-Verlag, 1985: 230-239.

CharacterString

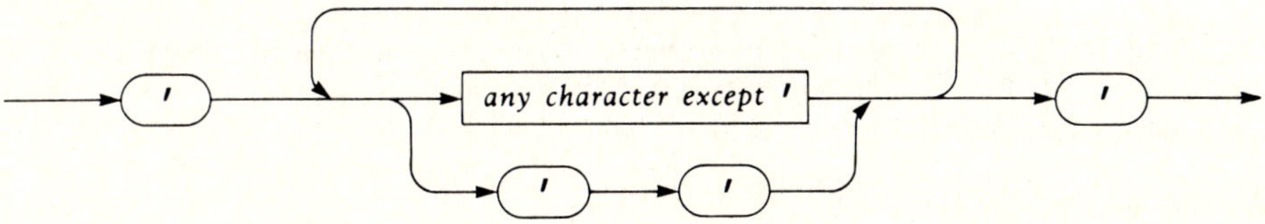

ConstantIdentifier, VariableIdentifier, FieldIdentifier, BoundIdentifier, TypeIdentifier, ProcedureIdentifier and FunctionIdentifier

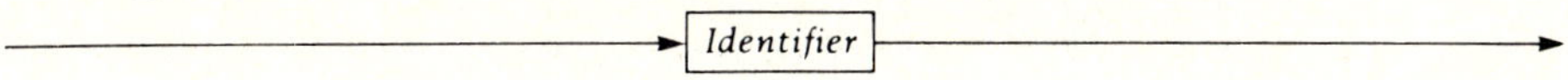

UnsignedConstant

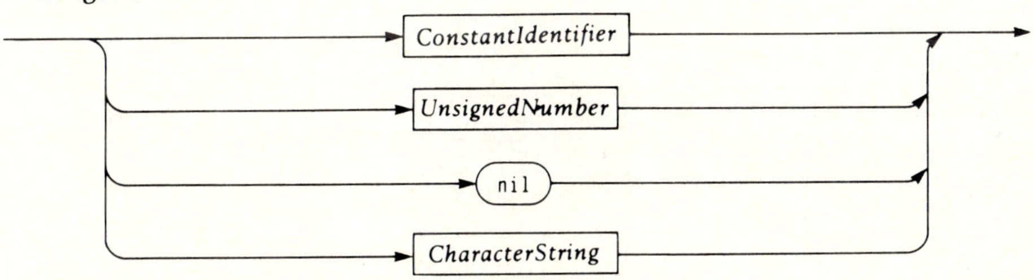

Constant

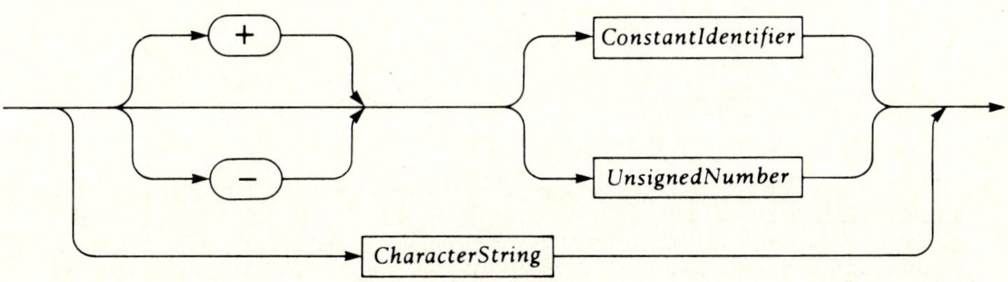

Variable

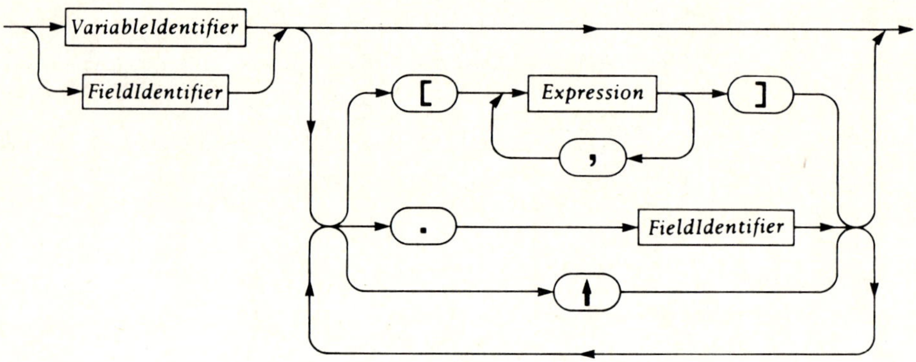

Factor

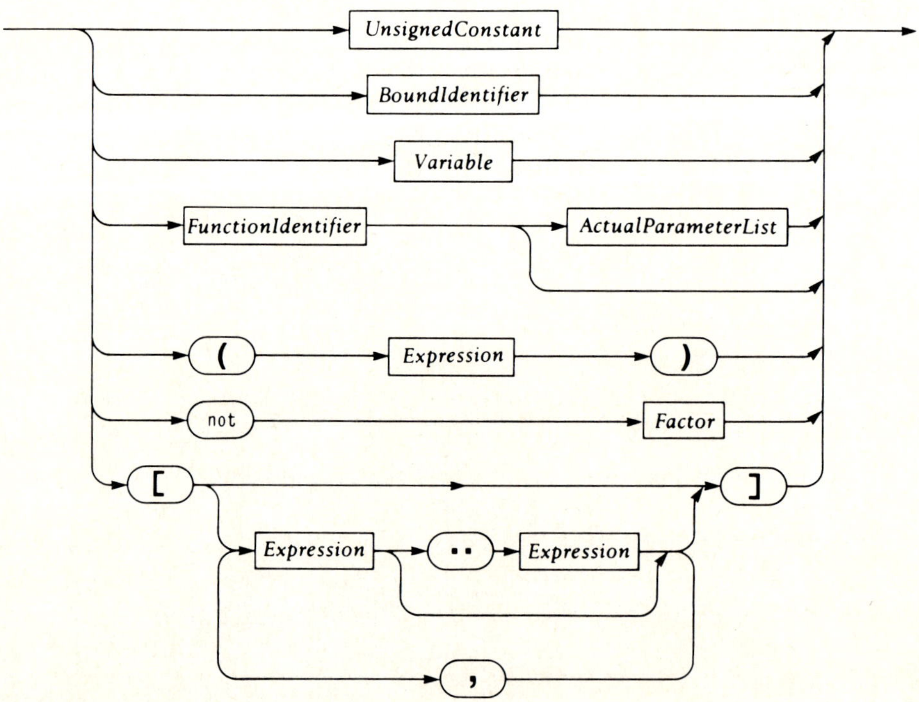

Term

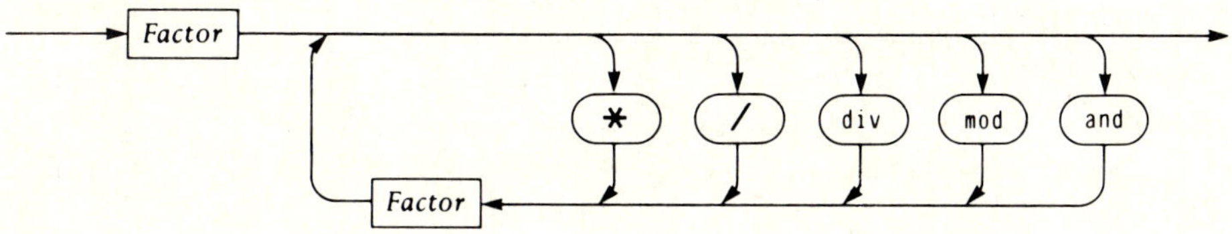

SimpleExpression

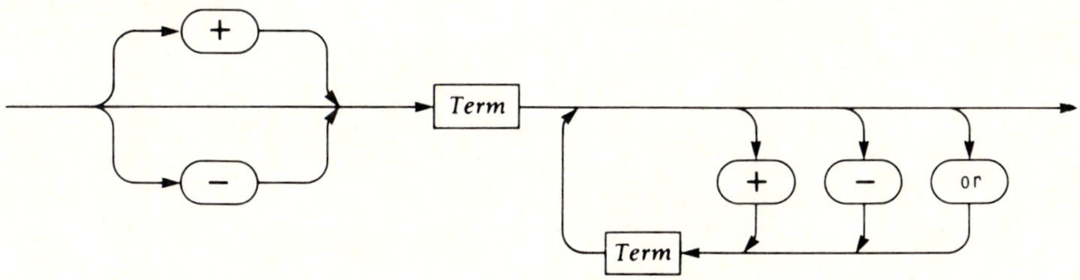

Expression

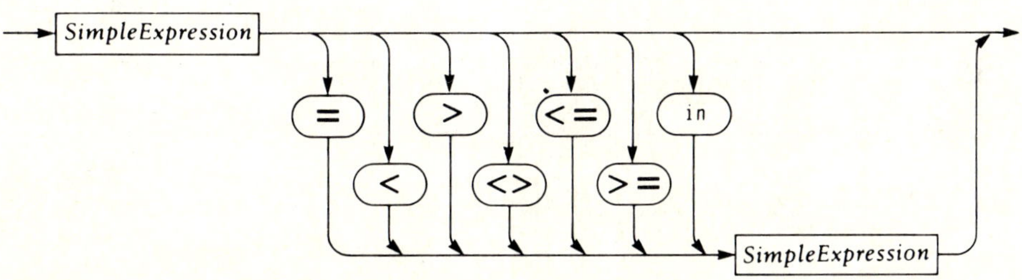

ActualParameterList

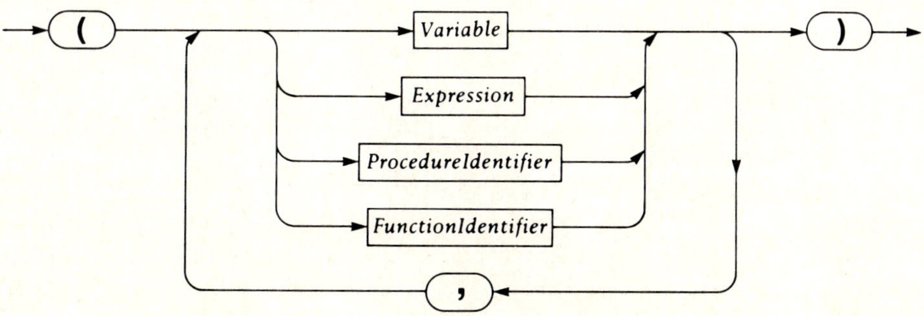

WriteParameterList

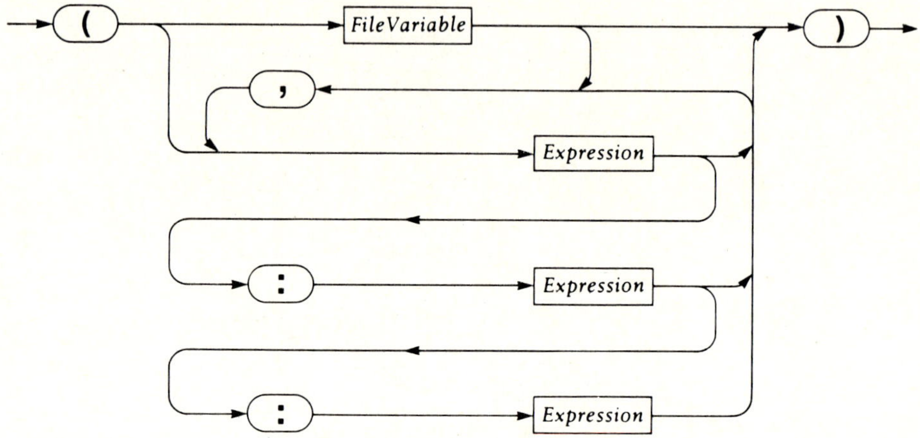

IndexTypeSpecification

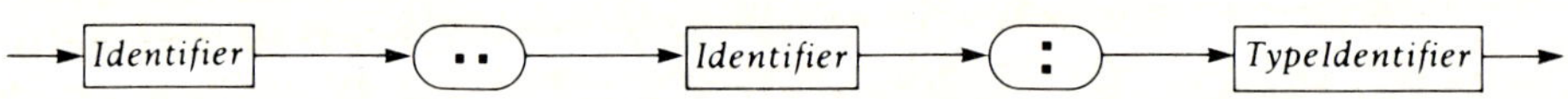

ConformantArraySchema

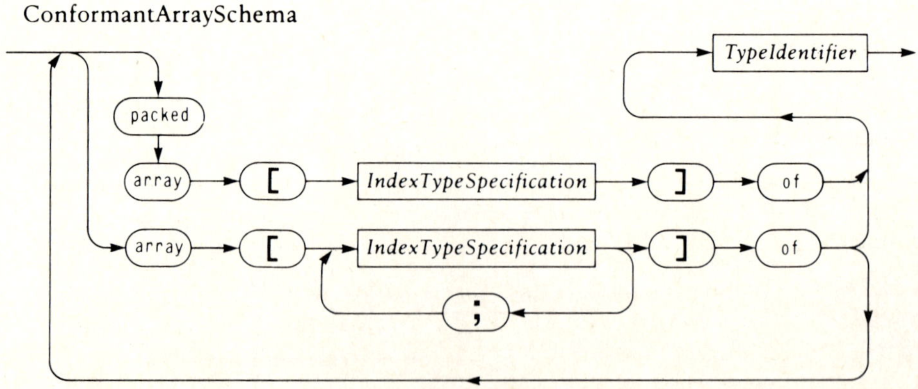

FormalParameterList

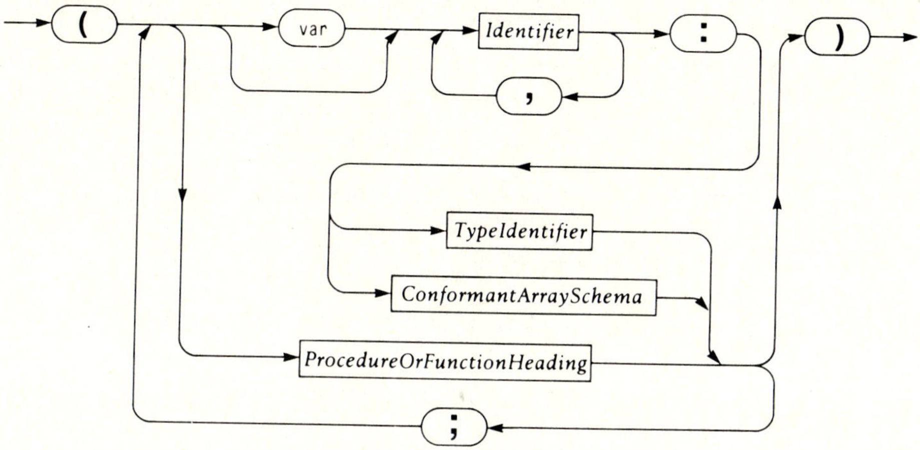

ProcedureOrFunctionHeading

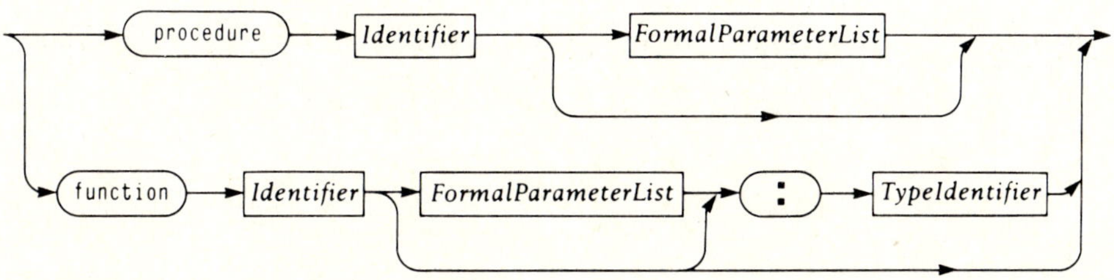

OrdinalType

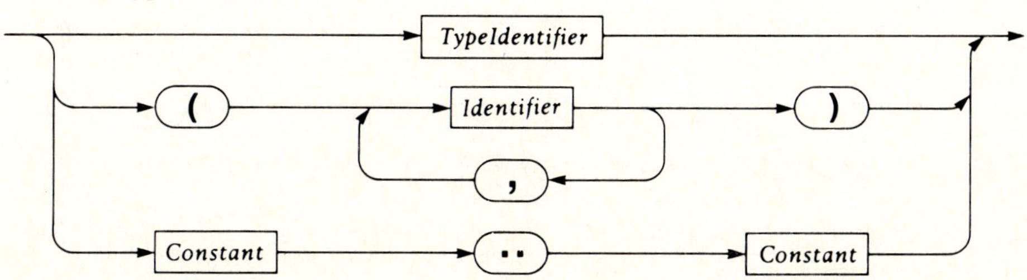

Type

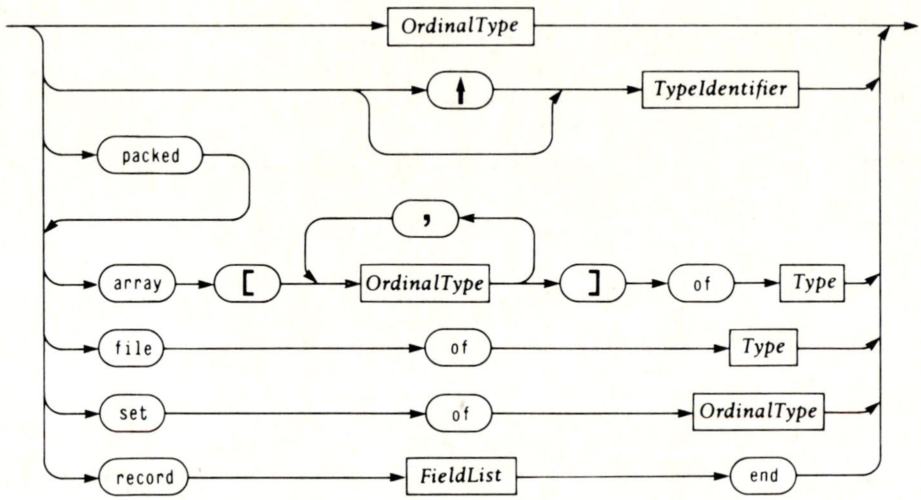

FieldList

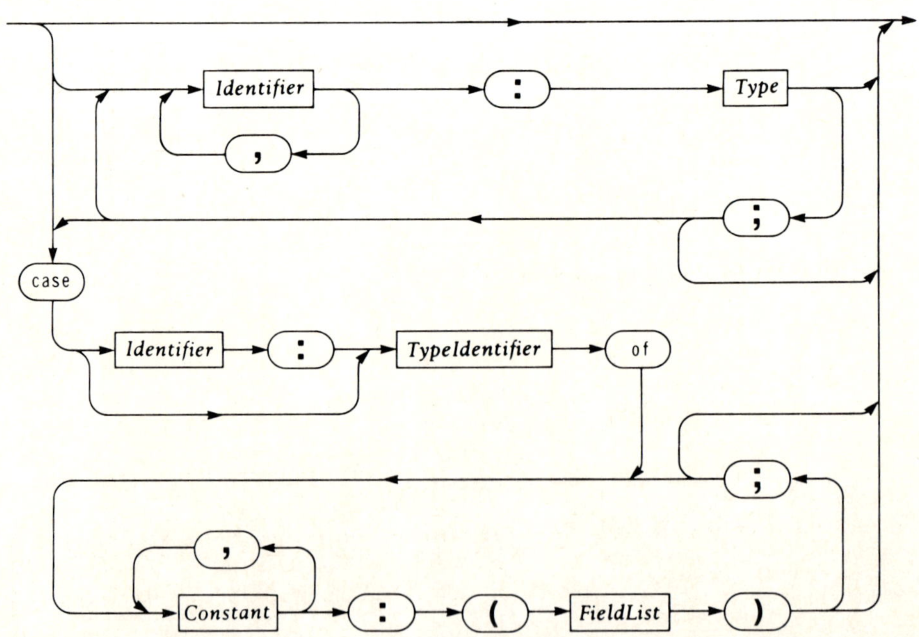

Statement

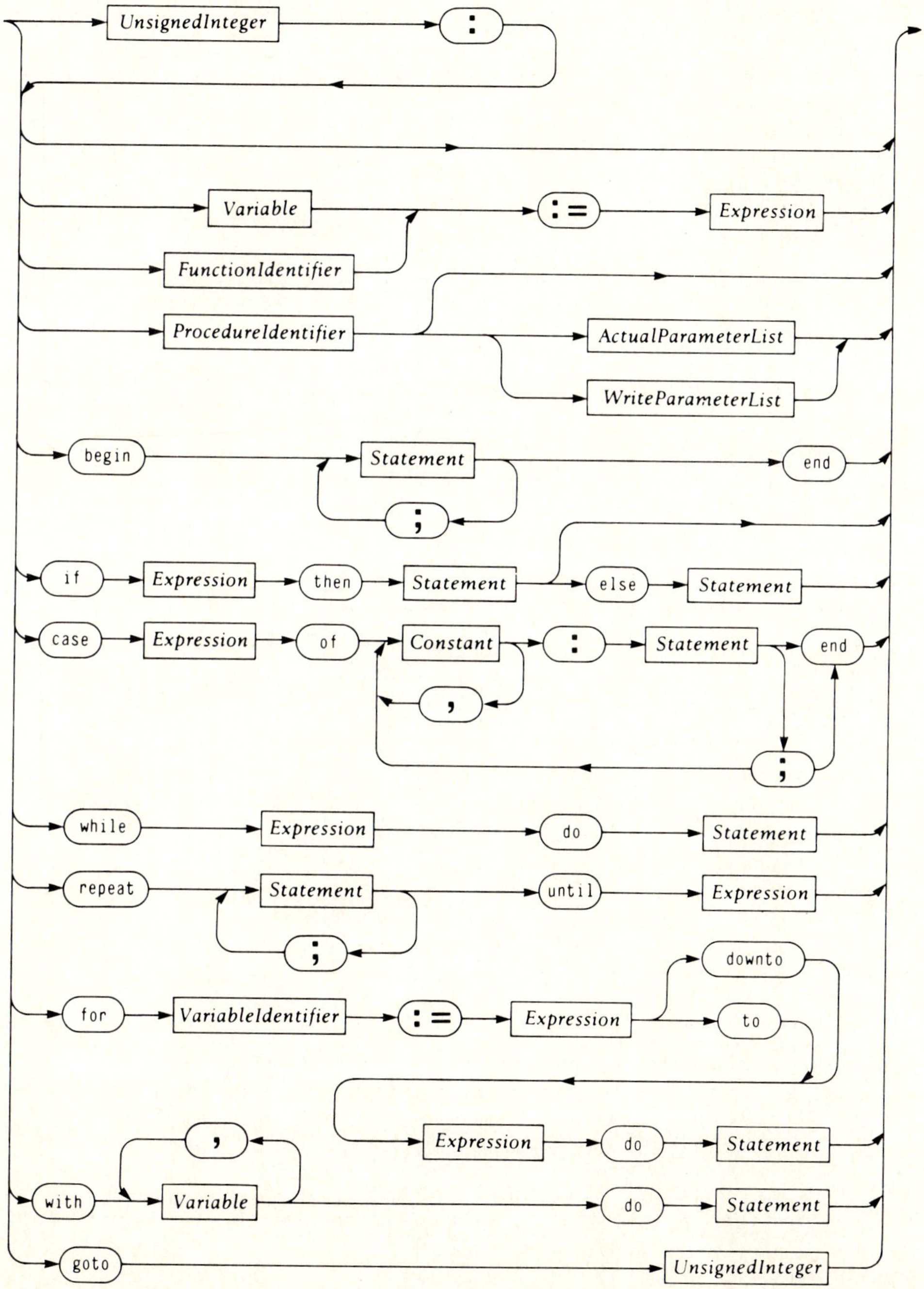
UnsignedInteger
:
Variable
:=
Expression
FunctionIdentifier
ProcedureIdentifier
ActualParameterList
WriteParameterList
begin
Statement
end
;
if
Expression
then
Statement
else
Statement
case
Expression
of
Constant
:
Statement
end
,
;
while
Expression
do
Statement
repeat
Statement
until
Expression
;
downto
for
VariableIdentifier
:=
Expression
to
Expression
do
Statement
,
with
Variable
do
Statement
goto
UnsignedInteger

Block

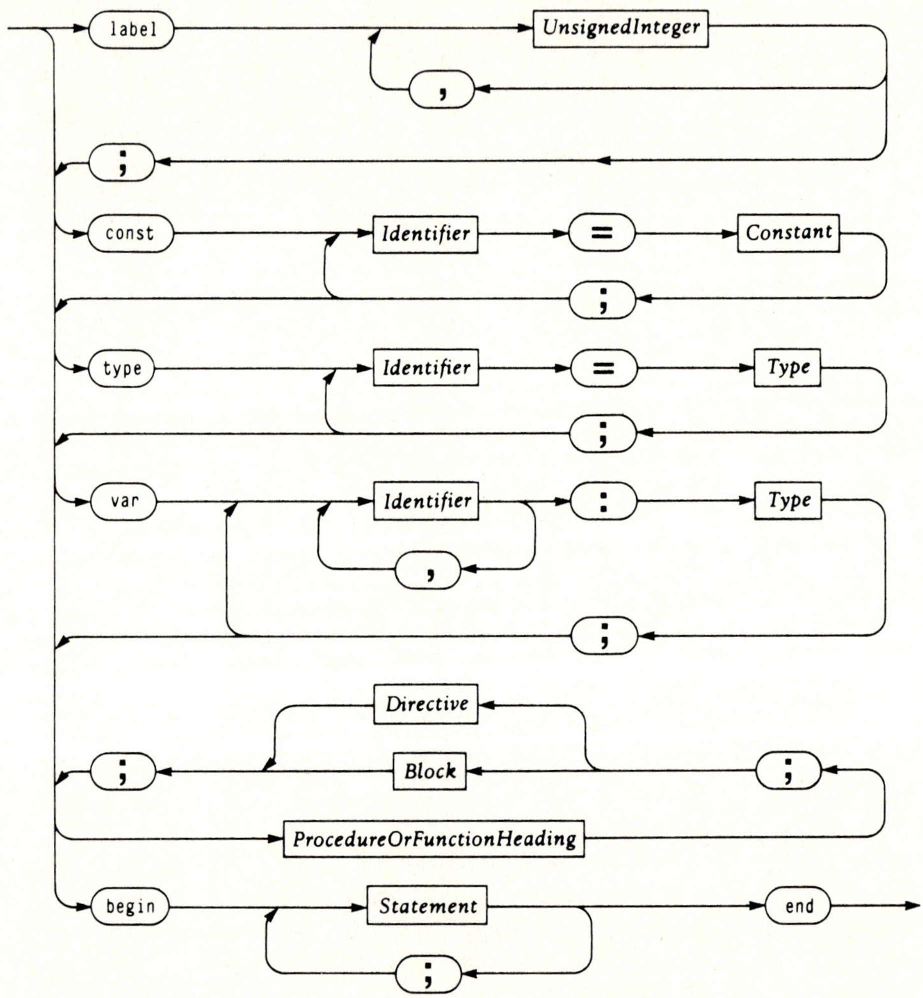

Program

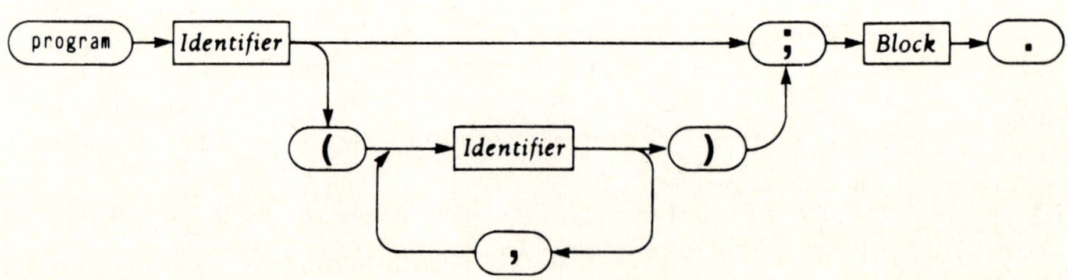

Key Term

APPENDIX B

PASCAL RESERVED WORDS, STANDARD INDENTIFIERS, AND OPERATORS

Reserved Words in Pascal

The following are reserved words in Pascal that cannot be used as identifiers in your program:

AND	DOWNTO	IF	OR	THEN
ARRAY	ELSE	IN	PACKED	TO
BEGIN	END	LABEL	PROCEDURE	TYPE
CASE	FILE	MOD	PROGRAM	UNTIL
CONST	FOR	NIL	RECORD	VAR
DIV	FUNCTION	NOT	REPEAT	WHILE
DO	GOTO	OF	SET	WITH

Standard Identifiers in Pascal

The following identifiers have a special meaning in Pascal. Although you could use these names as identifiers in your program, you are advised not to do so. This is because once you have done so, the original meaning and purpose of the identifier is lost for the remainder of the program.

Constants

FALSE   TRUE   MAXINT

Types

BOOLEAN CHAR INTEGER REAL TEXT

Files

INPUT OUTPUT

Functions

Name	Parameter Type	Function Type	Description
ABS(*X*)	INTEGER or REAL	Same as parameter	Absolute value of *X*.
ARCTAN(*X*)	INTEGER or REAL	REAL	Inverse tangent of *X*.
CHR(*X*)	INTEGER	CHAR	Character whose number in the collating sequence is *X*.
COS(*X*)	INTEGER or REAL	REAL	Cosine of *X*.
EOF(*F*)	FILE	BOOLEAN	End-of-file indicator.
EOLN(*F*)	FILE	BOOLEAN	End-of-line indicator.
EXP(*X*)	REAL or INTEGER	REAL	e^X
LN(*X*)	REAL or INTEGER	REAL	Natural logarithm of *X*.
ODD(*X*)	INTEGER	BOOLEAN	TRUE if *X* is odd; FALSE otherwise.
ORD(*X*)	CHAR	INTEGER	The integer in the collating sequence that corresponds to the character *X*.
PRED(*X*)	INTEGER, CHAR, BOOLEAN, or User-defined	Same as parameter	The value immediately preceding *X*.
ROUND(*X*)	REAL	INTEGER	*X* rounded up or down, whichever value is closer to *X*.
SIN(*X*)	REAL or INTEGER	REAL	Sine of *X*.
SQR(*X*)	REAL or INTEGER	Same as parameter	Square of *X*.
SQRT(*X*)	REAL or INTEGER	REAL	Square root of *X*.
SUCC(*X*)	INTEGER, CHAR, BOOLEAN, or User-defined	Same as parameter	The value immediately following *X*.
TRUNC(*X*)	REAL	INTEGER	*X* with the decimal point and all subsequent digits removed.

Procedures

Name (Parameters)	Description
`DISPOSE(P)`	Returns the storage space of the pointer variable referenced by *P* to the available space list.
`GET(F)`	Advances file *F* to the next element and places the value of that element in the buffer variable *F* ↑ .
`NEW(P)`	Creates a new pointer variable that is accessed by *P*.
`PACK(A, I, Z)`	Takes the elements beginning at subscript position *I* of array *A* and copies them into packed array *Z* beginning at the first subscript position.
`PAGE(F)`	Causes the printer to skip to the top of a new page before printing the next line of textfile *F*.
`READ(...)` `READLN(...)`	Reads information from textfiles.
`RESET(F)`	Positions file *F* at its beginning for reading.
`REWRITE(F)`	Clears file *F* and allows it to be written onto.
`UNPACK(Z, A, I)`	Takes the elements beginning at the first subscript position of packed array *Z* and copies them into array *A* beginning at subscript position *I*.
`WRITE(...)` `WRITELN(...)`	Writes information to textfiles.

Operators

Operator	Description	Type of Operand(s)	Type of Result
Arithmetic			
+	Addition or set union	INTEGER,	INTEGER (if both operands are INTEGER)
		REAL, or	REAL (if at least one operand is REAL)
		SET	SET (if both operands are SETs)
−	Subtraction or set difference	INTEGER,	INTEGER (if both operands are INTEGER)
		REAL, or	REAL (if at least one operand is REAL)
		SET	SET (if both operands are SETs)
*	Multiplication or set intersection	INTEGER,	INTEGER (if both operands are INTEGER)
		REAL, or	REAL (if at least one operand is REAL)
		SET	SET (if both operands are SETs)
/	Division	INTEGER or REAL	REAL

Operator	Description	Type of Operand(s)	Type of Result
DIV	Division (with no remainder)	INTEGER	INTEGER
MOD	Remainder on dividing	INTEGER	INTEGER
Relational			
<	Less than	INTEGER, REAL, BOOLEAN, User-defined	BOOLEAN
>	Greater than	INTEGER, REAL, BOOLEAN, User-defined	BOOLEAN
<=	Less than or equal to, or set inclusion	INTEGER, REAL, BOOLEAN, SET User-defined	BOOLEAN
>=	Greater than or equal to	INTEGER, REAL, BOOLEAN, User-defined	BOOLEAN
=	Equal to	INTEGER, BOOLEAN, SET, User-defined	BOOLEAN
<>	Not equal to	INTEGER, BOOLEAN, SET, User-defined	BOOLEAN
IN	Membership	Left Operand: INTEGER, REAL, BOOLEAN, User-defined Right Operand: SET	BOOLEAN
Boolean			
NOT	not	BOOLEAN	BOOLEAN
OR	or	BOOLEAN	BOOLEAN
AND	and	BOOLEAN	BOOLEAN

Precedence of Operators

Precedence	Operators
Done first (from left to right)	Expression in parentheses
↓	unary −, NOT
	*, /, DIV, MOD, AND
	+, −, OR
Done last (from left to right)	<, >, =, >=, <=, < >, IN

APPENDIX C

GOTO STATEMENTS AND LABELS

Until now, you have seen that the computer executes instructions in sequence—starting at the top and proceeding, statement by statement, until the last instruction is reached. So far, the only time an instruction might not be performed is when that instruction is part of an IF/THEN (or an IF/THEN/ELSE) statement, which is often called a **conditional statement.** In this appendix, you will learn about the GOTO statement, which is another method for telling the computer not to perform a group of instructions, and is often referred to as an **unconditional branch** in the program.

Conditional statement A statement whose "action" may or may not be performed, depending on the value of a prespecified condition, e.g., an IF/THEN or an IF/THEN/ELSE statement.

Unconditional branch A statement that instructs the computer to "jump" to another part of the program, and to continue executing instructions from that point on.

To illustrate the unconditional quality of the GOTO statement, consider one of its possible uses. Suppose that the pseudocode instructions

```
IF < the data are invalid> THEN
   WRITE 'Data invalid'
ELSE
   <Perform the rest of the program>
   .
   .
   .
```

were being used to verify the data and to perform the rest of the program only if the data are valid. The above statement, while technically correct, is a bit awkward. The reason is that "the rest of the program" must be viewed as one large compound statement that belongs to the IF/THEN/ELSE statement. In addition, each statement in "the rest of the program" would have to be indented (at least it would be if you are following a consistent indentation policy). Perhaps a better way to handle the data verification in pseudocode would be

```
IF <the data are invalid> THEN
   WRITE 'Invalid data'
   Skip the rest of the program

<Here is the rest of the program>
.
.
.
```

In the above situation, if the data are invalid, then the instruction

```
Skip the rest of the program
```

will be executed, thus preventing the computer from performing the rest of the program. On the other hand, if the data are valid, then, according to the way in which an `IF/THEN` statement works, the computer will not execute the compound statement consisting of

```
WRITE 'Invalid data'
Skip the rest of the program
```

Rather, the computer will proceed to perform the rest of the program.

An obvious question to ask is, how, precisely, do you instruct the computer to "skip the rest of the program"? The `GOTO` statement can be used to accomplish this objective. For example, in pseudocode you could write

```
IF <the data are invalid> THEN
   WRITE 'Data invalid'
   GOTO <the very last WRITE statement below>
Statement ⎫
.         ⎪
.         ⎬ Rest of the program
.         ⎪
Statement ⎭
WRITE 'This is the end of the program'
```

Label An unsigned integer (followed by a colon) that appears to the left of a statement. The computer will use the label to locate that particular statement.

Look, now, at the `GOTO` statement above. How will the computer know precisely which statement to proceed to; i.e., in the example above, how will the machine locate the last `WRITE` statement? Unlike a human, a computer cannot "see" which statement is the last one. In order to resolve this problem, you will need to attach a **label** to the desired statement. A label is an unsigned integer that appears to the left of the statement, followed by a colon (:). For example,

```
10: Statement
```

You can then instruct the computer to proceed to the appropriate statement by referring to that label in the GOTO statement.

Example

Using the number 10 as a statement label, the data-verification problem above could be written in pseudocode as

```
IF <the data are invalid> THEN
   WRITE 'Invalid data'
   GOTO 10
<Here is the rest of the program>
.
.
.
10: WRITE 'This is the end of the program'
```

You should note that a label must appear at the beginning of a statement, not in the middle. Thus, for example, in the IF/THEN/ELSE statement

```
IF Condition THEN
   Action 1
ELSE
   Action 2
```

you cannot put a label in front of the word ELSE, because the word ELSE is not a statement. A label could, however, appear to the left of the word IF in the example above.

In general, the pseudocode statement

```
GOTO Label
```

will instruct the computer to find the statement having the Label, and to perform that statement and all subsequent statements in order (until another GOTO statement is encountered).

One of the problems with using GOTO statements is that the program logic can become very difficult for the reader (or programmer) to follow because the instructions are being performed out of sequence. For this reason, many computer scientists feel that the use of the GOTO statement should be avoided as much as possible, or not used at all. For example, in the following program segment, it is not clear when (i.e., for what values of the variable *F*) the instruction in the statement with the label 30 should be performed.

```
    IF -0.1 ≤ F ≤ 0.1 THEN GOTO 10
    IF F > 0.1 THEN GOTO 20
    R := M
    GOTO 30
20: L := M
    GOTO 30
10: WRITE F
    GOTO 40
30: M := (R - L) / 2
40: .
    .
    .
```

This question could be answered more easily if the program were written without using a GOTO statement, as follows:

```
IF -0.1 ≤ F ≤ 0.1 THEN
   WRITE F
ELSE
   IF F > 0.1 THEN
      L := M
   ELSE
      R := M
   M := (R - L) / 2
```

In this form, it is much easier to see that the instruction

```
M := (R - L) / 2
```

is performed when the value of *F* is not between −0.1 and 0.1.

Declaring and Using Labels in Pascal

In order to label a statement in Pascal, you must choose an unsigned integer and place that number, together with a colon (:), to the left of the desired statement.

Example

```
15: WRITELN('This statement has the label 15')
```

The label can contain no more than four digits, and, again, it cannot appear in the middle of a statement. In addition, each integer that is used as a label must appear in a `LABEL` **declaration** in the declaration section of the program. Recall, from Section 3.1, that the `LABEL` declarations must follow the `PROGRAM` heading immediately, preceding all other declarations. The syntax for a `LABEL` declaration in Pascal is

`LABEL` declaration The process of providing the computer with the list of all labels used in a program.

```
LABEL Label, . . . , Label;
```

Example

```
LABEL 10, 85, 105;
```

Coding the GOTO Statement in Pascal

The syntax for a `GOTO` statement in Pascal is

```
GOTO Label
```

where the Label is the unsigned integer constant that appears to the left of the desired statement (and has also been declared in the declaration section of the program).

Example

```
PROGRAM Season(INPUT, OUTPUT);
LABEL 10;
VAR
   Month :INTEGER;
BEGIN
   WRITELN ('Enter an integer for the month');
   READ(Month);
   WRITELN('Month =', Month:3);
   IF (Month < 1) OR (Month > 12) THEN
      BEGIN
         WRITELN('The value of Month is invalid');
         GOTO 10
      END;
   WRITE('The season is ');
```

```
            CASE Month OF
                 1,   2, 12 : WRITELN('winter');
                 3,   4,  5 : WRITELN('spring');
                 6,   7,  8 : WRITELN('summer');
                 9,  10, 11 : WRITELN('fall')
            END {End of CASE statement.}
    10: END.
```

You should observe that technically the placement of the label 10 in the example above is incorrect. This is because a label should always appear to the left of a statement; yet, the word END (to the right of the label) is not a statement. However, in this situation, Pascal will automatically insert the empty statement (see Section 3.1) after the colon and before the END, thus avoiding a syntax error.

In this appendix you have learned how the GOTO statement can be used to instruct the computer to "jump" to a properly labeled statement. The labeled statement and all subsequent instructions are then performed in order (until another GOTO statement is encountered). However, since programs with "jumpy" logic are difficult to understand, you should use the GOTO statement only when doing so improves the readability of your program.

Key Terms

Conditional statement 457

Unconditional branch 457

Label 458

LABEL **declaration 461**

APPENDIX D

CHARACTER SETS

You might recall from Chapter 4 that a collating sequence is a list that associates an integer with each character on your computer. The computer uses the numbers in the collating sequence when comparing two characters to determine which one is "less" than the other. In this appendix, three of the many collating sequences are presented. In each table, the integer corresponding to a particular character consists of a left digit (or digits) and a right digit. The left digit is found by looking at the row number located on the far left in the row containing the character of interest; the right digit is found by looking at the column number located at the top of the column containing the character of interest.

CDC Scientific (With 64 Characters)

	Right Digit									
Left Digit	0	1	2	3	4	5	6	7	8	9
0	:	A	B	C	D	E	F	G	H	I
1	J	K	L	M	N	O	P	Q	R	S
2	T	U	V	W	X	Y	Z	0	1	2
3	3	4	5	6	7	8	9	+	−	*
4	/	(	)	$	=		,	.		[
5	]	%	≠	↱	∨	∧	↑	↓	<	>
6	≤	≥	¬	;						

ASCII (American Standard Code for Information Interchange)

	Right Digit									
Left Digit	0	1	2	3	4	5	6	7	8	9
3				!	"	#	$	%	&	'
4	(	)	*	+	,	–	.	/	0	1
5	2	3	4	5	6	7	8	9	:	;
6	<	=	>	?	@	A	B	C	D	E
7	F	G	H	I	J	K	L	M	N	O
8	P	Q	R	S	T	U	V	W	X	Y
9	Z	[	\	]	∧	–	`	a	b	c
10	d	e	f	g	h	i	j	k	l	m
11	n	o	p	q	r	s	t	u	v	w
12	x	y	z	{	|	}				

Codes 00 to 31 and 127 represent certain nonprintable control characters. Code 32 is the blank space.

EBCDIC (Extended Binary Coded Decimal Interchange Code)

	Right Digit									
Left Digit	0	1	2	3	4	5	6	7	8	9
6										
7					¢	.	<	(	+	|
8	&									
9	!	$	*	)	;	¬	-	/		
10							–	,	%	_
11	>	?								
12		`	:	#	@	'	=	"		a
13	b	c	d	e	f	g	h	i		
14						j	k	l	m	n
15	o	p	q	r						
16		~	s	t	u	v	w	x	y	z
17					[					]
18										
19			{	A	B	C	D	E	F	G
20	H	I							}	J
21	K	L	M	N	O	P	Q	R		
22							S	T	U	V
23	W	X	Y	Z	\					
24	0	1	2	3	4	5	6	7	8	9

Codes 00 to 63 and 250 to 255 represent nonprintable control characters. Code 64 is the blank space.

APPENDIX E

FLOWCHARTS

A **flowchart** is a pictorial method for representing the sequence of instructions that constitute a particular program. Specifically, using flowcharts, the algorithm is represented as a sequence of differently shaped boxes that indicate the type of operation being performed. The specific instructions to be performed are written in the boxes. The boxes are then connected by arrows that indicate the sequence in which the instructions are performed. The following is a summary of some of the standard flowchart symbols:

Flowchart A pictorial method for representing the sequence of instructions that constitutes a particular program.

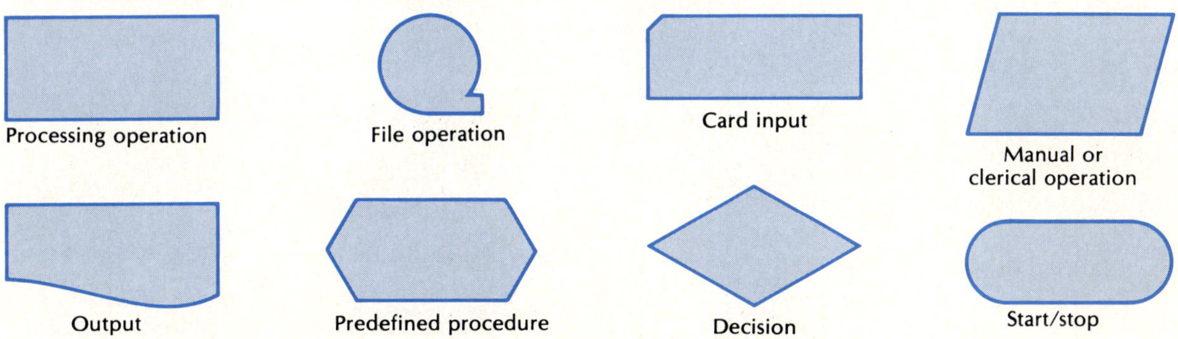

For example, recall the `IF/THEN` and `IF/THEN/ELSE` statements of Chapter 4, which have the following forms:

```
IF/THEN
IF Condition THEN
   Action
```

```
IF/THEN/ELSE
IF Condition THEN
   Action 1
ELSE
   Action 2
```

Those programming concepts could be represented by using flowcharts as follows:

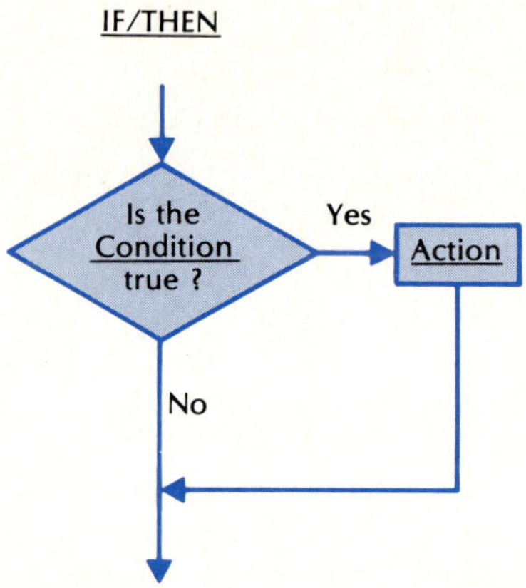

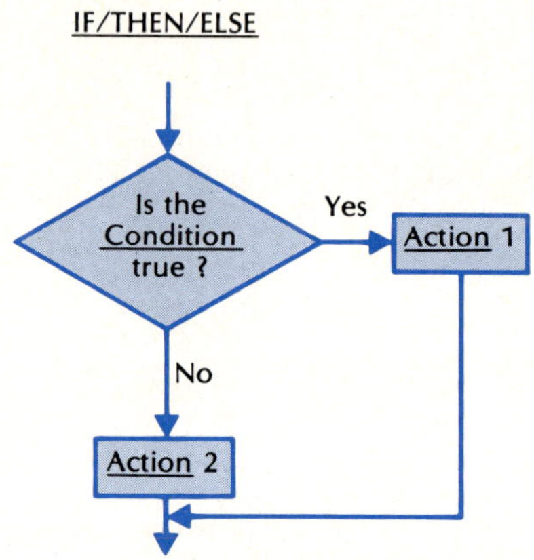

As another example, recall the FOR loop from Chapter 5, which has the following form:

```
FOR Variable := FirstValue TO LastValue DO
    Action
```

This programming concept could be represented by using the following flowchart:

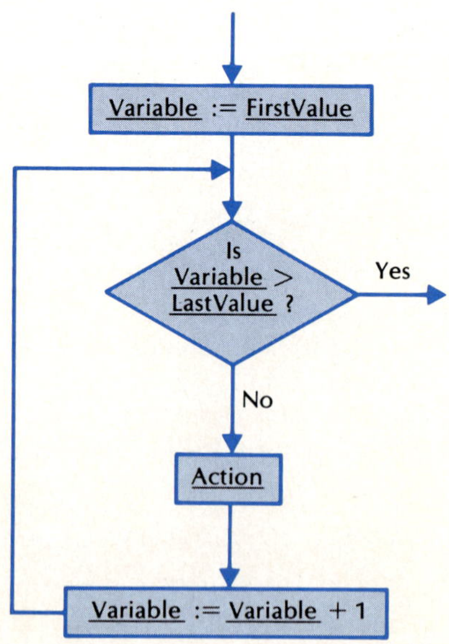

Similarly, recall the WHILE and REPEAT loops from Chapter 5, which have the following forms:

WHILE	REPEAT
WHILE <u>Condition</u> DO <u>Action</u>	REPEAT <u>Action</u> UNTIL <u>Condition</u>

These programming concepts can be represented by the following flowcharts:

WHILE

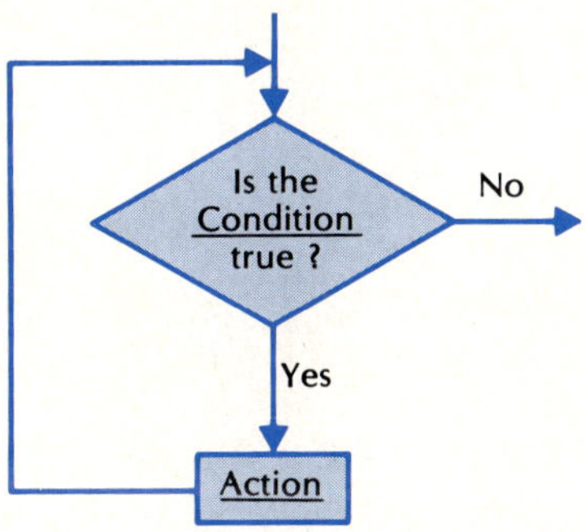

REPEAT

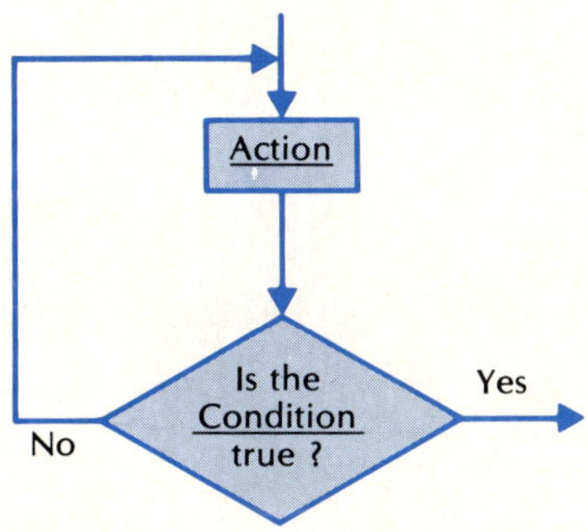

As a final example, the following flowchart represents an algorithm that reads a list of *N* numbers and finds the largest number in the list.

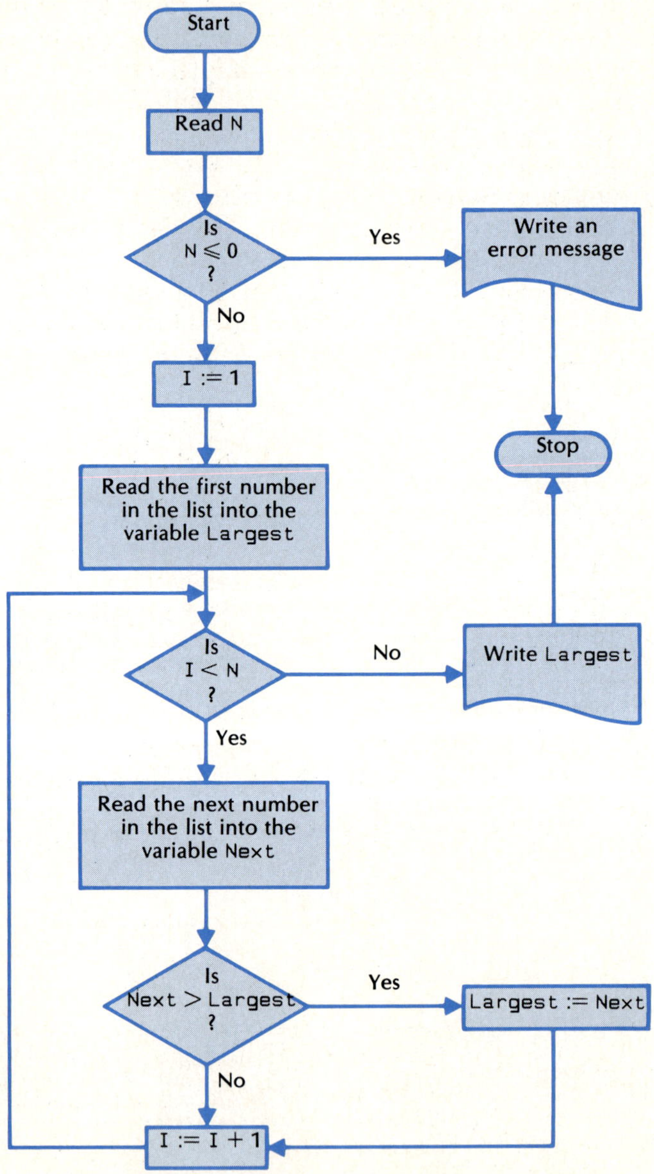

One of the major drawbacks of using flowcharts to represent an algorithm is that it can be very difficult to understand the underlying structure of the program (such as loops). The reason is that any box can, in theory, be connected to any other box. Consequently, it is possible (and common) to have flowcharts in which the arrows are so entangled as to make it virtually impossible to understand the program logic. There are, however, certain **structured flowcharts** that restrict the types of allowable operations and interconnections of arrows. These structured flowcharts are more readable.

Structured flowchart A flowchart that restricts the allowable operations and interconnections of arrows.

A second type of flowchart that appears in computer literature and manuals is called a **system flowchart.** System flowcharts are used in solving complex problems. They are used not so much to specify all of the individual instructions, but rather to identify the major tasks to be performed, their related sequence, and how and where the data will enter the program. For example, the following system flowchart might be used to describe the process of collecting the number of hours worked by a group of employees and computing and printing their paychecks.

System flowchart A flowchart that identifies the major tasks to be performed, their related sequence, and how and where the data will enter the program.

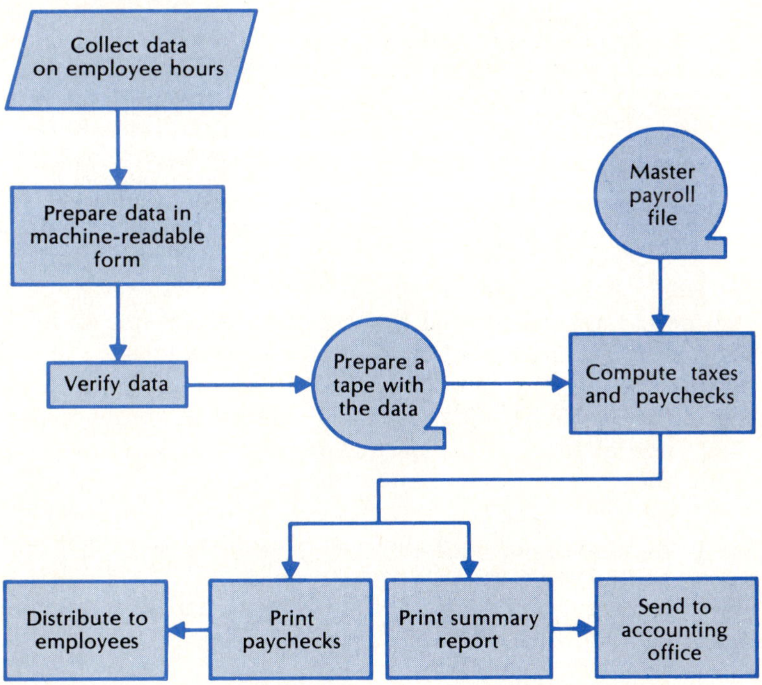

Key Terms

Flowchart 465
Structured flowchart 469
System flowchart 469

APPENDIX F

A DISCUSSION OF COMPUTER LANGUAGES

Throughout the history of the development of computers, different languages have been designed to communicate with the machine. Each language has its advantages and disadvantages, and was designed with special features and objectives in mind.

You should learn to select a language based on the specific type of job you want the computer to perform (assuming that those various languages are available on your computer). The reason is that a carefully chosen language can significantly reduce the programming task. For example, some languages, notably FORTRAN and BASIC, are more suited to performing great quantities of calculations on relatively small amounts of data. Such languages are referred to as *scientific* languages because they are frequently used in scientific applications. In contrast, other languages notably COBOL and PL/1, are more suited to handling large quantities of data that require a minimum amount of processing but a maximum amount of inputting and outputting. These types of languages are called *business* languages because they are frequently used in business applications. Still other languages, such as Pascal, are *general-purpose* languages.

The following is a chronological list of some of the more common programming languages available:

Language	Approximate Date of Introduction	General Application Areas
FORTRAN	1957	Numerically oriented language. Most applicable to scientific, mathematical, and statistical problem areas. Very widely used and available.

ALGOL	1960	Also a numerically oriented language but with additional features. Widely used in Europe.
COBOL	1960	The most widely used business-oriented computer language.
LISP	1961	Special-purpose language developed primarily for list processing and symbolic manipulation. Widely used by computer scientists in the area of artificial intelligence.
SNOBOL	1962	Special-purpose language used primarily for character and string processing, including such applications as text editors and language processors.
BASIC	1965	A simple interactive programming language widely used on microcomputers; often used to teach programming in high schools and colleges.
PL/1	1965	A complex, general-purpose language designed to incorporate the numeric capabilities of FORTRAN, the business capabilities of COBOL, and many other features into a single language.
APL	1967	An operator-oriented interactive language that introduced a wide range of new mathematical operations that are built directly into the language.
Pascal	1971	A general-purpose language designed specifically to teach the concepts of computer programming.
Ada	1980	A new systems-implementation language designed and built for the U.S. Department of Defense.

Glossary

Actual parameters The specific names and/or values that are specified when a procedure is called. Those names and/or values will replace the corresponding parameters in the procedure declaration.

Address of a variable The actual "page" number of the computer's memory that corresponds to a variable.

Algorithm A step-by-step method that can be used to solve a problem.

Array A collection of variables that is used for storing and processing a list of data.

Array name The common name that is given to each variable of an array.

Array subscript A value following the array name that is used to distinguish one array variable from the next.

Assignment statement The instruction that tells the computer to store a value into a variable.

Batch processing The original method developed for communicating with the computer.

Body of a loop The specific instructions of a loop that are to be repeated.

Body of a procedure The specific instructions that constitute a procedure.

Boolean expressions A sequence of comparisons and calculations whose final result is either of the values `TRUE` or `FALSE`.

Boolean operator Any of the three operators `AND`, `OR`, AND `NOT` that can be used to form boolean expressions.

Boolean values The values `TRUE` and `FALSE`.

Buffer variable A variable associated with each file, whose value is precisely that of the window of the file.

Built-in functions Functions that already exist in the computer and that you can use in your program without having to declare them.

Call-by-value parameter A dummy parameter in the declaration of a procedure that will be replaced with the *value* of the corresponding actual parameter when the procedure is called.

Call-by-variable parameter A dummy parameter in the declaration of a procedure that will be replaced with the *name* of the corresponding actual parameter when the procedure is called.

Calling a procedure The act of instructing the computer to perform the instructions in a procedure by referring to the name of the procedure in the program.

`CASE` statement A Pascal statement that can be used to instruct the computer to perform any one of an alternative number of actions based on the value of an expression that you can specify.

Character value Any letter, digit, or other symbol that is available on your computer.

Coding The final act of expressing the solution to a problem as a list of computer instructions in a specific language.

Collating sequence A list that associates an integer with each available character in the computer.

Compiling a program The act of translating a program into machine language.

Compound statement A group of statements that, when considered as a whole, can be thought of as one big statement.

Computer program A sequence of computer instructions written in a specific computer language.

Conditional statement A statement whose "action" may or may not be performed, depending on the value of a prespecified condition; e.g., an `IF/THEN` or an `IF/THEN/ELSE` statement.

Constant An identifier whose value will not change anywhere in the program.

Data Information provided by you to the computer in order to be able to solve a problem.

Data verification Testing whether the values of the data are within some allowable range.

Debugging The process of locating and correcting errors in a program.

Declaring a procedure Providing the computer with the specific instructions and the name that constitute a procedure.

Declaring a variable Telling the computer the name of a variable and the type of information that will be stored into that variable.

Decreasing `FOR` loop A `FOR` loop in which the loop-counter variable is decreased by 1 at each iteration.

Delimiter Any character used to separate values in a file.

Dummy parameters The parameters that appear in the procedure declaration. Those parameters will be replaced by the actual parameters when the procedure is called.

Echo printing The process of displaying the values of all variables that are obtained as a result of using a `READ` statement.

Element of an array One specific array variable consisting of the array name followed by the subscript of that variable.

Empty statement A Pascal statement that does nothing. This statement is sometimes inserted by the computer automatically so as to avoid a syntax error caused by incorrectly placing a semicolon before an `END`, for example.

End-of-file marker A special character used to indicate the end of a file.

End-of-line marker A special character used to indicate the end of each line in a file.

Expression A sequence of calculations that must be performed.

External file A file whose values are stored outside the primary memory of the computer—for example, on a disk or tape. Those values are saved even after the program is finished running.

Field names The various names given to the individual fields of a record.

Field width The number of columns used to display one value.

Fields of a record The various individual values that are stored in a record.

File A collection of information stored as a unit in some part of the computer.

Flowchart A pictorial method for representing the sequence of instructions that constitutes a particular program.

`FOR` loop A loop in which the stopping rule specifies precisely how many times the body of the loop is to be performed.

Function A programming tool, like a procedure, that enables you to perform a group of instructions many times while only having to write those instructions once. The primary output of a function is a single value that is stored into the function name.

Global variables Variables that are declared in the main program, and whose values can also be used (and changed) in the body of a procedure.

Identifiers Names that are used for various purposes in a program.

`IF/THEN` **statement** A statement that instructs the computer to perform an action only if a specified boolean condition is true.

`IF/THEN/ELSE` **statement** A statement that instructs the computer to perform one action if a specified boolean condition is true, and an alternative action if that condition is false.

Initializing a variable The process of assigning an initial value to a variable prior to beginning a loop.

Increasing `FOR` loop A `FOR` loop in which the loop-counter variable is increased by 1 at each iteration.

Infinite loop An error in a `WHILE` loop that causes the computer to perform the repetition "forever."

Input devices Electronic components from which the computer can obtain values for the data when instructed to do so in a program.

Inputting The process of supplying to the computer information (i.e., data) that will be needed when the program is used to solve a problem.

Inputting, processing, and outputting A problem-solving technique whereby you identify each of these three parts of a computer program.

Integer values Any of the positive and negative numbers that contain no decimal point.

Interactive processing A method of communicating with the computer that allows you to interact with the machine both as you prepare and as you run a program.

Iteration of a loop One complete execution of the body of a loop.

Label An unsigned integer (followed by a colon) that appears to the left of a statement. The computer will use the label to locate that particular statement.

`LABEL` **declaration** The process of providing the computer with the list of all labels used in a program.

Local file A file whose values are stored in the primary memory of the computer just like those of an array. Those values are lost after the program is finished running.

Local variables Variables that are declared within (and can only be used within) a procedure.

Logic error An error caused by giving the computer an incorrect sequence of instructions (although each instruction by itself can be performed by the computer).

Loop A group of instructions to be repeated together with an associated rule to indicate when the repetition should end.

Loop-counter variable A variable whose value represents the number of times the body of the loop has been performed. `FOR` loops automatically have such a variable associated with them; `WHILE` loops do not.

Microcomputer A form of interactive processing in which the computer will be working exclusively for you.

Multidimensional array An array in which each element can be referenced by more than one subscript.

Object code The machine-language translation that comes out of the compiler.

Output devices Electronic components on which a computer can display values when instructed to do so in a program.

Outputting The process of having the computer report to you the solution that the machine obtained during the processing phase.

Parameter A programming concept used with a procedure, which enables the computer to perform a group of instructions using different values and/or variables each time the procedure is called. There are two major types of parameters: *actual parameters* and *dummy parameters*.

Pascal A specific, general-purpose computer language.

Pointer (1) A method for keeping track of the next character to be read in a file. (2) The information associated with a specific element of a pointer-type data structure that specifies the preceding, the succeeding, or any other related elements.

Pointer-type data structure A data structure in which each element contains a value together with information that specifies the preceding, the succeeding, or any other related elements.

Precedence of operators The order in which the operators are performed.

Procedure A group of instructions that, as a unit, is given a name. By subsequently referring to that name in the program, you can instruct the computer to perform the instructions any number of times.

Procedure name The name you choose to give to a procedure.

Processing The method of using, manipulating, and/or performing computations with the data in order to obtain the solution to a problem.

Programming The process of giving instructions to the computer.

Pseudocode A limited English vocabulary used when applying stepwise refinement.

`READ` **statement** The instruction that tells the computer to obtain the value for a variable from somewhere outside the program.

Real value Any number that contains a single decimal point.

Record A Pascal data structure that allows you to store more than one type of value in each variable.

Record name The single name given to the record variable as a whole.

Recursion The process of having a procedure or function call itself.

Relational operators Any of the six operators (<, >, =, <=, >=, <>) used to compare two numbers, characters, or variables in Pascal.

`REPEAT` **loop** A loop that is similar to a `WHILE` loop except that the stopping rule is checked after the body of the loop is performed.

Repetition The process of repeating a group of instructions so as to solve a problem.

Reserved words Words that have a special meaning in Pascal and cannot be used as identifiers in your program.

Run-time error An error caused by asking the computer to perform an instruction that the machine cannot perform.

Sequential file A file in which the only way to find a particular element is to scan all elements sequentially to the right of the window.

Set A collection of individual values of the same type, referenced by a single name, that can be processed as a whole by using appropriate operators.

Source code The original program coded into a specific programming language.

Stepwise refinement The process of gradually expressing the original English solution to a problem in terms that can be understood by the computer.

Standard identifiers Words that have a special meaning in Pascal. Although you could use them as identifiers in your program, you should not do so.

Stopping rule A part of the loop that tells the computer when the body of the loop should no longer be performed.

Structured flowchart A flowchart that restricts the allowable operations and interconnections of arrows.

Subrange of values A specific portion of an existing set of values.

Syntax diagram A precise method for summarizing and for illustrating the syntax of a programming language.

Syntax error An error caused by not following the grammatical rules of a computer language. These errors usually arise from misspellings, bad punctuation, omitting special words, etc.

System flowchart A flowchart that identifies the major tasks to be performed, their related sequence, and how and where the data will enter the program.

Textfile A file that consists solely of printable characters, end-of-line markers, and a closing end-of-file marker.

Thinking through your solution The process of going over your initial solution very slowly and carefully in order to understand more precisely what individual steps you are performing to solve the problem.

Time sharing A form of interactive processing in which you share the computer with other users.

Top-down programming A technique designed to help you develop an algorithm for a complicated problem by decomposing the overall problem into smaller, more manageable subproblems.

Tracing The process of playing the role of the computer and performing the instructions of the program yourself.

Unconditional branch A statement that instructs the computer to "jump" to another part of the program, and to continue executing instructions from that point on.

User-defined values Names chosen by you that can be used in your program as actual values.

Value of a variable The information that is stored into the variable.

Variables Names that are used by you in a program to refer to specific memory locations of the computer.

`WHILE` **loop** A loop in which the body is performed an unspecified number of times, so long as a boolean condition is true.

Window of a file The one (and only) element of a file whose value is currently available for processing.

`WITH` **statement** A Pascal statement that enables you to refer to the fields of a record without having to specify the record name in the body of the statement.

Working through a specific example The process of choosing specific values for the data and solving the problem by hand. As you do so, attempt to describe the general computations that would have to be performed when the values of the data are not specified explicitly.

`WRITE` **statement** The instruction that tells the computer to display the value of a variable (or an expression).

INDEX